GWR No 4033 Queen Victoria *tops Filton Bank with an up Two-hour Bristol express.*(G.H. Soole)

LOCOMOTIVE PRACTICE
AND PERFORMANCE

LOCOMOTIVE PRACTICE AND PERFORMANCE

Highlights from the celebrated
Railway Magazine articles by O.S. Nock

Volume I: The age of steam, 1959~68

PSL

Patrick Stephens Limited

First published in 1989

These articles first appeared between January 1959 and
April 1974 in *The Railway Magazine*, whose co-operation
in the preparation of this reprint is gratefully
acknowledged.

British Library Cataloguing in Publication Data

Nock, O.S. (Oswald Stevens), *1905*
    Locomotive practice and performance.
    Vol. 1: The age of steam, 1959–68
    1. Great Britain. Railway services: British Rail.
    Locomotives, to 1984
    I. Title II. Railway magazine
    625.2'6'0941

    ISBN 1-85260-159-0

Patrick Stephens Limited is part of the Thorsons Publishing
Group, Wellingborough, Northamptonshire NN8 2RQ,
England.

Printed and bound in Great Britain by
Butler & Tanner Ltd, Frome and London

Typeset by Burns & Smith, Derby

10 9 8 7 6 5 4 3 2 1

Contents

Preface

Several years before the inauguration of *The Railway Magazine*, in July 1897, many of the so-called 'Railway-acs' had evidenced a considerable interest in the more intimate details of express train running other than start-to-stop average speeds as advertised in the public time-tables. The celebrated *littérateur* Charles Rous-Marten was already acknowledged as an expert in the train-timing art; indeed, his contributions to the technical press were considered so authoritative and influential by the top railway managements of the day that at the time of the exceedingly exciting 'Race to the North' in August 1895 he was given special facilities for travelling on the trains involved. When publication of *The Railway Magazine* began, he was inevitably an 'ace' contributor on the editorial list, though it was not until 1901 that he was invited to write a regular monthly serial article under the title 'British Locomotive Practice and Performance'. Already many of his contributions had borne the stamp of things to come: indeed, the last, in 1901, was a two-instalment piece entitled 'What Mr Webb's Compounds Have Done'.

Almost exactly 57 years later, the then Editor, Basil Cooke, told me that Cecil J. Allen was relinquishing the authorship of the now-famous series, and asked whether I would take over. My reactions to that invitation are recalled later. I carried on the authorship for another 22 years, and now in the evening of my life I am honoured that my present publisher should wish to reprint some of my *Railway Magazine* articles covering the most significant events in my time of authorship.

The 22 years' span, from the beginning of 1959 to December 1980, covered the transition on British Railways from steam to more modern forms of traction, and so it was suggested that the reprinting should first deal with the period up to 1968, the last year of steam traction on regular passenger services on British Railways, and that a second volume, concerned with subsequent developments both at home and overseas as covered in my *Railway Magazine* articles, might follow.

In choosing the individual articles for inclusion in this book, and in recalling the circumstances in which they came to be written, I recall no less, and re-echo, the sense of deep gratitude that I felt to all the fellow enthusiasts who helped me at the time. They were not only the correspondents who sent me logs of train running by the hundred, and wrote of their personal experiences in travelling, but also professional railwaymen of all grades. Locomotive Running Superintendents were unfailing in their generous responses to requests for footplate passes, while in the highest echelons of railway mechanical engineering I remember the friendship that was accorded to me by Sir William

Stanier, H.G. Ivatt, Kenneth J. Cook and Alfred Smeddle, among many others.

On a more personal basis, I have always valued the friendship of Mrs Violet Godfrey, daughter of Sir Nigel Gresley, and of the son and three daughters of C.J. Bowen Cooke, but above all there has been my dear Olivia, who for nearly 50 years fulfilled the multiplex rôle of wife, mother, grandmother, housewife, *cordon bleu*, gardener, typist, world travelling companion, literary critic (!) and secretary. The sustained encouragement she gave me throughout my professional work, of whatever kind, was a priceless asset.

O.S. Nock
Bath, 1989

Introduction

ONE day in mid-October I happened to be browsing through my files of *The Railway Magazine* for 1909 in search of some data I needed, and I came across the very first article written by Cecil J. Allen under the now famous title. I could not help pausing in my search to read that first article again. Little did I imagine, however, that the very next post would bring news of his impending retirement from the job of writing these articles, and an invitation to me to take over. At first I was non-plussed. One had come to regard the combination of Cecil J. Allen and 'British Locomotive Practice and Performance' as so much of an institution in the railway literary world that the idea of any severance of the association never entered one's head, though to be sure that severance must have come some time.

Even his immensely long run had ceased to cause surprise. Contributors and Editors might come and go; engines might be built, run their courses, and be scrapped; world wars might rage, and tear to shreds many a cherished institution; but Cecil J. Allen just went on clocking up the hundreds, and thinking back to my browsing of the previous day I realised that in August, 1959, it would be fifty years since his first contribution on the subject. *Fifty years*—just think of it. It takes us back to the days when single-wheelers were still in regular use on some crack British express passenger trains; when

Dugald Drummond was still in the saddle; when superheating was still in its infancy; and when a young man of 33, named Herbert Nigel Gresley, had just produced the first main-line articulated coaching stock to be seen in this country.

C. J. Bowen-Cooke had just succeeded George Whale as Chief Mechanical Engineer of the London & North Western Railway, and Allen's first article contained news of three locomotive exchanges that between them had a profound influence on future practice at Crewe:— 'Precursors' *versus* Great Northern Atlantics, between Euston and Crewe, on the one hand, and Kings Cross and Doncaster on the other; an 'Experiment' 4-6-0 *versus* the famous Caledonian 4-6-0 *Cardean*; and the through running between Rugby and Brighton on alternate days of the 'Precursor' No 7, *Titan*, and a Marsh superheater 4-4-2 tank engine of the 'I3' class, No 23.

But at the time of Cecil J. Allen's first contribution there were changes in the air, even then, more profound than the introduction of superheating, more profound than new personalities making their influence felt. From the opening of the second volume of *The Railway Magazine* for 1909, Cecil J. Allen shared the responsibility for these articles with J. F. Gairns and the Rev. W. J. Scott, and the latter, in his very first essay, rather shocked his readers by describing a footplate journey he had recently made on an electric locomotive!

He replied to a reader who thought that 'he could never feel much interest in the work done by an electric locomotive.' Scott continued: 'But he *could*, and will—if he live long enough. So those who wept over the death of the mail coach, with its team of spanking greys, thought that with it ended the romance of the road. But today we know better: as Rudyard Kipling sings: 'Romance brings up the nine-fifteen.' Accordingly, I this month give the times of a non-stop train on the District Railway, drawn by no engine at all, but by a mere 'motor-coach'—a name which brings visions of a machine having sparking-plugs as big as pineapples, and a vast radiator instead of a smokebox.

'Well, we may yet see a petrol-driven locomotive, fitted—let us hope—with an effective 'self-starter', and warranted not to 'back fire'. *I* find it hard to see what pleasure there will be in making timetables for airships, with all the blue ethereal sky to 'run' in, no gradients or station-slacks to take account of, where will the need for skilful arrangement come in? And yet, the first working-notice for the aeroplane *Entente Cordiale* London (Albert Memorial) to Paris (Place Vendôme) in 4 hr 0 min will be a historic document.' Today the very skies can become uncomfortably crowded with high-speed traffic—yet another reminder of the astonishing span of world affairs since Cecil J. Allen commenced his 49-year run.

In taking over the authorship of a 'feature' of such long standing, the new man must inevitably turn back the pages to the writings of his predecessors: for in addition to Cecil J. Allen, Gairns, and the Rev. W. J. Scott there was R. E. Charlewood, not to mention that unique personality of the railway literary world who founded the series, Charles Rous-Marten. It is with emotion and a feeling of deep humility that I take up the task, and in so doing I am reminded of the words of Joseph Locke, to whom it fell, as President of the Institution of Civil Engineers, to speak just after the death of Brunel. Coupling his name with those of the Stephensons and other pioneers he exhorted his fellow members of the Civils 'to honour their memory and emulate their example.' That, I feel, should be my own guiding principle in the writing of these articles.

Yet, as time goes on, there are bound to be changes. The new forms of motive power coming into service on British Railways do not lend themselves to mile-by-mile descriptions of individual runs; there is a fixed inexorable limit to their maximum achievement. Yet the steam locomotive has so strong an appeal to the emotions that it would be dangerously easy to slip back into nostalgic, imaginative putting-back-of-the-clock, dwelling on the past glories of *Cardean*, the Ivatt Atlantics, the 'Jersey Lilies', and so on, and tending to relate each new development to standards of the past, when in actuality the conditions are so different as to make direct comparison quite futile and illusory.

Today's accent is on modernisation, and our own generation has the good fortune to be witnessing and taking part in a scheme of development greater than anything previously seen in this country since the pioneer days when the Stephensons, Brunel, Gooch, Locke, Vignoles and others, were blazing the trail through the placid agricultural England of early Victorian times. At the same time, as the history of the steam locomotive begins to draw to a close, there is all the keener interest to complete our knowledge of this most fascinating of machines.

One last word, by way of introduction: I do hope to establish personal contact, through the post, with those readers who may be kind enough to write to me, or send in details of runs. I can recall in the past many contacts, first made through mutual interest in British Locomotive Practice and Performance, that have blossomed into close personal friendships, and I recall no less those evenings, before 1939, when half-a-dozen or so kindred spirits used to foregather at R. E. Charlewood's flat in London, and how we used to talk trains to our hearts' content. But it is time we were done with preliminaries and taking the road.

West Coast Main Line — Euston to Carlisle

From 1951, British Railways began publishing the reports of locomotive performance and efficiency tests carried out on certain specified classes, both of the new Standard BR types and also Regional designs that by reason of their quantities and widespread utilisation were likely to remain in use for many years. I was commissioned by *The Engineer* to write commentary reports on each of the test bulletins as they were published. In some of the later ones, notably that dealing with the one and only 'BR8' Pacific No 71000 *Duke of Gloucester*, published in 1957, the test data was supplemented by 'Cost of Energy and Performance Computers' covering the whole of the West Coast Main Line between Euston and Carlisle. The predicted performance of engine No 71000 led me to analyse the actual performance put up by various LMS Pacific engines, including No 71000, in the following article.

ONE of the most fascinating channels into which the recording of train running can lead us is the assessment, or attempted assessment, of the ultimate capacity of the locomotive concerned. From such studies comes, of course, comparison of the various engine designs, and there is scarcely one among us who does not tend to grow hot under the collar when the capabilities of his favourites are challenged.

The bulletins issued from time to time by the British Transport Commission, describing in very full detail the performance and efficiency tests carried out on one or other of the stationary testing plants, have satisfied our natural curiosity over certain designs, but only whetted our appetites for more. Unfortunately from the viewpoint of locomotive history some of the most

controversial designs are no longer in existence, and in any case the testing plants are so fully occupied with work of vital importance to the future of British Railways that academic researches would be out of the question, even if examples of these enigmas of past years were still available.

In another respect, however, some of the later bulletins issued have included data of much interest to the ordinary compiler of logs, in the form of the 'Cost of Energy and Performance Computers' worked out for certain definite stretches of line. These computers have been prepared primarily for the use of those engaged in timetable compilation, and their nature will be best appreciated from an actual example. In the bulletin dealing with the tests on engine No

The up 'Royal Scot' soon after leaving Carlisle on its non-stop run to Euston in 1935, with engine No 6205 Princess Victoria. (Rail Archive Stephenson, F.R. Hebron)

71000, *Duke of Gloucester*, computers were included for the sections Euston to Rugby, Rugby to Crewe, and Crewe to Carlisle, with loads varying between 200 and 600 tons, and various overall average speeds.

To take the Euston-Rugby section as an example: on the 80-min schedule worked until recently by the 'Royal' and 'Midday Scots,' one could read off from the computer what the coal consumption would be in pounds per ton mile for any load that might be required. But of greater interest, perhaps, to readers of these articles are the intermediate times based on a constant rate of steaming throughout. When logging a run from the carriage, rather than the footplate, one can often sense when a locomotive has been definitely eased; but it is more difficult to detect subtler changes in the working. Comparison of the logs of day-to-day running with point-to-point times calculated on the basis of a constant rate of steaming can lead to a more precise assessment of engine performance, and thus to the interest and enjoyment to be derived from the art.

It is interesting first of all to compare some ac-

tual schedules, with the times evaluated on a constant steam rate basis.

Reference		A		B		C	
Overall time (min)		92		86		80	
		Cal min	Actual min	Cal min	Actual min	Cal min	Actual min
Euston	...	0	0	0	0	0	0
Willesden Jc	...	9.2	9.6	8.9	9	8.8	9
Watford Jc	...	24.0	24.0	22.5	22	21.2	21
Tring	...	41.9	40.8	38.9	38	36.1	35
Bletchley	...	55.3	54.3	51.6	51	48.1	47
Roade	...	68.1	67.5	63.6	63	59.3	58
Blisworth	...	71.4	70.8	66.6	66	62.1	61
Rugby	...	92.0	92.2	86.0	86	80	80

Of the data set out in the table above, 'A' was an actual run with an LNWR locomotive on the 1.30 pm from Euston showing remarkably close approximation to the calculated times; 'B' was the 1939 schedule of the 'Merseyside Express'; and 'C' the recent schedule of the 'Royal' and 'Midday Scots'. Both these latter show a striking similarity to the calculated values for constant evaporation working. In actual working, however, one can often note an almost traditional variation from the point-to-point times laid down in the working timetables where some local circumstance intervenes, and it is in-

LONDON MIDLAND REGION: 1.30 pm EUSTON–CREWE (THE 'MIDDAY SCOT')

Dist	Run No Engine No Load, tons tare Load, tons gross	Sched	1 46212 409 440	2 71000 453 485	3 46211 459 490	4 46201 455 490	5 45532* 468 500	6 46231 474 510
miles		min	m s	m s	m s	m s	m s	m s
0.0	EUSTON	0	0 00	0 00	0 00	0 00	0 0	0 0
5.4	WILLESDEN JUNC	9	9 34	9 19	10 48	10 27	8 55	10 31
			—	—	pws	—	—	—
11.4	Harrow		15 16	15 16	19 17	16 41	14 33	16 07
17.5	WATFORD JUNC	21	20 58	21 31	27 00	22 39	20 16	21 32
24.5	Hemel Hempstead		27 15	28 23	33 58	29 11	26 22	27 34
			—	pws	—	—	—	—
31.7	TRING	35	33 58	38 14	42 00	36 02	32 56	34 12
40.2	Leighton Buzzard		40 57	45 20	49 05	42 58	39 40	41 00
			—	—	—	—	—	psw
46.7	BLETCHLEY	47	46 11	50 27	54 18	48 08	44 55	49 59
52.4	Wolverton		50 46	54 51	58 53	52 40	49 49	55 52
59.9	ROADE	58	57 10	61 17	65 30	59 13	56 53	62 17
62.8	BLISWORTH	61	59 45	63 50	68 12	61 54	59 34	64 43
			pws	sigs	—	pws	—	—
69.7	Weedon	67	66 38	70 21	74 06	70 08	65 31	70 07
78.8	Kilsby Tunnel North		77 45	78 29	82 11	79 29	74 02	77 35
			sigs	sigs	—	sig stop	sigs	sigs
82.6	RUGBY	80	82 24	83 47	86 36	87 35	79 12	82 35
0.0			0 00	0 00	0 00	0 00	0 00	0 00
			3 checks	2 checks	1 check	2 checks	—	2 checks
75.5	CREWE	77	78 15	76 24	76 50	74 42	74 35	75 45
	Net times: to Rugby to Crewe		78 70½	78 71¼	83 74	81 73½	78½ 74¼	77½ 72½

* Piloted by Stanier class '5' 4–6–0 No 44780

teresting to see how a very hard schedule like that of the 'Midday Scot' works out in practice, particularly in relation to the steam rates involved.

I have therefore tabulated details of six runs on this train. Of these the one with No 71000 was clocked from the footplate by Mr Ronald I. Nelson, and all the rest were experiences of my own. As a supplement to the usual form of log I have tabulated additionally the calculated point-to-point times, from the computer published in the test bulletin for engine No 71000, and the actual times made on the six journeys concerned. In the first place it will be seen that it was only on the double-headed trip, No 5, that anything approaching the calculated time was made to

Willesden, even though we were banked to Camden on every occasion. But once through Willesden there were substantial gains on the calculated time on the long adverse stretch to Tring on four out of the six journeys. Against the rated time of 27.3 min for this distance of 26.3 miles the actual times on these same four runs were 24.4, 25.6, 24.0 and 23.7 min.

From the computer contained in the test bulletin it is clear that if the engines concerned had been worked uniformly hard all the way to Rugby, steaming with the same vigour as from Willesden to Tring, their overall times would have been in the region of 75 min start to stop. A comparison of actual times with those of the computer, however, makes it clear that drivers

COMPUTER AND ACTUAL POINT-TO-POINT TIMES, EUSTON TO RUGBY

Run No Engine No	Computer times	1 46212	2 71000	3 46211	4 46201	5 45532†	6 46231
	min	min	min	min	min	min	min
Euston							
	8.8	9.6	9.3	10.8	10.4	8.9	10.5
Willesden							
	12.4	11.4	12.3	16.2*	12.2	11.3	11.0
Watford							
	14.9	13.0	16.7*	15.0	13.4	12.7	12.7
Tring							
	12.0	12.2	12.2	12.3	12.0	12.0	15.8*
Bletchley							
	11.2	11.0	10.8	11.2	11.1	12.0	12.3
Roade							
	2.8	2.6	2.5	2.7	2.7	2.7	2.4
Blisworth							
	5.8	6.9*	6.5*	5.9	8.2*	6.0	5.4
Weedon							
	12.1	15.8*	13.4*	12.5	17.5*	13.7*	12.5*
Rugby							

* Includes either signal or pw check. † Piloted by 4–6–0 No 44780. Engine names: Nos 45532, *Illustrious* ('Patriot' class); 46201, *Princess Elizabeth*; 46211, *Queen Maud*; 46212, *Duchess of Kent*; 46231, *Duchess of Atholl*; 71000, *Duke of Gloucester*

deliberately take things easy in starting out of Euston, to lessen the chance of slipping on Camden bank, and in Primrose Hill Tunnel, and generally giving their engines a chance to warm up. Then they go really hard out to Tring, with a reversion to somewhat easier running afterwards.

So far as individual runs are concerned, No 1, with *Duchess of Kent*, was an excellent performance; Willesden Junction was passed at 60 mph, and thereafter the speed lay between a maximum of 68½ through Watford Junction and a minimum of 62 mph right up to Tring. Passing this summit more than 2 min ahead of the computer time of 36.1 min and running closely in accordance with it afterwards we passed Blisworth in the fine time of 59¾ min from Euston. But there was not sufficient in hand to offset the effect of a very heavy permanent way slack near Weedon, and the arrival in Rugby was 2½ min late.

In connection with this very hard schedule I have always wondered why it should ever have been laid down. Again referring to the com-puter, with a tare load of 450 tons the coal consumption for No 71000 is 0.12 lb per ton mile, or 54 lb per train mile; by contrast, the continuation schedule of 77 min for the 75.5 miles from Rugby to Crewe required no more than 40 lb per mile. The coal consumption of other London Midland Pacifics may not be the same as that of No 71000, but the relative consumptions would be approximately the same. I should add that the coal figures given are those for traction only; to this would have to be added small extra for steam heating in the winter months.

The run with No 71000, in column 2, affords a very interesting comparison with the data given in the computer. The start was the fastest of all the Pacific runs, with reasonably close correspondence to the computer times to Watford. As soon as the train was fairly on the move the regulator was opened to the full; cut-off was at first 54 per cent, then 40, and finally 27 per cent on passing the top of Camden bank. Gradual linking up continued till on passing Willesden the gear was in 13 per cent and the adjustments varied between 10 and 13 until steam was shut off for the permanent way check at Hemel Hempstead. Speeds up to this point had been 67½ mph on the level after Willesden, 55½ after Hatch End, and 66½ at Watford Junction. This showed a rather wider variation in speed than is usual on this schedule. With the *Duchess of Kent*, on run No 1, the corresponding speeds had been 65, 62 and 68½ mph.

From the slack, speed had been worked up to 59 mph at Tring, and then the point-to-point times correspond once again closely with those of the computer. The cut-offs were very short on this stretch, varying between 7 and 11 per cent until well past Castlethorpe, and on to the incline to Roade cutting. Again the variations in speed were unusual. Normally one expects the maximum to occur nearing Leighton Buzzard, but although the cut-off was 7½ per cent down from Tring and 7 per cent between Bletchley and Wolverton, the maximum speeds were 78 before Leighton and no less than 83 nearing Wolverton.

No 71000, with Caprotti valve gear, is an ex-ceptionally free running engine, and I have myself timed her at 83 mph between Swindon and Reading from the Western Region dynamometer car, with a load of 610 tons. But for all the short cut-off working, and free running, the coal consumption in ordinary service seems very much on the high side. Careful reading of the water indicator on the tender showed a consumption of about 49 gal per mile; this would correspond to a feed water rate of approximately 30,000 lb per hour, or practically up to the maximum obtained with this engine on the Swindon tests. The coal consumption could not be measured with any accuracy, but it is fairly safe to assume it was at least 70 lb per mile. The check between Blisworth and Weedon was not severe, but it was enough to spoil what promised to be another piece of very fast running. Working in 10 per cent the speed just beyond Blisworth was 78½ mph and still rising; even after the check, which was to 50 mph, speed was worked up to 70 mph at Weedon.

The third run, as a personal experience, was

The up 'Coronation Scot' passing Oxenholme with engine No 6220 Coronation. (Rail Archive Stephenson, F.R. Hebron)

One of the first non-streamlined LMS Pacifics, No 6231 Duchess of Atholl, *in 1938 at Polmadie shed, as originally built before smoke deflecting screens were added.* (Rail Archive Stephenson, T.G. Hepburn)

rather disappointing. I was on the footplate myself, and hoped to secure an interesting record to compare with that of No 71000 and that of the brilliant run of the 'Duchess' No 46231 that I had enjoyed on the footplate some little time earlier. But No 46211, *Queen Maud*, was not in the best of form. I must admit that in quite a lot of recent travelling over the West Coast route, I have had a number of indifferent runs with the 'Princess Royal' class engines—the 'Lizzies', as they are popularly known among the men.

I have the feeling that footplate psychology cannot be entirely ruled out in assessing some of the poor work that one nowadays sees with these engines. In their earlier days, before the building of the 'Duchess' class, the 'Lizzies' were always good, and sometimes utterly brilliant. There is no denying they needed careful handling, and good firing, but when the 'Duchesses' began to come into general use the men quickly found that the newer engines did their work with an ease, and a margin in reserve that was never pre-

sent with the 'Lizzies'; the loading limits for both classes have, however, remained the same, though an attempt has always to be made to provide 'Duchesses' for the hardest turns. When one of the earlier Pacifics has been rostered for a really crack train, such as the 1.30 pm from Euston, one has frequently heard the comment 'You need a "Duchess" for this job,' in a way that the onlooker half expected time to be lost in any case.

Of the 3 min net lost on my footplate run with No 46211, nearly 2 min had gone before we passed Willesden. Certainly the loss, as compared with the computer times, was small from Watford onwards. The fourth run showed one of these engines much nearer to its true form, particularly in the fine uphill work from Watford to Tring; but even this was not quite enough to recover the initial loss, and the net time to Rugby was 81 min. As might be expected the double-headed train, with so lavish a provision of engine power, showed considerable variation in effort on the various point to point timings.

The morning Birmingham–Glasgow and Edinburgh express in 1947, passing Wigan hauled by engine No 6234 Duchess of Abercorn. (W. Philip Conolly)

To Tring the times were the fastest of the series, and Bletchley was passed in even time; but after that the effort was much eased down. It is nevertheless a significant commentary on the sharpness of this schedule that it was only on this one journey that the train was strictly punctual in arriving at Rugby. As the table shows, however, every engine—even including No 46211—showed an appreciable net gain on the easier timing from Rugby to Crewe.

On the first stage of the journey it is the sixth run that claims most of the honours. I was on the footplate of No 46231, *Duchess of Atholl*, on this occasion, and after a traditionally slow start we got away in most thrilling style from Willesden onwards. The engine was worked in 25 per cent cut-off with regulator opened well out on to the second valve, and after just topping the '60' mark at Brent Junction she went on steadily accelerating all the way up the 1 in 335 past Harrow and Hatch End to top the bank at 67 mph. Although cut-off was reduced to 15 per cent at Bushey we reached no less than 75 mph through

Watford, and a subsequent increase to 20 per cent beyond Kings Langley was enough to take us over Tring summit at a minimum speed of 64 mph.

Even with running of this quality we should not have had sufficient time in hand to offset the effects of the long permanent way slowing north of Leighton Buzzard, and with signals 'on' outside Rugby into the bargain we were 2½ min late in. But the *Duchess of Atholl* was a grand engine to ride. There was ample steam available for her biggest outputs of power, and as I listened to her crisp, businesslike beat I could not help reflecting that in the absence of the exhaust 'music' of the steam locomotive, rail travel in the future will lose a good deal of its emotional appeal. The cab of a diesel may be ideal for railway sightseeing, but I for one shall miss that narrow, cramped, but fascinating view of the line ahead beside the boiler of a steam locomotive.

This engine made considerably the fastest running north of Bletchley. From the long permanent way check near Stoke Hammond Box

Down West Coast express near Bourne End, Herts, hauled by engine No 46209 Princess Beatrice *in May 1962.* (Rail Archive Stephenson, D.M.C. Hepburne-Scott)

there was a fine recovery to 75½ mph at Wolverton; Roade summit was cleared at 68 mph, and we ran splendidly at 77 to 78 mph on the level between Blisworth and Weedon. Again, the minimum speed at Kilsby Tunnel was only a shade under 70 mph. The cut-offs here were 20 per cent from Castlethorpe to Roade, 17 per cent to Weedon, and 20 per cent up to the tunnel. In passing, it is interesting to note the maximum and minimum speeds roughly corresponding to the times evaluated by the computer; these are 78 mph at Leighton Buzzard, 62 at Roade, 73 at Weedon, and 63 at Kilsby Tunnel. These figures alone are enough to underline the difficulty of the schedule, and even the relatively poor run of No 46211, with its net start-to-stop time of 83 min for the 82.6 miles from Euston to Rugby, would have been considered a very fine performance in 1933, when the 'Lizzies' were first introduced.

According to the computer, engine No 71000,

worked to the maximum rate of continuous steaming, should be able to run from Euston to Rugby in 73 min start to stop with a tare load of 480 tons; but this would probably involve a coal rate that would need two firemen, and in any case the 80-min schedule presented difficulties enough in actual operation. Details of the running between Rugby and Crewe have been shown in no more than skeleton detail, as every engine concerned was being driven more easily. The continuation from Crewe to Carlisle presents some most interesting contrasts, in comparison between the point to point times shown in the computer, based on a constant rate of evaporation, and the running performed in actual service. At the times my runs were made the 'Midday Scot' was allowed 163 min for the 141.1 miles from Crewe to Carlisle, divided between 90 min for the 78.2 miles to Carnforth, and 73 min for the 62.9 miles through the Westmorland hill country. First of all there is comparison between the actual schedule and the computer times:

Section		Dist	Sched	Comp
		Miles	min	min
Crewe–Winsford Jc	...	8.8	11	12.2
Winsford–Warrington	...	15.2	15	14.7
Warrington–Winwick Jc	...	3.5	4	3.5
Winwick Jc–Wigan ...	...	8.3	12	10.2
Wigan–Standish	...	3.3	7	5.3
Standish–Euxton Jc	...	6.4	7	7.6
Euxton Jc–Preston	...	5.5	8	5.0
Preston–Oxheys	...	1.3	3	3.2
Oxheys–Garstang	...	8.1	8	10.0
Garstang–Lancaster	...	11.6	10	12.2
Lancaster–Carnforth	...	6.2	5	6.1

The most notable differences are in the approaches to Wigan and Preston, where the actual schedule allows for easier running, and on the level north of Preston. Here the actual schedule demands much harder running than the computer—equivalent, indeed, to an effort that, if sustained throughout, would yield an overall time of about 76 min from Crewe to Carnforth, instead of the actual 90 min. Between Carnforth and Carlisle, on the other hand, the computer and the actual schedule are in much closer agreement:

Section		Dist	Sched	Comp
		Miles	min	min
Carnforth–Oxenholme	...	12.9	15	14.2
Oxenholme–Tebay	...	13.1	17	19.0
Tebay–Summit	...	5.5	10	10.5
Summit–Penrith	...	13.6	13	13.2
Penrith–Plumpton	...	4.7	5	4.4
Plumpton–Carlisle	...	13.1	13	11.7

It has always been traditional, ever since North Western days, to have a very sharp point-point allowance between Oxenholme and Tebay; but on my last northbound run with the 'Midday Scot', despite the hindrance of a permanent way check to 30 mph right at the foot of the Grayrigg bank, and a similar check over Tebay troughs, engine No 46246, *City of Manchester*, took a thirteen-coach train of 431 tons tare from Carn-

forth to Shap Summit in 40½ min, against 42 min scheduled, and the 43.7 min of the computer. I have an ever-growing collection of runs over this most interesting route, and rather than compress details of a few into my remaining space this month, I will save them for more extended description later.

To conclude, there is no doubt that we shall inevitably find ourselves comparing steam and diesel performance to an increasing extent in the next few years—not only in details of times and speeds, but in the fundamental characteristics of the two forms of motive power. The performance of the diesels may be predicted with certainty and *finality*; there is no means of extracting that little extra in times of the greatest need. But with steam there are occasions when a driver and fireman will so set about things as to make any constant evaporation test results, and any 'computer' figures, look small.

One such occasion took place on the Grayrigg bank in 1944 of all years, on the wartime 10.5 am *ex*-Euston, when Mr Cecil M. Furst was a passenger. Following the recent tests on engine No 46225, *Duchess of Gloucester*, at Rugby, and the study of some results communicated to me by Mr R. C. Bond, Technical Adviser to the British Transport Commission, I was curious to know how near that run of 1944 came to the maximum capacity of the locomotive. Mr Bond was kind enough to have the details of this run analysed at Rugby, with some rather astonishing results.

During the trials of the *Duchess of Gloucester*, the maximum rate of continuous steaming attained slightly exceeded 40,000 lb per hour—a figure substantially exceeding the maximum attained with No 71000. But taking 40,000 lb of steam per hour as a basis, a graph was plotted to show the anticipated performance of the engine from a signal stop just south of Oxenholme. The calculation assumed a continuous steaming rate of 40,000 lb per hour, which would require a firing rate of 6,500 lb per hour—2.9 tons of coal per hour! The following table shows the predicted speeds, from such strenuous working, and the almost unbelievable effort actually made.

GRAYRIGG BANK: LMSR Engine 6244

Location	Predicted speed 40,000 lb/hr	Actual speed
	mph	mph
Passing Oxenholme	30	29½
Milepost 21	46½	43
Milepost 22½	50	54
Milepost 24½	52½	60
Milepost 25½	53	56
Grayrigg	53	55

Predicted time Oxenholme–Grayrigg   9 min 24 sec
Actual time Oxenholme–Grayrigg   8 min 20 sec

Thus it is evident that while initially the engine was worked at a little under the 40,000 lb per hour rate, the effort was afterwards stepped up to a truly terrific standard. It could not have been sustained indefinitely, but it was an outstanding example of what an expert crew can get out of a steam locomotive by mortgaging the boiler, in view of the respite to come immediately after passing Grayrigg in the six miles of almost level track before tackling the final ascent to Shap. In the Rugby trials with engine No 46225, *Duchess of Gloucester*, the established indicated horsepower on level track at a steam rate of 40,000 lb per hour and a speed of 50 mph was 2,660, giving 2,260 at the tender drawbar at the same speed. I calculate that No 6244 on the Grayrigg bank was developing about 2,600 *drawbar* horsepower—the equivalent value, that is, related to level track; so that this represented a substantial advance on the Rugby figures. The indicated horsepower on the run with No 6244 was probably in excess of 3,000, though even this does not surpass the maximum of 3,300 attained during the trials of engine No 6234, in 1939, when some exceptionally high outputs were obtained over short periods.

East Coast Main Line — pre and post war

For 14 years of my life as a professional engineer, from 1925 until 1939, I worked in the head office and engineering headquarters of the Westinghouse Brake and Signal Company Ltd, which was then a building overlooking the locomotive yard at King's Cross. On the weekly pay packet of a graduate-trainee, lunches were necessarily brief, and the entrance to the cab rank alongside No 1 Platform at King's Cross provided a convenient entrée to the station itself for some post-luncheon walks. The staff lunch hour at Westinghouse was an ideal time for railway observation, for between 1 and 2 o'clock there were three main-line departures, and four arrivals. In my article of July 1959 I continued thus:

FOR many years it was a tradition of the Great Northern to arrange the long-distance express passenger train departures in three groups during the day. There were the 10 am and 10.10; the 1.15, 1.30 and 1.40 pm; and the 5.30, 5.35 and 5.45 pm expresses. There were variations in the actual minutes, over the years, but the only definite breaks were made by the 4 pm combined Yorkshire and Newcastle express, and between the wars, the Pullman trains at first leaving shortly after 11 am. But even then, until the 'Harrogate Pullman' was extended to Glasgow and became the 'Queen of Scots', if one missed the 'Flying Scotsman' there was not another train to Newcastle and Edinburgh for more than three hours.

The value of this policy from the operating point of view was shown during the first world war, when the Great Northern was carrying an unprecedented volume of freight traffic. South-bound trains were dispatched from Peterborough as soon as they were ready, all running to a standard schedule, and with the express passenger trains running in tightly-confined groups it was a far easier matter to keep the line clear for them for a short period, and then the freights could once again have the line largely to themselves, for a couple of hours or more. Of course the passenger loadings were enormous, and the tradition of Great Northern loadings was accepted by the locomotive department and carried into LNER days. It was publicly announced that the first Gresley Pacifics were designed to haul 600-ton trains.

Today the contrast is absolute. From 7.50 am

Class 'A1' Gresley Pacific No 2565 Merry Hampton *near Drumlithie on an up express fish train from Aberdeen.* (E.R. Wethersett)

there is a fast express from Kings Cross at approximately hourly intervals to 6 pm running to Newcastle, or beyond, and it is rare to see any of them loaded to much more than 400 tons, tare. From the passenger's point of view this is admirable, and in my own business journeyings to York and Newcastle I have found the morning trains most useful. I can, for example, leave my home in Bath shortly before 8 am and be in York at 2.34 pm in time for an afternoon conference, with the opportunities of joining my London colleagues and spending some useful time in discussion with them on the way down. In the old days it would have meant staying overnight in London and travelling down on the 'Flying Scotsman'.

The locomotive work, of course, is generally not nearly so strenuous as of old. The faster trains, such as the 'Talisman' and the 9 am, load to no more than nine coaches; but while it was certainly great fun to clock the work of the Gresley Pacifics with Brobdingnagian loads the present arrangement, giving a frequent service of lighter trains, is far more convenient to the user. Although a very far cry from the 600-ton loads envisaged by Sir Nigel Gresley, much of

the present-day performance is very smart, and worth recording in full detail. The interest of today's running has been enhanced recently by the rebuilding of the 'A3' Pacifics with twin-orifice blast pipes and double chimneys, and the use of these engines turn and turn about with the Gresley 'A4s' and the Peppercorn 'A1s,' on the most severe duties.

After his appointment as Chief Mechanical & Electrical Engineer of the Eastern and North Eastern Regions, Mr K. J. Cook introduced the practice of optically lining-up the frames, cylinders, and horn guides of locomotives passing the shops for general repairs, a practice with which he had been so closely associated in his earlier days at Swindon. Pacifics, on which it has been my privilege to ride, have been beautifully turned out, as quiet and sweet as sewing machines—with no trace of irregular, syncopated beats all too familiar at the end of the second world war, nor the frightful knocking and banging that suggested that these famous engines were in many cases worth little more than scrap metal price! Judging from my recent experiences the 'A3s' in particular have been given another lease of very useful life.

It was in 1937 that a design for a twin-orifice blastpipe and double chimney was worked out for the 'A3' engines. The first Gresley locomotives to be so fitted, the 'P2' class 2–8–2s, *Cock o' the North* and *Earl Marischal*, had proved astonishingly free runners; *Cock o' the North* in particular ran up to 85 mph with ease on its early trials on the Great Northern main line, and a similar arrangement was also prepared for the 'A4s,' and later fitted to the four engines originally numbered 4468, 4901, 4902 and 4903, and named *Mallard, Capercaillie, Seagull* and *Peregrine*. Only one 'A3' was fitted, No 2751, *Humorist*, and like the 'P2s' and the 'A4s' this engine had the full Kylchap arrangement, with double petticoats extending down to the level of the blastpipe orifice.

It is the same arrangement that is now being fitted to all the 'A3s' and by the courtesy of Mr K. J. Cook, I am able to include the accompanying drawing, prepared from a Doncaster drawing of June, 1937. The original 'A3s' had a blastpipe orifice of 5¼ in dia, and this was subsequently increased to 5½ in with a lower blastpipe top. As will be seen from the drawing the new arrangement includes twin orifices of 5¼ in dia. No change has been made in the valve setting as a result of the modified draughting, though of course the cut-off in full gear has for some time been 75 per cent instead of the 65 per cent provided in the original Gresley design. In its original form with double-chimney, *Humorist* looked exactly like the present rebuilds, externally at any rate; but in a subsequent modification the engine was fitted with an ugly fabricated affair without any lip, and to check any tendency for exhaust steam to blow down and obscure the driver's look-out,

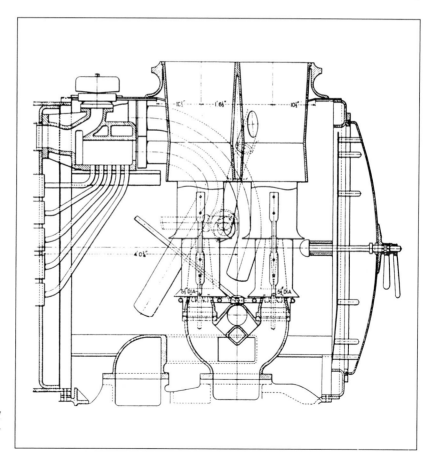

Twin-orifice blastpipe and double chimney arrangement for an 'A3' Pacific.

small deflector shields were fitted. In the arrangement now standardised on the 'A3s,' no shields have been provided, and judging from my own footplate experience in cold wintry weather, when the exhaust was at its most profuse, none appeared necessary.

As this article has so far been concerned with contrasts between past and present, I am continuing, in Table I, with details of four runs between Kings Cross and Grantham, all of my

TABLE I
EAST COAST ROUTE: KINGS CROSS–GRANTHAM

Run No			1			2			3			4		
Year			1959			1959			1937			1939		
Train			9 am			7.50 am			10.5 am			10.5 am		
Engine No			60048			60021			2571			4464		
Engine Name			Doncaster			Wild Swan			Neil Gow			Bittern		
Engine Class			A3			A4			A1*			A4		
Load, tons (E/F)			315/330			309/320			491/525			473/510		
Dist miles		m	s	mph	m	s	mph	m	s	mph	m	s	mph
0.0	KINGS CROSS	0	00	—	0	00	—	0	00	—	0	00	—
2.6	Finsbury Park	6	20	—	6	18	—	6	53	—	6	56	—
5.0	Wood Green	9	17	60	8	56	64	10	08	53½	10	12	53½
						pws	15						
12.7	Potters Bar	17	54	52	19	05	47	20	15	42½	20	26	44½
17.7	Hatfield	22	22	75	23	36	73½	25	25	72	25	17	76½
23.5	Woolmer Green Box ...	28	00	58	28	31	67½	30	57	56	30	17	64
28.6	Stevenage	32	47	—	32	37	80/76	35	50	68/65	34	41	75/69
		sig	sev	5									
31.9	HITCHIN	38	33	—	35	00	88	38	36	80½	37	12	85
35.7	Three Counties	43	02	—	37	33	90/86	41	15	86½	39	47	91
										76½	sigs	and	pws
41.1	Biggleswade	47	32	76	41	15	90	45	23	80	45	29	15
51.7	St Neots	55	55	73½/79	48	34	81½/87	53	57	68½/75	57	20	63/75
58.9	HUNTINGDON	61	36	—	53	49	80	59	56	72	63	20	72
		pws		10									
63.5	Abbots Ripton	69	13	—	57	42	70½ min	64	29	56 min	67	29	62½ min
					pws		20						
69.4	Holme	74	27	79	63	49	76/64	69	18	77½	71	52	86½
									sigs				
75.0	Fletton Junction	79	07	—	68	43	72½	74	45	—	76	08	—
									sigs				
76.4	PETERBOROUGH ...	80	57	(slack)	70	38	(slack)	77	15	—	77	54	(slack)
								sig	stop				
79.5	Werrington Junction ...	85	03	63	75	02	64	86	06	50	82	35	59
84.8	Tallington	89	50	70	79	42	71½	90	53	61½	87	39	68½
88.6	Essendine	93	10	66	82	54	69/72	95	43	57/59	91	09	63/65
97.1	Corby Glen	101	08	61/64	90	13	66/69	105	18	46/50	100	09	50½
									sigs				
100.1	Stoke Box	104	08	57	92	55	63½	109	30	—	103	53	45½
				72			77		sigs				61
105.5	GRANTHAM	109	07	—	97	16†	—	117	52	—	110	16	—
	Net times ... ... (min)		100			94½‡			111			105	
	Net average speed (mph)		63.4			67.1			57.0			60.3	

* Original Gresley 'A1' with 180 lb boiler. † Passing time. ‡ Equivalent net time to stop

own recording, that can be said fairly to typify the old order and the new. The modern runs are both quite recent experiences, while the older ones were made during the period in the summer when the 'Flying Scotsman' was running non-stop to Edinburgh, and the so-called 'Junior Scotsman' left immediately afterwards. The 'group' policy was still continued even when extra trains were run, and at the height of the summer the 'ten o'clock group' consisted of departures at 10, 10.5, 10.10 and 10.15, and on Saturdays a *fifth* train was sandwiched in from York northwards leaving immediately afterwards, when the 'non-stop' had passed. Run No 1, on the present-day 9 am, was no more than a moderate performance, with a double-chimneyed 'A3.' After the very bad check at Hitchin, right down to 5 mph, I would have expected some faster running, but in actual fact we did not exceed 79 mph anywhere, and the climb to Stoke was not unduly energetic in the circumstances. Nevertheless a net time of 100 min to Grantham, with its start-to-stop average speed of 63.4 mph, would have been considered quite fast for an *ordinary* East Coast express twenty years ago. At Grantham, *Doncaster* was exchanged for another rebuilt

'A3,' No 60063, *Isinglass*, and much livelier running ensued, giving net times of 47 min from Grantham to Doncaster (65 mph) and 30½ min from Doncaster to York (63.2 mph). Due to checks, however, we were still 1 min late in arriving at York.

On the morning 'Talisman', Run No 2, the 'A4' No 60021, *Wild Swan*, was handled brilliantly. We had a late start of 2½ min, and were checked at Greenwood Box, near Potters Bar, where the connections to the lines through the new tunnels were being laid in. Thus Hatfield was passed 4 min late. Over the next 41.2 miles, to Huntingdon, the timetable requires an average speed of 74.5 mph but *Wild Swan* was driven in a style that was not merely reminiscent of the pre-war streamline days—she gave me the fastest time I have *ever* recorded between Knebworth and Huntingdon. Four pre-war runs on the 'Silver Jubilee,' and one on the 'Coronation,' gave me times, over this 33.9-mile stretch, of 24 min 47 sec; 25 min 43 sec; 25 min 19 sec; and 25 min exactly, with

Left *'A4' Pacific No 4902* Seagull *leaving Grantham with the 1.20 pm ex-King's Cross Scottish express in 1938.* (O.S. Nock)

Right *The 'Tees–Tyne Pullman' crawling over the widening works at Potters Bar behind engine No 60029* Woodcock *with the author on the footplate.* (M.W. Earley)

average speeds varying between 79 and 82 mph. *Wild Swan* took 23 min 58 sec—an average of all but 85 mph. We clocked our first '90' just north of Wymondley automatic signals, but then eased slightly through Hitchin, to regain 90 mph at Three Counties, and again north of Biggleswade.

The check at Abbots Ripton was a bad one, but so swift was the recovery that it did not cost more than 1½ min, and Peterborough was passed dead on time. Our net time to this point, 67 min, was not much more than the old streamline allowance of 63½ min when speeds through Hatfield were much higher and there was no speed restriction over the Fenland stretch from Holme to Yaxley. With a brisk climb to Stoke box, Grantham was passed nearly 2 min early. Having done so well up to this point the rest of the run could be taken more easily. York was passed 5 min early, with plenty in hand to offset a permanent way check to come at Northallerton. But a signal check at Tollerton was not expected and the driver had to 'step on it' thereafter, to reach Darlington, as we did, dead on time. Net time for the complete run of 232.3 miles was 220 min.

The first point to be emphasised about the pre-war runs is that they were both made on Saturdays—that with *Neil Gow*, indeed, was made at the August Bank Holiday weekend. The starts at that period, with these heavy trains, were always very strong and vigorous, and the times out to Finsbury Park made by *Neil Gow* and *Bittern*, namely 6 min 53 sec and 56 sec, would have been considered a little on the slow side by the best standards then current. On a trip with the 1.20 pm Scotsman, when I rode on No 4476, *Royal Lancer*, with a load of 483 tons tare, we entered the first tunnel with the engine going literally 'all-out'—full regulator, full forward gear—and the cut-off had not been reduced below 47 per cent when we entered the second tunnel, just beyond Belle Isle box. On this occasion we passed Finsbury Park in 6 min

33 sec, and that was not by any means the fastest I had recorded with 500-ton trains.

On Tuesdays, Thursdays and Saturdays at that time the 10.5 am was worked by Heaton men, and their Pacifics, *Bayardo, Dick Turpin* and *Neil Gow*, were familiar sights in London. In 1939 the 'A4' No 4464, *Bittern*, was added to their stud, and the run tabulated in column 4 is a grand specimen of her work. She began to draw away from *Neil Gow* after Hatfield, and gave us the usual 90 mph running north of Hitchin. The 'A1,' despite her splendid running, was keeping no more than dead time, as the allowance for this train was then 38½ min to Hitchin and 60 min to Huntingdon. Holiday congestion caused a series of checks in the Peterborough district, and eventually we were nearly 7 min late into Grantham; there was, however, no time to be booked against the engine.

North of Hitchin, *Bittern* was making such excellent time that we ran into the signals of the 'Flying Scotsman' at Biggleswade. There was a heavy permanent way slack on at Sandy, and the 'Scotsman,' running at much reduced

speed, was evidently not clear when we sighted the Biggleswade 'distant.' In recovering from the permanent way check our driver did not press the engine at first, allowing the 'non-stop' to draw well ahead; but from St Neots we were at it again 'hammer and tongs,' and with speeds of well over 80 mph sustained right across the fens we were less than a minute late through Peterborough. A good climb to Stoke brought us into Grantham comfortably on time. Though I must not be tempted to dwell on the continuation of these runs north of Grantham, I must refer once again to the vigour of the pre-war starts. On my recent run with the 9 am, *Islinglass*, hauling 330 tons, took 7 mins 15 sec for the 4.2 miles from Grantham to Barkston; *Bittern* with 510 tons took 6 min 52 sec; and *Neil Gow* with 525 tons took 6 min 27 sec!

To follow up in more detail the working of the newly-rebuilt 'A3s,' by the courtesy of Mr G. F. Fiennes, Line Traffic Manager, Great Northern, I was privileged to ride on one of them from Newcastle to Kings Cross on the up 'Flying Scotsman.' We had the usual load for today, eleven coaches of 377 tons tare, and the engine was one of the 'general service' batch of Gresley 'A1s' built in 1925, after the decision had been taken to standardise the Gresley rather than the Raven type of Pacific. The engine concerned,

No 60061, *Pretty Polly*, was in first rate nick, and we had some good coal on the tender. Kings Cross men were on the job, Driver Eldridge and Fireman Rutt, with Eastern Region Head-quarters Inspector Dixon riding as my guide and philosopher. I was interested to see that another 'A3' brought the train into Newcastle, but this use of the older engines is no more than typical of East Coast workings today.

The overall schedule time of 286 min for the 268.3 miles from Newcastle to Kings Cross is the same as that worked for a short time at the end of the summer service of 1936, when the 'Scotsman' had ceased to be non-stop, but was calling at Newcastle before the beginning of the normal winter working of those days with stops at Darlington, York and Grantham. A run I had on the train at that time is of such interest, by way of comparison, that I have tabulated it alongside my recent footplate journey. The engine diagrams were the same as during the non-stop period, with one Pacific working through from Waverley to Kings Cross; but instead of crews changing over through the corridor tender the engines were remanned at Newcastle. This enabled engines with non-corridor tenders to be used, and on this particular run we had the then-well-known Kings Cross 'A1' No 4474, *Victor Wild*. It is

TABLE II
EAST COAST ROUTE: NEWCASTLE–KINGS CROSS
The 'Flying Scotsman'

Year						1936			1958		
Engine No						4474			60061		
Engine Name						*Victor Wild*			*Pretty Polly*		
Engine Class						A1*			A3		
Load, tons (E/F)						445/475			377/400		
Dist miles						Sched min	m s	mph	Sched min	m s	mph
0.0	NEWCASTLE	...	...	...	...	0	0 00	—	0	0 00	—
2.5	Low Fell ...	...	...	...	...	—	5 15	—	—	5 29	51
							pitfall				55/47½
8.2	Chester-le-Street ...	...	...	...	—	11 58	56/44	—	12 00	56/51½
14.0	DURHAM	...	...	...	...	20½	19 17	(slack)	18	18 37	(slack)
18.2	Croxdale	...	...	...	...	—	—	—	—	24 20	65
23.1	Ferryhill ...	...	...	.....	...	—	32 11	—	29	29 32	—
30.6	Aycliffe ...	...	...	...	...	—	40 36	60 max	—	36 14	74/55

Engine Name		Victor Wild			Pretty Polly		
36.0	DARLINGTON	48	46 02	56	44	41 22	72
38.6	Croft Spa	—	48 41	64½	—	43 29	76
41.2	*Eryholme*	—	51 20	57	49	45 37	69½
50.1	NORTHALLERTON	63	60 17	63/58	56	53 32	74/57
57.9	Thirsk	70	67 32	69	63	59 59	79½
64.0	Pilmoor	—	73 02	66	—	64 38	80½
68.9	Alne	—	77 17	72	72	68 05	84
						pws	20
78.5	*Skelton Junction*	—	85 42	—	80	78 33	58
80.1	YORK	90½	88 50	(slack)	83	81 32	(slack)
84.3	Naburn	—	95 24	56	—	87 59	60
89.8	Riccall	—	100 56	64½	—	92 55	73
93.9	SELBY	108	105 36	(slack)	98	98 09	(slack)
102.3	Balne	—	115 20	66	—	108 05	63
108.1	*Shaftholme Junction*	—	120 43	64½	116	113 09	69
112.3	DONCASTER	128	125 04	53	121	117 49	eased
120.6	Bawtry	—	easy	—	—	126 48	64
129.7	RETFORD	145	144 02	56	138	137 00	64/50
134.3	*Milepost 134*	—	149 50	44	—	142 03	56
140.9	Crow Park	—	155 58	76½	—	147 30	82
						sigs	20
148.2	NEWARK	163½	162 02	68½	155	155 28	—
152.9	Claypole	—	166 22	64	—	160 44	63
156.8	Hougham	—	170 17	58½	—	164 19	66
158.6	*Barkston N Junction*	—	172 21	46	168	165 59	60
162.8	GRANTHAM	179	177 44	51	172	170 12	57
168.2	*Stoke Box*	—	185 18	38	178	176 00	50
171.2	Corby Glen	—	188 35	71½	—	178 51	72½
176.1	Little Bytham	—	192 32	82	—	182 32	86
179.7	Essendine	—	195 09	84	187	184 56	90
183.5	Tallington	—	198 03	77	—	187 48	77
188.8	*Werrington Junction*	—	202 27	—	199	192 19	—
191.9	PETERBOROUGH	207	205 54	(slack)	204	196 17	(slack)
198.9	Holme	—	214 15	69	—	205 39	62½
204.8	Abbots Ripton	—	219 49	53	—	211 35	55½
209.4	HUNTINGDON	226½	224 21	76½	222	216 00	75/60
216.6	St Neots	—	230 23	62½	—	222 44	62
224.2	Sandy	—	237 14	70/63	234	228 53	78/74
229.7	*Langford Bridge*	—	242 33	57 / 61	—	233 30	65
						pws	
236.4	HITCHIN	251	249 38	48½	245	244 39	47½
239.7	Stevenage	—	254 12	40½	—	249 02	—
243.3	Knebworth	—	258 33	51	254	252 57	56
250.6	HATFIELD	266	265 29	74	262	260 28	easy
						sigs	
255.6	Potters Bar	—	270 18	60	269	266 12	—
						sigs	
263.3	Wood Green	—	276 49	76½	—	275 49	—
						sig stop	
265.7	Finsbury Park	—	279 00	—	281	282 02	—
268.3	KINGS CROSS	286	283 20	—	286	289 52	—
	Net time (min)		283¼			269	

* Original Gresley 'A1' with 180 lb boiler

interesting to compare the past and present point-to-point times, making up the same over-all allowance. The older schedule, for example, was based on a relatively fast finish from Hatfield.

A big detail that will immediately strike those familiar with present running conditions is that apart from a slight pitfall slack in the Team Valley there was not a single check anywhere between Newcastle and Kings Cross, and the day was a Saturday—September 27, 1936, to be precise. The driver was able to take things quite quietly and steadily throughout, going moder-ately uphill, and letting the engine show the usual Gresley speedworthiness on the favourable stretches, with close point-to-point timekeeping all the way. The uphill minimum speeds of 44 mph at Plawsworth and Markham, 38 at Stoke, and 40½ at Stevenage tell their own tale, while I have little doubt that the maxima, including that of 84 mph near Essendine, were achieved under quite easy steaming conditions. It would have been interesting to have a full analysis of the engine working on this run, as I feel sure that the coal consumption on such a nicely balanced performance would have been very low. Only at the very end did the driver open up a little, to clear Potters Bar at 60 mph and to make a fast and undelayed time of 13 min 2 sec over the last 12.7 miles. I may add that the Gateshead driver who worked the train down from Edinburgh did equally well, stopping at Newcastle 4¼ min early, in 139 min 46 sec from the start.

On my recent run *Pretty Polly* had to be worked much more vigorously. The point-to-point timings are faster, aggregating to a lead of 10 min by Selby. There are recovery time allowances approaching Doncaster and Peter-borough, and 4 min longer than previously are allowed for the final run in from Hatfield.

One naturally expects more in the way of relaying slacks in the winter than during the period in the summer service, and three were in operation on this trip; those at Beningbrough and Arlesey were severe, while the slack over the viaduct at Bawtry was just one of those niggling hindrances that break up a spell of sustained steaming. Despite much harder running than on my journey of 1936 we were no more than a minute early at Retford, and ultimately our time in hand at Hatfield was insufficient to offset the effects of the concluding checks. It was a day of weather characteristic of the winter of 1958–9—a tendency for fog in places, some stretches of clear, beautiful sunshine, and a murky night awaiting us in London.

We started gently out of Newcastle, and although the engine was given full regulator once we were round the curve at King Edward Bridge Junction cut-off was quickly brought back to 18 per cent and we did not exceed 55 mph at Lamesley. But a reversion to 25 per cent at Chester-le-Street took us up the 2½ miles of 1 in 150 past Plawsworth box at the excellent minimum speed of 51½ mph, and from that point, with the fire thoroughly warmed up, the performance was immaculate. The section from Newcastle to Darlington, once so infested with pitfall troubles, is now quite clear, and the only hindrances are the very severe permanent way slack at Durham, made worse by the sharp ensuing rise of a mile at 1 in 120–101 to Relly Mill Junction, and the moderate slack for the curve at Aycliffe. Working in 15 per cent cut-off *Pretty Polly* sustained 74 mph over the Bradbury moors, slackened to 55 at Aycliffe, and had regained 72 mph when we passed Darlington.

The use of 15 per cent cut-off all the time with full regulator was continued from Darlington, taking us up the two miles of 1 in 391 of 'Croft Bank,' as the local enginemen call it, and past Eryholme at a minimum of 69½ mph. Then came the usual easing over Wiske Moor troughs, and with Northallerton passed at 57 mph the regulator was once again to the full and cut-off advanced to 17 per cent. In response, *Pretty Polly* gave us a grand burst of speed, reaching 80 mph just after Thirsk and averaging 82 mph for 12½ miles till steam was shut off for the Beningbrough check. The road here is of course one of the finest stretches in the country, and the whole action of the engine at this high

Sir Nigel Gresley in its last years as a regular traffic department engine at Grantham. (K.H. Leech)

speed was as good as one could wish for. Near Alne we passed the down 'Flying Scotsman,' headed by a diesel-electric locomotive, and imagining the snug comfort inside the cab on that cold winter's day I must confess to rejoicing in the wilder and more boisterous conditions on our own footplate. In this, of course, I am a heretic of contradictions and inconsistency, for as a motorist I should hate the idea of an open car in the winter!

But to return to the footplate of *Pretty Polly*, the permanent way check near Beningbrough was a bad one, and we had not recovered afterwards to more than 58 mph when it was time to ease off for York. We passed through with time comfortably in hand, and we could afford to drop a little on the next stage, to Selby, as there would be the Doncaster recovery allowance soon available to us. With the Bawtry check following we were a minute early through Retford, the net time to this point being 131½ min—an excellent average speed of 59.3 mph from the start. From Retford southwards we enjoyed the assistance of the new British standard atc, and what a sense of additional security it gives on a hard, fast run! At the time of my trip the apparatus was in operation throughout from Retford to London, and its sphere of activity has since been extended northwards to York.

The engine was worked hard up to Markham summit with the cut-off in 25 per cent; she responded with a sustained 56 mph up the 1 in 200 to Askham Tunnel, and her crisp, even beat was a joy to hear. The regulator was eased back a little for the descent to the Trent valley, but we reached 82 mph, and held this speed across the level towards Newark until the regulator was eased further back in readiness for Muskham troughs. We were heavily checked by signal at the level crossing with the Lincoln line, though this check gave an opportunity for a further display of the engine's prowess in a splendid uphill recovery. From Newark the cut-off was 20 per cent right up to Stoke box, with full regulator except for an easing through Grantham. The minimum speed at Peascliffe Tunnel was 60 mph but because of the easing of the regulator there was a drop to 57 mph in the approach to Grantham. Again we were holding 54 mph on the 1 in 200 above Great Ponton, but the driver then eased back the regulator to lessen the chance of a slip in Stoke Tunnel. This accounted for a rather rapid fall to 50 mph at Stoke summit.

The point-to-point from Stoke to Essendine, 11.5 miles in 9 min, involves an average speed of 77 mph and it was interesting to see the engine working necessary for its almost exact observance. The cut-off was kept in 20 per cent for the first mile over the summit; then it was reduced to 15 per cent, with the regulator not quite full open. Approaching Little Bytham at 85 mph the driver made a very slight increase, to 16 per cent, and this gave us a maximum of exactly 90 mph. After Essendine the regulator was eased back to give 180 lb steam-chest pressure, against 210 lb per sq in in the boiler, and with a reversion to 15 per cent cut-off, speed gradually tailed off to 77 mph at Tallington, and 75 mph at Helpston box. So, with the aid of recovery time, we were 7¾ min early through Peterborough, though most of the time in hand was to be needed to off-set the effects of the very heavy check we knew to be in store for us at Arlesey.

Before coming to that check, however, we had two further examples of the way in which present-day running is handicapped, as compared with that of pre-war years. Between Peterborough and Langford Bridge box,

37.8 miles, the times made were 36 min 39 sec by No 4474 and 37 min 13 sec by No 60061. The latter engine had to observe the speed restriction over the fenland stretch, and did not exceed 62½ mph beyond Holme, as compared with 69 mph by No 4474; and again the latter engine went through Offord at full speed and took the rise to St Neots in her stride, whereas No 60061 reduced down below the present 70 mph limit and *accelerated* up the subsequent rise to pass St Neots at 62 mph. So that despite considerably harder work intermediately, and much faster running from St Neots southwards, No. 60061 made the slower overall time. Little remains to be told. After the Arlesey check we were on time through Hitchin, and ahead once again at Hatfield; but checks came so thick and fast afterwards that our ultimate arrival was nearly 4 min late. But from the locomotive point it had been a grand run, with a net gain of 17 min on schedule.

Someone will be sure to ask, what is the effect of the double blast-pipe and chimney—has it had any appreciable effect? The Gresley Pacifics were always free-running engines, even in their earliest days when they had short-lap, short-travel valves; but even bearing this in mind my own impression is that they are still freer, and the concensus of opinion among the men is that they steam more readily when fuel and other conditions are adverse. In the Swindon dynamometer car I have seen the effect of putting twin-orifice blastpipes on the 'Kings,' in the considerable reduction in pressure difference in the exhaust between the root and the tip of the blast pipe, with consequently greater freedom of exhaust. The same order of improvement has undoubtedly taken place on the rebuilt 'A3s'; but quite apart from the finer points of technical achievements, Mr Cook's rebuilding of these engines has provided the East Coast Route with a fine stud of rejuvenated express passenger motive power for the difficult days of transition that lie ahead.

Midland — doing the 'ton'!

My school days were spent within sight of two important routes of the Midland Railway; one was the far-famed Settle and Carlisle, and the other was the important cross-country route, which from its bifurcation at Wennington led to the Furness Line at Carnforth, and to Lancaster, Morecambe and Heysham Harbour. Later, ensconced at Westinghouse in London, in many a lunch hour I found time to tear myself away from the attractions of King's Cross to see what was going on at St Pancras, but then there was little of interest. There were express arrivals from Bradford and Manchester, usually compound hauled, but so lightly loaded that they never needed pilots. At that time of day there was rarely a sight of a 2-4-0, or a single wheeler. In the 1950s all was changed, and, as my September 1959 article tells, Pacifics were in regular use — and how!

IN the next year or so, when more and more important services will be changed over to diesel or electric traction, it seems likely that we shall find ourselves paying one farewell tribute after another to steam. And generations later, when enthusiasts read about the historical aspects of railways, there may be some who find themselves wondering why we ever *did* change. Certainly it cannot be said that the British steam locomotive is staggering, overburdened and broken-backed, to its extinction. I was never more conscious of this than at the conclusion of an extensive journey on the Continent, during which I sampled the running in France, Switzerland and Italy. The fastest running of the whole round was made not on any of the foreign lines but on the up 'Golden Arrow,' from Dover to Victoria, by one of the rebuilt 'Merchant Navy' class 4-6-2s, heavily loaded, and turning a late start of 4 min into an arrival a minute early.

This month it is the turn of the Midland main line between St Pancras and Leicester. This is a route over which I do not often have the opportunity of travelling personally, and such experiences as I have had recently have not been particularly fortunate. But from a number of correspondents I have received such a wealth of data, much of it showing locomotive performance of an outstanding quality, that it has been the greatest pleasure to collate these records and comment on them. At the same time it is clear that not all running on the main line to and from St Pancras is of the same high order. Some of my friends have written to tell of experiences that tally more closely with some of my own. In presenting details, however, inevitably one picks out the star runs, and the collection contained in this article does constitute a magnificent tribute to the Midland enginemen of today, and no less to the design and workmanship put into the engines concerned. It may be no more than a coincidence, but the majority of the runs that I have chosen for tabulation have been made with Kentish Town men. I can only use the data that has come to hand; but from past experience on the Midland I can hardly think that the drivers and firemen of Leeds and of Trafford Park are anything if at all behind their London *confrères* and this tribute of mine is offered to the line as a whole.

During the years in which I was perhaps more closely acquainted with Midland running, between 1925 and 1935, the timings between St Pancras and Leicester were almost entirely static. The non-stop time of the fastest Scottish and Manchester expresses was 107 min, in the up direction—never quite regaining the 105 min of days before the first world war. On that schedule the compounds were at first limited to a maximum tare of 240 tons, but following trials of those engines against North Western and Caledonian designs of comparable power that old Midland limit was relaxed, and I have notes of journeys made in 1931 on which ten, and even eleven bogies were taken unassisted. At that time the Manchester expresses changed engines at Derby, while the up 'Thames-Clyde Express,' and the 12 noon up from St Enoch both changed engines at Leicester. Today the locomotives work through, either from Manchester or Leeds, and by comparison with the work on the up Scottish expresses of former days they have an advantage in starting, in that they are not getting away 'cold' from Leicester. I mention this particularly, because in looking over details of my older runs I find that on quite a number of the finest examples time was frequently dropped on the initial booking of 20 min for the 16.2 miles from Leicester to Market Harborough.

In turning now to recent work over this route, I should like at the outset to express my best thanks to Messrs M. G. Boatman, W. O. Knight, F. G. Lodge, M. Palmer, K. R. Phillips, and N. Rimes, whose letters have been helpful to me in the preparation of this article. In Table I are details of seven runs on the up 'Palatine,' leaving Leicester at 4.31 pm, and in contrast to former Midland days when the engine of the principal expresses was almost invariably a compound, no fewer than four different classes are concerned. In studying the work over this route it must be borne in mind that while the intermediate gradients are in places quite severe there are normally no appreciable speed restrictions in the 60 miles between Wellingborough and Cricklewood, other than the overall limit of 90 mph, and the regulation slacks at Market Harborough and Wellingborough are not severe, even though they are followed in each case by stiff rising gradients.

Between Wigston Magna and Hendon, over which stretch I have shown the average speeds for each run, the overall tendency of the line is slightly falling, and if account be taken of the slight hindrances at Harborough and Wellingborough, the aggregate effect could be considered as roughly level. On the majority of these runs very full use was made of the down gradients, again in striking contrast to pre-1914 days; then, with the light trains then in vogue, the uphill running was often such that steam could be shut off entirely when running downhill and still leave sufficient margin in hand to keep time. When, however, drivers are registering net gains of 12, 13 and 14 min on a schedule of 99 min from Leicester to St Pancras, there has clearly been no loitering on the way!

Coming now to the runs themselves, on the first, the 'Jubilee' class 4-6-0 *Uganda* was 10 min late away from Leicester, and by a start of the utmost vigour her driver had practically halved this considerable lateness by Kettering. A speed of 63 mph had been attained after Wigston, and sustained over Kibworth summit, while the acceleration to 85 mph at East Langton was in the traditional manner of up Great

TABLE I
LONDON MIDLAND REGION: LEICESTER–ST PANCRAS

Run No		1	2	3	4	5	6	7
Engine No		45636	73073	45589	70014	70021	45530	45530
Engine Name		Uganda	—	Gwalior	Iron Duke	Morning Star	Sir Frank Ree	Sir Frank Ree
Engine Class		LM6	BR5	LM6	BR7	BR7	LM7	LM7
Load, tons (E/F)	Sch	243/265	302/330	304/330	304/325	301/330	304/330	306/330
Dist miles	min	m s	m s	m s	m s	m s	m s	m s
0.0 LEICESTER	0	0 00	0 00	0 00	0 00	0 00	0 00	0 00
—		—	—	—	—	pws	—	—
3.7 Wigston Magna		5 45	6 32	6 16	6 27	7 30	5 56	6 16
7.5 Great Glen		9 36	11 16	10 37	10 13	11 30	9 44	10 23
9.4 Kibworth North		11 12	13 56	12 40	11 55	13 16	11 27	12 05
12.8 East Langton		13 55	16 18	15 43	14 32	15 59	14 07	15 00
16.2 MARKET HARBOROUGH	19	16 31	19 14	18 26	17 08	18 59	16 45	17 51
20.6 Desborough North		20 59	24 18	23 13	21 30	23 35	21 27	22 30
24.5 Glendon S Jc		24 17	—	26 39	24 39	—	24 37	25 50
27.1 KETTERING	31	26 14	29 49	28 31	26 35	29 09	26 32	27 52
30.9 Finedon		29 00	32 55	31 24	29 40	32 05	29 33	30 42
—		sig stop						—
34.1 WELLINGBOROUGH	37	34 27	35 38	33 47	32 12	34 30	32 08	33 00
39.4 Milepost 59¾	43	40 34	40 31	38 23	36 58	39 08	37 16	37 30
42.4 Sharnbrook		43 17	43 07	40 56	39 28	41 41	39 47	40 03
—			—	sig stops	—	—	—	—
49.2 Bedford N Jc	51	48 34	48 28	50 14	44 26	46 45	44 42	44 45
—						sigs		
57.3 Ampthill		55 03	55 33	61 35	51 10	54 10	51 34	51 11
61.8 Harlington		58 47	59 34	65 53	55 03	58 42	55 40	54 56
66.3 Leagrave		62 35	63 51	70 26	59 10	63 00	59 59	59 00
68.9 LUTON	70	64 35	65 59	72 39	61 28	65 10	62 02	61 10
74.5 Harpenden		68 39	70 26	77 09	66 28	69 47	66 18	65 44
—		—	—	pws	—	—	—	—
79.2 ST ALBANS	79	71 56	74 09	81 13	70 23	73 30	69 55	69 25
83.9 Radlett		75 12	77 42	85 45	74 03	76 45	73 22	72 43
86.7 Elstree		77 13	79 56	88 05	76 18	78 45	75 26	74 48
—		—	—	—	sigs	—	—	—
92.2 Hendon	90	81 17	84 19	92 20	80 26	82 44	79 38	78 48
94.0 Cricklewood		—	85 50	94 09	sigs 84 33	84 13	sig stop	80 10
—		pws	—	—	—	—	pws	—
97.6 Kentish Town	96	86 25	89 16	97 37	88 40	87 38	89 49	83 10
—		sig stop	—	—	—	—	sigs	sigs
99.1 ST PANCRAS	99	95 11	92 05	100 00	91 04	90 18	93 48	87 22

	1	2	3	4	5	6	7
Net time, min	84½	92	89	87½	87½	87½	85½
Average speed, Wigston to Hendon (88.5 miles)	74.6	68.2	70.8 (net)	72.1	71.7 (net)	72.0	73.2
Min speed Leagrave, mph	68	61	58	63	63	60	65
Max speed on trip, mph	89 (at Radlett)	83 (at Sharnbrook)	89 (at Sharnbrook)	95 (at Sharnbrook)	90 (at Radlett)	91½ (at Sharnbrook)	91 (at Sharnbrook)

Engine classes: – LM6, Stanier 'Jubilee' 4–6–0: LM7, Rebuilt 'Patriot' 4–6–0 ('Royal Scot' boiler); BR5, Standard Class '5'
4–6–0; BR7, 'Britannia' 4–6–2

One of the first 6 ft 9 in compounds, No 1047, on a down Manchester Express near Matlock. (M.W. Earley)

Northern expresses on passing Stoke Summit! A dead stand for signals outside Wellingborough hardly helped matters, but evidently this driver was beyond discouragement. After a relatively moderate descent of Sharnbrook bank, not exceeding 82½ mph, he and his fireman really began to pile it on. From Bedford North Junction up to Leagrave the average speed was 73.3 mph, while the ensuing 25.9 miles on to Hendon took no more than 18 min 42 sec—an average speed of 83 mph. Actually the maximum did not exceed 89, and this occurred near St Albans. The engine was evidently eased a little here, as speed fell slightly on the continuation of the descent toward Radlett. Passing Hendon in such a time as 81 min 17 sec the recorder could reasonably have been expecting a punctual arrival, despite the Wellingborough stop and the late start; but checks intervened, and the arrival was 6 min late.

The remaining runs all relate to the working of nine, rather than eight-coach trains. The standard class '5', 4-6-0 No 73073 had a clear road throughout, and steadily gained time without any special fireworks, while the same driver made a still finer run with a 'Jubilee' class engine, *Gwalior*, in column 3 of the table. Particular interest, however, attaches to the work of the 'Britannias,' in columns 4 and 5, and it is evident that these engines are being used to the utmost advantage on the Midland line. At one time one might have been disposed to think that the 'Britannias' would go down in locomotive history as controversial engines. Certainly they have not won universal acclaim, though one feels that much of the opposition to them has arisen from long familiarity with different designs. One is reminded of the engineer who once said: 'I am all for universal standardisation, so long as it is my designs that

A relief Anglo-Scottish express climbing Shap Incline hauled by 'Jubilee' class three-cylinder 4-6-0 No 45606 Falkland Islands. (Derek Cross)

are standardised'! It would be little short of a miracle if a standard locomotive design pleased everybody. Today, with the magnificent running of the Midland men to reinforce what has already been done with these engines in East Anglia, the reputation of the 'Britannias' is becoming even more secure.

No 70014, *Iron Duke*, a former Stewart's Lane (Southern Region) boat-train engine, put up some tremendous running, in column 4. The start from Leicester was 7½ min late, but such uphill speeds as 68 mph over Kibworth, 62 at Desborough North, and 60 at Sharnbrook summit, combined with maxima of 88 at East Langton, 87 before Glendon Junction, and 95 down Sharnbrook bank had almost wiped out the lateness by Bedford. Speed was eased carefully at Harborough and Wellingborough,

and also through Kettering, while once the train was running on time the driver refrained from further very fast work. In the adjoining column is the work of *Morning Star*, on which, some years ago, I recorded some exceedingly fine hill-climbing between Newton Abbot and Plymouth. On the up 'Palatine,' the running was a little slower than that of *Iron Duke* until the signal check at Ampthill; then there came a fast finish, with the luxury of a clear road right into the terminus. On this run the maximum speed of 90 mph at Radlett took the train by impetus over Elstree summit at the rather extraordinary minimum speed of 78 mph.

The engine concerned in the runs tabulated in columns 6 and 7, or rather its name—*Sir Frank Ree*—brings back very early railway memories of mine. I suppose I shall always associate that name with the original bearer of it, the LNWR 'Claughton' No 1191, for many years stationed at Camden, and used turn and turn about with No 1161, *Sir Robert Turnbull*, for the haulage of the old 2 pm 'West Coast Corridor.' When my family moved north in the early days of the first world war we travelled by that train, and sure enough *Sir Frank Ree* was on the job. This engine, as LMSR No 5902, was the first of the 'Claughtons' to be rebuilt as a 'Baby Scot,' a true rebuild in that case as many parts of the original LNWR engine were used; but in the more recent conversion, to class '7P,' with the 'Royal Scot' type boiler, little, if anything, of either of the two previous 'incarnations' can remain.

Two magnificent runs were made. The first included an extremely vigorous start, with a speed of no less than 67 mph over Kibworth summit, and 86½ mph at East Langton. Again, very hard running was done up to Sharnbrook summit, topping the bank at 58 mph after a careful reduction to 60 mph through Wellingborough. The second run had by this time fallen more than a minute behind, though still representing splendid work in itself; but after easing to 72 mph through Kettering the driver on No 7 run pressed his engine to a maximum of 90 mph between there and Wellingborough—a most unusual spurt. Speed was checked down again through the later station; Sharnbrook summit was cleared at 60 mph, and then the second '90' was reached below Sharnbrook Station. There was every reason for haste on this trip, as Leicester had been left 9 min late, and from Bedford onwards engine and crew 'went in a perisher' for it—to quote a memorable phrase of the late Charles Rous-Marten!

From Bedford, passed at 75 mph, the speed was increased to 82 near Elstow Box, after which on six miles of almost continuous 1 in 200 climbing there was a gradual fall to 71 mph at Ampthill Tunnel. The brief easing of the gradient, and a mile of level past Flitwick brought an acceleration to 76 mph, after which the second six miles of 1 in 200 were cleared at a minimum of 65 mph. At Luton the train was practically on time, but the effort was continued without the slightest 'let-up.' Two more 'nineties' were recorded, at both Radlett and Hendon, and with a clear road through the inner suburban area

Kentish Town was passed in the remarkable time of 83 min 10 sec. The concluding check was not severe, and the train arrived in St Pancras 2¾ min early. This is indeed a worthy concluding effort in a most exhilarating series of runs.

In the down direction the runs that I have received relate to a variety of trains, but for detailed tabulation I have chosen five on the down 'Palatine,' which has regular stops at Luton and Wellingborough, and some sharp intermediate bookings. On this train, and others, speeds of 90 mph and more are nowadays common on the long descent between Leagrave and Bedford; but what is perhaps even more stimulating is to study the logs of lesser trains, and to see the vigorous and enterprising work put up by enginemen from a diversity of sheds. Space does not permit of the inclusion of an unlimited number of logs, but it is evident from the mass of data reaching me that enterprise in running is widespread, including semi-local trains between St Pancras, Luton and Bedford.

Principal interest in Table II centres round the very free running of the locomotives concerned between Luton and Bedford. Naturally I have picked out the best from the collection of runs sent to me by various correspondents, and to the five on the down 'Palatine' can be added one on the 2.25 pm down, non-stop from St Pancras to Leicester on which another 'Jubilee,' hauling 308 tons tare, reached 96 mph at Flitwick, and after a slight drop to 92 in Ampthill Tunnel was doing 95 again when a sight of adverse signals compelled a slowing to 40 mph at Houghton Conquest Box. The frequent attainment of speeds of 90 mph and more, by 'Scots,' 'Jubilees' and 'Britannias' alike, is as much a tribute to the free-running and good riding qualities of the engines themselves as to the enterprise of their enginemen. In the course of fast and arduous turns such as these drivers do not spur on their locomotives for the sheer delight of high speed. One can take it fairly safely for granted that the speeds of 90 mph were attained in the natural way, by engines being driven fast and skilfully,

TABLE II
LONDON MIDLAND REGION: 7.55 am ST PANCRAS–LEICESTER

			1	2	3	4	5
Run No			46116	45618	70014	70014	45579
Engine No			*Irish*	*New*	*Iron*	*Iron*	*Punjab*
Engine Name			*Guards-*	*Hebrides*	*Duke*	*Duke*	
			man				
Engine Class		Sch	LM7	LM6	BR7	BR7	LM6
Load, tons (E/F)			264/280	264/280	273/290	282/300	296/315
miles		min	m s	m s	m s	m s	m s
0.0	ST PANCRAS	0	0 00	0 00	0 00	0 00	0 00
1.5	Kentish Town	4	3 34	3 58	4 12	4 25	4 05
—			—	—	—	sig stop	—
6.9	Hendon	10½	11 02	11 25	11 02	14 42	12 04
—			—	—	pws	—	pws
12.4	Elstree		16 42	17 04	18 14	20 12	17 50
15.2	Radlett		19 15	19 34	21 25	22 30	21 12
—				pws			
19.9	ST ALBANS	23	23 11	24 34	25 30	26 05	25 25
—				sigs		pws	
24.6	Harpenden		27 48	31 48	29 50	32 27	29 50
30.2	LUTON	34	33 02	37 02	34 58	37 10	34 42
2.6	Leagrave		4 28	4 12	4 31	4 11	4 22
7.1	Harlington		8 28	8 14	8 24	8 00	8 40
11.6	Ampthill		11 38	11 30	11 40	11 00	11 54
—			pws				
19.7	*Bedford N Jc*	18	19 32	17 17	17 24	17 00	17 30
26.5	Sharnbrook		27 32	22 25	22 29	21 42	22 37
29.5	*Milepost 59¾*	27½	30 48	25 20	25 39	24 10	25 39
32.5	Irchester		33 17	27 40	28 21	26 12	28 04
34.8	WELLINGBOROUGH	34	35 42	30 21	31 07	28 21	30 18
3.2	Finedon		—	4 28	5 28	5 25	—
—				sigs	—	—	
7.0	KETTERING	8½	8 09	8 15	8 56	8 48	8 58
—				—	—	pws	
9.6	*Glendon S Jc*		10 55	11 38	11 30	14 00	11 45
—				—	—	pws	
13.1	Desborough		14 40	15 32	15 05	20 30	15 31
17.9	MARKET HARBOROUGH	20½	19 10	20 00	19 28	25 15	19 58
21.3	East Langton		22 32	22 57	22 51	28 28	23 10
23.9	Kibworth		24 58	25 11	25 10	30 38	25 38
—				pws	—	—	—
26.6	Great Glen		27 52	28 30	27 29	32 42	28 08
—			sigs	—	sigs	—	—
30.4	Wigston Magna		31 58	31 48	32 10	35 27	31 12
				sigs	—	—	
34.1	LEICESTER	38	36 38	36 48	38 18	40 06	35 18
Net times:- St Pancras–Luton			33	33	32	31	33
Luton–Wellingborough			31	30¼	31	28¼	30¼
Wellingborough–Leicester			35	35	35	34	35¼
Max speed on trip, mph			90	92	92	98	93½
			(before	(before	(before	(before	(before
			Bedford)	Bedford)	Bedford)	Ampthill)	Bedford)

Engine classes:- LM6, Stanier 'Jubilee' 4–6–0; LM7, 'Royal Scot' (rebuilt) 4–6–0; BR7, 'Britannia' 4–6–2

Left *A Euston–Manchester express near Leighton Buzzard hauled by 'Converted Scot' class 4-6-0 No 46153* The Royal Dragoon. *(Ian S. Pearsall)*

Below *Euston–Perth express, relief to the 'Royal Scot', climbing Shap, hauled by 'Converted Scot' class 4-6-0 No 46136* The Border Regiment. *(E.D. Bruton)*

in the manner best calculated to produce the best overall results.

Of individual runs, that of the 'Britannia' *Iron Duke*, in column 4 was outstanding. Due to the checks on the first stage the train was 3½ min late away from Luton. The start was good, but then the engine really got going, to a maximum of 98 mph before Flitwick. It would indeed have been interesting to see what maximum this splendid engine would have attained below Ampthill Tunnel; but this was a service run, not a stunt, and the speed was eased to 80–83 mph on what is normally the fastest part of the descent. Having reached almost level track, however, the engine was opened out again; Bedford was passed at 90 mph, speed was held at 82 to 88 right on to Sharnbrook Station, and the three-mile bank at 1 in 119 was cleared at the astonishing minimum speed of 73½ mph. At the summit, marked by milepost 59¾, the train was once again on time, yet a further '90' was recorded at Irchester.

The train was heavily checked between Kettering and Desborough North, thereby losing another 5 min on schedule; but again there was a most thrilling recovery. Slowing carefully at Market Harborough speed was worked up to 73½ mph at East Langton, but then, up the 3½ miles to Kibworth North, mostly steeper than 1 in 200, and including two miles at 1 in 130–114, the speed never fell below 70 mph. This was followed by a swift acceleration to yet another '90' before the Wigston slack. A notable feature of this run was the care with which the speed restrictions were observed, despite the vigour with which the engine was being driven in order to recover lost time.

I have not tabulated the running on the 'Palatine' north of Leicester, but on this same trip, following a late start of 2½ min, the 17.2 miles to passing Kegworth were covered in 14 min 58 sec, with yet another '90'—93 this time—at Loughborough. I should not imagine, even with present driving enterprise from some Midland engine crews, that one can often record *five* individual maxima of 90 mph or more in one single journey, between Luton and Derby—not

to mention an '85' at Chiltern Green. The locations were 98 before Flitwick, 90 at Bedford North, Irchester, and Great Glen, and 93 at Loughborough. As will be seen from the tabulated times the other four engines featured in Table II were all doing excellent work though none quite so spectacular as that of the *Iron Duke*.

A study of these twelve runs on the 'Palatine,' seven up and five down, certainly gives a brilliant view of present-day running on the Midland line, though it is only fair to add the almost inevitable reminder that there is another side to the coin. While I was writing this very article I saw some of that other side. I had occasion to travel over the Midland line from Cheltenham to Birmingham, and with a 'Jubilee' class engine we, too, had a nine-coach load. It was soon pretty clear that the engine was painfully short of steam. The crew were doing what they could, flailing the engine for brief periods to try and liven up the fire; but it was of no avail and then, to add to our troubles, although there were five bank engines in the sidings at Bromsgrove, a full 3 min elapsed after we had stopped before one of them even made a move to come out and assist us. In this period more time was lost, and the train was 8 min late into Birmingham after a start practically on time.

The reputation of the 'Jubilee' class for fast and hard running is not impaired by an experience of this kind, which was probably due to an ill-prepared individual engine. It was all the more surprising in that the train in question was the morning Cardiff-Newcastle express, and the LMR engine would have come on 'fresh' at Gloucester. To more than restore the balance, however, I have tabulated five runs with 'Jubilees' on the 12.15 pm from St Pancras to Leeds, as between Leicester and Trent. The schedule is one of the many very smart bookings on the Midland, and to cover the 20.8 miles in 21 min, start to stop, some hard running was needed with nine-coach trains. This table represents the work of five different drivers, all from Kentish Town shed, and except for No 3 show a striking uniformity in speed.

TABLE III
LONDON MIDLAND REGION: LEICESTER–TRENT

Run No Engine No Engine Name						1 45682 Trafalgar		2 45694 Bellerophon		3 45694 Bellerophon		4 45618 New Hebrides		5 45639 Raleigh	
Load, tons (E/F)						296/310		292/310		300/320		302/320		304/320	
miles						m	s	m	s	m	s	m	s	m	s
0.0	LEICESTER	...	...	...	...	0	00	0	00	0	00	0	00	0	00
4.7	Syston	...	...	...	...	6	19	6	09	6	42	6	14	6	18
9.8	Barrow-on-Soar	...	...	...	...	10	29	10	24	11	19	10	34	10	30
12.5	LOUGHBOROUGH	...	...	...	...	12	28	12	26	13	34	12	42	12	34
15.3	Hathern	...	...	...	...	14	36	14	37	15	48	14	56	14	44
17.2	Kegworth	...	...	...	...	16	11	16	12	17	24	16	32	16	20
20.8	TRENT	...	...	...	...	20	07	20	02	20	56	20	38	20	13
Max speed, mph		...	...	...	...	83		80		77		77		79½	

And now, in conclusion, I come to the 6.50 pm down from St Pancras, which has a sharp booking of 21 min for the 19.6 miles from Luton to Bedford. This might perhaps be thought an easier proposition than the same time over the 20.8 miles from Leicester to Trent, but in actual fact, with the uphill start to Leagrave, and the slow finish into Bedford, involving a crossover from fast to slow lines, it is quite a proposition. Furthermore, it often loads up to eleven bogies, which with heavy passenger complements means a gross load of 390 to 400 tons. Timekeeping from one cause or another is not too good and details of six successive runs with 'Jubilee' class engines gave the following results on the opening stage to Luton, booked in 36 min, for the 30.2 miles:

Engine No	Load, tons (E/F)	Total time	
		m	s
45628	279/308	35	02
45652	366/395	37	59
45620	366/395	38	11
45675	333/355	46	50
45622	345/375	41	47
45562	368/390	45	04

Only the first of the six was completely free of checks, but the engines had little margin for

recovery with such loads. My correspondent did not travel beyond Luton on the first run, but on the remainder the times to Bedford were, in order: 19 min 51 sec; 19 min 51 sec, again; 21 min 23 sec; 21 min exactly; and 21 min 42 sec. Only engine No 45652 reached 90 mph on any of these runs, and she gave a fine exhibition, averaging 85 mph, from Flitwick to Elstow Box.

More recently 'Britannias' have taken a turn on this job, and my correspondents were pardonably enthusiastic to see what would happen when so mettlesome an engine as the *Iron Duke* was put on. They were not

TABLE IV
LONDON MIDLAND REGION:
LUTON–BEDFORD

Load: 9 coaches, 296 tons tare, 320 tons full
Engine: 'BR7' 4-6-2 No 70014, *Iron Duke*

Dist			Sch	Actual		Speeds
miles			min	m	s	mph
0.0	LUTON ...	...	0	0	00	—
2.6	Leagrave ...	...		4	55	53
7.1	Harlington	...		8	47	82
10.1	Flitwick ...	...		10	48	90
11.6	Ampthill ...	...		11	48	90
13.6	Milbrook Box	...		13	08	92
17.1	Elstow Box	...		15	18	101
19.6	BEDFORD	...	21	19	21	—

Liverpool–Glasgow express in the Lune Gorge, between Low Gill and Tebay, hauled by rebuilt 'Patriot' class 4-6-0 No 45545 Planet. *(Derek Cross)*

disappointed. On the remarkable trip set out in Table IV there were no fewer than *three* recorders on the train, two travelling together and checking each other's note taking, and a third working independently. The times passed to me were in almost precise agreement, and particularly over the critical length from milepost 45 to Elstow Box, 2.3 miles in 1 min 23 sec. This gives an average speed of 99.6 mph, and fully bears out the claim of a maximum speed of 101 mph. It is interesting to see, however, that on this run the start from Luton was slower by 48 sec to Ampthill than the fastest of the 'Palatine' runs, and it was only

north of this point that the *Iron Duke* was allowed really to have his head. In any case the 'Britannias' can now be included among the select band of British locomotives that have attained 100 mph.

Speaking of running at 100 mph, the congratulations of all locomotive enthusiasts will be extended to Driver Hoole of the Eastern Region for his fine running with the Stephenson Locomotive Society special on May 23 last, when a maximum of 112 mph was attained with the famous 'A4' Pacific No 60007, *Sir Nigel Gresley.* Some day I must also tell the full story of how the same driver gave me a maximum of 103 ½ mph when I was riding on the footplate of the up 'Tees-Tyne Pullman' train. Maximum speeds of this order don't just happen!

Dover boat trains — LCDR and BR

Steamer services across the English Channel were many and various in the days of the pre-Grouping British Railways; indeed, in the nineteenth century there were two routes in hot competition from London to the same pier at Dover! With Grouping and then Nationalisation, affairs became more rationalised, though less exciting, and in this article I recalled the days of the London Chatham & Dover boat expresses in contrast to some more modern journeys.

THE completion of the first stage of the electrification of the Kent Coast lines of the Southern Region has been accompanied by some interesting developments in motive power. The multiple-unit trains put on to the fast services between Victoria, Margate, and Ramsgate are modern developments of the express stock used in earlier Southern projects, but their use on the 10 am Ostend Boat Express and the corresponding inward service from Dover has once more brought the Chatham line into the picture as a principal, as well as a relief boat train route, and while describing my first experiences with the new trains, it is interesting to recall some of the past exploits of the London, Chatham & Dover Railway, and no less some later achievements of Southern Railway locomotives over the same route.

Although before the setting up of the joint Managing Committee both the Chatham and the South Eastern companies ran to Dover, it is not perhaps generally realised today that the Chatham was then unquestionably the principal route, and that company owned the English packets plying from Dover. The South Eastern boats operated from Folkestone. The Chatham line for much of its length closely followed the historic route of the Dover Road (A2)—the Roman Watling Street; east of Rochester, the only appreciable deviations from its straight course were to ease the gradients of the railway, between Faversham and Canterbury, and again over the high ground south-east of Canterbury. Nevertheless the gradients are severe east of Faversham, with summit points at Selling Tunnel and near Shepherdswell reached only after long climbs at 1 in 100 to 132. Fortunately the track is for the most part well aligned, and, unlike the neighbouring South Eastern Railway, there was apparently no restraint on downhill running in LCDR days.

The continental expresses from Victoria to Dover Pier called at Herne Hill to connect with the City line from Holborn Viaduct, and at the

TABLE I
LCDR: HERNE HILL–DOVER PIER

Train		9.14 pm			11.14 am		
Engine, 4–4–0 No		25			13		
Load, coaches		10			15½		
Load, tons (approx)		130			200		
Dist miles		m	s	mph†	m	s	mph†
0.0	HERNE HILL	0	00	—	0	00	—
1.0	Dulwich ...	2	32	—	2	36	—
1.8	Sydenham Hill	3	52	32.7	4	12	27.3
3.2	Penge ...	6	02	40.5	6	33	35.0
3.8	Kent House	6	44	53.5	7	17	51.0
4.7	Beckenham	7	39	56.5	8	10	58.5
6.0	Shortlands ...	9	17	48.7	9	49	48.5
6.9	BROMLEY ...	10	14	52.1	10	46	52.1
8.0	Bickley ...	11	37	47.7	12	13	45.5
10.8	St Mary Cray	15	03	50.7	15	52	47.7
13.7	Swanley ...	18	10	54.7	19	01	54.0
16.5	Farningham Rd	20	57	61.2	21	50	60.5
19.4	Fawkham ...	23	56	57.3	24	51	56.9
22.0	Meopham ...	27	11	47.8	28	19	44.7
22.9	Sole Street ...	28	24	45.5	29	39	42.5
29.0	Strood ...	34	21	61.2	35	49	59.1
29.8	Rochester ...	35	29	41.7	36	59	40.4
30.4	CHATHAM	36	14	50.0	37	47	46.8
32.0	New Brompton*	38	31	41.7	40	10	39.9
35.0	Rainham ...	42	06	50.3	43	53	48.6
37.6	Newington ...	44	53	57.1	46	50	54.0
40.8	SITTINGB'RNE	48	18	54.7	50	20	53.2
44.0	Teynham ...	52	10	50.3	53	54	54.6
48.0	FAVERSHAM	56	42	52.9	58	48	47.9
51.3	Selling ...	60	42	49.7	63	53	39.1
57.9	CANTERBURY	67	57	53.8	72	20	46.0
60.7	Bekesbourne	71	30	52.3	75	52	52.4
						sigs	
63.8	Adisham ...	75	10	50.0	80	45	37.4
67.7	Shepherdswell	80	21	45.1	90	21	24.1
71.1	Kearsney ...	83	56	57.6	94	05	55.3
73.3	Dover Priory	86	25	53.6	96	21	59.5
74.0	Dover Harbour	87	21	41.0	97	07	49.8
74.5	DOVER PIER	88	25	26.7	98	22	22.8
Net times,‡ min		87¾			93		

* Now Gillingham. † Average speeds from exact chainages. ‡ Allows for slight bridge slack at Sittingbourne on each run.

close of the nineteenth century the down night mail was allowed only 91 min to cover the 74.5 miles from Herne Hill to Dover Pier. The loads were not heavy it is true, but the locomotive work done by the Kirtley 4–4–0s appears to have been most excellent. By comparison, the electrically-hauled Ostend Boat Train of today is allowed 85½ min from passing Herne Hill to arrival at Dover Marine. Two logs of LCDR boat trains are of interest in comparison with modern running; the first of these relates to the old night mail, while the second was on the popular 11 am from Victoria. The engines concerned were both of the latest type of Kirtley 4–4–0, with 6 ft 6 in coupled wheels, and 18 in by 26 in cylinders. The logs do not include any maximum and minimum speeds, so I have worked out the station-to-station averages from the official chainages then quoted.

As far as Faversham the going was very even, with the night train gradually drawing ahead. The running averages over the 44.8 miles between Penge and Faversham were 53.0 mph by engine No 25, with 130 tons, against 51.5 mph by No 13 hauling some 200 tons. Up to this point the latter engine had done the harder work, especially as no attempt had been made to snatch seconds by faster running downhill. It is interesting to see from the average speeds that neither engine was unduly pressed along the level after New Brompton, and that the good time had been made, rather, by excellent uphill work. Although the gradient profile looks like a violent switchback in its alternation of rising and falling stretches the tendency is markedly uphill from the start to Sole Street, and the average speeds of the two engines from Dulwich to Sole Street, 50.7 and 48.5 mph respectively, were indeed excellent.

East of Faversham No 25, on the night mail, continued in great style, and the average speed of 49.7 mph between that point and Selling suggests a speed of well over 40 mph at Selling summit, on 1 in 100; while, up the concluding ascent from Adisham to Shepherdswell, on 1 in 132 the speed was again above 40 mph. No fast running appears to have been attempted on the long descent from Shepherdswell to Dover, almost entirely at 1 in 132; but the train was by then comfortably ahead of time. One can imagine, however, that a very brisk run was made over the single-track line over the cobblestones on to the Admiralty Pier, to cover the last half mile in 64 sec pass to stop! Engine No 13, with the day train, was evidently eased considerably after Faversham but then, unfortunately, she was brought almost to a stand by adverse signals at Adisham. Recovery had to be made with this relatively heavy train up the grade to Shepherdswell and the arrival on the pier was 2¼ min late.

The foregoing runs were typical examples of performance by the Kirtley engines in ordinary service, but in June, 1896, two special trips were made, non-stop between Victoria and Dover Pier, which stand easily as the records with steam, in each direction, over this route. They are nowadays of enhanced interest, in view of the possibilities with electric traction over this route. The logs are detailed in Tables II and III, and in each case I have again worked out the average speeds from the official chainages of that time. Coming so soon after the 'Race to the North' of 1895 these runs are of additional interest in the differences they reveal from the style of running that came to distinguish the northern lines towards the end of the 1895 affair. On the down journey, for example, the start was extremely vigorous, and the travelling through the outer suburbs lively for the passengers. And having passed Bickley in the very fast time of 14 min 5 sec anything might have seemed possible when the train got on to the really fast stretches of the line.

In actual fact the going beyond Bickley appears to have been nothing very much out of the ordinary, having regard to the lightness of the load; and whereas locomotives of the LNWR, of the Caledonian, and of the North Eastern had been running at 70 and even 75 mph on level track the LCDR engine No 16 averaged only 60 mph from New Brompton to Faversham. The hillclimbing was certainly very good, and the whole run was much in advance of anything done south of the Thames up to that time.

On the return journey it is evident that the train started from a point on Dover Pier considerably short of that to which the official

TABLE II
LCDR: VICTORIA–DOVER PIER
JUNE 12, 1896

Engine: Kirtley 4-4-0 No 16
Load: 70 tons

Dist miles					m	s	mph
0.0	VICTORIA	...	...	...	0	00	—
0.72	Grosvenor Road	...	...	1	11	36.3
1.21	Battersea	...	...	...	1	56	39.2
2.31	Clapham	...	...	...	3	16	49.5
3.17	Brixton	...	...	...	4	19	49.3
3.97	HERNE HILL	...	...	...	5	10	56.5
5.0	Dulwich	...	...	...	6	29	47.0
5.72	Sydenham Hill	...	...	7	24	47.0
7.19	Penge	...	...	...	9	08	50.6
7.81	Kent House	...	...	9	49	54.5
8.67	Beckenham	...	...	...	10	35	67.3
10.0	Shortlands	...	...	...	12	02	55.0
10.82	BROMLEY	...	...	...	12	51	60.2
11.92	Bickley	...	...	...	14	05	53.5
14.81	St Mary Cray	...	...	17	02	58.8
17.65	Swanley	...	...	...	19	53	59.8
20.49	Farningham	...	...	...	22	28	66.0
23.35	Fawkham	...	...	25	13	62.3
25.94	Meopham	...	...	...	27	50	59.5
26.86	Sole Street	...	...	...	28	56	50.1
32.94	Strood	...	...	...	34	39	64.0
33.72	Rochester	...	...	...	35	40	46.5
34.35	CHATHAM	...	...	...	36	23	52.8
35.94	New Brompton	...	...	38	26	46.5
38.96	Rainham	...	...	...	41	38	56.5
41.61	Newington	...	...	...	44	09	63.5
44.72	SITTINGBOURNE	...	...	47	03	64.5
47.98	Teynham	...	...	...	50	20	59.6
51.99	FAVERSHAM	...	...	54	25	58.7
55.30	Selling	...	...	...	58	09	53.1
61.82	CANTERBURY	...	...	64	49	58.6
64.70	Bekesbourne	...	...	67	46	58.5
67.76	Adisham	...	...	...	70	41	63.7
71.66	Shepherdswell	...	...	74	56	55.0
75.09	Kearsney	...	...	...	78	05	65.2
77.31	Dover Priory	...	...	80	14	61.9
77.95	Dover Harbour	...	...	81	04	46.1
78.43	DOVER PIER	...	...	...	81	56	32.5

chainage relates—probably from a spot roughly equal in distance to the present position of engines starting the up boat trains from the Marine station. The old 'Harbour' station is roughly marked by the present Hawkesbury Street Junction Signalbox. But although the initial passing time of 42 sec to the Harbour sta-

TABLE III
LCDR: DOVER PIER–VICTORIA
JUNE 14, 1896

Engine: Kirtley 4–4–0 No 16
Load: 70 tons

Dist miles				m	s	mph
0.0	DOVER PIER ...	...	...	0	00	—
0.48	Dover Harbour	...	...	0	42	—
1.12	Dover Priory ...	...	...	1	41	38.6
3.34	Kearsney	...	...	4	40	44.7
6.76	Shepherdswell	...	...	9	14	44.9
10.66	Adisham	...	...	13	13	58.7
13.72	Bekesbourne ...	...	...	15	57	67.8
16.60	CANTERBURY	...	...	18	38	64.3
23.13	Selling	...	...	25	53	54.0
26.44	FAVERSHAM ...	...	...	28	39	75.8
30.45	Teynham	...	...	32	28	62.8
33.70	SITTINGBOURNE ...	...	...	35	33	63.3
36.81	Newington	...	...	39	15	50.4*
39.46	Rainham	...	...	41	51	61.5
42.49	New Brompton	...	...	44	39	65.3
44.08	CHATHAM	...	...	46	20	56.7
44.70	Rochester	...	...	47	03	51.8
45.49	Strood	...	...	48	08	43.4
51.56	Sole Street	...	...	55	39	48.3
52.49	Meopham	...	...	56	45	50.5
55.08	Fawkham	...	...	59	05	66.7
57.94	Farningham	...	...	61	27	72.3
60.78	Swanley	...	...	64	13	62.0
63.61	St Mary Cray ...	...	...	66	53	63.7
66.50	Bickley	...	...	69	32	65.5
67.60	BROMLEY	...	...	70	28	70.8
68.43	Shortlands	...	...	71	13	66.5
69.75	Beckenham	...	...	72	34	58.7
70.61	Kent House	...	...	73	27	58.3
71.24	Penge	...	...	74	08	55.3
72.70	Sydenham Hill ...	...	...	75	45	54.3
73.43	Dulwich	...	...	76	29	59.7
74.45	HERNE HILL ...	...	...	77	29	60.0
75.25	Brixton	...	...	78	35	43.5†
76.12	Clapham	...	...	79	34	52.3
77.21	Battersea	...	...	80	40	59.5
77.70	Grosvenor Road	...	...	81	15	50.4
78.43	VICTORIA	...	...	82	33	—

* Bridge slack near Sittingbourne. † Speed reduced
through Herne Hill

tion cannot be compared truly with the quoted mileage, the running onwards admits of no doubt. A speed of 45 mph was quickly attained on the 1 in 132 ascent to Lydden Tunnel, and sustained unbrokenly to the summit. The downhill running was a little more free in this direction, though some reduction appears to have been made through Canterbury. Again, however, after a dash down from Selling Tunnel that probably involved a maximum of over 80 mph, the going along the coast was comparatively mediocre.

The curves in the neighbourhood of Chatham and Strood were taken at just about the utmost limit for safety, and then some of the finest work of the whole round trip came in the ascent of Sole Street bank, with its average speed of 48.3 mph from Strood to the summit—1 in 100 practically throughout. There was some fast running inwards from this point, with an average speed of all but 66 mph from Meopham to Shortlands; again, too, the final run-in from Herne Hill was extremely brisk. At that time it was generally considered that the up journey from Dover was the harder of the two by three or four minutes, so that in making a time of 82 min 33 sec inwards the crew of engine No 16 had accomplished a very fine performance. Like some of the greatest runs in the Race to the North it was made during the night. The train left Dover Pier at 11.38 pm and arrived in Victoria at a shade after 1 am.

From these feats of more than sixty years ago we can now turn to the present day, and through the courtesy of the Southern Region I was privileged to ride down to Dover and back in the motorman's cab. The 10 am Ostend Boat Train consists of fourteen vehicles: three four-coach 'express' sets, coupled in multiple unit, and two motor luggage vans conveying registered luggage, which latter, however, on Paris boat trains is still carried in containers on open trucks as in SECR days. Power available on this train is greater in proportion to its total weight than that of the ordinary Kent Coast express sets. On the latter there are two motors, each of 250 hp, on a four-car set, making a total of 1,500 hp on a 12-car train of 435 tons tare. The 14-car Ostend Boat Train weighs 528 tons tare, and has motors aggregating 2,000 hp. Comparing the weights of the ordinary cars and the motor coaches one can say that each motor and its equipment is roughly equal to an additional 10 tons, so that if comparison is made to a locomotive and train, the 14-coach assembly could be likened to a locomotive of 80 tons, hauling a train of roughly 450 tons tare.

The power available, 2,000 hp, is greater than that of any steam passenger locomotive running on the Southern Region, and one could naturally expect enhanced standards of running. This point is important, because there is a tendency in some quarters to state that the improvement is due merely to the change from steam to electric traction. In fact, trains of vastly increased power have been put on the road, and that power is very conveniently provided by electricity, with all the advantages in cleanliness, convenience in operation, and interchangeability of units between one service and another. It would have been difficult to design coal-fired steam locomotives within the limitations of the British loading gauge capable of such performance as I am about to describe, particularly with present-day qualities of coal.

After the elaborate cab equipment of the most modern steam locomotives, and the array of dials, indicators, switches and what-not in the driving compartments of the new non-steam locomotives, the utter simplicity of the driving cabs of the Southern electrics could well take the privileged visitor by surprise. Ever since the inauguration of electric traction on the constituent companies of the Southern Railway the multiple-unit trains have been worked by one man, and the Ostend Boat Express is no exception. Like all the Southern 'electrics' it is equipped with the Westinghouse air brake, and like the latter ones the control is electro-pneumatic, giving instantaneous application throughout the train. On the occasion of my journey the train was worked by Motorman Tibbles, while Inspector Polling travelled with me throughout my round trip.

Traffic to the Continent was heavy, and practically every seat was taken; the gross load would have been about 565 tons. The equiva-

London, Chatham & Dover Continental boat express near Bickley, hauled by 2-4-0 engine No 54 of the 'Europa' class. (LGRP)

Above *SE & CR Kirtley 'M3' class 4-4-0 No 473, built at Longhedge Works by the LCDR in 1892.* (British Railways)

Below *Southern Railway down extra Continental boat train passing Bromley in 1936 hauled by Maunsell rebuilt 'E1' class 4-4-0 No 1507 and rebuilt Stirling 4-4-0 No 1233.* (H.C. Casserley)

Down Continental Pullman car express on the Chislehurst junction spur, hauled by 'King Arthur' class 4-6-0 No 764 Sir Gawain. (Real Photos Co Ltd)

lent trailing load in a locomotive-hauled train would have been about 480 tons, and with existing steam power on the Southern Region the checks we experienced *en route* would have been serious. We were slackened severely by signal in the approach to Herne Hill, right at the foot of the stiff rise to Penge Tunnel; there were permanent way checks at Shortlands and Bickley Junction, and a check that could have been devastating in its effect—namely a momentary dead stand for signals on the steep climb from Farningham Road to Sole Street. Then again the permanent speed restrictions were most carefully observed, through the Chatham area, and at Canterbury, and right at the finish there was a signal check to 20 mph at Kearsney. Despite all this we glided gently into the Marine station to stop in 88 min 50 sec from Victoria.

In starting away we certainly did not equal the time of the 1896 special to Grosvenor Road, and the succession of restricted aspects from the colour-lights south of Factory Junction, culminating in the sight of a 'red' after Brixton, brought us down to 25 mph before it cleared.

Then the controller was put over to full power, and we had a first taste of what that could produce in an acceleration, up the continuous 1 in 101 to 54 mph at the entrance to Penge Tunnel. Such was the recovery, indeed, that Beckenham was passed on time, and the two permanent way checks followed. Then we got away magnificently over the fine, new quadruple line reaching a maximum speed of 75 mph at St Mary Cray. A further slack to 40 mph was necessary over Swanley Junction, and then, just as I was anticipating a good spin over the stretch where steam locomotives would be really showing their paces, in the dip past Farningham Road, we sighted adverse signals ahead.

The line is equipped with colour-light signals throughout to Faversham, and between Swanley and Rochester the spacing of the signals is such as preserves a uniform headway between trains. The new signal locations do not necessarily correspond with the position of the intermediate stations, and we were brought momentarily to a stand at a colour-light signal adjacent to Milepost 21, half a mile beyond Farningham Road Station and right on the

TABLE IV
SOUTHERN REGION:
VICTORIA–DOVER MARINE

10 am Ostend Boat Express
Load: 14 vehicles (3 four-car sets, and two motored vans),
529 tons tare, 565 tons gross.

Dist		Sched	Actual		Speeds
miles		min	m	s	mph
0.0	VICTORIA	0	0	00	—
0.7	Grosvenor Rd (site)	—	1	40	—
			sigs		
3.2	Brixton	—	5	23	25
			sigs		
4.0	HERNE HILL ...	6½	6	53	—
5.0	West Dulwich ...	—	8	13	49
5.7	Sydenham Hill ...	—	9	00	55
7.8	Kent House	—	11	07	65
8.7	Beckenham	12	11	57	eased
10.0	Shortlands ...	13½	13	35	35
			pws		
10.9	BROMLEY SOUTH	—	14	42	51
			pws		15
12.6	Bickley Junc	—	17	58	—
14.8	St Mary Cray ...		20	14	75
17.7	SWANLEY	—	22	30	40 (slack)
			sigs		
20.5	Farningham Road ...	—	25	43	—
			sigs		
21.0	Milepost 21	—	26	57	sig stop
			27	02	
23.4	Fawkham	—	31	01	56
25.9	Meopham	—	33	42	—
26.9	Sole Street	30	34	33	67
30.9	Cuxton Road... ...	—	37	59	75(max)
34.3	CHATHAM	39¼	43	00	(slack)
35.9	Gillingham	—	45	05	53
38.9	Rainham	—	47	56	71
41.6	Newington	—	50	05	75
			—		60 (slack)
44.7	SITTINGBOURNE	51	52	55	75
48.0	Teynham	—	55	30	76
			sigs		45
52.0	FAVERSHAM ...	58	59	22	58
55.2	Selling	—	62	32	62
	Chartham	—	—		72 (max)
61.8	CANTERBURY ...	69¾	69	10	30 (slack)
64.7	Bekesbourne ...	—	72	27	72
67.8	Adisham	—	75	03	70 (eased)
69.7	Snowdon Halt ...	—	77	03	—
71.7	Shepherdswell ...	81¼	78	55	62
			—		69 (max)
			sigs		
75.1	Kearsney	—	82	45	—
77.3	Dover Priory... ...	—	85	50	—
78.4	DOVER MARINE	92	88	50	—

rising 1 in 100 gradient. The motorman had reduced speed to little more than walking pace as we approached the signal, and had the brakes released as we came up to it. Had it remained 'on' the brakes would have been applied again to hold the train on that 1 in 100 gradient, but as it was the signal cleared, and without a second's delay we were able to restart.

From that signal there is a climb of 5.9 miles to Sole Street. Intermediately there are two short lengths, each of about half a mile, descending at 1 in 100, to Fawkham Junction and after Longfield Siding Box; otherwise the rise is mostly at 1 in 100–132. The inclination from the point of our stop to Sole Street Station averages 1 in 170; yet from the restart we passed Sole Street in 7 min 31 sec at 67 mph!—an astonishing display of the power of these trains. Down the famous Sole Street bank power was shut off altogether and the train coasted freely up to 75 mph. Speed was held to this maximum by the brakes and then gradually reduced in readiness for the normal slow passage through Rochester and Chatham. Due to the various checks we were running about 4 min late, but steady recovery now commenced.

Attaining 53 mph up the 1 in 132 through the tunnels to Gillingham speed was then worked up to 75 mph on the level between Rainham and Newington, and after a slight slack to 60 mph over a curved length of line a maximum of 76 mph was reached at Teynham. A 'yellow' nearing Faversham compelled a reduction to 45 mph, but we were able to begin the climb to Selling Tunnel at 58 mph and on the continuous 1 in 100 gradient speed rose to 62 mph. We coasted down towards Canterbury, speed being restrained by brakes to a maximum of 72 mph, and easing further to 30 mph through the station we passed through on time. The schedule as can be seen from the log in Table IV includes the refinement of quarter minutes, and on this reckoning we were half a minute early.

Reverting once more to full power we made fast time up the more broken ascent to Shepherdswell. The maximum gradient of 1 in 103 extends only for a short distance from

Down 'Golden Arrow' Pullman boat express leaving Martello Tunnel between Folkestone and Dover in May 1959 behind Bulleid Pacific No 34089 602 Squadron *of the 'Battle of Britain' class.* (Derek Cross)

Canterbury and there are downhill stretches near Bekesbourne and Adisham. The final pull includes a mile at 1 in 110 and 2½ miles at 1 in 132, and here the minimum speed was 62 mph. The working had been eased somewhat after Adisham. So we passed Shepherdswell 2 min early, and despite the final check came into Dover in just short of 89 min from Victoria. It is of interest to note that the 57.4 miles from that very difficult restarting point near Farningham Road had been covered in 61 min 48 sec start to stop. The net time for the whole run was about 83 min, assuming nothing more than sectional timekeeping between Beckenham and Sole Street.

I returned to London by the 1.10 pm train from Dover Priory—a four-car set, calling at the principal stations to Chatham and then running fast to Bromley South. We were combined with the Ramsgate portion at Gillingham, and went forward as a 12-car train. I have tabulated the section between Chatham and Bromley in brief detail alongside a fine example of steam running on the 7.45 pm from Ramsgate to Victoria.

It was, of course, in the ascent of Sole Street bank that the electric train showed so overwhelming an advantage, though it is not entirely fair to compare the weights, seeing that the power for driving the electric train is not generated on the locomotive but in a distant power station. Nevertheless the comparison is illuminating. The 'King Arthur' I may add, the one-time crack Stewarts Lane engine No 30768, *Sir Balin*, was in the hands of that great footplate

TABLE V
SOUTHERN REGION:
CHATHAM–BROMLEY SOUTH

Power		Steam		Electric	
Total load (including motive power), tons		508		455	
Weight of tractive units		138		60	
Class of power		'King Arthur'		Multiple-Unit	
Dist miles		m s	mph	m s	mph
0.0	CHATHAM ...	0 00	—	0 00	—
3.4	Cuxton Rd Box	7 01	35	5 01	58
7.4	Sole Street ...	14 29	30	9 17	54½
8.4	Meopham ...	16 01	49	10 17	—
10.9	Fawkham ...	18 34	73	12 40	71
13.8	Farningham Rd	20 54	84	15 09	71
16.6	Swanley Junc ...	23 32	51½	18 09	50*
19.5	St Mary Cray ...	26 21	68	20 34	72
		sigs			
21.7	Bickley Junc ...	29 16	—	22 34	—
23.4	BROMLEY STH	32 58	—	24 42	—

* Eased to this speed for junction

TABLE VI
SOUTHERN REGION:
DOVER MARINE–VICTORIA
'The Golden Arrow'

Engine: Rebuilt 4–6–2 No 35015, *Rotterdam Lloyd*
Load: 404 tons tare, 425 tons full

Dist miles		m s	mph
0.0	DOVER MARINE	0 00	—
7.0	FOLKESTONE CENTRAL	13 12	49
11.5	Sandling Junction	18 35	53
12.7	Westenhanger	19 56	—
16.5	Smeeth	23 20	75
20.8	ASHFORD	26 55	(eased)
26.5	Pluckley	31 17	82
31.7	Headcorn	35 00	88
35.0	Staplehurst	37 17	86/81
37.5	Marden	39 06	85
42.1	Paddock Wood	42 25	80
47.4	TONBRIDGE	46 50	(slack)
49.9	Hildenborough	49 43	50
51.8	Weald	52 22	39
54.2	Sevenoaks Tunnel exit ...	56 08	38
54.8	SEVENOAKS	56 52	—
56.3	Dunton Green	58 26	65
60.3	Knockholt	62 51	44
63.1	Orpington	65 51	62
65.4	Bickley Junction	68 35	(slack)
67.1	BROMLEY SOUTH	70 46	—
69.3	Beckenham	73 38	—
70.2	Kent House	74 28	—
72.3	Sydenham Hill	76 55	—
74.0	HERNE HILL	80 05	—
78.0	VICTORIA	87 05	—

character Sammy Gingell, and was being driven with the vigour that we came to regard as no more than typical of his working.

To conclude I have another splendid example of Southern boat train working, steam this time, on the up 'Golden Arrow.' It seems the fashion sometimes to denigrate our railways at the expense of those of other countries, and after a foreign visit travelling over railways far less heavily worked than our own the complications under which the Southern, in particular, has to operate its passenger train services are underlined. The boat trains do not always get through on time, and one sometimes overhears remarks from fellow travellers who do not stop to think, or enquire, such as: 'We're home all right; we're running late!' On this journey, however, which began at Venice, the running honours were fairly and squarely with Great Britain, judged quite apart from the operating conditions in which the runs were made.

We had a substantial load; in addition to the seven Pullman cars the rake included two ordinary coaches, one eight-wheeled van, and two six-wheeled vans with the registered luggage, 404 tons tare, and 425 tons with the heavy

complement of passengers. The 'Merchant Navy' class locomotives have lost none of their speedworthiness in the extensive rebuilding and this was certainly a good example of their prowess. After a moderate start up to Westenhanger, and a somewhat restrained descent to Ashford, the engine was given her head and made an average speed of 84 mph over the 15.6 miles from Pluckley to Paddock Wood. Thus we were through Tonbridge in well under 'even time,' and the late start had already been recovered. Although this run was made on Whitsun-Tuesday, and traffic into London was heavy from all directions, we got a wonderfully clear road and apart from one slight check at Herne Hill were entirely undelayed.

The days of steam on the railways of Kent are now indeed numbered, and when stage two of the electrification is completed through Tonbridge to Ashford, Folkestone and Dover a long and honourable chapter in transport will be virtually closed. In the meantime, alongside the multiple-unit express trains the new freight diesels, and the 2,500-hp electric locomotives, are getting into their respective strides. Before long I hope to describe some of the work of the latter on the 'Night Ferry' train, and then it will be time also for a farewell tribute to the Maunsell 'Schools' and 'King Arthurs,' at any rate so far as Kentish services are concerned. As my Table V shows, the 'Arthurs' are completely outclassed by the new electrics, but in their heyday there were few better engines on the road, anywhere in the country.

JANUARY 1960

Euston–Liverpool — past and present

In the year 1959, in the course of my business travelling to and from Euston, I experienced my first runs over that route when we were hauled by diesel-electric locomotives of the type that were later designated Class '40'. Several of my runs were made on the down 'Merseyside Express' which in steam days ran the 189.6 miles from Euston to Mossley Hill non-stop in 200 minutes, an average of 57 mph. Over the years, in the course of journeys between Euston and Liverpool, I had amassed quite a collection of runs on that train, together with some timed by friends extending back into the greatest days of the London & North Western Railway. It will be well imagined how keenly I compared the running of the new diesels with what had gone before.

THE New Year is inevitably a time for taking stock of things, and in looking back over AD 1959, even without the passage of time that will give the true retrospect of history, it can already be seen as one of the greater years in the ever-unfolding story of the locomotive, regardless of the means of propulsion. Some of the highlights of new development, the Kent Coast electrification, and the change to diesel-hydraulic traction on 'The Bristolian,' have already been discussed in these articles; alongside such evidences of the march of time has been the restoration of several more pre-grouping steam locomotives to their old glory. The sight of Midland compound No 1000 not merely revives memories of that class in its heyday, but is a reminder of what all Midland express locomotives, whether of class '1,' '2,' '3'

or '4,' looked like, so far as immaculate turnout was concerned; while the restoration of that grand old warrior of the West Highlands, *Glen Douglas*, should settle, once and for all, in the minds of present-day enthusiasts what the colour of North British passenger engines really was!

References to the new power have raised among many readers questions as to how the nominal horsepower values quoted for some diesel and electric locomotives compare with their actual output on the road. There is a natural desire to see how the performance characteristics compare with those of well-known steam locomotives, and early this year I hope to present a survey of potential capacities, including those of the latest multiple-unit electric trains. The introduction of many new type '4' diesel-electric locomotives of English Electric

LNWR—the first of the post-war 'Claughton' class, No 1914 Patriot, *designated as a War Memorial engine.* (Author's Collection)

design to the Euston–Liverpool and Euston–Manchester expresses inevitably invites comparisons with the past, but on this route the performances of the diesels themselves will be passing into history before so many years are out.

Travelling to Liverpool early in October by 'The Merseyside Express' I had my first trip on the train behind a diesel, and with a heavy load of fifteen coaches the job provided an interesting test of the capacity of the locomotive. In Table I are set out summary details of the run, in comparison with runs of steam locomotives at various stages in the history of the service. Of these, No 1 was made in the greatest days of the LNWR just before the first world war; No 2 was typical of the best work of the original 'Royal Scots,' after they had been fitted with solid valve heads and narrow piston rings, and had the Great Western type of coupled wheel axleboxes; and No 3 was one of the best of many I had with the 'Princess Royal' class of Stanier Pacific just before the second world war. The locomotives were thus of 1913, 1927 and 1935 vintage, the last named representing the 6203–6212 batch of Pacifics having high-degree superheating.

Turning now to the engines in more detail, the 'Claughton' class 4–6–0 No 1327, *Alfred Fletcher,* was one of the first batch, built at Crewe in 1913. It was sent new to Edge Hill, and for rather more than a year was the only 'Claughton' stationed there. Out of the first batch, two were at Camden, and the remaining seven at Crewe North. Engine No 1327 was named after a popular and energetic director of the London & North Western Railway, resident in Liverpool, who was Chairman of the Passenger Traffic Committee originally set up in 1891. It was that committee, under the enthusiastic leadership of Mr Alfred Fletcher, that brought the majority of North Western mainline express schedules up to the 55 mph standard, after the more leisurely running enforced during the time that Sir Richard Moon was Chairman of the LNWR. No 1327 was the pride of Edge Hill, and in those first years certainly earned her keep. For months on end she ran the 11 am from Lime Street to Euston, returning with the 5.55 pm on the same day—thus making a weekly mileage of 2,328. The up train called at Crewe, Stafford and Rugby, and conveyed a

TABLE I
EUSTON–LIVERPOOL: 'THE MERSEYSIDE EXPRESS'

Run No							1		2		3		4	
Year							1914		1935		1937		1959	
Engine No							1327		6142		6211		D220	
Engine Name							Alfred Fletcher		Lion		Queen Maud			
Engine Class							'Claughton'		'Royal Scot'		'Princess Royal'		Type '4' diesel-electric	
Load, tons gross							435		505		535		535	
Dist miles							m	s	m	s	m	s	m	s
0.0	EUSTON	...	...	...	...	...	0	00	0	00	0	00	0	00
5.4	Willesden Jc	...	...	...	...	...	9	30	10	13	9	42	10	29
—							sigs				sigs		pws	
17.5	Watford Jc	...	...	...	...	...	26	00	22	48	22	59	24	18
—													pws	
31.7	Tring	...	...	...	...	...	40	10	38	45	39	52	39	17
46.7	BLETCHLEY	...	...	...	...	...	53	00	51	49	52	00	51	30
—													pws	
59.9	Roade	...	...	...	...	...	65	00	63	23	63	19	63	52
—											sigs			
82.6	RUGBY	...	...	...	...	...	88	10	85	44	85	30	85	05
—							sigs							
97.1	NUNEATON	...	...	...	...	...	106	10	100	38	101	21	100	35
110.0	Tamworth	...	...	...	...	...	119	30	112	19	113	37	110	05
127.1	Colwich	...	...	...	...	...	134	05	129	25	126	37	123	29
133.6	STAFFORD	...	...	...	...	...	140	50	136	15	133	30	129	22
—									sigs		sigs		sigs	
158.1	CREWE	...	...	...	...	...	166	50	164	00	160	00	163	52
—													sigs	
174.3	*Weaver Jc*	...	...	...	...	...	184	00	179	45	176	46	186	38
—											sigs			
189.6	Mossley Hill	...	...	...	...	...	sigs		198	37	196	51	207	57
192.2	EDGE HILL	...	...	...	...	...	205	45						
	Net time						195*		195¾		188½		182	

*Equivalent time to stop at Mossley Hill

load of about 330 tons from Liverpool to Stafford, and about 430 tons southwards from Stafford.

The 'Claughton' made a fine start out to Willesden, and as with the other three runs no rear-end banking assistance was taken up to Camden. Then came a bad signal check at Harrow, costing at least 3 min; the recovery from this was extremely vigorous, with speed averaging 60 mph from Watford to Tring, and with a brisk run down the north side of the Chiltern Hills the train was on time through Bletchley. A

second signal check, equally severe, was experienced at Nuneaton, but again the recovery was swift and to some purpose, passing Stafford a shade before time, and in a net time of 134¾ min. At the time this run was made there was no stop at Mossley Hill, and the allowance to Edge Hill was 208 min; despite a further signal check the arrival was 2¼ min early, equivalent to a net time of 195 min to a stop at Mossley Hill.

The run with the 'Royal Scot' class 4-6-0, *Lion*, was made on the Friday before Whitsun,

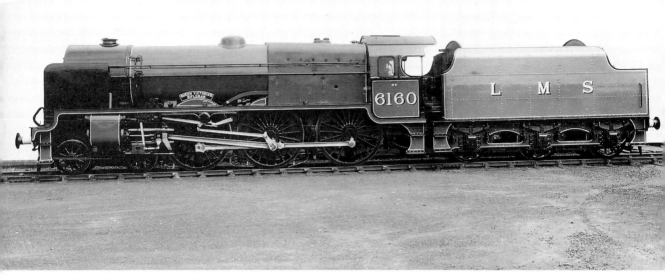

'Royal Scot' class 4-6-0 No 6160 Queen Victoria's Rifleman, *in the last, pre-1940, style of painting.* (BR)

and it is a fine tribute to the LMSR operating authorities that we got so good a road, seeing that many extra trains were running. It was only in the approach to Crewe that any signal checks were experienced, and these were not severe. The booked time to passing Stafford was then 139 min and we were comfortably ahead of time at this point, though for some reason the driver chose to open out with great vigour on the gradual climb to Whitmore; having reached the fine speed of 64 mph at Standon Bridge the summit was cleared at 60½ mph. Despite the checks nearing Crewe that station was passed a minute early, and we were 1½ min early at Mossley Hill. This run was typical of several I had with unrebuilt 'Royal Scots' on 'The Merseyside Express.' Only once, when we had the tough combination of a heavy side wind and a load of 545 tons was there any time to book against the engine.

The 'Princess Royal' class engine No 6211, *Queen Maud*, made some very fine running with a gross load of 535 tons behind the tender. We had sustained 61 mph steadily up the 1 in 335 from Wembley, and were already up to 68½ mph at Bushey when there came a very

bad signal check at Watford. Nevertheless, speed had topped 60 mph again before we reached Tring summit, and an average speed of 71 mph from Tring to Weedon put us back on time. Over the Trent Valley section we fairly romped away, passing Whitmore 5½ min early, but then came the seemingly inevitable check outside Crewe. There was another check to come, at Runcorn, but the driver had an ample margin in hand, and Mossley Hill was reached just over 3 min early.

From these earlier experiences it will be appreciated with what interest I settled down to log my first trip on the train behind a diesel-electric locomotive. The start was inclined to be slow, in comparison with those of the Stanier Pacifics, and the permanent way check through Willesden Junction Station put us still further back. The climbing to Tring was further delayed by a relaying slack north of Berkhamsted Tunnel, but after that we had two spells of very fast running. From Cheddington to Castlethorpe, 18.7 miles, we averaged 80.7 mph, while over the 36 miles from Bulkington to Milford we averaged 78 mph. Maximum speeds were 85 mph near Wolverton and 86 between Polesworth and Tamworth. The sustained uphill speeds, and the recovery from regular slacks, as at Rugby, were not greatly different from the normally good

steam performance; but the locomotive was evidently given her head downhill, where there is usually some relaxation in the effort on a steam locomotive. The checks north of Stafford were severe; but the schedule has been eased out as compared with pre-war running, and despite the checks, and further delays that caused us to take no less than 23¼ min over the last four miles from Mossley Hill, we were still a minute early on arrival at Lime Street.

From the actual runs a further table has been prepared to obtain a broad comparison between the basic performances of the four locomotives. For this comparison I have taken the net average speeds between Willesden Junction and Staf-

'Princess Royal' class 4-6-2 No 46204 Princess Louise *climbing Madeley bank, south of Crewe, with a relief Glasgow–Euston express in 1960.* (Derek Cross)

ford, and the average drawbar horsepowers have been worked out from the latest British Railways figures of train resistance. I cannot imagine there would be a great deal of difference in the resistance of the fine, electrically-lighted stock run on the principal LNWR expresses just before the first world war. On this basis of comparison there was not a great deal of difference between the three steam locomotives in horsepower per ton of engine and tender, though when the comparison is related to the nominal

TABLE II
EUSTON–LIVERPOOL EXPRESSES: 1914–1959
HORSEPOWER COMPARISONS
WILLESDEN JUNCTION-STAFFORD

Date of engine design	Engine No	Load, tons gross	Net average speed, mph	Assumed train resistance, lb per ton	Calculated db-hp	Weight of locomotive, tons	Db-hp per ton of locomotive	Db-hp per ton of te
1913	1327	435	61.7	9.5	680	116*	5.85	68†
1927	6142	505	61.2	9.4	775	139½*	5.55	52.5†
1935	6211	535	65.3	10.5	980	160*	6.12	54.5†
1958	D220	535	68.8	11.2	1,100	133	8.28	47.2‡

* Including tender. † Based on nominal te at 85 per cent boiler pressure. ‡ Based on max te value of 52,000 lb

tractive effort it is revealed that the 'Claughton' was being worked by far the hardest. The diesel shows a notable increase in the power-weight ratio, for in making this comparison one must include the tenders in the total weight of the steam locomotives; the diesel carries its own fuel, and the means of conveyance of the fuel for the steam locomotives must also be included in the comparison.

Viewing the work of the class in retrospect there are few locomotive designs in British railway history that have aroused more controversy than the 'Claughtons,' and on studying the performance of No 1327 and my analysis of its results there are sure to be some readers who will tend to belittle it by suggesting it is unrepresentative of average work in the post-grouping period. No one would agree more heartily than I on this point, but this is not the place to try and set fourth the causes for that deterioration. There were times, right down to the year 1930, when the 'Claughtons' were brilliant, and others when individual engines of the class were positively shocking. One could understand it if observers taking notes from a seat in the train were mystified, but the results of dynamometer car tests taken since 1923 seem equally inconclusive, to me at any rate. The class provides one of the most fascinating of historical studies, as so many facets of performance seem to be involved, and the data bequeathed to us contains so many pitfalls for those who would draw sweeping conclusions.

In Table III are given the official results of five sets of dynamometer car trials made in LMSR days with locomotives in various stages of modification. At the outset one should be warned not to take too much notice of the figures of coal consumption per drawbar horsepower hour. This *should* take account of the variations in running conditions from day to day, because presumably one is measuring coal consumption against actual work done. But the extent to which this ratio can vary was shown vividly during some dynamometer car trials on the LNER in 1928. One of the locomotives under test was the Gresley Pacific No 4473, *Solario*, and within a single week this engine, worked throughout by the same crew and on the same duties, showed values of coal per drawbar horsepower hour varying between a minimum of 2.89 lb and a maximum of 3.44, an increase of 19 per cent between minimum and maximum. In Table III it will be noticed at once that *Thalaba*, working test trains of 402 tons, gave considerably better results than the other standard engine, the *Charles J. Cropper*, showing a reduction in basic coal consumption of practically 10 per cent.

Test No 3 relates to the original Caprotti engine, equipped while carrying the standard LNWR boiler. Engine No 1093, *Sir Guy Calthrop*, was the 'guinea-pig' for the '5X' paral-

TABLE III
DYNAMOMETER RESULTS WITH 'CLAUGHTON' 4–6–0s

Ref No				1	2	3	4	5
Engine No (LNWR)				1567	30	1327	1093	—
Engine Name				Charles J. Cropper	Thalaba	Alfred Fletcher	Sir Guy Calthrop	—
Boiler				Standard	Standard	Standard	Standard re-tubed	Large class '5X'
Valve Gear				Walschaerts standard	Walschaerts standard	Caprotti	Walschaerts standard	Walschaerts solid valve heads
Test route				Crewe and Carlisle	Preston and Carlisle	Crewe and Carlisle	Crewe and Carlisle	Euston and Manchester
Load, tons tare				316	402	316	327	417
Average speed, mph				49.5	50.4	50.7	50.0	52.7
Coal per mile, lb				44.5	52.7	33.3	40.0	38.2
Coal per dhp hr, lb				5.22	4.74	4.10	4.34	3.25

'Duchess' class 4-6-2 No 46245 City of London *with an Eastern Region special from Doncaster to King's Cross climbing to Stoke summit, south of Grantham, in June 1963.* (Rail Archive Stephenson, T.G. Hepburn)

lel-boiler design, used on twenty 'Claughtons,' and subsequently on the 'Baby Scots.' In overall dimensions the boiler of No 1093 on Test No 4 was the same as the original, externally, but it had the small tubes re-spaced, and larger air spaces were provided through the ashpan and grate.

On the tests in question this engine showed a marked improvement over No 1567, but not so much over No 30. The most astonishing result, however, is that obtained with one of the large-boilered engines on the Manchester service, when the basic coal consumption came down to the kind of figure one would expect from the best modern engines of the present day. The important thing to emphasise here is that the engine retained the original LNWR valve dimensions, with no more than 1 in steam lap and a maximum travel in full gear of $4\frac{5}{16}$ in. The difference, and it is a big difference, too, is that the old Schmidt type of wide piston rings, with trick ports, had been replaced by solid valve heads

with six narrow rings. This change greatly reduced the loss due to steam leakage past the valves which bedevilled all engines fitted with the Schmidt type of ring after some months of running. It would have been interesting to see test results on engines of the original 'Claughton' design, modified only in respect of the valve heads.

This has been, I fear, a long digression on the subject of 'Claughton' performance, arising from the excellent running shown by No 1327 in Table I; but the past achievements of well-known steam locomotives will continue to have the close and enthusiastic attention of students of practice and performance, and I have been surprised and gratified by the number of letters I have received since the logs of running on the London, Chatham & Dover boat trains were published in my article for October last. Mr H. Dixon Hewitt writes to say that the special runs of June, 1896, were made in connection with a visit of members of the Jockey Club to Paris for the Grand Prix races. Both Mr Hewitt and Mr O. J. Smith refer in their letters to a still faster run, in the up direction, made with a 'special' run for a Russian Grand Duke *en route* for Windsor. This latter train, weighing 80 tons tare, was worked from Dover Pier to Windsor (LSWR) in 2 hr 2 min, inclusive of a 2 min stop at Clapham Junction, and a 3 min stop at Lavender Hill, about 0.3 mile short of Clapham Junction. The LCDR engine was No 15, and she passed Herne Hill, 74.5 miles, in 80 min inclusive of *four* permanent way checks. The net time was approximately 72 min—a grand piece of running.

Reverting now to more recent topics, on the fast-running main lines it does seem increasingly rare to see a modern locomotive *driven* really hard. That is not to say there is not a great deal of fast running being made on many routes, but more often than not it seems to arise from locomotives that are in first class 'nick,' and steaming well, being given their heads and allowed to make their own pace. On the return journey of my recent visit to Liverpool we were also diesel-hauled, but this was not my first of such trips. I had a good run with the pioneer British main-line diesel-electric locomotive, the LMSR No 10000, on this same train as long ago as 1952. Earlier in 1959, however, I had what will probably be my last run on the up 'Red Rose' with a steam locomotive, and if this should indeed prove eventually to be the last I could not wish for a grander finale. The crew had no preliminary advice that they were to be 'clocked' in full detail—in fact when I joined the train at Crewe it was already so full that I was far too concerned in finding a seat to have any conversations with driver or fireman. It was a hot sultry evening in mid-July when a driver might very well have run a little easier than usual out of consideration for the physical labour to be done by his mate. On the contrary, no 'George the Fifth,' no 'Prince of Wales,' or no 'Claughton' can ever have been flailed more wholeheartedly than was the *Princess Margaret Rose* that evening. The log is detailed in Table IV, but so memorable an effort deserves a special comment.

The start was good, though without giving much indication of what was to follow; but after reaching 80 mph below Standon Bridge, and then easing over the curve at Norton Bridge, speed was worked up to no less than 83 mph before Stafford. We had scarcely got going after the moderate slack over Trent Valley Junction when we were pulled up to 15 mph for permanent way work near Rugeley. The recovery from this check showed truly the calibre of driver, fireman and engine. With a continuous roar from the exhaust No 46203 was whipped into speed; a second maximum of 80 mph was reached before Tamworth and the uphill work towards Rugby was superb, especially the minimum speed of 67½ mph at Bulkington, after nearly four miles rising at 1 in 320. Speed was carefully reduced through Rugby, but after that the driver and fireman put the engine to it harder than ever. Two more 'eighties' were registered, and when we took the rise from Castlethorpe troughs to Milepost 48½ at a minimum speed of 73½ mph, I thought we were in for a record ascent to Tring.

Unfortunately, adverse signals brought us down to 10 mph in the approach to Bletchley; however, it was no more than a local check, and it must have been something of a record in itself to climb the 15 miles from Bletchley to Tring in 14¼ min from practically a standing start! The acceleration from that check was terrific, and in the steadily maintained speed of 66½ mph up the 1 in 335 to Tring the engine must have been developing at least 1,660 drawbar horsepower, based on a train resistance, at that speed, of 10 lb per ton. So despite the two severe checks Tring was passed 4 min inside even time, and as we dashed away down the grade towards Watford, with speed up to 80 mph once more as early as Berkhamsted, I was looking forward to an exceptionally fast finish to this very hard run. But then what happens? Bourne End 'distant' was at caution; we slowed down, the 'home' being pulled off when speed was no more than a walking pace, and we were flagged to a stop at the box to be warned by the signalman to go cautiously, as some children had been placing stones on the rails!

TABLE IV
LONDON MIDLAND REGION: CREWE–EUSTON
'THE RED ROSE'

Load: 13 coaches; 456 tons tare, 495 tons full
Engine: 46203, *Princess Margaret Rose*

Dist		Sch	Actual		Speeds
miles		min	m	s	mph
0.0	CREWE	0	0	00	—
4.7	*Betley Road*		8	30	47½
7.9	*Madeley*		12	35	46½
10.5	Whitmore	15	15	36	—
14.6	*Standon Bridge*		19	23	72
19.2	Norton Bridge	23	22	57	80*
21.2	*Great Bridgeford*		24	25	83
24.5	STAFFORD	33	27	05	53 (slack)
31.0	Colwich		33	29	69
—			pws		15
33.9	RUGELEY	43	38	04	—
37.0	Armitage		41	50	61
41.8	Lichfield	50	46	15	72
48.0	TAMWORTH...	56	51	05	80
55.7	Atherstone		57	40	63
60.9	NUNEATON	70	62	10	72
64.6	*Bulkington*		65	19	67½
70.0	Brinklow		69	47	76
75.5	RUGBY	86	74	50	40 (slack)
79.3	*Kilsby Tunnel North*		79	52	56
88.4	Weedon	100	88	01	80½
95.3	BLISWORTH	106	93	33	70
98.2	ROADE	109	96	03	66½
103.3	Castlethorpe		100	03	84
109.6	*Milepost 48½*		104	43	73½
—			sigs		10
111.4	BLETCHLEY	121	108	02	30
117.9	Leighton Buzzard		114	53	71
122.0	Cheddington		118	23	68½
126.4	TRING	137	122	17	66½
130.1	Berkhamsted		125	19	80
—			sigs		—
—	*Bourne End Box*		sig stop,		—
			42 sec		
133.6	Hemel Hempstead		134	33	49
140.6	WATFORD JUNCTION...	150	141	30	72/69
144.8	Hatch End		145	07	72
146.7	Harrow		146	38	76
150.0	Wembley		149	10	79
152.7	WILLESDEN JUNCTION	161	151	13	72
155.7	South Hampstead		153	50	—
—			sigs		—
158.1	EUSTON	170	159	50	—

Net time 144 min (65.7 mph)

* Speed before service slack

One of the first English Electric Type 4 diesel-electric locomotives. (British Railways)

I must confess I am rather at a loss for words to comment on this incident. It is not that a fine piece of engine performance was cut short, nor that the results of the hard work by this keen driver and fireman to regain several minutes of a late start were thrown away by these little hooligans; it is the disturbing thought of what such acts might lead to if they pass unchecked. As long ago as June, 1900, *The Railway Magazine* published a cartoon, in cynical vein, of a species of 'rake's progress'—a headstrong youth, unchecked by any parental control, who progressed in his adventures from torturing cats, and stoning engine-drivers to train wrecking on the grand scale. This cartoon was titled 'A Question of Training,' and each time I have come across it, when referring to the particular volume, I had, until fairly recently, passed it over as a caricature of an age happily passed. But after the Bourne End episode, and other items reported from time to time in the press, I am not sure that age has passed.

After such a set-back it would not have been surprising if the crew had given up trying. On the form they were showing it cost fully 9 min in running; but, although not pressing the engine so hard as previously, they won back nearly 2 min between Watford and Euston, to finish 10¼ min inside schedule. All in all, it was a grand run, with a net time of 144 min from Crewe to Euston. I must add, however, that running of this kind, while common enough with the 'Princess Royal' class engines in the years 1935–1939, has been notable by its rarity in recent years. The record of the class has in some ways been analogous to that of the Crewe superheater express passenger engines of LNWR design in LMSR days. Like the 'Princess Royals,' no one doubted their basic ability to work prodigious loads at standard express speed, but few of them were able to rise to such heights in those latter days, due to lack of maintenance, and as a whole the breed became discredited. My own recent experiences with the 'Princess Royals' have been the same, particularly north of Crewe, and Nos 46200, 46205 and 46211 have all given me runs on important expresses that are really best forgotten!

Lest I should blacken the present-day character of these engines too much, however, I am very glad to be able to mention summary details of yet another very fine run on the up 'Red Rose,' that have just reached me from a correspondent. Although the 'Red Rose' is now normally worked by diesel, my friend was travelling on a Saturday evening in November, when the train carries a Manchester portion, and calls additionally at Watford Junction. The engine was once again No 46203, *Princess Margaret Rose*, and the load from Crewe was one of 15 coaches, weighing 506 tons tare, and about 545 tons full. The Manchester portion was late at Crewe and the train left 10 min late.

There were four checks between Crewe and Rugby, two of them severe, and far from regaining any of the lost time, a further $3\frac{3}{4}$ min had been lost by the time Nuneaton was passed. After that, however, the engine performance must have been magnificent to the last degree, for with this very heavy train, the 79.7 miles from Nuneaton to the stop at Watford were covered in $68\frac{3}{4}$ min. The average speed over the 31.1 miles from Blisworth to Tring was no less than 73.3 mph and, as a result, the train pulled into Watford $2\frac{1}{2}$ min early.

Deterioration in older locomotives is not entirely a matter of maintenance. No stud of locomotives has been repaired more thoroughly, nor re-erected more accurately, than the Swindon four-cylinder 4-6-0s; and it has been a joy to record the work of ripe old veterans like *Caerphilly Castle* and *Cardiff Castle* thirty years after the original time of construction. But although engines of this vintage have been put on to the road in spanking condition it has been noticeable how much more quickly they deteriorate after each general overhaul than later engines of the class. At the moment of writing another of the 1923 batch, No 4079, *Pendennis Castle*, is doing some splendid work on the Bristol expresses, but the chassis seems the governing factor, and in due course its age is reflected in the engine getting rough, fastenings working loose, and in cracks developing. An individual locomotive may receive a new boiler and have very careful

mechanical repairs carried out on the cylinders and running gear; but more often than not it is the condition of the frames that decides what kind of work the engine can be put to. In this respect, of course, the LNWR express passenger locomotives suffered. Their frames were relatively light, and the 'George the Fifth's' in particular got terribly rough.

Today, veteran locomotives with so high a reputation as the 'Castles' are showing traits that to me are strangely reminiscent of the later days of the 'Claughtons.' Quite recently I had a run on one of the Paddington-Bath non-stops, with a load of 414 tons tare, on which there was a net loss of 15 min to engine, whereas another engine, and driver, worked a load of 473 tons tare, 515 tons full to Bath in $108\frac{3}{4}$ min start to stop, despite nearly 5 min delay *en route*—a magnificent net average speed of 61.7 mph with this heavy train. Today, with steam on the way out, I feel it is important that we remember the famous classes that have served us so well by the work of their heyday, rather than by some of the depressing experiences we suffer from time to time. Some classes, like those amazing little SECR 'D1' and 'E1' 4-4-0s, seem evergreen, and we can still rejoice in their prowess, while with others their present running is a mere travesty of former achievement.

I have been interested to receive a number of letters asking for running details of classes long since scrapped, and I can assure all those who have written in this vein that I will do my best. The opportunities must necessarily be few, for there is so much new to be recorded and discussed, and the running of the new forms of motive power is not by any means showing that extreme and dull uniformity that many expected. The keen interest and careful observations of many enthusiasts show a reappraisal of this subject, of nearly sixty years' standing, as fresh and thoroughgoing as the rejuvenation of the railways themselves. From time to time I hope to give something of the technical background to modernisation that will help readers to a better appreciation of the running that can be noted from the trains.

Scottish topics — the 'Postal' — on the Highland line

The introduction of diesel-electric traction on British Railways was providing a frequent topic for discussion around 1960 while recent developments in the use of the steam power then available provided another. North of Glasgow, the introduction of ex-LNER locomotives on some of the fastest trains on the former LMS route to Aberdeen gave some quite exciting runs on the southbound 'Postal' which carried a passenger portion as far south as Perth, while on the Highland line the Locomotive Interchange Trials of 1948 were still a vivid memory that could invoke some forward speculations.

THE introduction of diesel-electric locomotives on the Edinburgh-Aberdeen route stimulates thought as to how the new form of motive power might be used on other famous Scottish routes. The publication by the British Transport Commission of the Test Bulletin relating to the Brush Traction type '2' locomotives of the A1A–A1A wheel arrangement, now doing such good work on the Great Eastern Line, happened to coincide with a number of journeys I had to make to Scotland; there were plenty of opportunities for studying it while I was in the North, and the passage of trains to and from the Highland line, as seen from the high vantage point of the temporary control tower in the new marshalling yard north of Perth, suggested an application of the data in the bulletin towards the age-old problem of getting heavy trains over the Drumochter and Slochd summits.

Before leaving the Aberdeen road completely, however, this present article can appropriately include some notes on an interesting example of the integration of motive power studs, previously quite separate in their activities, yet using the same shed; I refer to Ferryhill, Aberdeen, where the former LMSR and LNER workings, and locomotives, are now pooled. One result of this arrangement is that the up 'West Coast Postal' express now begins its southward journey behind an East Coast engine, almost invariably a Gresley 'V2' 2-6-2, and the transition from Aberdeen to the Highland line can be fittingly made by reference to some runs on this train. Several times recently I have seen it arrive in Perth dead on time, and while this article was in contemplation, as if to satisfy my hitherto unspoken curiosity, a correspondent who has been living near to the East Coast main line for some little time, Mr D. Springall, sent me a number of carefully compiled logs.

To add the spice of comparison between East Coast and West Coast motive power on this train, I have looked up some logs of my own, and some clocked by Mr Ronald I. Nelson, and these are included in Table I. In the ordinary way the 'Postal' is not an unduly difficult train to work; but within my own experience, I have found that at the Aberdeen end of the journey drivers would appear to make it a point of honour to arrive in Perth on time, and the incidence of delays has often led to some very fast running. The two runs with 'V2' engines were, however, fairly free from checks. On the first of these engine No 60824 made a good start, with an average speed of 42½ mph between mileposts 238 and 234, and a better time to Muchalls than any of the steam runs detailed in my May article. The companion run was considerably less energetic in the early stages, but having passed Stonehaven only a shade ahead of time the driver of No 60970 opened out to make a splendid climb of the Dunnottar bank.

From Stonehaven Station the rising gradient

TABLE I
SCOTTISH REGION: ABERDEEN–FORFAR
The 'West Coast Postal'

Run No Engine No Engine Class Load, tons (E/F)				Sch	1 60824 'V2' 294/315	2 60970 'V2' 303/325	3 45580 LM:6P 299/315	4 44727 LM : 5 321/345
Dist					Actual	Actual	Actual	Actual
Miles				min	m　s	m　s	m　s	m　s
0.0	ABERDEEN	...	...	0	0　00	0　00	0　00	0　00
—					—	—	sigs	—
0.6	Ferryhill Jc ...	...	...	2	2　43	2　42	2　51	2　33
4.8	Cove Bay　...	...	...		9　27	10　25	9　54	9　26
7.0	Milepost 234	...	...		12　37	14　22	13　27	12　40
11.6	Muchalls　...	...	...		17　07	18　50	17　46	16　53
13.5	Milepost 227½	...	...		19　04	20　34	19　34	18　37
16.2	STONEHAVEN	...	...	23	21　24	22　43	pws 22　47	pws 21　25
18.8	Dunnottar　...	...	...		24　21	25　37	26　58	25　33
20.8	Milepost 220¼	...	...		27　21	27　59	30　02	28　43
23.3	Drumlithie　...	...	...		30　26	31　14	33　12	31　44
— 30.6	LAURENCEKIRK	...	...	40	36　52	pws 38　58	— 39　04	— 37　49
— 33.8	Marykirk　...	...	...		39　55	— 42　13	pws 42　29	40　53
38.0	Kinnaber Jc ...	...	...	48	— 43　25	45　58	pws 46　37	pws 45　36
— 41.9	Bridge of Dun	...	...		pws 47　25	— 49　17	— 50　42	49　38
— 45.0	Farnell Road ...	...	...		50　46	— 52　08	pws 54　55	pws 53　32
48.3	Glasterlaw　...	...	...		55　58	56　18	59　42	58　12
50.3	GUTHRIE　...	...	...	60	58　21	58　31	61　50	60　23
— 54.9	Clocksbridge	...	...		63　13	— 63　04	sigs 66　21	— 64　42
— 57.3	FORFAR　...	...	...	68	66　05	— 66　13	— 69　24	sigs 68　13
Net times, min	...	...	...	...	65	65	62	63

Flashback to the Aberdeen road of the inter-war years: a Gresley Mikado, No 2006 Wolf of Badenoch, *climbing the bank out of Aberdeen with an express for Edinburgh.* (M.W. Earley)

averages 1 in 100 for two miles; then there is an easing to 1 in 423 for three-quarters of a mile, followed by a final 1½ miles at 1 in 102 to near Carmont platform at milepost 220¼. On No 1 run engine No 60824 passed Stonehaven at 71 mph, and came down finally to 40 mph at Carmont summit. No 60970, on the other hand, began the climb at 69½ mph and had not fallen below 50 mph at Dunnottar box. There was, indeed, a rise to 53 mph on the 1 in 423 pitch, but speed was allowed to fall off rapidly to 40½ mph at Carmont summit. Fast downhill running, which is usually so conspicuously absent from the progress of the East Coast trains, seems the rule with the 'Postal.' On No 2 run, for example, No 60970 recovered from a permanent way slack near Drumlithie to reach a maximum speed of 76 mph near Marykirk, while No 60824 touched 82½ mph at the same point. Neither engine was driven energetically up the Farnell Road bank, but both trains reached Forfar comfortably inside schedule time.

The first of the companion runs with the *ex*-LMSR locomotives, run No 3, included some extremely vigorous working. There were no fewer than four permanent way checks between Aberdeen and Forfar alone, and with two signal checks in addition it was indeed surprising that the loss was no more than 1½ minutes. There was a check before each of the heavy inclines, yet the minimum speeds were as good as 35½ mph at Cove Bay, 36½ at Dunnottar and 39½ up the four miles of 1 in 100 from Farnell Road to near Glasterlaw. At the same time maximum speeds of 83 mph at Muchalls, 84 at Fordoun, and 69 mph on the level after Guthrie showed a resolve to keep time, if it were humanly possible. The last run, with an extra coach, and a 'Black Five' to haul a gross load of 345 tons, included a particularly fine start, and although there were three permanent way checks in operation, for all practical purposes time was kept. Even though Stonehaven was passed at no more than 42 mph the minimum up the Dunnottar bank was

34½ mph, while up Farnell Road bank the minimum was 40 mph from an initial speed of only 50 mph.

On the basis of these four runs the Stanier engines had the greater opportunities for 'showing off,' and their drivers took full advantage of them. Engine No 44727, for example, averaged 39 mph up the Dunnottar bank, and did still better above Farnell Road, when the speed was practically sustained at 40 mph on 1 in 100. This run was timed jointly by Mr Nelson, riding on the footplate, and myself, in the train. From Stonehaven the engine was being worked in 35 per cent cut-off, with full regulator, while on Farnell Road bank the cut-off was the same, but the regulator not quite opened to the full. On both these ascents the equivalent drawbar horsepower was in the neighbourhood of 1,100

to 1,200, a fine achievement for an engine of these proportions.

In Table II are shown the continuations of three of the runs forward to Perth. The run that had started so well from Aberdeen with No 44727, was made on a Saturday afternoon, and south of Forfar we caught up the preceding Glasgow train, and suffered so many checks that the log was of little interest. I have therefore included instead another excellent 'Black Five' run from Mr Nelson's collection. Modern locomotives of whatever type always seem to excel in running over a fast and level road, and the average speeds sustained on these four runs between Glamis and Stanley Junction are alone sufficient evidence of this. The three-cylinder 4-6-0 *Burma* in particular seemed to be in tremendous form, and her maximum speed of

TABLE II
SCOTTISH REGION : FORFAR–PERTH
The 'West Coast Postal'

Run No Engine No Engine Class Load, tons (E/F)						1 60824 'V2' 294/315	2 60970 'V2' 303/325	3 45580 LM : 6P 299/315	4 44704 LM : 5 271/285
Dist					Sch	Actual	Actual	Actual	Actual
Miles					min	m s	m s	m s	m s
0.0	FORFAR	...	...	...	0	0 00	0 00	0 00	0 00
2.9	*Kirriemuir Jc*		...	...	4	4 32	5 09	4 35	4 57
5.7	Glamis	...	...	...		7 13	7 50	7 09	7 33
7.9	Eassie	...	...	...		9 08	9 45	8 59	9 22
12.0	ALYTH JC	...	...	...	12	12 39	13 25	12 21	12 43
14.2	Ardler	...	...	...		14 33	15 32	14 13	14 34
16.7	COUPAR ANGUS		...	...	16	16 33	17 46	16 09	16 33
21.2	Cargill	...	...	...		20 26	21 59	19 51	20 18
23.1	*Ballathie*	...	...	...		21 57	23 36	21 13	21 44
—						—	—	pws	—
25.3	STANLEY JC	...	...	...	24	23 52	25 40	24 33	23 33
28.3	Luncarty	...	...	...		26 16	28 10	27 30	25 56
30.9	*Almond Valley Jc*		...	...	30	28 20	30 24	29 44	27 58
—						—	pws	—	—
32.5	PERTH	...	...	...	34	31 00	34 14	32 29	30 49
Net times, min	...	...	...	...		31	33	30¼	30¾
Average speed, Eassie–Ballathie		...	...	...		71.3	65.8	74.5	73.8
Max speed, mph	...	...	...	...		78½	77	88½	85

Note:—At time of 'V2' runs schedule was 14 min to Alyth Junction, and 2 min more than shown at all points forward to Perth

88½ mph at the Tay viaduct, near Cargill, was perhaps *the* highlight of the collection. On all four runs the arrival in Perth was punctual or early.

And now for the Highland line. In view of the advances in locomotive engineering technique during the intervening years the maximum load permitted to be taken unassisted, northbound over Drumochter, and in both directions over the Slochd pass, has not risen greatly since the introduction of the 'Castle' class 4–6–0s in 1900. Those excellent engines were rostered to haul tare loads up to 200 tons unassisted, on schedules considerably faster than anything booked today, whereas the 'Black Fives' are limited to 255 tons. As a basis for comparison, 'The Hill,' as enginemen call the long incline from Blair Atholl to Dalnaspidal, provides a good background. From near Struan the gradient is 1

in 70, with only the slightest intermission, for ten miles, and here the climbing speed on a good average run needs to be around 26 to 28 mph.

At a speed of 27 mph the Brush 1,250-hp diesels develop an equivalent drawbar horsepower of 970 when 'flat-out'. It is possibly fair to assume that the 1,160-hp machines now working on the Aberdeen road have a performance proportionately less, say 900 equivalent drawbar horsepower. At 27 mph the resistance of modern coaching stock, in still air, can be taken at about 4½ lb per ton, and from these figures the load that one of the 1,160-hp diesels can probably take up a 1 in 70 gradient at 27 mph works out at 255 tons; this is the same as that now permitted to the class '5' 4–6–0s, except that in the latter case the load is the tare weight of the train, whereas with the diesel it is the gross. On test, one of the 'BR5' 4–6–0s, No 73008, sustained an output of slightly over 1,200 equivalent drawbar horsepower when fired with Grade 1A coal up to the maximum rate agreed for a single fireman, namely 3,000 lb an hour,

'V2' 2-6-2 No 856 on a down East Coast express north of Potters Bar. (M.W. Earley)

though this output was reduced to a little under 1,100 dhp with Grade 2B coal (Blidworth).

In first-class working conditions, therefore, a class '5' 4–6–0, whether a Stanier or 'BR5,' should have a comfortable margin in hand with a 255-ton load, though naturally the tonnage was fixed as an all-weather, all-the-year-round figure. It does tend to emphasise, however, the extraordinarily tough tasks set to the old Highland engines, with 200 tons taken unassisted by a 'Castle,' and 220 tons by one of Christopher Cumming's 'Clans'.

The accompanying table certainly underlines the point that refinements in design, such as those embodied in modern locomotives do not count for much in actual haulage capacity where

HIGHLAND 4–6–0 LOCOMOTIVES
Power Output at 27 mph—1 in 70 Gradient

Class		Load, tons	Equiv dhp	Nom te, lb	Dhp, per ton of te
Castle	...	200	790	21,550	82
Clan	...	220	845	23,900	79.3
BR5	...	255	960	26,120	82

such heavy gradients are concerned. It is sheer strength, in the form of nominal tractive effort, that counts in such conditions.

From theoretical values it is interesting to study details of some actual runs on the Highland line, and in Table III are shown the times made on two journeys of my own on the 12

TABLE III
SCOTTISH REGION : PERTH–AVIEMORE

Engine No Bank engine, from Blair Load, tons (E/F)					44699 2-6-4T 286/305		44998 4-4-0P 349/375	
Dist					Actual	Speeds	Actual	Speeds
Miles					m s	mph	m s	mph
0.0	PERTH	...	...	...	0 00	—	0 00	—
4.2	Luncarty	...	...	...	7 35	45	7 34	44
7.2	Stanley Jc	...	...	...	12 03	30*	11 45	30*
10.3	Murthly	...	...	...	17 45	51	17 13	—
12.9	Kingswood Box	...	...	...	22 05	26	21 34	28
15.6	Dunkeld	...	...	...	25 45	54½	25 06	58
23.6	Ballinluig	...	...	...	36 15	48/52	35 21	49
28.5	PITLOCHRY	...	...	...	42 50	38	42 20	36½
30.0	Milepost 30	...	...	...	46 23	26½	45 29	31
					—	—	sigs	15
32.2	Killiecrankie	...	...	...	49 41	—	49 17	—
35.3	BLAIR ATHOLL	...	...	...	55 05	—	54 53	—
1.7	Milepost 37	...	...	...	0 00	—	0 00	—
13.7	Milepost 49	...	...	...	3 42	—	4 37	—
15.7	Dalnaspidal	...	...	...	27 24	—	29 43	—
17.7	Milepost 52¾	...	...	...	30 47	42½	33 35	43½
23.3	Dalwhinnie	...	...	...	33 59	28	36 46	30
—					41 11	66 max	44 00	60 max
33.4	Newtonmore	...	...	...	pws	10	—	—
36.3	KINGUSSIE	...	...	...	55 12	56	56 20	—
—					60 45	—	59 40	—
42.1	Kincraig	...	...	...	62 35	—	—	—
48.0	AVIEMORE	...	...	...	71 04	58½ max	66 38	56 max
					78 50	—	75 00	—

T: Stanier tank; P: Pickersgill ex-Caledonian type. *Speed restriction.

'V2' 2-6-2 No 60845 on a special dynamometer car test run during the period of trials by the Western Region testing team at Swindon, here seen passing Hullavington. (K.H. Leech)

noon express from Perth. On the first of these runs I was on the footplate, and the engine working gave a very good impression of the extent to which the Stanier 4-6-0s have to be opened out to maintain schedules that to outward appearances might be considered easy. By way of comparison, it may be recalled that before 1914 this train, then leaving Perth at 11.50 am, was booked non-stop to Newtonmore, 68.7 miles in 114 min. It was rare that the run was made literally non-stop, as it was frequently necessary to call at Blair Atholl to pick up a bank engine, and to stop at the County March summit to set this engine down. The overall times to passing Newtonmore on the two runs tabulated were 115½ and 116¼ min respectively, inclusive of stops of 5¼ and 7 min at Blair Atholl.

On the first of the two runs engine No 44699 was in good nick, and we had some good hard

Fife coal on the tender. The work of Fireman Ford, of Perth, was a joy to watch. With skilful use of the injector he managed to keep a very free steaming engine just below blowing off point all the way. My readings of boiler pressures kept monotonously at 215, 218 and 220 lb per sq in, and the only time pressure fell below a momentary 210 was nearing Dalwhinnie, where we had a long permanent way check to observe, and pressure was let down to 190 lb per sq in. With no more than nine coaches on, the task was not difficult. On the harder banks that were taken unassisted, such as Murthly to Kingswood Crossing, and up the 1 in 85 past Pitlochry, Driver Tulloch used 35 per cent cut-off, with the regulator just opened on to the main valve.

As far as Blair Atholl the second run, on which I was travelling as a passenger, involved much harder running. With two additional coaches on the train the uphill speeds were consistently better, and the minimum speed of 31 mph up Pitlochry bank was practically a sustained one. This was an extremely fine effort with 375 tons

TABLE IV
HIGHLAND LINE: BLAIR ATHOLL–DRUMOCHTER

Rly	Train engine	Assistant engine	Class	Load, tons	Time: Blair start, to Summit
HR	*Ballindalloch Castle*	*Sutherland*	A	220	32 42*
HR	*Gordon Castle*	*Stafford*	B	265	35 47*
HR	*Beaufort Castle*	*Sir George*	C	300	36 44*
ScR	No 44699	2–6–4T	—	305	33 59†
ScR	No 44998	14467	P	375	36 46†

*: Start to stop. †: Start to pass. A: 'Duke' class (1874 type 4–4–0). B: 'Clyde Bogie' (1886 type 4–4–0). C: 'Strath' class (1892 type 4–4–0). P: Caledonian Pickersgill 4–4–0

behind the tender. But from Blair the positions were reversed, not because of any change in tactics on the train engines, but in the calibre of the bank engines provided to assist us in rear up to Dalnaspidal. On my footplate run we got a modern 2–6–4 tank, while on the second, made in June, 1950, the bank engine was an *ex-*Caledonian Pickersgill 4–4–0. When the guard saw this engine he remarked: 'Ay, a thr-r-ee; an' it's no' steamin'.' Certainly the assistance from rear on this occasion was not of the most vigorous. To afford some comparison with the way 'The Hill' was climbed in former days, I have shown in Table IV some details of three runs on the old 11.50 am when the train engine stopped at Blair Atholl for a pilot, and that engine was put off at the County March. *Ballindalloch Castle* had only just over the rostered load for her class—indeed, on another occasion *Duncraig Castle* took a 220-ton load without assistance, averaging 27 mph from Blair Atholl to the County March, pass to pass. The pilots were all relatively small engines, with cylinders

no larger than 18 in diameter and 24 in stroke. On my footplate trip the cut-offs used on No 44699 varied between 32 and 37 per cent, with the regulator opened well out on to the second valve. This gave us an average speed of 30.4 mph over the 12 miles between mileposts 37 and 49. On the second run the corresponding average was 28.7 mph, but it is significant of the effectiveness of the respective bank engines that after Dalnaspidal, when the train engines were left to themselves to climb the last mile at 1 in 78 up to Drumochter summit, the more heavily loaded engine showed the higher minimum speed.

During the Interchange Trials of 1948, some fine performances were recorded on 'The Hill.' With the scheduled loads of 350 to 360 on the 4 pm train from Perth assistance was needed, but with the bank engines in rear the dynamometer car recorded only that proportion of the work that was being done by the train engines. In Table V I have set out the best climbing performances of the competing locomotives, from

TABLE V
TEST RESULTS: BLAIR ATHOLL–DALNASPIDAL

Railway	Engine No	Load, tons tare	Distance of recording, miles	Average mph	Actual dhp	Equivalent dhp	Proportion of total load, tons
LMS	44973	353	10	27½	600	900	225
LNE	61292	353	9½	31½	800	1,130	257
Southern	34004	360	10	36¼	1,115	1,550	315

Highland Railway: southbound mail train at Aviemore behind 4-6-0 No 53 Clan Stewart. (Author's collection)

which it will be seen that the Stanier 4-6-0 No 44973 put up what might be called a normal Highland performance on 'The Hill,' and her effort was equivalent to hauling a train of 225 tons. Both the visiting engine crews, impressed no doubt by the pilotmen as to the severity of what was coming, put their engines to it with considerably greater vigour. The 'B1' 4-6-0 sustained for 18 minutes an effort well above the maximum demanded from the *ex*-LMSR 4-6-0s by the 255-ton maximum load limit, while the Bulleid Pacific, in the most enthusiastic hands of Driver Swain and Fireman Hooker, of Nine Elms, put up a magnificent show. It was this ascent that led to the story of the bank engine getting left behind! On such form engine No 34004 could quite comfortably have taken the full 360 tons up without any assistance at all.

With all due respect to the severity of the weather conditions that can develop on the line north of Blair Atholl, one always feels that load limits in recent years have been fixed a little on the cautious side. So far as grading is concerned, the stretch of unbroken severity begins roughly a mile before Struan Station, at the 49th milepost, and continues for exactly 10 miles. There is then an easing to 1 in 85 for 1½ miles, before the definite break in the ascent, past Dalnaspidal Station. This bank is really little more difficult than Beattock, or the tremendous climb out of Liddesdale, to Whitrope summit, on the Waverley Route. An ascent that is probably more testing than either, coming so near to the start of a run, is the southbound climb to Falahill, also on the Waverley Route, where the gradient is 1 in 70 for 8½ miles, with no more than two very brief intermissions. Yet over the latter route the North British Atlantics were rostered to take 290 tons tare, before assistance could be claimed. The northbound ascent to Drumochter is of course not the worst of the Highland banks. Without any doubt, the immediate start from Inverness to the summit point two miles above Daviot is the most gruelling, in that no less than 8½ miles out of 12 miles climbing is inclined at

1 in 60; another 2½ miles are at 1 in 70, and there is only the three-quarters of a mile, steeply downhill across the valley, at Culloden Moor, that provides the slightest respite. During the Interchange Trials the best trains were made up to the full class '5' unassisted load over this stretch, but it is significant that the best climbing performances recorded in the dynamometer car occurred not on the first gruelling test of capacity, but on the final pull from Tomatin up to Slochd summit, when the locomotives had had time to warm up. There, the rival engines gave these results, climbing on 1 in 60:

Railway	Engine No	Load, tons tare	Speed, mph	Actual dhp	Equivalent dhp
LMSR	44973	241	25¾	780	1,082
LNER	61292	251	26	742	1,030
Southern	34004	251	37¼	1,202	1,730

The performance of the Southern locomotive again leaves one somewhat bereft of comment, and I may add that, later in the same run, No 34004 and her crew made a final triumphant salute to the Highland line by taking the full 360-ton load southbound over Drumochter summit unassisted, at a minimum speed of 47 mph, reaching an equivalent drawbar horsepower of 1,950 in the process!

Writing of interchange trials reminds me of what must have been an interesting event right back in 1910, when the 4–6–0 No 146, *Skibo Castle*, was tested against a North British 4–4–0, both on the Highland itself, between Blair Atholl and Dalwhinnie, and over the NBR line between Perth and Kinross, so as to include the formidable Glenfarg bank. No factual data at all has ever leaked out concerning these trials, and there has even been some confusion as to the actual North British engine involved. I have seen it written that this latter was a superheated 'Scott' 4–4–0, which class was not however introduced until two years after the trials. The actual engine involved was No 867, one of the so-called 'intermediate' class, with 6 ft coupled wheels.

These excellent engines were the non-superheated forerunners of the well-known 'Glen' class, and bore the same relation to the latter as the original 'Scotts' of 1909 did to the superheated version of 1912. From their being unnamed, the 'intermediates' were never very well known outside their own system.

The *Locomotive Magazine* of 1910 reported that No 867 showed a slight advantage over *Skibo Castle*, though no technical details were given; but like all W. P. Reid's 4–4–0s the 'intermediates' were capable of being thrashed indefinitely, and, as in 1948, one can be sure that the visiting enginemen in 1910 were anxious to give a good account of themselves on the long climb from Blair Atholl to Drumochter summit. The 'intermediates' were considerably more powerful engines than Peter Drummond's own 4–4–0s, of the 'Big Ben' class, having 19 in-diameter cylinders against 18 in, and larger boilers. It is interesting to recall that, when they were first built at Cowlairs, in 1907, they were known officially as the '19 in intermediate goods engines.'

So we come, finally, to the southbound run from Aviemore down to Perth, and in Table VI I have set out details of three runs made in the years 1912, 1927 and 1952 respectively. The first was a magnificent performance by one of the 'Castles' on the old 8.40 am up from Inverness, and was recorded by Mr B. Purvis. It illustrates not only excellent climbing, with an average speed of 35 mph between Newtonmore and the summit, but the very brisk running then made on the favourable stretches of the Highland Railway. Note particularly the 5.8 miles from Kincraig to the Kingussie stop covered in 6 min 5 sec pass to stop, and the average speed of 52.5 mph from Pitlochry to Dunkeld. On the ascent to Drumochter, it was only on the 2¾ miles at 1 in 80 after Dalwhinnie that speed fell below 30 mph, and then only momentarily. The non-stop run of 35.3 miles from Blair Atholl to Perth showed an average speed of 48 mph.

The second of the up runs was one of my own, on the Edinburgh portion of the up mail, with

TABLE VI
HIGHLAND LINE: AVIEMORE–PERTH

Run No		1	2	3
Year		1912	1927	1952
Engine No		140	14762	44997
Engine Name		Taymouth	Clan	
		Castle	Campbell	
Load, tons (E/F)		195/205	274/295	328/345
Miles		m s	m s	m s
0.0	AVIEMORE ...	0 00	0 00	0 00
5.9	Kincraig ...	8 15	10 50	10 25
11.7	KINGUSSIE ...	14 20	18 15	17 25
0.0			0 00	0 00	0 00
2.9	Newtonmore	4 30	7 15	6 11
—		—	9 50	6 52
			sig stop	pws
13.0	Dalwhinnie ...	20 45	38 35	27 25
18.6	Summit ...	31 30	52 30	38 35
20.6	Dalnaspidal ...	33 45	54 55	41 02
—		—	—	pws
31.8	Struan ...	47 00	68 00	54 45
36.3	BLAIR ATHOLL	53 00	74 35	61 02
0.0		0 00	0 00	0 00
6.8	PITLOCHRY	9 15	11 20	10 55
0.0		0 00	—	0 00	0 00
4.9	Ballinluig ...	14 00	7 20	—
—		—	pws	—
12.9	Dunkeld ...	24 00	13 10	17 28
15.6	Kingswood ...	—	18 20	21 53
18.2	Murthly ...	31 00	21 40	25 22
21.3	Stanley Jc ...	34 20	26 40	30 40
24.3	Luncarty ...	39 00	30 40	34 28
28.5	PERTH ...	44 00	36 30	41 05
Net times:				
Kingussie–Blair ...		53	64*	56*
Pitlochry–Perth ...		—	40*	41

* On basis of a non-stop run over the section

the engine *Clan Campbell*, then immaculate in 'Derby red.' From the viewpoint of hard hillclimbing we were rather handicapped by the schedule, which allowed as much as 70 min from Kingussie to Blair Atholl. This included a booked stop for crossing purposes at Inchlea loop, but we were stopped at Newtonmore in addition, and so passed Dalwhinnie 4½ min late. From there, mostly on 1 in 80, we averaged 24 mph up to Drumochter summit, and as customary no attempt was made to regain lost

time down 'The Hill.' But the subsequent running was quite smart, and with gains on schedule of 1¾ min to Pitlochry, another 1¾ min to Ballinluig, and a final 2½ min, we clocked into Perth on time. Some of the best work lay in the recovery from a 25-mph permanent way check near Inchmagranachan loop to 45 mph at Dunkeld, and a subsequent minimum of 24 mph up the 2¼ miles at 1 in 80 to Kingswood crossing. Maximum speed on the descent from Stanley Junction towards Perth was 62½ mph.

On the third run I was a passenger on the summer Edinburgh express leaving Aviemore at 4.35 pm, and the Stanier 4–6–0 No 44997 gave us some excellent running. After a good start to Kingussie we were once again stopped at Newtonmore to cross a down train, and so had to get away from a dead start up the 2½ miles of 1 in 95 to Etteridge crossing. Here we attained 30 mph, and increased this to 44 mph on the more broken grades past Inchlea crossing. Any advantage from this good progress was nullified immediately afterwards, however, by a permanent way check compelling a reduction to 5 mph at the 60th milepost, so that we approached and passed Dalwhinnie at much below the normal speed. In consideration of the two checks, both severe, the time of 27 min 25 sec from Kingussie to Dalwhinnie was excellent, with a load of 345 tons behind the tender.

Fine work was now done up to Drumochter summit. A maximum of 33½ mph was attained on the short length of 1 in 300 through Dalwhinnie, and the six miles of steep ascent between mileposts 58¾ and 52¼ took only 11½ min, an average speed of 31.2 mph. On the longest stretch of 1 in 80 speed fell to 25½ mph; but the recovery on no more than half a mile of 1 in 150 and level beyond Balsporran box was to 34½ mph, and the minimum on the final 1 in 80 was not below 32 mph. Twice on the descent to Blair Atholl we touched, or slightly exceeded, 60 mph, but there were two permanent way checks in operation, one to 10 mph near Edendon box in the gorge of the River Garry, and another to 15 mph at Struan.

Leaving Pitlochry on time there was no par-

One of the ubiquitous 'Black Five' 4-6-0s No 44997 on an up express goods train at Hilton Junction, south of Perth. (Derek Cross)

ticular need for hurry, and we rolled placidly down Strathtay barely exceeding 50 mph anywhere, while the time to Dunkeld, quite unchecked, was longer than the running time of *Clan Campbell*, which had a permanent way check thrown in, and the disadvantage of stopping and starting from Ballinluig. But the driver of No 44997 had a final thrill in store for us. We were drifting through Dunkeld at 46 mph when the exhaust opened up into such a roar that I immediately took up my stopwatch and notebook again. We cleared the 1 in 80 to Kingswood at a minimum of 30 mph, touched 53 down to Murthly, but then slacked heavily to 35 mph through the loop; and this was the prelude to another thunderous, but this time brief ascent, up the 1 in 108 to milepost 9. We came, as usual, very slowly through Stanley Junction, and a final 62 mph at Luncarty rounded off an excellent run.

The 'Night Ferry' — 'Merchant Navy' dynamometer car test

Ever since its introduction, the 'Night Ferry' was a very popular service and more often than not required to be double headed in steam days. After electrification, loads sometimes went up to nearly 700 tons, though it was not so heavy as that when I was privileged to ride in the cab of one of the new Bo-Bo electrics one morning. The run made a great contrast to that recorded on one of my last trips on a 'King Arthur'. Even more contrasting were the dynamometer car test runs on one of the rebuilt 'Merchant Navy' 4-6-2s, which I was invited to join.

A N interesting foretaste of the standards of locomotive performance we may expect on the electrified main lines of the future is provided now by the working of the 'Night Ferry' train on the Southern Region, with the new 2,500-hp Bo-Bo locomotives of the E5000 series. On this popular service the loads hauled daily are in excess of 600 tons, and at peak periods often exceed 700. Use of the Chatham route provides an excellent test of haulage capacity on steep rising gradients, while the schedule of the inward-bound service, with 87 min for the 65.8 miles from Dover Marine to passing Bickley Junction, calls for some hard work on the banks. From Shortlands Junction this train is routed *via* the Catford loop line, and has an allowance of 23 min for the remaining 13.7 miles into Victoria.

By the courtesy of the Southern Region authorities I was recently permitted to make a journey in the cab of one of these fine locomotives, on a day when the load was one of 608 tons tare, and as comparisons form one of the major interests in a study of locomotive practice and performance I am setting the stage, as it were, by some reference to an excellent trip I enjoyed some six years ago, over the same route with a relief boat train off one of the Belgian services. On that occasion I was also on the footplate, but that time in dungarees and happily dirty, on one of those grand old stalwarts of the Southern, a 'King Arthur' class 4-6-0. It took place on a Saturday in July, and the train was packed, so much so that our tare load of 389 tons would have been increased to fully 425 tons with passengers and their luggage. The engine, No 30769, *Sir Balan*, was manned by Driver P. Tutt and Fireman R. Wilks, of Stewarts Lane shed, and I have never enjoyed pleasanter or more enthusiastic company on the footplate. I have

TABLE I
SOUTHERN REGION:
DOVER MARINE–VICTORIA

2.50 pm Relief Continental Boat Express
Load: 12 cars, 389 tons tare, 425 tons full
Engine: 4–6–0 No 30769, *Sir Balan*

Dist		Sch	Actual		Speeds
Miles		min	m	s	mph
0.0	DOVER (Hawkes-bury St) ...	0*	0	00†	—
0.7	Dover Priory ...	4	3	07	—
2.9	Kearsney ...	—	9	28	30½
6.3	Shepherds Well	—	15	50	33½
10.2	Adisham	—	20	43	72½
			sig stop		
16.2	CANTERBURY	24	29	55	—
18.0	*Milepost 60* ...	—	33	16	34½
21.0	*Milepost 57* ...	—	38	30	34½
22.8	Selling ...	—	41	06	55½
24.0	FAVERSHAM ...	38	44	17	65
			sigs		40
30.0	Teynham ...	—	49	03	54
33.3	SITTINGBOURNE	48	52	52	48½
35.0	*Milepost 43* ...	—	55	10	37
39.1	Rainham ...	—	60	09	54
42.1	Gillingham	—	63	40	eased
43.7	CHATHAM ...	61	65	39	—
46.0	*Milepost 32*	—	69	13	39
			sigs		5
51.1	Sole Street ...	77	85	40	—
57.5	Farningham Road	—	93	08	71½
			sigs		
65.4	*Bickley Jc* ...	96	103	08	—
			sigs		
74.0	HERNE HILL ...	113	124	23	—
			sig stop		
78.0	VICTORIA ...	120	143	50	—

* Schedule from Marine Station.
† Times from restart at Hawkesbury Street.

tabulated this run in detail no further than Chatham, for after that we got involved in the Saturday afternoon procession up the Kent Coast line and suffered many delays.

One of the characteristic features of steam locomotive working on the Continental boat trains of the Southern is the different fuel used on the outward and inward journey. At Stewarts Lane shed the tenders are loaded with hard Yorkshire, or East Midlands coal, while at Dover they are replenished with soft Kentish.

The latter needs a technique in firing similar to the Welsh varieties used in most parts of the Western Region, and before backing on to the train Wilks had built up a big fire, quite in the Great Western style, so as to have a thick and thoroughly hot firebed which he could build on further during the heavy ascent to Shepherds Well, and again during the shorter, but equally hard, climb from Canterbury up to Ensden Tunnel. The climb to Shepherds Well, which begins at the very entrance to Dover Tunnel, and continues for 6¾ miles at 1 in 106–132, is indeed a gruelling start, particularly as the junctions and sharp curvature out of the Marine station and past Hawkesbury Street box preclude any taking of a run at it.

On a day of such heavy traffic it was something of an achievement by the operating folks at Dover to get us away from the Marine station on time. But we were immediately involved in checks, and it was not until nearly 5 min after our first start that we got away from Hawkesbury Street, and it is from this second start that the tabulated log commences. There were no half measures on the footplate of *Sir Balan*. Once we were through Dover Tunnel, and passing the Priory station, the regulator was put full open, and cut-off shortened a little, to 50 per cent. We then had six solid minutes of this tremendous pounding. The gradient eases from 1 in 106 to 1 in 132 at Buckland Junction, and at Kearsney, where speed was just coming up to 30 mph, the cut-off was shortened to 42 per cent. The fireman had done his preliminary work well, and all the way up the bank the needle of the pressure gauge was rock-steady.

At the mouth of Lydden Tunnel we reached our maximum speed on the ascent, of 34 mph, representing an equivalent drawbar horsepower of 1,030, but in the tunnel there was a slight falling back, and we topped the summit at 32½ mph. On this ascent the sense of effort, on this relatively old engine, was ever-present and enthralling; the heavy exhaust beat; the frequent, careful firing; the keen attention to steam and water gauges—all combined to build up that atmosphere of strenuous human endeavour that

A celebrated boat train engine of former years, Maunsell 'E1' class No 31504, on a Kent Coast train near Bellingham on the Catford loop line. (E.D. Bruton)

is synonymous with the finest work on steam locomotives. A maximum speed of 72½ mph was easily attained down the well-aligned descent towards Canterbury, but we were brought to a dead stand for signals outside, having run the 15 miles from Hawkesbury Street in 26 min start to stop.

Fortunately we got a clear run through Canterbury East Station, and so were able to commence the bank to Ensden at about 30 mph. The climbing here was finer than ever, with a speed of 34½ mph steadily maintained on the 1 in 132 gradient, giving an equivalent drawbar horsepower of 1,080. The fireman was steaming the boiler right up to blowing-off point, 200 lb per sq in, and the cut-off was 37 per cent, with full regulator. It is interesting to compare this performance with the test results obtained at Rugby with the 'BR5' 4-6-0 No 73008, for to produce 1,080 equivalent dhp at 35 mph the cut-off necessary was also 37 per cent, and required a coal consumption of about 2,400 lb per hr. The all-out performance of the 'BR5,' with a

coal rate of 3,620 lb per hr, gave an equivalent dhp of 1,350 at 35 mph. At the same time, when I read the modern test bulletins it is always with a tinge of regret that the old stalwarts like the 'King Arthurs,' the Great Northern Atlantics, the Great Eastern '1500' class, and others, ran their courses too early in railway history to be subjected to scientific testing on one or other of the stationary plants.

To revert to the work of *Sir Balan*, however, nothing special was done along the coastal section to Gillingham, but with the unusual luxury of a completely clear road through Chatham and Rochester I was hoping for a fine ascent of the Sole Street bank. We certainly started off in great style, doing nearly 40 mph approaching Cuxton Road box. There, however, our troubles started, and checks came so repeatedly afterwards that detailed consideration of the running is not worth while. As the log in Table I shows we were eventually 29½ min late in arriving at Victoria. The first portion of the train, hauled by a 'Merchant Navy' 4-6-2 and travelling *via* Ashford, had fared no better; her actual overall time was 2 hr 25 min.

The 'Night Ferry' train has exactly the same allowance to passing Chatham, though curiously enough the initial booking to Faversham is 4½ min easier than that of the relief boat train worked by *Sir Balan*; but the capacity of the new electric locomotives was evidently taken into account in allowing no more than 9 min for the 6½ miles from Rochester Junction to Sole Street, as compared with 13½ min for the earlier run. The cab of No E5002 was typical of the Southern 'electrics' in its utter simplicity,

TABLE II
SOUTHERN REGION:
DOVER MARINE–VICTORIA

The 'Night Ferry' Train
Load: 608 tons tare, 620 tons full.
Engine: Bo-Bo Electric No E5002

Dist		Sch	Actual		Speeds
Miles		min	m	s	mph
0.0	DOVER MARINE	0	0	00	—
1.1	Dover Priory ...	—	3	50	—
2.0	*Buckland Jc* ...	6¼	5	58	—
3.3	Kearsney ...	—	7	58	40
6.7	Shepherds Well...	14½	12	46	45
10.6	Adisham ...	—	17	04	68
16.6	CANTERBURY...	29	23	32	30
					(slack)
18.4	*Milepost 60* ...	—	26	28	—
21.4	*Milepost 57* ...	—	31	06	44
23.3	Selling ...	—	33	26	58
24.4	FAVERSHAM ...	42½	36	23	70
			sigs		30
33.7	SITTINGBOURNE	50½	44	27	35
35.4	*Milepost 43* ...	—	—		40
			sigs		—
42.5	Gillingham ...	—	56	22	—
44.1	CHATHAM ...	61	58	50	5
46.4	*Milepost 32* ...	—	63	53	37
50.4	*Milepost 28* ...	—	69	39	43
			sigs		
51.5	Sole Street ...	73	71	13	30
57.9	Farningham Road	—	78	40	70
60.7	SWANLEY ...	82	82	02	42
63.6	St Mary Cray ...	—	84	57	62
65.8	*Bickley Jc* ...	87	87	20	eased
			sigs		5
68.4	Shortlands ...	90	92	01	—
73.4	Nunhead ...	98	98	50	—
76.0	*Milepost 3½* ...	—	103	35	sig
			104	18	stop
77.3	*Factory Jc* ...	—	108	25	—
			sigs		2
79.5	VICTORIA ...	110	114	15	—

and it was difficult to believe one was travelling on the most powerful single locomotive unit yet in regular service in this country. The master controller has 33 running notches, thus providing for quite fine adjustment of the power output, and like the earlier Southern main-line electric locomotives Nos 20001–20003 these new locomotives are equipped with the 'booster' control system.

A characteristic of the British railway system that is only too familiar in country districts is the frequency of occupation level crossings. Over these there must be a complete break in the conductor rails, and the booster set is designed to provide continuity of supply to the traction motors while the locomotive is passing over the gap. With multiple-unit trains these gaps are of no consequence as only one collector shoe is over the gap at any one time. The 'booster' consists of a motor-generator set, the armature shafts of which each carry a heavy flywheel, which help to maintain the speed of the set during the interruptions of supply from conductor rails. The output of the booster generator is approximately 1,250 hp at 1,750 rpm. The starting of the booster set was the only preparation for the run that had to be made prior to our getting the 'right away.'

The start out of the Marine station was made very cautiously, winding round the curves to Hawkesbury Street, with the master controller advanced to no further than the ninth notch. But entering Dover Tunnel Driver Dudley opened up, and we were soon gathering speed. There was, however, one slight pause in the acceleration up the continuous 1 in 132 gradient, when the booster motor cut out momentarily just after Kearsney; but the going thereafter was excellent, and we threaded the long Lydden tunnel at a steady 45 mph. Here the controller was in notch 27, and the equivalent drawbar horsepower would have been approximately 2,000. Downhill towards Canterbury we were coasting for most of the way, reaching a maximum speed of 68 mph at Adisham. Then came the 30 mph slack through Canterbury, as an awkward preliminary to the climb to Ensden Tunnel.

At relatively low speeds the effect of the conductor rail gaps over the occupation level crossings was quite marked; for although the booster generator continued to supply the traction motors the supply available across the gaps was considerably below that normally taken from the conductor rail on this heavy ascent, and the result was a gentle backward surge as the gaps were crossed. Apart from these brief interludes we steadily gathered speed on the climb, and topped the summit at 44 mph. So far as times are concerned there was not a great deal of difference between the steam and electric locomotive on this ascent; the times between Canterbury East and Milepost 56½ were 9 min 51 sec by No 30769, and 8 min 42 sec by No E5002, with the steam locomotive passing Canterbury at considerably the slower speed.

Once through Ensden Tunnel No E5002 was put into the coasting position, and we ran freely downhill, reaching a full 70 mph as Faversham was neared. Here, following the old main line of the London, Chatham & Dover Railway, we ran through at full speed, and continued under relatively light power, with the master controller in the seventeenth notch. Then came a whole succession of signal checks, which continued right through to Chatham; so that although we had passed Faversham with 6 min in hand we lost some 4 min on the delayed section. We got the road once again from Rochester Junction, and as I expected the ascent of Sole Street bank was of great interest. With the controller in notch 30 we reached a maximum of 43 mph on the continuous 1 in 100 gradient, with the equivalent drawbar horsepower rising to 2,165. Right at the summit, however, we got signals 'on,' through a goods train shunting at Meopham, and speed had to be reduced to 30 mph.

Up Pullman boat train in the Folkestone Warren hauled by 'Lord Nelson' class 4-6-0 No 859 Lord Hood. (M.W. Earley)

The point-to-point timings of this train are considerably sharper inwards from Rochester than those of the relief train on which I travelled earlier, and with the effects of the Sole Street check we were only just on time at Swanley, and again at Bickley Junction. From Farningham Road we were going fairly hard, with the master controller in notch 23, until power was shut off at Bickley Junction. The signal check at Shortlands came in a very awkward place. We were practically stopped in the station, and then had to get away up a sharp rise to the junction, and pass over a considerable 'gap,' in crossing over to the Catford Loop line. A misjudgment here on the part of the driver might easily have led to the stalling of so heavy a train. The loop line is no place for speeding. There are many restrictions, though we were no more than a minute late

The down 'Golden Arrow' on the re-aligned junctions at Petts Wood, with 'Battle of Britain' No 34085 502 Squadron. (R.C. Riley)

through Nunhead. A dead stand for signals at Cambria Junction and a check to walking pace on Grosvenor Road bridge made us eventually 4¼ min late into Victoria.

From a study of a log in Table II it will be appreciated that this particular run gave little opportunity for the sustained capacity of the locomotive to be displayed. The 'Night Ferry' comes into London at a time when the lines are very heavily occupied with suburban trains; a fast schedule would be quite impracticable, and it is the ability of these locomotives to accelerate rapidly with the heaviest trains that is their greatest attribute in these circumstances. When the Tonbridge-Ashford route to Dover is electrified we may look forward to some considerably more spectacular running with the boat trains that are locomotive hauled.

Since I last wrote of Southern steam locomotives, the official test bulletin for the rebuilt 'Merchant Navy' class 4–6–2s has been published, and it is interesting to compare the

performance of these engines with that of other modern types. At a steam rate of 25,000 lb per hour the equivalent drawbar horsepower at various speeds was measured thus:

Speed, mph	30	40	50	60	70	80
Equiv dhp	1,310	1,340	1,300	1,200	1,050	840

At the lower speeds this performance lies close to that of a 'King,' but it becomes a little higher at speeds of over 60 mph. The locomotive was steamed up to a maximum of 38,000 lb of steam per hour, at which the maximum sustained drawbar horsepower was a shade over 2,000, at 45 mph.

Having regard to the relative sizes of boiler and firebox, the 'King' maximum, reached in the 1953 trials with No 6001, having then a single chimney, was remarkably high at 33,600 lb per hour. The comparative power outputs of 'King' and 'Merchant Navy' at this steam rate, 33,600 lb per hr, are interesting, thus:

Speed, mph	30	40	50	60	70	80
Dhp 'King'	1,810	1,800	1,680	1,520	1,310	1,080
Dhp 'MN'	1,760	1,840	1,810	1,710	1,550	1,350

The test bulletin sets out very complete details of the speeds one of the rebuilt 'Merchant Navy' class engines should be able to maintain in various service conditions. Taking the maximum service coal rate of 3,000 lb per hr, the sustained speeds to be expected on certain gradients are shown in Table III:

TABLE III

Gradient (rising)	Speeds, mph	
	400-ton train	500-ton train
Level	72	67
1 in 300	55	49
1 in 200	47½	42
1 in 100	30	25
1 in 70	21	18

From this table it is evident that on many sections of modern Southern runs the standard maximum coal rate was substantially exceeded for intermittent periods. During the trials with engine No 35020 two remarkable runs were made with the 3 pm down express from Waterloo, as between Templecombe and Sidmouth Junction. The load in each case was 394 tons tare, and the times as recorded in the bulletin were:

Dist, miles		Sch min	June 26, act min	June 28, act min
0.0	Templecombe	0	0	0
10.7	Yeovil Junc	12½	13	13
35.8	Seaton Junc	37½	33½	32
47.4	Sidmouth Junc	51	46½	43

The times quoted are in no more detail than the above, but the records of power output are most impressive. The following figures are taken from the bulletin:

Location	June 26		June 28	
	Speed, mph	Equiv dhp	Speed, mph	Equiv dhp
Yeovil Junc	78	1,427	75	1,328
Milepost 126	65	1,571	67	1,484
Crewkerne	71	1,374	80	1,191
Hewish Summit ...	60	1,686	63½	1,459
Axminster	—	—	95	1,345
Milepost 150	56	1,583	67	1,645
Entering Honiton Tunnel	42	1,538	48½	1,494

There was some tremendous running on the second trip after Sutton Bingham bank had been cleared. The power output in relation to speed suggests that the boiler was not steamed uniformly, which would be done by increasing cut-off as speed fell in the ascent of Honiton bank; instead, the cut-off was kept unchanged at about 27 per cent. The characteristic curves show that with a constantly maintained cut-off of 27 per cent the corresponding values of equivalent drawbar horsepower are:

Speed, mph	45	65	80	90
Equivalent dhp	1,490	1,600	1,440	1,300

The running between Hewish summit and the foot of Honiton bank on this occasion provides one of the very rare examples of a locomotive being 'pushed' really hard downhill. At the maximum speed of 95 mph the actual horsepower on the drawbar was no less than 1,480, and as the train was running downhill the equivalent value was less than the actual, as the effect of gravity on engine and tender had in this case to be deducted. So far as the steaming rate was concerned the engine was practically 'all-out'—with the rate of usage slightly exceeding the maximum sustained capacity of the boiler, until the speed had fallen below 80 mph.

Such a performance makes one ask what maximum speed one of these locomotives might achieve in the most favourable circumstances, with a lighter load, for example, or on a steeper gradient. Strange though it may seem, however, there are certain conditions in which the weight of the train makes no difference, as the power needed to overcome the rolling and wind resistance of the coaches is exactly equalled by the effect of gravity. On a falling gradient of 1 in 100, for example, at any speed up to 100 mph, the effect of gravity easily outweighs the rolling

The down 'Golden Arrow' passing Chelsfield behind 'West Country' class 4-6-2 No 34092 City of Wells. (Derek Cross)

An up Continental boat express emerging from Abbots Cliff Tunnel in the Folkestone Warren, hauled by 'Battle of Britain' class 4–6–2 No 34067 Tangmere. (Derek Cross)

resistance of modern coaching stock. The nearest approach to equality is at a speed of 80 mph on a falling gradient of 1 in 200. In still air the horsepower necessary to overcome the rolling resistance of the stock is 2.66 lb per ton of train weight, while the assistance from gravity is 2.4 lb per ton. On a fine downhill stretch like that from Stoke Tunnel to Essendine on the East Coast main line practically no power is needed from the locomotive to keep even the heaviest train rolling at 80 mph.

At higher speeds it is another matter, and the following figures have been worked out, taking the latest BTC figures for coach resistance in still air:

Horsepower at Drawbar.   Gradient at I in 200 falling.

Speed, mph	Load behind tender tons	Dhp
80	500	130
90	500	400
100	325	585

The effects of adverse winds are surprisingly severe. A head wind of no more than 7½ mph blowing obliquely to the line at an angle of 45 deg puts the coach resistance at 90 mph up from 14.6 to 16.2 lb per ton, or in other words makes a 450-ton train pull exactly like 500 tons in still air.

One of the most interesting items in the bulletin on the rebuilt 'Merchant Navy' class locomotive is the series of results of engine and tender resistance, as these enable us to calculate the power used in driving the locomotive itself. The following table relates to running on level track:

Speed, mph	60	70	80	90	100
Hp to overcome total loco resistance	520	710	950	1,210	1,575

From this one can make a rough estimate of the probability of one of these engines reaching 100 mph on that splendid stretch from Round-wood Tunnel down towards Southampton, with a 400-ton train. Roughly 1,800 horsepower would be needed to overcome the rolling resistance of the train; the effect of gravity on engine, tender and train would contribute 1,315, thus leaving 485 hp to be added to the power needed to get the engine along—2,060 in all. The test bulletin shows that this would be easily possible, on a steam consumption of roughly 30,000 lb per hr.

Such calculations are all very well, theoretically; but they are of interest in showing what could be done if all the running conditions were ideal. The state of the track, and the state of the engine, are factors that can weigh heavily against the attainment of theoretical optima, as a rough-riding engine is a very much greater deterrent to high speed than any traction or rolling resistances, or adverse winds. But to conclude this article, I cannot do better than quote details of two runs with engines of the rebuilt 'Merchant Navy' class, sent me by two different correspondents on which very high speeds were run. Neither, curiously enough, was on that famous West of England speedway between Salisbury and Exeter, where the maximum of 95 mph was reached during the trials of engine No 35020, but their very attainment is enough to show the superb condition of modern permanent way on the lines in question.

The first run was clocked by Mr H. F. Maybank, on the 8.20 am from Waterloo, with engine No 35019, *French Line*, and a gross load of 400 tons behind the tender. For some months the bridge renewal slack at New Malden had been a serious hindrance, but on this run two further checks were experienced, putting the train 5½ min behind time at Worting Junction, and passing that point at no more than 15 mph. But once over Roundwood summit some terrific speed developed. Passing Micheldever at 76½ mph the engine romped up to 96 mph in five miles, but was then eased to 88 mph through Winchester. A further maximum, of 93 mph, was attained near Shawford, and in all the 19.2 miles from Micheldever to St Denys

TABLE IV
SOUTHERN REGION:
WATERLOO–SALISBURY

The 'Atlantic Coast Express'
Load: 12 cars, 397 tons tare, 425 tons full
Engine: 4–6–2 No 35016, *Elders Fyffes*

Dist		Sch	Actual		Speeds
Miles		min	m	s	mph
0.0	WATERLOO ...	0	0	00	—
7.3	Wimbledon ...	—	12	15	60
			pws		15
12.0	Surbiton ...	—	20	04	51
13.3	*Hampton Court Jc*	18	21	33	60
19.1	Weybridge ...	—	26	55	72
21.7	West Byfleet ...	—	29	05	73
24.4	WOKING ...	—	31	19	73
28.0	Brookwood ...	—	34	24	69/70
31.0	*Milepost 31* ...	—	36	58	69
33.2	Farnborough ...	—	38	48	73
36.5	Fleet ...	—	41	26	76½
42.2	Hook ...	—	45	53	77/80
47.8	BASINGSTOKE	—	50	27	—
			slight		
			check		50
50.3	*Worting Jc* ...	51	53	34	—
59.2	Whitchurch ...	—	60	07	77½
61.1	Hurstbourne	—	61	29	81
66.4	ANDOVER JUNC	—	65	19	85
72.8	Grateley ...	—	70	46	62
78.3	Porton ...	—	75	10	85
82.7	*Tunnel Junc*	80½	79	02	—
83.8	SALISBURY ...	83	81	10	—

were covered at an average speed of 88.5 mph. As my correspondent suggests, had not the engine been eased below Waller's Ash Tunnel, a maximum of 100 mph or more might easily have been attained, such was the rapidity of the acceleration.

On the second of these runs, on the 'Atlantic Coast Express,' Worting Junction had been passed 3½ min late, and the driver put on a great spurt west of Overton, to reach 94 mph at Andover Junction and to clear Grateley Summit at 66 mph. After that the day was won, and nothing more than 90 down the final steep descent into Salisbury was needed to make a punctual arrival. To conclude, I have tabulated details of yet another first-class run on the 'Atlantic Coast Express' recorded by a correspondent living at Chapel-en-le-Frith, and he comments: 'This may be an exceptional timing, or a common occurrence...' It was certainly very commendable, in the vigour of the uphill work and, this time, in the moderation of the downhill running. On this journey the average speed between mileposts 17 and 81—64 miles in all—was 74 mph, inclusive of the slowing to 50 mph at Worting Junction.

East Coast —
on the footplate of *Mallard*

Following the 1988 celebrations surrounding the 50th anniversary of the establishment of the world record for maximum speed by a steam locomotive, and the restoration of *Mallard* to her original appearance and working efficiency, it is interesting to recall what those famous engines were doing in the last years of steam on the East Coast route, and in particular what *Mallard* herself could do in her last days working as a regular traffic department engine.

FROM a number of letters I have received recently it is evident that there is considerable interest in the economics of the new diesel locomotives as compared with the steam power they are replacing. It is the use of diesel-electric locomotives in multiple-unit, as on the Aberdeen route and on the Midland line on certain services between St Pancras and Manchester, that seems to have aroused the greatest curiosity. Referring particularly to the Aberdeen road, one correspondent writes that the combined effort of two 1,160-hp diesels could easily be matched by one Gresley Pacific, and asks pointedly where the economy and modernisation come in. His question would appear to have added force in that many of the new three-hour Edinburgh-Aberdeen trains are loaded up to no more than six coaches. On the face of it two diesels weighing 77 ½ tons apiece would seem a retrograde form of motive power, seeing that one Reid Atlantic sufficed for trains of equiva-lent weight when the three-hour service was introduced 54 years ago.

Now I do not hold any particular brief for the diesels, but it is only fair to say that the process of dieselisation is only just taking shape. The present utilisation of the new power does not, one would imagine, represent the arrangements when steam is completely superseded. The ultimate aim, that of securing maximum utilisation of the entire locomotive stock, naturally envisages the intensive diagramming of individual units to passenger, mixed-traffic and freight duties alike, working to the very minimum of turn-round times, with all power massed in common-user pools at a few large depots, to be handled by each and every engineman on the strength, as need be. For this purpose it is abundantly necessary to have locomotives of a general utility kind, that will not be excessively powerful for the lighter duties; in Scotland, in particular, it has been a matter of major policy to

The preserved Flying Scotsman *in 1966, backing down to Victoria Station preparatory to hauling a special on Southern Region* (P.H. Groom)

invest in the type '2,' and run them in pairs on the heavier duties.

It is important to appreciate that the latter form of usage is not double heading. The locomotives are coupled in multiple unit, and handled by a single crew, so that although one does double up on the machinery there is not the expense of two sets of men. Even so, two 1,160-hp Bo-Bo, or two 1,200-hp Bo-Co locomotives, as used on certain Midland turns, cost a good deal more than the present price of a North British Atlantic, or even a Gresley Pacific. The question is, does the higher utilisation offset the greatly increased capital cost? On some services where the operating staff have become thoroughly accustomed to the new locomotives it has been found possible to effect very considerable economies by having one engineman. Of this the Liverpool Street-Kings Lynn route is a good example. The overall journey time is less

than three hours; there are no lengthy non-stop runs; and the drivers are relieved by a two-man crew on arrival at Liverpool Street. The latter men do all the manoeuvring in the station yard, and the train engineman does not take over again until the locomotive has been backed on and coupled up ready to go.

Another correspondent, writing on a further aspect of costs, suggests that, if fuel supply and servicing conditions sounded the death knell of steam, a complete modernisation of the servicing and cleaning facilities at major depots could have been achieved at a mere fraction of the cost of dieselisation, and that coal difficulties could have been overcome by oil-firing. In this connection he cites the excellent performance of Great Western locomotives converted soon after the second world war, which steamed with the utmost freedom and consistency. I can certainly confirm this latter assertion from personal experiences on the footplate. I have never seen 'Castles' worked harder or steam better than on some journeys in Cornwall in the summer of 1947.

Gresley 'A4' Pacific No 4482 Golden Eagle *in 1938 on an express at Newcastle Central.* (W.B. Greenfield)

The steam *versus* diesel argument is likely to be prolonged for many years. So much publicity has been given to this part of the modernisation plan that enthusiasts are bound to look on critically as successive phases of the plan take effect. In this respect it is interesting to find the majority of letters reaching me on the subject are devoid of any upholding of steam that is based only on sentimental grounds. In nearly every case there is a seeking after enlightenment based on strictly economic factors. Their interest in the railways of this country is obviously friendly, but in view of the present financial situation they, like many others, are puzzled by what they see. Whether we like it or not the diesels are with us for some time to come, and as individual units their overall performance, as measured by work done in relation to the heat energy latent in the fuel, is highly efficient.

At the present time the railways are in the throes of a very difficult and complicated half-way house. There are not sufficient diesel locomotives to provide for the exclusive haulage of certain well-defined groups of trains. Some trains must remain steam hauled for a time, and so the schedules and the locomotive diagramming remains on a steam basis; steam facilities must remain while new diesel depots are built, and the men, who must be prepared to work either, inevitably tend to get the worst of both worlds. At the same time one can hardly subscribe to the facile optimism sometimes heard, that once steam is finally abolished all will be well. The operating arrangements on British Railways in many districts leave much to be desired, and the lack of any over-riding supervisory control is painfully apparent.

I had an example of this kind of trouble on the very day of writing this article. I was travelling by an express usually worked by a diesel; but a most unusual mishap on the outward working, quite unconnected with the locomotive itself, put the rostered locomotive out of action, and a steam 4–6–0, of class '5' capacity, was provided for the return. This was a mixed-traffic unit, hastily commandeered, but although departure was 10 min late, smart running, and smart station working at the two intermediate stops saw the train only 5 min late away on the final run of 70 miles, non-stop. The engine was not in the condition to recover any more time, but from the running over the first 20 miles nothing would have been lost. Instead, through bad operating, 15 min was lost, and the arrival was thus 20 min late. One would not have minded so much if someone had not commented on arrival: 'Well, what can you expect; we've got a 'steamer' on!'

Apropos of diesels, it is with something of a pang that one realises this has probably been the last summer in which the principal East Coast expresses have been steam hauled, and that a fleet of 'Deltics' will be operating in 1961. In a number of recent articles in this series many references have been made to the power output of various Western, Southern and London Midland locomotives, and so this month it is the turn of the most famous of all British Pacifics, the Gresley 'A3s' and 'A4s.' I write the last sentence in full appreciation of all that has been done by the Stanier 'Duchesses,' and the Southern 'Merchant Navys'; but the 'A3s'—or at any rate those originally built with 180-lb boilers—were veterans before the 'Duchesses' were laid down at Crewe, and yet today they are still responsible for a very high proportion of the workings into and out of Kings Cross.

At the same time it is only on the night expresses that one regularly finds anything approaching the Gargantuan loads of old, but while the runs I have to describe are mostly with the nine-coach trains, most popular today, I have looked through my earlier records to find examples of sustained power output that can compare with the best performed on the Western side of the country. A splendid example of present 'A3' performance on the down 'West Riding' is detailed in Table I, with an engine of 1923 vintage, No 60110, *Robert the Devil*. Because of permanent way and signal checks nothing very much could be done as far as Peterborough, but some grand running followed. Up the long

TABLE I
EASTERN REGION: HITCHIN–RETFORD
'The West Riding'
Load: 9 cars, 301 tons tare, 320 tons gross.
Engine: Class 'A3' 4–6–2 No 60110, *Robert the Devil*

Dist			Actual		Speeds
Miles			m	s	mph
0.0	HITCHIN	... ...	0	00	—
3.8	Three Counties	...	5	01	66½
			sigs		50
9.2	Biggleswade	... ...	10	11	78
			pws		20
12.2	Sandy	... ...	12	52	—
19.8	St Neots	... ...	20	30	64/77½
24.1	Offord	... ...	23	58	68
27.0	HUNTINGDON	...	26	29	70
31.6	Abbots Ripton	...	30	55	58 (min)
	Milepost 67	... ...	—		85
			pws		30
37.5	Holme	... ...	36	52	67 (max)
44.5	PETERBOROUGH		43	59	(slack)
47.6	*Werrington Jc*	...	47	50	64½
53.0	Tallington	... ...	52	20	82
61.1	*Milepost* 93	... ...	58	47	64½/69
68.2	*Stoke Box*	... ...	65	07	64½
73.6	GRANTHAM	... ...	69	24	82*
83.5	Claypole	... ...	76	58	86
			sigs		—
88.2	NEWARK		80	52	—
			sigs		—
95.5	Crow Park	... ...	89	40	75
99.4	*Dukeries Jc*	... ...	92	54	64½ (min)
			—		75½
106.7	RETFORD	... ...	99	40	—

* Eased to 70 mph through station

gradient from Tallington to Stoke summit speed averaged no less than 72 mph; with a minimum of 64½ mph past Stoke, the eventual net time of 90¼ min from Hitchin to Retford showed a start-to-stop average speed of 71 mph. This strikes me as a most excellent performance and I am much indebted to Dr J. A. Dew for the details.

Next, in Table II, come three runs on the afternoon 'Talisman,' as between Newcastle and Edinburgh. The first of these, which was an experience of my own, shows the kind of work that is required for ordinary timekeeping, and recovery from no more than a modest amount of delay from out-of-course reasons. Again the

TABLE II
EAST COAST ROUTE: NEWCASTLE–EDINBURGH
The 'Talisman'

Run No			1		2		3	
Engine No			60057		60009		60043	
Engine Name			Ormonde		Union of South Africa		Brown Jack	
4–6–2 Class			'A3'		'A4'		'A3'	
Load, tons (E/F)			271/285		304/320		311/325	
Dist		Sch	Actual	Speed	Actual	Speed	Actual	Speed
Miles		min	m　s	mph	m　s	mph	m　s	mph
0.0	NEWCASTLE　...	0	0　00	—	0　00	—	0　00	—
5.0	Forest Hall　...	—	10　15	40	9　12	53½	8　06	53
9.9	Cramlington　...	—	15　50	60	13　56	63	12　32	69
13.9	Stannington　...	—	19　25	75	17　22	76	15　33	85½
16.6	MORPETH　...	20½	22　18	40*	20　06	36*	18　10	40*
			pws	20	—	—	—	—
23.2	Widdrington　...	—	31　17	—	26　34	70	23　59	77
28.5	Acklington　...	—	35　47	—	30　48	77½	27　51	87
34.8	ALNMOUTH　...	37	41　47	55*	36　32	60*	32　35	slack
39.4	Little Mill　...	—	46　51	51½	40　52	65/61	36　31	66
46.0	Chathill　...	—	52　41	—	46　16	80½	41　26	92½
51.6	Belford　...	52	57　20	75	50　51	70	45　15	87
58.6	Beal　...	—	62　27	86	56　15	80½	49　50	95
63.5	Scremerston　...	—	66　17	64	60　11	65	53　06	73
66.9	BERWICK　...	69½	69　40	slack	63　50	40*	56　44	40*
72.5	Burnmouth　...	—	76　32	49	70　14	57¼	63　56	53
78.1	Reston Jc　...	82	81　34	71½	75　15	72	69　04	71½
83.1	Grantshouse　...	88	86　09	63	80　16	55	73　55	60¼
							sigs	—
87.9	Cockburnspath　...	—	90　05	82	84　31	75	78　16	—
				eased	—	eased	sigs	45
95.2	DUNBAR　...	98	96　22	—	90　43	—	86　26	—
101.0	East Linton　...	—	102　20	—	96　02	67½	92　27	63
106.6	DREM JC　...	108	107　10	72	100　29	80	97　14	77
114.9	Prestonpans　...	—	115　15	66	106　57	75/79	104　07	69/76
							pws	—
118.3	Monktonhall Jc　...	120	118　24	—	109　40	—	108　27	—
			sigs	—	sig stop	—	sigs	—
121.4	Portobello　...	123	123　00	*	114　37	—	112　24	—
					sig stop	—	sig stop	—
124.4	WAVERLEY　...	129	128　33	—	123　29	—	122　04	—
Net times, min			124½		119		112½	

* Speed restriction

engine was an old one, originally of the 1925 batch of Gresley 'A1s,' and probably written down to a very low capital value. Newcastle was left on time, after a fine run down from London behind another 'A3,' and the going at first was on the leisurely side, but there was some excellent work north of the border, particularly in the minimum speed of 63 mph at Grantshouse.

The second and third runs in this table were both clocked by Mr Ronald Nelson. That in column two, with an 'A4,' was admittedly a piece of *joie de vivre* on the part of the driver. The train was on time from Newcastle, and having run hard to keep the fast sectional time to Belford he continued in the same style to the outskirts of Edinburgh, with the result that Monktonhall

Junction was passed 10 min early. Then came a succession of signal checks that caused the last six miles into Waverley to take nearly 19 min. One could perhaps criticise this driver from the viewpoint of good operating, saying that he was running unnecessarily hard from Berwick and using more coal than the schedule required; but a good free-running engine tends to make its own stride, and no long-distance passenger minds arriving at destination a little before time.

Although the engine was skating along in the best 'A4' style on the level stretches, there was some fine uphill running on this journey. At Alnmouth, for example, speed was carefully reduced to 60 mph through the station, and then the engine was opened out to such an extent as to average 63½ mph up the 1 in 170 of the Longhoughton bank. It was the same following the pronounced slack at Berwick. Here the train came off the Royal Border Bridge and passed through the station at no more than 40 mph, yet speed was rapidly worked up afterwards to 57¼ mph on a continuous ascent of 1 in 190. The equivalent drawbar horsepower on the

Longhoughton bank was at least 1,450, and in accelerating between Berwick and Burnmouth the power output probably exceeded 1,600. On the continuation of the climb, between Reston Junction and Grantshouse, the effort was somewhat relaxed, as on a 1 in 200 gradient speed fell from 66¾ to 55 mph in five miles.

On the third run there was every incentive to high speed, as the train was leaving Newcastle 11½ min late. High speed was developed in very truth, for despite the vigour required by the initial stages of this journey the train passed Berwick just over a *minute early*! The uphill work in general was no harder than on the previous run, but this driver certainly let fly on the favourable stretches. All the same he was as careful as his colleague on the *Union of South Africa* at points requiring a definite reduction in speed, such as Morpeth, Tweedmouth Junction and Berwick. Between the slacks the going was truly fierce, and the maximum speeds of 85½ mph near Stannington and 87 near Acklington were mere curtain-raisers to what was to follow. Not since the days of the 'Coronation' have I seen such

The southbound 'Coronation' near Low Fell in 1938 with Class 'A4' 4-6-2 No 4482 Golden Eagle. *(W.B. Greenfield)*

running north of Alnmouth, where the average speed over the 17.8 miles from Christon Bank to Goswick was exactly 90 mph. Through this magnificent effort the train which had left Newcastle 11½ min late was actually 1½ min early through Berwick.

Although still continuing to do very well the work was not quite so exceptional north of the Border, and a succession of signal checks hindered the approach to Dunbar. Nevertheless the running through the Lothians was exactly on time, until signal checks recommenced and made the arrival 4½ min late in Edinburgh. One gets rather tired of commenting on the numerous occasions when signal checks nullify splendid work on the footplate, and there is nothing to be gained in this case by dwelling on the miserable sequel to a magnificent piece of locomotive running. Instead it is interesting to compare this run with the classic performance of the North Eastern 'M' class 4-4-0 No 1620 on the last night of the 1895 Race to the North. The principal times are shown alongside in Table III, and it will be seen that after the immediate start

TABLE III
NEWCASTLE–EDINBURGH RECORDS

Run No		1	2
Year		1895	1959
Engine		1620	60043
Engine Class		'M'	'A3'
Load, tons tare		101	311

Dist, Miles		m s	m s
0.0	NEWCASTLE ...	0 00	0 00
5.0	Forest Hall ...	6 45	8 06
16.6	Morpeth ...	18 00	18 10
34.8	Alnmouth ...	33 30	32 35
51.6	Belford ...	48 00	45 15
66.9	BERWICK ...	60 00	56 44
83.1	Grantshouse ...	77 30	73 55
		—	sigs
95.2	DUNBAR ...	88 00	86 26
101.0	East Linton ...	93 15	92 27
106.6	DREM Jc ...	98 00	97 14
		—	pw sigs
121.4	Portobello ...	110 00	112 24
		—	sig stop
124.4	WAVERLEY ...	113 00	122 04
Net times, min ...		113	112½

Mallard in 1938 after the commemorative plaques had been fitted to mark the exploit of 3 July. (British Railways)

Brown Jack was drawing clean away from the North Eastern 4–4–0 to Grantshouse, and would have done so to a still greater extent beyond Dunbar if by that time all the initial lateness had not been wiped out.

If for nothing else the Gresley Pacifics will always be remembered for their work on the London–Edinburgh non-stops, and I have just received some notes from Baron Vuillet of two runs he was privileged to make during the past summer on the footplate of engine No 60027, *Merlin*. These runs were just what we have come to expect from the 'A4s' on this crack working, and I feel that the summary set out in Table IV is perhaps more eloquent than pages of detailed description. In his letter to me Baron Vuillet concludes with the comment 'steaming superb.'

TABLE IV
'THE ELIZABETHAN' — SUMMER, 1960
LONDON–EDINBURGH
Engine: Class 'A4' 4–6–2 No 60027, *Merlin*

Direction			Down	Up
Load, tons (E/F)	...	...	361/390	361/385
Distance, miles	...	...	392.7	392.7
Schedule time, min	...		395	395
Actual time, min	...	...	392	380
Net time, min	...	...	371	362
Net average speed, mph	...		63.5	65.1

On the down run the average speed up the long bank from Tallington to Stoke Box was 72 mph, and this leads me to an analysis of some uphill performances on which some high outputs of power were sustained. These are shown in Table V. In general these disclose maximum ef-forts considerably less, in equivalent drawbar horsepower, than the maximum efforts of all the Stanier 'Duchess' class 4–6–2s. Putting all partisan feelings aside one could hardly expect it otherwise. The Crewe engines have a considerably higher nominal tractive effort; their fireboxes are larger, and both types are excellently designed so far as valves, ports, internal passages and all details that contribute to ensure the freest possible flow of steam. One would certainly expect the 'Duchess' to have the better of it when both classes are being worked really hard for short periods.

So far as hill climbing is concerned the biggest effort I have ever seen from an 'A4' was with *Silver Link*, when with the redoubtable Ted Hailstone at the regulator she was taken up the Stevenage bank at an absolutely sustained 61 mph with a load of 505 tons behind the tender. The equivalent drawbar horsepower was a shade over 1,900, and it needed full regulator and 33 per cent cut-off to do it. In pre-war years, when 500-ton trains were the general order of the day on East Coast expresses, the normal cruising speed of the 'A4s' on level track and working in 15 per cent cut-off was about 75 mph. This involved an output of about 1,200 drawbar horsepower. On the memorable occasion when engine No 4490 (now 60011), *Empire of India*, worked the 'Flying Scotsman' on its fast 1939 schedule with a 635-ton load, the power output was between 1,200 and 1,400 equivalent drawbar horsepower for long periods.

I made my first footplate journeys on the Gresley Pacifics in 1935, and very complete

TABLE V
Class 'A4' Gresley Pacifics
Uphill Performance

Engine number	Engine name	Load, tons gross	Locality	Average speed mph	Average dhp (equivalent)
60014	*Silver Link*	400	Helpston Box–Stoke	74.0	1,655
60027	*Merlin*	390	Helpston Box–Stoke	72.0	1,530
60033	*Seagull*	425	Helpston Box–Stoke	73.1	1,700
60014	*Silver Link*	505	Stevenage	61.0*	1,900

* Sustained minimum speed on 1 in 200

details of the engine working on these and later trips were published by Mr Cecil J. Allen at various times. But as the time of their withdrawal from the East Coast express services comes nearer the moment has come for another set of full working details. There could scarcely be a more appropriate locomotive for such an occasion than *Mallard*, and I am indebted to Mr Ronald Nelson for very complete notes of a footplate journey he was recently privileged to make on the 1.30 pm express from Newcastle to Kings Cross. To give the fullest details of the whole journey would take up too much space, so I have shown, in Tables VI, VII, and VIII, representative sections in the fullest detail. On the first stage the 36 miles from Newcastle to

Darlington were covered in 44 min 3 sec start to stop, and then there followed the fine run from Darlington to York shown in Table VI.

The scheduled time of 6 min from Darlington to passing Eryholme, 5.2 miles, is a counsel of perfection indeed; yet so vigorously was the engine driven away from Darlington that the actual time was only 43 sec outside schedule. During this fine acceleration the equivalent drawbar horsepower exceeded 1,500. Signals hindered the northern part of the great racing stretch through the Plain of York, but from Thirsk onwards *Mallard* found her true stride. From the table it will be seen that the regulator remained full open at speeds of over 80 mph, and that steam-chest pressure was within 5 lb per sq in of

TABLE VI
NORTH EASTERN REGION: DARLINGTON–YORK

Load: 12 cars; 411 tons tare, 435 tons full
Engine: Class 'A4' 4–6–2 No 60022, *Mallard*

Dist			Schd	Actual		Speed	BP	SCP	Regulator	Cut-off
Miles			min	m	s	mph	psi	psi		per cent
0.0	DARLINGTON	...	0	0	00	—	205	180	$\frac{1}{2}$	45
							200	185	$\frac{5}{8}$	35
							210	205	full	25
2.6	Croft Spa	... ...	—	4	13	$59\frac{1}{2}$	215	210	,,	,,
5.2	*Eryholme Jc*	... ...	6	6	43	$64\frac{3}{4}$	210	205	,,	18
6.9	Cowton	... ...	—	8	17	$70\frac{3}{4}$	225	220	,,	15
						79	230	0	shut	25
10.4	Danby Wiske	... ...	—	11	10	—	235	0	,,	,,
					sigs	55*	210	165	$\frac{1}{2}$	,,
							215	210	full	15
14.1	NORTHALLERTON		14	14	51	$69\frac{1}{4}$	230	225	,,	,,
						$72\frac{3}{4}$	240	0	shut	25
					sigs	40*	235	200	$\frac{1}{2}$	30
17.5	Otterington	... ...	—	18	19	$48\frac{1}{2}$	220	215	full	25
						63	210	205	,,	15
21.9	THIRSK	... ...	21	22	20	$71\frac{1}{4}$	230	225	,,	15
26.1	Sessay	... ...	—	25	41	78	240	235	,,	,,
28.0	Pilmoor	... ...	—	27	07	$81\frac{1}{2}$	230	225	,,	12
30.7	Raskelf	... ...	—	29	03	84	240	235	,,	10
32.9	Alne	... ...	30	30	36	$84\frac{1}{4}$	235	230	,,	,,
34.4	Tollerton	... ...	—	31	38	$83\frac{3}{4}$	230	225	,,	,,
						$82\frac{1}{4}$	220	0	shut	25
38.6	Beningbrough	...	—	34	51	—	215	0	,,	,,
					sigs	27*	205	180	$\frac{3}{4}$	30
						$61\frac{1}{2}$	185	0	shut	25
42.5	*Skelton Jc*	... ...	38	40	01	—	190	0	,,	,,
44.1	YORK	... ...	42	43	33	—	—	—	—	—

* Speed restriction

TABLE VII
EASTERN REGION: YORK–PETERBOROUGH

Load: 12 cars; 411 tons tare, 435 tons full
Engine: Class 'A4' 4–6–2 No 60022, *Mallard*

Dist			Schd	Actual		Speed	BP	SCP	Regulator	Cut-off
Miles			min	m	s	mph	psi	psi		per cent
0.0	YORK ...	...	0	0	00	—	—	—	—	—
				sigs		—	—	—	—	—
13.8	SELBY ...	...	16	17	12	—	—	—	—	—
32.2	DONCASTER	...	39	34	21	—	—	—	—	—
				pws		—	—	—	—	—
49.6	RETFORD	...	56	55	48	—	—	—	—	—
68.1	NEWARK	...	75	73	28	$53\frac{3}{4}$	225	170	$\frac{1}{2}$	20
							225	220	full	15
71.3	*Balderton*	...	—	76	58	61	230	225	,,	,,
72.8	Claypole	...	—	78	26	$62\frac{1}{4}$	230	225	,,	,,
74.7	*Milepost 113½*	...	—	80	14	$60\frac{1}{2}$	225	220	,,	,,
						65	230	225	,,	,,
76.7	Hougham	...	—	82	06	$64\frac{1}{4}$	235	230	,,	,,
78.5	*Barkston South Jc*		87	83	49	63	225	220	,,	,,
79.7	*Milepost 108½*	...	—	85	01	$59\frac{1}{4}$	235	230	,,	,,
82.0	*Barrowby Road*	...	—	87	23	$63\frac{1}{2}$	235	230	,,	,,
82.7	GRANTHAM	...	91	88	02	$64\frac{3}{4}$	225	220	,,	,,
86.2	Great Ponton	...	—	91	21	59	230	225	,,	,,
86.9	*High Dyke*	...	—	92	09	$56\frac{3}{4}$	225	220	,,	,,
88.1	*Stoke*	...	97	93	25	55	220	215	,,	$7\frac{1}{2}$
91.1	Corby Glen	...	—	96	07	$77\frac{3}{4}$	230	225	,,	,,
96.0	Little Bytham	...	—	99	40	$85\frac{1}{2}$	220	140	$\frac{3}{8}$	,,
						$87\frac{1}{4}$	215	200	$\frac{3}{4}$	,,
99.6	Essendine	...	106	102	11	85	210	195	,,	,,
103.4	Tallington	...	—	104	52	$80\frac{3}{4}$	200	185	,,	,,
						$77\frac{1}{2}$	210	0	shut	25
106.3	*Helpston*	...	—	107	15	—	205	0	,,	,,
108.7	*Werrington Jc*		116	109	34	47*	190	170	$\frac{3}{4}$	20
110.4	*New England North*		—	111	36	53	200	0	shut	25
111.8	PETERBOROUGH		122	114	41	—	—	—	—	—

* Speed restriction

boiler pressure. As the speed mounted so the cut-off was reduced, to a minimum of 10 per cent at 84 mph. Net time from Darlington to York was 38¾ min, an average speed of 68.4 mph start to stop.

From York the good work continued, and I have included full details of the section south of Newark. Checks up to this point had cost 6¾ min in running, so that already the net time was well inside even time. The climb from Newark to Stoke Box was an admirable example of what the 'A4' locomotives can do on what can be considered their standard method of work-

ing—full regulator and 15 per cent cut-off. The average speed over this 20 miles of ascent was exactly 60 mph, and working against an average gradient of 1 in 420 the equivalent drawbar horsepower would be approximately 1,200. Acceleration was extremely rapid once over the summit, while the same working continued, and speed rose from 55 to 77¾ mph in three miles. Then the cut-off was shortened to as little as 7½ per cent and the engine ran very freely and sweetly up to a maximum of 87 mph. Here the regulator was eased back somewhat from the full open position. This was an interesting example

TABLE VIII
EASTERN REGION: PETERBOROUGH–KINGS CROSS

Load: 12 cars; 411 tons tare, 435 tons full
Engine: Class 'A4' 4–6–2 No 60022, *Mallard*

Dist		Schd	Actual		Speed	BP	SCP	Regulator	Cut-off
Miles		min	m	s	mph	psi	psi		per cent
0.0	PETERBOROUGH ...	0	0	00	—	—	—	—	—
			pws		—	—	—	—	—
17.5	HUNTINGDON ...	20	21	40	70½	220	160	⅜	15
20.4	Offord ...	—	24	04	73¼	245	240	full	17
22.6	*Paxton*	—	25	49	75	240	235	''	''
24.7	St Neots ...	—	27	28	72¾	230	225	''	12
28.9	Tempsford ...	—	30	41	82½	240	235	''	''
32.3	Sandy ...	32	33	12	78¼	250	245	''	''
35.3	Biggleswade ...	—	35	29	79	245	240	''	14
37.8	*Langford Bridge*	—	37	29	72½	230	225	''	''
39.4	Arlesey ...	—	38	48	76¼	240	235	''	''
40.7	Three Counties ...	—	39	50	78	245	240	''	16
43.1	*Cadwell* ...	—	41	46	71¾	240	235	''	''
44.5	HITCHIN ...	46	42	59	68½	250	245	''	''
47.8	Stevenage ...	—	46	07	60¾	240	235	''	''
					64	250	0	shut	25
					60*	235	200	⅝	15
49.7	*Langley Jc* ...	—	47	56	63	230	225	full	12
51.4	Knebworth ...	55	49	32	59¾	245	240	''	''
52.9	*Woolmer Green* ...	—	51	00	62½	235	200	½	''
					68	220	0	shut	25
54.4	Welwyn North ...	—	52	22	67	215	200	¾	13
56.1	Welwyn Garden City	—	53	55	63¼	210	205	full	''
					74½	220	0	shut	25
			sigs		28*	205	150	⅜	30
58.7	HATFIELD ...	64	57	12	34	200	195	full	25
			sigs		—	—	—	—	—
			pws		—	—	—	—	—
73.9	Finsbury Park ...	81	76	52	—	—	—	—	—
			sigs		—	—	—	—	—
76.4	KINGS CROSS ...	86	83	07	—	—	—	—	—

* Speed restriction

of the supreme ease with which a well-designed steam locomotive will attain spectacularly high rates of speed.

On restarting from Peterborough the engine primed badly, as it had done to a lesser degree from Newcastle, and as far south as Abbots Ripton boiler pressures were under 200 lb per sq in. Then, from Huntingdon *Mallard* got going again, and details of the working are shown in full in Table VIII. Time was being gained in order to offset the effect of permanent way checks to come at Potters Bar and New Southgate, and eventually the run ended 3 min early after a late start of 3 min and checks aggregating 21½ min *en route*. In sending the run to me Mr Nelson commented: 'I do not believe that there can be many engines—even "A4s"—that can put up so fine a performance with so little effort.' It only remains for me to add that the crew responsible were Driver R. Turner and Fireman T. Kirkby of Kings Cross, with Headquarters Locomotive Inspector G. A. Harland also riding on the footplate.

Before leaving the subject of the 'A4s' and their high-speed capacity I think it can now be revealed, in some detail, how the highest speed I

The now preserved 'A4' No 60009 Union of South Africa *climbing to Kinghorn, Fife, with a special in 1973.* (W.B. Greenfield)

have personally recorded on the footplate was actually achieved—a speed of 103½ mph by the 'A4' *Woodcock* on a southbound run. It took place several years ago, on the 'Tees-Tyne Pullman' express, when the underline bridge works at Potters Bar were at their worst, so far as delays to traffic were concerned, and when we were specially stopped at York. There was plenty of lost time to be made up; but in addition the driver and fireman were both anxious to show off what the engine could do. They succeeded so well that I was asked not to publish the details—at any rate for some little time to come. Even now I am confining my notes to the technical rather than to the personal details of the occasion.

We had not travelled far before I realised that *Woodcock* was running up to the finest 'A4' standards. With the usual load of eight Pullmans, weighing about 335 tons full, we ran from Darlington to York in 39 min 35 sec start to stop, including a very slow, signal-delayed approach to York. Speed had been extraordinarily even south of Otterington, so that although we averaged 87 mph for 21 miles the maximum did not exceed 89 mph. After the York stop things continued normally, with careful observation of the various speed restrictions, and then at Newark the build-up began for the effort that was to be made down the Stoke bank. We passed Newark at 64½ mph working in 15 per cent cut-off, and fast running was made over the approach grades, touching a maximum of 72 mph at Claypole, and still running at 67 mph approaching Barkston South Junction.

Between Newark and Barkston firing was deliberately heavy, to build up a thick body of fire to sustain the high rate of steaming that would be needed south of Stoke summit. With the fire in first-class shape and a full boiler, cut-off was increased to 20 per cent on passing Barkston; Pearscliffe Tunnel was cleared at 66 mph, and with this working continued there was a very rapid acceleration to 75 mph through Grantham. The regulator was not quite full open, and the steam-chest pressures were generally about 20 lb per sq in below boiler pressure. Stoke summit was cleared at 65½ mph, and the hard working was continued for a mile beyond. By this time speed had risen to 75 mph, and the cut-off was shortened to 15 per cent. What followed can best be described by giving a complete tabulation of the milepost readings, together with the relevant average speeds:

Milepost	Time from Post 100		Average Speed
	m	s	mph
99	0	51	70.6
98	1	36½	79.2
97	2	18	86.8
96	2	58½	88.9
95	3	37½	92.3
94	4	15½	94.8
93	4	52½	97.5
92	5	28½	100.0
91	6	03½	102.7
90	6	40	98.7
89	7	17½	96.0

We were doing 100 mph as early in the descent as Little Bytham, and the rate of acceleration was steady and swift. The engine was riding with the utmost steadiness, and the only minor and incidental discomfort was an absolute whirlwind of coal dust on the footplate. If allowed to continue, I am of the opinion that the speed would have reached about 110 mph below Essendine; but this was a service train and not a speed trial, and having reached the hundred so easily and so early in the descent the engine was severely eased at the 91st milepost, dropping the steam-chest pressure from 215 to 140 lb per sq in. Speed began to fall at once. The slight rise

past Essendine brought us down to 87 and we continued at 86 to 88 mph on to Tallington. The maximum speed near the 91st milepost was 103½ mph.

One can say that this major effort lasted for 15 min, from passing Barkston to Milepost 91, and during that time the steaming was perfect. When the engine was eased down, boiler pressure was 235 lb per sq in and the water level was barely an inch from the top of the glass. At a speed of 75 mph, working in 15 per cent, the indicated horsepower of the 'A4' engines is about 2,000; at 100 mph it would be nearly 2,800. It must not be forgotten that the effort would have been considerably greater during the spell from Barkston when the cut-off was 20 per cent, so that quite apart from the indescribable thrill of the occasion this was indeed a performance to remember.

The displacing of the Gresley Pacifics from the East Coast Route has already proceeded someway, but locomotive enthusiasts will be most interested in one new duty found for at least some of the 'A3s,' namely on the double-home workings between Leeds and Glasgow St Enoch. The Leeds-Carlisle section of this route is certainly unique in that its first-line motive power has at various times been of Midland, London & North Western, and now of Great Northern design. More than this, the period between the innings of the 'Claughtons' and that of the 'A3s' is bridged by locomotives that, in their most important feature—the boiler—were derived directly from Great Western practice. I have already enjoyed an interesting trip on the footplate of 'A3' 4-6-2 No 60077, *The White Knight*, working the down 'Thames-Clyde Express,' with a heavy train of 420 tons behind the tender, and I am hoping to include this in a retrospect of running over this famous route, incorporating not only service journeys, but some dynamometer test trips with such strangers as the Southern 'Merchant Navy' 4-6-2 and the LMR 4-6-2 No 46225, *Duchess of Gloucester*.

Great Western — 'Castle' retrospect, Paddington–Bath

By the end of the Second World War, I was living in Bath and Westinghouse headquarters were re-established in London, affording me ample opportunities of clocking Western Region expresses. Until the coming of the diesels, the motive power was almost exclusively Great Western. From 1951 some sporadic attempts were made to introduce the British Railways Standard types, but most of the enginemen hated the 'Britannia' Pacifics, and none of them was stationed at Bristol Bath Road shed. For most of the Bristol-London workings, the 'Castles' were left in almost complete possession.

IN my article in the December, 1959, issue of *The Railway Magazine* I began with these words: 'By next autumn it seems that the whole pattern of train service between Paddington and Bristol will be in process of change.' It is indeed! What with the Pullmans, and with many trains worked by the new diesel-hydraulic locomotives, the traditional Great Western 'look' that survived so long after nationalisation is at last disappearing, and so far as the Bristol services are concerned the time has come to pay something of a farewell tribute to one of the most famous engine classes of all time, the 'Castles.' I do so however in no spirit of unreasoning adulation. The 'Castles' in their prime were good engines—very good engines!—but no better than some of their contemporaries of the same wheel arrangement.

They have had a wonderfully long innings. They fitted in ideally with the express train policy of the Great Western Railway, which was to run a frequent service of fast, moderately-loaded trains, and they became the standard express passenger type for the whole system, with a route availability that excluded them only from the old Cambrian line. If necessary they could deputise for the 'Kings' on the heaviest West of England and Birmingham services. The sterling quality of their performance had an influence that extended far beyond the confines of the Great Western Railway. Readers of these articles need no reminder of the effects of the locomotive interchange trial of 1925 with the LNER, or of that of 1926 with the LMSR: but before either of those events R. E. L. Maunsell of the Southern had sent his assistant James Clayton to ride on a 'Castle,' to Plymouth on the 'Cornish Riviera Express,' and it was this experience that helped to settle the general size and capacity of the 'Lord Nelson' class 4–6–0.

And now the pioneer engine of the class, No 4073, *Caerphilly Castle*, is to be a museum piece. It is a matter for gratification that an engine so widely known in her day should be spared from the scrap heap, and should be placed in the Science Museum at South Kensington. In her later days she was stationed at Bristol, and I shall always be glad that in the course of my footplate work I was twice privileged to ride on her. One fine example of her running is included in the present article wherein I have endeavoured to summarise some of the best work of the 'Castle' class in hauling the ordinary Bristol expresses, as distinct from the high-speed 'Bristolian.' The runs detailed in Tables I and II represent the cream of my collection, amassed in twelve years of regular travelling between Bath and Paddington.

Naturally I have picked some of the best examples I can find in my note books. The records I have are very many, seeing that I have made between forty and fifty journeys every year. For uniformity of presentation I have confined the present comments to the non-stop trains in each direction, but while one could hardly expect the standard of running shown in these tables to be sustained week in, week out, all the year round it is rare that time has been booked against any engine, until quite recently. Now, alas, the quality of steam locomotive performance between Paddington and Bristol seems very much on the decline. Most of the runs tabulated were made on the 9 am up and the 5 pm down, both trains that have disappeared since the introduction of the diesel Pullmans.

At one time both these trains were allowed 109 min non-stop for the 106.9 miles between Bath and Paddington. The down journey was the harder of the two, with the long gradual rise to Swindon giving little respite, and made

An up Two-hour Bristol express topping the summit of Filton bank, with engine No 4033 Queen Victoria (G.H. Soole)

against the prevailing wind. It is true that in the reverse direction there are the Box Tunnel and Dauntsey banks to be climbed; but if the steaming is not quite up to standard it is much easier to regain a little time on the fast stretches east of Swindon, especially if there is a following wind, than to hold one's own in adverse conditions over the same stretch on the down line. The schedule of the 5 pm, which was fixed at 109 min at the time of the 1954 accelerations, has since been eased slightly to a working time of 110½ min. Curiously enough the two trains had a different loading classification in the working timetable. The 9 am up was 'four star,' on which the limit of load for a 'Castle' was laid

down as 300 tons, and the 5 pm down was 'three star,' with a 350-ton limit. It will be seen that these limits were exceeded on every run of the 9 am up and the 5 pm down expresses between Bristol and Paddington.

At the time of the 1954 accelerations, the 9 am express from Bristol to Paddington was a fairly heavy train, with a minimum formation of eleven coaches. The putting on of an additional London express at 8.30 am from Temple Meads enabled the 9 am to be cut to a minimum formation of eight coaches and since that time, of course, much of the interest of the locomotive work has vanished. Most of the runs in Table I were made before this alteration. The first run of

TABLE I
WESTERN REGION: BATH— PADDINGTON

Run No		1	2	3	4	5	6	7	8
Engine No		4056*	7019	4073	5096	5063	5064	5077	5077
Engine Name		Princess Margaret	Fowey Castle	Caerphilly Castle	Bridg-water Castle	Earl Baldwin	Bishops Castle	Fairey Battle	Fairey Battle
Load, tons (E/F)		310/325	341/365	349/375	376/405	379/410	411/440	409/440	445/475
Dist		Actual	Actual	Actual	Actual	Actual	Actual	Actual	Actual
Miles		m s	m s	m s	m s	m s	m s	m s	m s
0.0	BATH	—	0 00	0 00	0 00	0 00	0 00	0 00	0 00
2.3	Bathampton	—	4 17	4 20	4 19	4 41	4 44	4 36	5 05
5.0	Box	—	7 23	7 24	7 12	7 54	8 04	7 56	8 34
8.6	Corsham	—	12 25	11 44	11 24	12 49	13 11	13 03	13 53
				pws			pws		
12.9	CHIPPENHAM	0 00	17 00	16 29	15 27	19 28	18 10	17 42	18 46
15.9	Milepost 91	4 58	19 46	19 48	18 33	pws	21 26	20 20	21 35
					19 00				
		—	—	—		—	—	—	—
19.2	Dauntsey	8 19	22 54	22 59	24 11	27 02	24 39	23 09	24 37
				pws					
24.0	Wootton Bassett	13 27	28 15	28 46	29 26	32 35	29 52	28 10	29 44
		sigs					pws		
29.6	SWINDON	20 16	33 42	34 44	34 49	38 17	38 48	33 50	35 27
35.4	Shrivenham	26 05	38 35	39 52	39 52	43 27	44 45	39 04	40 44
								pws	
40.4	Uffington	30 28	42 28	44 11	44 19	47 38	49 02	47 05	45 05
46.5	Wantage Road	35 30	47 08	49 17	49 23	52 29	53 59	52 26	50 11
		sigs	pws						
53.8	DIDCOT	42 18	56 27	55 21	55 14	58 05	59 44	58 12	56 20
				pws					
58.4	Cholsey	47 03	60 31	61 13	59 02	61 38	63 26	61 53	60 17
		pws	pws						
65.4	Pangbourne	54 53	68 46	67 24	65 00	67 09	69 19	67 51	66 36
							sigs		

Engine Name		Princess Margaret	Fowey Castle	Caerphilly Castle	Bridg-water Castle	Earl Baldwin	Bishops Castle	Fairey Battle	Fairey Battle
Dist		Actual	Actual	Actual	Actual	Actual	Actual	Actual	Actual
70.9	READING ...	62 18	74 31	72 07	69 40	71 36	74 49	72 29	71 39 sigs
75.9	Twyford	66 42	79 12	76 38	74 04	75 44	79 47	76 45	79 29
82.7	Maidenhead ...	72 11	85 19	82 14	79 39	81 14	85 38	82 10	86 31 sigs
88.4	SLOUGH	76 48	89 56	87 04	84 24	85 53	90 26	86 43	93 32 sigs
93.7	West Drayton ...	81 10	94 09	91 37 sigs	88 58	90 25	94 53	91 03	100 36
97.8	Southall	84 39	97 32	97 24	92 44	94 00	98 30	94 40	104 58 sigs
103.6	Old Oak West Jc	89 59 pws	102 27 pws	103 27	97 51 sigs	99 19 sigs	103 30 sigs	99 56	112 25 sigs
106.9	PADDINGTON	96 38	109 07	108 50	105 23	105 31	112 15	104 52	124 00
Speeds (mph) at:-									
Box	... ...	—	55	57	61	55	53	51	50½
Corsham	... ...	—	33	43	44	35	33	33	32
Post 91	... ...	56/61½	66	62	70½	64	61½	70	65
Incline Box	... ...	51½	48	47½	49	47	50	53	51½
Average speeds (mph), Shrivenham-Southall		71.6†	72.6†	71.3†	70.7	74.0	72.3†	72.7†	67.8†
Max speeds (mph)	...	76	79	73½	75	78½	76½	76	72
Net time (min)	... ...	88½*	100	101½	100	100	102	101	106

*From Chippenham; 8.30 am ex-Bristol; 'Star' class locomotive   †Net average speed

all, however, was made on the new 8.30 am with the last engine of Churchward's 'Star' class to remain in traffic. This run was made in the autumn of 1955 when the *Princess Margaret* was newly out of the shops from what was to prove her last general overhaul. I was privileged to ride on the footplate, and a memorable last experience of the 'Stars' it was. The *Princess Margaret* had always been a favourite among Bristol enginemen, and I shall always remember an occasion, several years previous to the run in Table I, when a top link driver remarked: 'She's the best "Castle" we've got!'

Before commenting on the actual runs, I should like to pay a special tribute to the enginemen. The 'mileage men,' as they were known at Bath Road shed, worked, and still do work, to every point of the compass: to Newton Abbot, to Weymouth, to Salisbury, to Paddington, to Shrewsbury, and into South Wales,

with so varied a range of activities that each turn came round only once in every 26 weeks. In the course of my regular travelling, I came to know many of these splendid fellows, and to ride with a number of them on the footplate, and the runs detailed in Tables I and II are a fine tribute to them, collectively. At the same time, as most of these runs were made in the ordinary course of business travelling, it was rare that the men themselves knew what a detailed record was being taken of their work on any particular occasion.

On the first run I have not shown the details of the Bath-Chippenham stage in the table. We were right on the heels of the preceding stopping train, and were stopped by signal at Box. There could not have been a more awkward place for a signal stop, with the climb at 1 in 100 through the wet atmosphere of Box Tunnel immediately following; but we had a first-class driver in Bert

Giles, and he got No 4056 cleanly away, and climbed the 2½ miles to Milepost 99 in 5¾ min from the dead start, attaining 30 mph on the gradient. Through the tunnel, cut-off was 27 per cent, with the regulator about three-quarters open. The restart from Chippenham was very brisk, with speed up to 56 mph at the crossing of the River Avon, three miles out. Acceleration continued up the 1 in 660 rise to Dauntsey, and there, an increase in cut-off from 22 to 24 per cent took us sailing up Dauntsey Bank with speed falling only from 61½ to 51½ mph in 1½ miles of 1 in 100. Then came a couple of signal checks, approaching and passing through Swindon.

We had a pleasant spin down the Vale of the White Horse, working in 20 per cent, with only the first valve of the regulator. Speed rose to a

One of the most famous of the 'Castles', No 5069 Isambard Kingdom Brunel, *at Bristol having worked down on an express from Paddington.* (M.W. Earley)

steady 75 mph from Wantage Road onwards until we were checked again by signal at Didcot. There was scarcely time to recover from this before there came the last of the checks—the long and severe relaying slack through Pangbourne. Then came a grand piece of high-speed running, wherein the 23.6 miles from Twyford to Hanwell were covered at an average speed of 73 mph. The maximum was 76 mph approaching Maidenhead, and for some ten miles of level track the speed was held at 75 mph with a cut-off of 15 per cent and the main valve of the regulator just cracked. This train used to be allowed 101 min for the 94 miles up from Chippenham, and in recovery from the various checks the driver had 12½ min to his credit. The coal consumption was approximately 30 lb per mile—a thoroughly typical example of 'Star' performance at its best.

On the 9.19 am (from Bath) express, run after run that I have recorded gave net times of 100 min or very little over, and the next three

journeys tabulated could be regarded as typical examples of the variation in work one could note with the various drivers. With *Fowey Castle*, the climb through Box Tunnel was taken easily, and things did not begin really to liven up until after Swindon. Then there were fine spells of running before and after the two permanent way checks, and Paddington was reached on time. The next run features *Caerphilly Castle* herself, and this time I was on the footplate with Driver W. H. Brown and Fireman A. Hares. For once the wind was contrary to the prevailing direction, and we were driving into a fierce and icy east wind that developed into a full-scale blizzard by the time we had passed Didcot. Such was the cold that on arrival at Paddington the head lamps were frozen to the irons, and it needed a coal pick to get them free. The famous engine was in grand form, and although the adverse weather conditions made the speed east of Swindon a little slower than usual on this train we clocked into Paddington dead on time. On this trip the start had been much more vigorous and

The 5.5 pm Paddington–Plymouth express near Thingley Junction, Chippenham, hauled by 4-6-0 No 5081 Lockheed Hudson. (K.H. Leech)

the minimum speed climbing through Box Tunnel was 43 mph.

On Run No 4, with *Bridgwater Castle* and Driver Johns, the conditions could hardly have been more contrasting, with a calm and beautifully-fine summer's day. The start was very fast, but then we were flagged down at a permanent way restriction at the Avon bridge and stopped momentarily. The restart was brilliant, with speed worked up to 57½ mph in 3¼ miles of 1 in 660 rising gradient, and Dauntsey Bank cleared at 49 mph. Then we had a brisk and undelayed run till approaching Westbourne Park, where we were stopped a second time. The 89.3 miles between the two stops had however been covered in 80 min 57 sec start to stop, an average speed of 66.3 mph, and we reached Paddington 3½ min early, with two dead stands on the way!

The fastest sustained speed east of Swindon that I have recorded on this train took place on a journey that is not tabulated. Two bad checks had made us some 7 min late through Swindon, and then the driver of No 5057, *Earl Waldegrave*, really opened out. From Uffington to South Stoke signals a distance of 20 miles was covered at an average of 78.8 mph, with a sustained maximum of 82 past Didcot. But a shocking series of signal checks followed, and eventually we reached Paddington 10 min late. On the form displayed from Uffington the lateness at Swindon could very easily have been recovered. I should add this engine, and all others featuring in Tables I and II, had the original single blastpipe and chimney at the time my runs were made. They all had the so-called 'improved draughting,' with the Churchward jumper cap on the blastpipe removed, and a slightly reduced blastpipe orifice.

At the time of the 1954 accelerations, a group of 'Castles' in specially good condition was transferred to Bristol Bath Road shed. No 5057, just mentioned, was one of these, and there were also Nos 5027, 5063, 5077 and 5085. At that time, Bristol did not provide the engine for the up 'Bristolian,' as at first both down and up trains were worked by a 'King' from Old Oak Common shed. The 9 am up from Temple Meads usually got the best engine on the strength at Bath Road shed, particularly in view of the return working on the very fast 1.15 pm down, second only to the 'Bristolian' itself in booked speed. In actual fact, however, there was little to choose between the new arrivals at Bath Road shed, while the best of the existing stud at that time, notably Nos 5096 and 7034, were engines one could scarcely fault on any score. In the fifth column of Table I, No 5063, *Earl Baldwin*, driven by Woolford, made another excellent run, on which we enjoyed the longest and fastest spell of undisturbed fast running in the whole table.

On the next two runs the load had risen to twelve coaches, and the gross load to 440 tons in each case. Yet on the seventh run we made the fastest overall time of the whole series. Apart from the incidence of the checks these two runs were very similar. I have not a note of the name of the driver of *Bishops Castle*, but *Fairey Battle*, on the seventh run, was driven by Iles, with whom I once rode up from Newton Abbot on the *Princess Margaret*. The run of *Bishops Castle* was made on a Saturday morning, when the train is not worked by the regular mileage men but by the 'spare link'; but as the log shows, there was little to choose between this work and that of the regulars. Despite the checks earlier in the run, and the 440-ton load, *Bishops Castle* had time for an arrival less than a minute late, but we were stopped dead at Portobello Junction because of another train crossing to the relief line at Subway Junction.

On the last run *Fairey Battle* was again the engine, with a load of 145 tons over the official limit; yet time would have been kept quite easily but for the signal checks that dogged our path east of Reading. Things were taken steadily in the early stages with this big load, but at Dauntsey the engine was opened out in such a style as to clear the 1 in 100 bank at a minimum speed of 51½ mph, with 475 tons behind the tender. East of Swindon we ran at a beautifully even speed, and by Reading we were getting close to 'level time.' Ahead of us however the line was crowded. The 'Capitals United Express' was running in duplicate, and eventually the reaction spread back to such an extent that we were 15 min late into Paddington. Yet as this table shows, 'Castle' class locomotives in good condition had a margin in reserve of 8 to 9 min on this fast schedule, with loads up to 400 tons tare.

On the down road Table II commences with two runs on the 1.15 pm. In the accelerations of 1954, the schedule of this train was cut from 106 min to 97 min for the 106.9 miles from Paddington to Bath, and the load was reduced to a basic formation of seven coaches. The first run in the table is only one of many similar trips I have enjoyed on this train, but I have chosen it because of the engine concerned. It is 37 years now since *Caerphilly Castle* was completed at Swindon, and I can remember how impatiently we enthusiasts waited for news of her perfor-

TABLE II
WESTERN REGION: PADDINGTON–BATH

Run No		1	2	3	4	5	6	7	8
Engine No		4079	7034	5093	5027	7015	7015	7014	4075
Engine Name		Pendennis Castle	Ince Castle	Upton Castle	Farleigh Castle	Carn Brea Castle	Carn Brea Castle	Caerhays Castle	Cardiff Castle
Load, tons (E/F)		250/265	335/350	379/400	379/410	412/435	444/475	443/475	444/485
Dist		Actual	Actual	Actual	Actual	Actual	Actual	Actual	Actual
Miles		m s	m s	m s	m s	m s	m s	m s	m s
0.0	PADDINGTON	0 00	0 00	0 00	0 00	0 00	0 00	0 00	0 00
5.7	Ealing Broadway	8 27	8 56	9 03	9 20	9 07	10 20	10 06	9 21
9.1	Southall ...	11 41	12 24	12 37	13 03	12 37	14 35	14 07	13 02
			pws			sigs			
13.2	West Drayton	15 20	17 51	16 37	17 17	17 51	19 22	18 35	17 04
				sigs					
18.5	SLOUGH	19 40	24 26	24 00	22 03	23 19	24 37	23 35	22 05
					sigs				
24.2	Maidenhead	24 19	29 52	29 45	27 32	28 32	30 18	28 55	27 19
								pws	
31.0	Twyford ...	29 49	35 56	35 51	34 25	34 39	37 07	35 36	33 40
				pws					
36.0	READING ...	33 48	40 18	44 10	38 57	39 10	41 58	41 03	38 18
					sigs	pws			
41.5	Pangbourne	38 18	45 08	51 03	44 53	47 07	47 06	46 26	43 23
48.5	Cholsey ...	44 16	51 23	57 51	51 32	55 55	53 33	53 02	49 50
					sigs				sigs
53.1	DIDCOT ...	48 13	55 34	62 17	56 14	60 15	57 52	57 32	55 58
					sig stop				
60.4	Wantage Road	54 28	62 17	69 10	70 30	66 59	65 11	65 02	64 26
66.5	Uffington	59 44	68 03	74 57	76 35	72 44	71 34	71 22	70 17
			pws						
71.5	Shrivenham ...	64 04	74 12	79 29	81 29	77 29	76 44	76 33	75 00
								pws	
77.3	SWINDON...	69 05	82 08	84 44	86 55	83 02	82 38	82 53	80 20
82.9	Wootton Bassett	73 42	87 00	89 32	91 56	88 05	88 04	88 20	85 18
87.7	Dauntsey ...	77 23	90 35	93 18	95 44	91 56	92 04	92 20	89 13
94.0	CHIPPENHAM	82 05	94 56	98 06	100 29	96 56	96 59	97 22	94 15
98.3	Corsham ...	85 48	98 23	101 51	104 11	100 58	100 58	101 53	97 58
101.9	Box ...	88 48	101 24	104 55	107 11	104 21	104 10	105 14	100 52
104.6	Bathampton	91 04	104 10	107 14	109 27	106 50	106 37	107 32	103 05
						sigs	sigs		sigs
106.9	BATH ...	94 15	106 56	110 00	112 11	110 15	110 20	110 08	108 20
Max speed to Reading (mph)		77	70½	68	67½	70	64½	65	67
Average speed, Slough–Swindon (mph) ..		71.4	65.7*	66.2*	64.0*	64.6*	60.7	60.8*	64.3*
Max speed at Dauntsey (mph)		84	90	85	85	83	79	80	82
Net time (min) ...		94½	99	100	102½	103½	109¼	108	102
Net average speed (mph)... ...		68.1	65.0	64.2	62.6	61.9	58.7	59.3	62.8

*Net average speed, Slough to Swindon

mance in these articles. We had to wait for over a year, but then, in December, 1924, the 'Castles' fairly hit the headlines. Mr Cecil J. Allen had been down to Plymouth on the footplate of the engine working the 'Cornish Riviera Express,' and *Pendennis Castle* was the engine on which he rode. I cannot think of any other locomotive type that made its *debut* in these columns in more brilliant style.

In much more recent times, *Pendennis Castle* was stationed in Gloucester, and was kept in the immaculate condition traditional of that shed; and still more recently she came to Bristol. Her run on the 1.15 pm was entirely unchecked, and with fast, even running throughout she finished 2¾ min early. This is not by any means the fastest run I have had on the train; that honour belongs to *Caerphilly Castle*, with a net time of 91½ min. Truly the veterans were distinguishing themselves in the years 1955–1957, but

on this latter run we were victims of a shocking blunder in traffic regulation. A moderate permanent way check, and a signal check at Didcot, had cost us 4½ min between them, but the intermediate work had been magnificent, and with a sustained 75 mph up the gradual rise to Shrivenham we were approaching Swindon dead on time. We had indeed covered the 73¾ miles to Marston East box in 68 min from the start, despite the two checks. Then, just in front of us, some fool allowed a slow freight out of the Swindon yards, and sent it dawdling right through to the Hay Lane loop! As a result this crack Bristol express lost *fourteen minutes*, from this one cause alone, and eventually took 110½ min to reach Bath.

The second run in Table II was made just before the accelerations of 1954, again on the 1.15 pm when the schedule time was 106 min to Bath. As far as Swindon the work was brisk,

The up 'Bristolian' passing Hullavington, hauled by 4-6-0 No 7018 Drysllwyn Castle *fitted with a double chimney.* (K.H. Leech)

without any special distinction, and speed fell to 63½ mph on the rise to Shrivenham. After the second permanent way check the driver fairly went for it, reaching 90 mph at the foot of Dauntsey Bank, and the speed was held at 88 mph right to the Avon bridge. An absolutely punctual arrival was within our grasp at Corsham, but the engine was much eased on entering Box Tunnel, and the finish was comparatively slow. A short time afterwards I had another run behind *Ince Castle* that included some even faster running; but the signal checks were crippling, and a maximum of 92 mph at Dauntsey was cut short by a check at Chippenham arising from a purely local movement.

The third run in the table, with *Upton Castle*, was on the 5 pm, and was the last stage in a long journey that began at Berne. For once the running on the SNCF had been uninteresting, and the Southern put up a poor show with the boat train from Folkestone to Victoria. The honours were definitely with the Western Region on this trip. It was indeed one of the best runs I have ever had on the 5 pm. The start out of Paddington was vigorous, and speed had reached 68 mph no further out than West Drayton. Then came bad signal checks at Iver, and at Reading, preceding a permanent way check in the latter case. The recovery from this second check might have been more vigorous had we not been right on the tail of the 4.55 pm Cheltenham express, and as far as Wantage Road speed ranged round 62 to 63 mph. Then the driver evidently judged that the preceding train was clear, for we gradually accelerated uphill to 67 mph at Shrivenham, and after Swindon we went like the wind to arrive in Bath just inside the working time and 2 min early by the public timetable.

At the outset there was no particular need for

No 7018 Drysllwyn Castle *on a dynamometer car test run with the down 'Torbay Express' approaching Reading.* (H.J. Ashman)

haste on the fourth run, this time with *Farleigh Castle*, and a very dependable driver, Tanton by name. There were slight signal checks at Maidenhead, and again at Tilehurst, both arising from our proximity to the 4.55 pm ahead. But then, after a long preliminary slowing, we were stopped at Foxhall Junction, and held for 2 min to be warned to go carefully through the next section. There had been a door open on the 4.55 pm. Because of this, it was Wantage Road before we had regained 60 mph, and with the other train still not far ahead, *Farleigh Castle* was not pressed up the remainder of the rise to Shrivenham. We passed Swindon at 65 mph, running 5 min late, and then, with no train ahead of him, Driver Tanton made a real dash for Bath. We touched 85 mph at Dauntsey, fell to nothing less than 69 at Corsham, and with a fast finish reached Bath at the public time of 6.52 pm.

The fifth run was another example of the fine work of Driver Giles. For several months before this run, *Carn Brea Castle* had been the regular engine for the up 'Bristolian,' and she had just been demoted to a general service unit. She was still in good nick, and with a train one coach above normal gave us some splendid running. Between the West Drayton and the Pangbourne checks, speed rose to 70 mph, and the recovery after the latter, which had been to 15 mph, showed no fear of catching up the 4.55 pm. Through Swindon we were only a minute late, and the driver was able to ease right up after Chippenham, and still be in Bath on time. The net time of 103½ min was particularly good with a gross load of 435 tons.

On the sixth and seventh runs the load was increased to thirteen coaches, and with these heavy trains of 475 tons gross good time was made by *Carn Brea Castle* and *Caerhays Castle*, but the last run of all was perhaps the crowning achievement of this whole collection. It was made on a Saturday afternoon in the height of the summer, and before we got away the prospect as viewed from the Paddington platform was anything but encouraging. A mishap in Old Oak Common yard delayed the departure of the empty coaches and

the start was 22 min late. With such a train, packed with passengers and well out of its proper path, one could hardly expect much, save for one thing—Driver W. H. Brown was on the job. Everyone concerned was so anxious to get that long train out of the station that we were signalled away the moment he had coupled on, and there was no opportunity for even the briefest word with him, or his mate. But the moment we were away it was evident that he was going for it in his usual determined way.

No 4075, *Cardiff Castle*, another veteran of 1923, was not by any means a 'star' engine at that time, but we were soon storming along in thrilling style and the average speed from Slough to Reading was 65½ mph. The steaming must have been rock-steady, for we continued up the Thames valley at a fine even pace, and notwithstanding the 485-ton load were getting within measurable distance of 'level time' by Cholsey. Fortune had certainly favoured us at Reading by giving us a clear path amid the swarm of Saturdays-only expresses up from the West of England, but a bad signal check came at Didcot, down to 20 mph, after we had covered 35 miles at an average speed of 64¾ mph.

The vigour of the recovery was typical of the whole run. I suppose there is an impressiveness about a diesel or an electric locomotive working almost silently into speed, but their working cannot convey the sense of real effort and endeavour that comes from the sound of a steam locomotive being worked hard into speed after a check. And on this occasion Driver Brown and his fireman, and *Cardiff Castle*, gave us this audible thrill in full measure. By the now-closed signalbox at Lockinge we were back to 60 mph, and up the gradual rise to Shrivenham speed gradually rose to 66 mph. With a 485-ton load this was grand work, and when we came to the more favourable stretches of line there was no let up. Touching 82 mph at Dauntsey, speed did not fall below 67 mph up the seven miles of 1 in 660 to the entrance to Box Tunnel, and a final maximum of 77½ mph was attained at the western end.

Despite the Didcot check, we were well inside 'level time' at Bathampton, and our net time of

86½ min for the 95½ miles from Southall to Bathampton showed an average speed of 66½ mph. Even a second bad signal check, in the approach to Bath, did not prevent us from bettering the schedule time. This splendid run forms a fitting conclusion to this series of performances by the 'Castle' class locomotives. The final curtain has not yet fallen on the long and varied pageant of steam locomotive running on the crack express trains between Paddington and Bristol, but the time is surely drawing quite near now. When it does, and this applies no less to other famous express routes in this country, an age of human endeavour will be ended. The work required in the cabs of the diesels, and of the multiple-unit Pullmans, belongs verily to another world.

If the age of steam is ending on the Bristol and West of England routes of the former Great Western Railway, the running of certain special trains still gives opportunities to show that the locomotives and their crews can still run as of old. The working of race specials has always been given preferential treatment from Paddington and many a time seeing the well-polished 'Kings' and 'Castles' on the Newbury specials I have wondered whether those trains ever got a chance for some real speeding. This query is answered by the remarkable run detailed in Table III, which was clocked by an old friend of the 'Members and First Class Only' special during the October meeting at Newbury in 1960.

With two severe permanent way checks to come, engine No 6025, *King Henry III*, was taken out of Paddington in a style that in many ways eclipsed the greatest days of the 'Cornish Riviera Express' between the wars, with a speed of 60 mph as early as Ealing, and 72½ mph before the first of the checks. At the second the

TABLE III
WESTERN REGION:
PADDINGTON–NEWBURY RACECOURSE

11.50am Race Special
Load: 13 coaches, 446 tons tare, 465 tons full
Engine: No 6025, *King Henry III*

Dist		Sch	Actual		Speeds
Miles		min	m	s	mph
0.0	PADDINGTON	0	0	00	—
1.3	Westbourne Park	—	3	11	—
5.7	Ealing Broadway	—	8	45	60
9.1	Southall ...	13½	12	00	66
16.2	Langley ...	—	18	14	72½
			pws		17*
18.5	SLOUGH ...	22½	20	39	—
			pws		3*
24.2	Maidenhead ...	28½	30	00	64
31.0	Twyford ...	—	35	48	77½
			—		75
36.0	READING ...	40	40	06	33*
37.8	Southcote Junc	—	43	33	50*
41.2	Theale ...	—	47	20	64
44.8	Aldermaston	—	50	32	68
49.6	Thatcham ...	—	54	30	60*
		—	—		64
			sigs		—
52.4	Newbury Racecourse	62	60	05	—

Net time, 54 min *Speed restriction

train was practically stopped, by Farnham Royal Signalbox, and it was from this check that a really terrific acceleration took place, to 64 mph at Maidenhead and to no less than 77½ mph before Twyford. As a result, the train was on time passing Reading and, following an exceptionally cautious run over the junctions there, the recovery up the Kennet valley was again most vigorous. Because of this grand running, Newbury Racecourse was reached 2 min early. As my friend aptly remarks, for him, this was by far the best and most thrilling race of the day!

APRIL 1961

Seaside expresses to Folkestone, Dover and Deal

In the far-off days before the First World War, the premier express trains of the South Eastern & Chatham Railway were the 'Continentals'. All others ranked definitely in a class below, both as regards engine and status generally. But in the rebuilding of services from 1920 onwards, all was changed. While the SE&CR and Southern certainly introduced fine new locomotives for the Boat Trains, the Folkestone and Dover service was notably accelerated, and with the 'Schools' three-cylinder 4-4-0s the running became absolutely top class. Enhanced power came after the Bulleid Pacifics were built, and then there were the diesels as a first step towards the complete modernisation with full electrification.

THE replacement of steam by diesel locomotives in Great Britain was originally put forward as an interim measure, pending full electrification. Now, it seems, there are many trunk lines on which diesel haulage is likely to remain for many years, though this month I am turning to one important route where the reign of diesels is likely to be very brief, namely the old South Eastern main line to Dover, *via* Tonbridge. Diesel-electric locomotives were introduced on these trains last summer, but the relatively simple preparations that are necessary for the low-voltage dc system of electrification used on the Southern Region are going ahead so rapidly that the 'diesel age' on the Folkestone and Dover expresses is not likely to be more than two years at the most.

When this work is completed, only the line

between Tonbridge and Bo Peep Junction at West St Leonards will remain out of the whole main-line network of the former SECR, and for civil engineering reasons this stretch is unlikely to be electrified, at any rate for some time to come. The difficulty lies in the tunnels between Tunbridge Wells and Wadhurst where the clearances are seriously restricted. This line was one of the earliest parts of the old South Eastern system, and had been open since 1851. In view of the extreme care and vigilance exercised by William Cubitt over other major engineering works on the line, one would not expect trouble in this case. In fact, however, though the specification called for four rings of brickwork in the tunnels, in the long one near Wadhurst the contractor, presumably to save money, put in only one, and this departure from specification apparently went unnoticed until the year 1862, when reports were received from the district engineer of caving in! After a lengthy and protracted examination the re-lining of the tunnel was finally authorised, but to cut the cost of the repair work some of the new lining was put *inside* the old profile, thus reducing the clearances.

It was not until the days of the Southern Railway that the restrictions in this tunnel had any serious effects on locomotives and rolling stock, though as it turned out connoisseurs of locomotive history may well be grateful for those restrictions. Had the clearances permitted the use of the 'King Arthurs' between Tonbridge and Hastings, in all probability the 'Schools' would never have been designed and built, and locomotive practice and performance would have been the poorer by the non-existence of one of the best locomotive classes ever to run south of the Thames. In more recent times the restriction has led to a most interesting piece of modernisation by the engineers of the Southern Region, the outcome of which was described recently in a paper read before the Institution of Locomotive Engineers by Mr W. J. A. Sykes, Chief Mechanical & Electrical Engineer of the Southern Region. This paper described the origin of, and operating experience with, the diesel-electric multiple-unit train sets on the Hastings line.

Mr Sykes recalled how, in 1955, it became necessary to take urgent steps to meet increasing public pressure for the improvement of train services on this route. The 'Schools' class locomotives were the largest steam power permissible because of the clearances; the increasing loads of the business trains made an acceleration of the schedules impracticable and as priority in electrification was to be given to the Margate, Ramsgate and Dover lines it would have been the year 1963 at the earliest before electrification between Tonbridge and Hastings could be contemplated. As Mr Sykes said: 'Diesel electrification was the only system under which the desired improvement could be provided in a minimum of time.'

Down Folkestone and Dover express near Chelsfield hauled by Class 'E' ex-SE & CR 4-4-0 No 175. (Rail Archive Stephenson, F.R. Hebron)

It was achieved by a carefully-designed synthesis of well-tried operational units.

At the time 32 new coaches for locomotive haulage on the Hastings line were under construction. These were being built to the maximum dimensions permitted by the engineering clearances, and by the length of the platforms at Cannon Street and Charing Cross—8 ft 0¾ in wide, by 56 ft 11 in. A decision was taken to convert these into five six-car diesel-electric multiple-unit train sets. The traction motors were to be identical in all respects to those used in the latest Southern express and suburban multiple-unit electric stock, while power for the traction motors was provided by 500-hp diesel engine-generator sets of an existing English Electric design that had been well tried in service overseas. The result was extremely successful, though when the scheme was extended to provide for complete dieselisation of the Hastings services, *via* Tunbridge Wells, the additional 18 six-car sets were built on the standard Southern 63 ft 5 in underframes, because with multiple-unit working there was no longer any need to provide for the length of the locomotive in the overall length permitted by the platform lengths at the London termini.

In his paper Mr Sykes gave some interesting details of the calculated performance of the new trains, provided with 1,000 engine horsepower per six-car unit, and weighing 248 tons tare, thus:

Gradient	Balancing speed, mph
Level	69
1 in 250 rising	58
1 in 100 rising	40
1 in 50 rising	23

For those who are unfamiliar with the term, I should add that the balancing speed is that which would be attained, and sustained, under full power conditions on a continuous length of such a gradient. Although the Hastings line has practically no lengths of even gradient where the speed can settle down to a steady figure, I understand that on a trial run to Southampton that was made in 1957 the calculated figures of performance were very accurately reproduced in practice.

One point brought out in Mr Sykes's paper emphasises that the difficulties of the Hastings line are not by any means confined to gradients. On the most difficult section, between Crowhurst and Tunbridge Wells, there are speed restrictions due to curves. To make sure that a reasonable amount of tractive power has been provided, the schedule over this section was recalculated, assuming 50 per cent additional power. The original calculated schedule for 23.2 miles from Crowhurst to Tunbridge Wells was 29 min start to stop, but even with 50 per cent more tractive power this time could not be cut to less than 27½ min. In the light of this investigation it was felt that the original power was adequate, and that any increase would not be justified. The restrictions, all to 40 mph, extend for 1¼ miles approaching and through Mountfield Tunnel; at Milepost 52; for the last 1½ miles up to Wadhurst Tunnel; and for nearly two miles north of Wadhurst itself.

The effect of these restrictions is shown in a log detailed in Table I herewith, which was part of a run recorded by Mr Ronald Nelson not long after the service was first introduced, with one of the original sets, No 1006. These have a tare weight of 225 tons, against the 248 tons of the standard six-car sets. Full power was used from the start up the moderate rise to Battle, after which the train coasted downhill before the 40 mph slack through Mountfield Tunnel. Then full power was used again over the fast stretch past Robertsbridge and Etchingham, and continued up the bank towards Wadhurst until the restricted lengths were reached. It was only over the nine miles between Mileposts 51½ and 42½ that full power could be used for any length of time, and as the average speed over this stretch was 62 mph Mr Sykes's statement that fifty per cent extra power would be needed to clip 1½ min off the Crowhurst–Tunbridge Wells time can be well appreciated. Any im-

TABLE I
SOUTHERN REGION: 3.30 pm
HASTINGS—CHARING CROSS

Multiple-unit diesel-electric set No 1006
Load: 6 cars, 225 tons tare, 240 tons full

Dist			Schd	Actual		Speeds
Miles			min.	m	s	mph
0.0	CROWHURST	...	0	0	00	—
2.0	Battle	... ...	3½	3	42	49¼
						68
						70¼
4.8	*Mountfield* ...	...	—	6	24	—
5.5	*Milepost* 52 ...	...	—	7	20	40*
7.9	Robertsbridge	...	—	10	08	68
						70¼
10.1	ETCHINGHAM	...	12	11	56	67½
						77½
12.0	*Milepost* 45½	...	—	13	34	68
13.7	Stonegate	...	—	15	09	61
15.0	*Milepost* 42½	...	—	16	30½	56¾
						40*
18.2	Wadhurst	... ...	21½	20	49	46¾
19.5	*Milepost* 38 ...	...	—	22	39	40*
20.8	Frant	... ...	—	24	34	41¾
						55¾
				sigs		15*
23.1	TUNBRIDGE WELLS		29	28	22	—

* Speed restriction

provement would have to be confined almost entirely to the stretch between Milesposts 51 ½ and 42½, and to cut 1½ min would entail an average of nearly 75 mph.

On the Folkestone expresses, by the courtesy of the Southern Region authorities I have been privileged to observe the working of the diesel-electric locomotives at first hand, from the cab. In comparing their road performance with that of the steam locomotives that preceded them it is important to appreciate their designed capacity, at full power. The type '2' locomotives of the D5000 series, built at Derby, and having Sulzer engines, have a nominal horsepower of 1,160. The input to the generator at full engine output is 1,085 hp, and at various speeds this gives the hp at the rail shown in the accompanying table. The difference between the rail hp and that available for hauling the train is accounted for by the resistance of the locomotive itself:

DESIGNED RAIL HORSEPOWER
'D5000' Class, Type '2' Diesel-Electric Locomotive

Speed mph	Tractive effort at wheels, lb	Rail hp
20	16,600	886
30	11,000	882
40	8,200	875
50	6,550	873
60	5,300	848
70	4,550	848

It can be seen, therefore, that over the complete range of running speeds the rail hp is roughly constant at a little below 900, though of course the drawbar hp diminishes with increasing speed. On one of the runs I made we sustained 70 mph on the level between Staplehurst and Headcorn, with a load of 325 tons behind the locomotive, and assuming, on the calm, fine day it was, a coach resistance of 10.5 lb per ton, this gives a dbhp of 635. On another occasion the same locomotive sustained 34 mph on the 1 in 122 gradient between Hildenborough and Sevenoaks Tunnel, with a load of 355 tons. Taking the coach resistance at 4.8 lb per ton this works out at 850 equivalent dbhp. The air resistance of the locomotive would be quite low at this speed.

The horsepower figures quoted are enough to show that it would be quite unreasonable to expect one of these type '2' diesels to compete on level terms with some of the steam locomotives that have previously been used on the service. During the Interchange Trials of 1948 the 'West Country' Pacifics were regularly producing peak equivalent dbhp figures of 1,500, and more, while on the Great Central line there is a recorded instance, with engine No 34006, of an equivalent drawbar horsepower of slightly above *two thousand*. This, of course, was only a transitory peak and could not have been sustained for any appreciable time. My own best records with the 'Schools' show edbhp rates of about 900 at 75 mph. At speeds of 50 mph and over, the old South Eastern & Chatham superheater 4-4-0s of classes 'D1', 'E1' and 'L,' on their past records, would show up almost as well as the new type '2' diesels, and the Maunsell 'L1' 4-4-0s appear definitely better; it is at lower speeds that the diesels are superior. So far as the 'E1' class is concerned, one of the best runs with the 11 am Continental boat express shows an actual average speed of 59 mph from Paddock Wood to Sandling Junction with a load of 298 tons tare. The net average was 61 mph. On my own recent run with the 4.10 pm from Charing Cross, the net average speed over the same stretch, with a tare load of 305 tons, was 63 mph.

The type '3' diesel-electrics of the 'D6500' class have a nominal horsepower of 1,550, and are intended primarily for goods working. During the summer of 1960, however, some of these locomotives were being used on express passenger trains and on a journey when I was travelling up from Folkestone one of them put up some excellent hill-climbing work. With a load of 395 tons behind the locomotive a speed of 46 mph was sustained for about three miles on the 1 in 122 ascent of Sevenoaks Tunnel, and this gives an equivalent drawbar horsepower of about 1,400—more nearly type '4' rather than

type '3' performance. This, of course, does not approach my own record up this bank, when one of the unrebuilt 'Merchant Navy' class 4-6-2s gave me a sustained 53 mph on the 1 in 122 with a 425-ton train—this is 1,950 edbhp.

From this preliminary discussion the actual runs can be studied in their proper perspective. The present schedules are slower than the best maintained between the two world wars. It was in the summer of 1922 that the South Eastern & Chatham Railway accelerated four of the Folkestone expresses to an 80-min run over the 69.9 miles between Charing Cross and Folkestone Central. At first, with the 'L' class engines, there was no intermediate stop, but soon after the introduction of the excellent Maunsell 'L1' class 4-4-0s a stop at Waterloo was included, leaving the 69.2 miles between that station and Folkestone to be covered in 76 min. Today the 4.10 pm down is allowed 81½ min from Waterloo to Folkestone Central, while the up morning 'Man of Kent' is allowed 85 min for the same run. The first of my diesel runs was made as a passenger on the 9.10 am from Charing Cross. It was somewhat delayed by adverse signals, but east of Paddock Wood we got a fine

TABLE II
SOUTHERN REGION: TONBRIDGE–ASHFORD

Run No		1		2		3		4		5	
Engine No		31739		30922		34017		30932		D6504	
Engine Class		4-4-0 'D1'		4-4-0 'S'		4-6-2 'WC'		4-4-0 'S'		Bo-Bo 'DE'	
Load, tons (E/F)		267/290		357/380		357/380		366/390		362/395	
Dist		Actual	Speeds	Actual	Speeds	Actual	Speeds	Actual	Speeds	Actual	Speeds
Miles		m s	mph	m s	mph	m s	mph	m s	mph	m s	mph
0.0	TONBRIDGE ...	0 00	—	0 00	—	0 00	—	0 00	—	0 00	—
		—	56	—	—	—	—	—	—	sig stop	63/0
5.3	Paddock Wood ...	8 21	53	7 47	68	7 34	69	7 37	70½	9 39	—
9.9	Marden	13 10	57	11 49	67	11 34	65	11 31	77/72½	14 52	61
12.4	Staplehurst ...	15 37	63	14 01	73	13 50	68	13 36	76	17 10	66
15.7	Headcorn ...	18 35	69	16 48	72	16 41	72	16 15	80½	19 00	72
		—	—	—	—	—	—	pws	15	—	66½
20.9	Pluckley	23 25	65	21 20	—	21 25	—	22 45	49	24 27	72
24.4	*Chart Siding* ...	26 47	58	—	67	—	65	26 52	57½	27 34	66
		—	—	—	—	—	—	—	66	sig stop	—
26.6	ASHFORD ...	30 11	—	27 15	—	27 29	—	29 51	—	34 35	—

Engine names: 30922, *Marlborough*; 30932, *Blundells*; 34017, *Ilfracombe*.
Classes: 'D1' = ex-SECR 4-4-0. 'S' = 'Schools.' 'WC' = 'West Country.' 'DE' = Type '3' diesel-electric.

run to the outskirts of Ashford. This run is shown in Table II in company with four runs with steam locomotives, in which the work of a Maunsell rebuilt 4–4–0 of class 'D1,' two 'Schools' and a 'West Country' Pacific are contrasted.

The schedule for this run is 31 min. The little 'D1' 4–4–0, clocked by Mr A. F. Mercer, started somewhat slowly, but ran splendidly from Marden onwards with a sustained speed of 69 mph on the level at Headcorn, and a minimum of 58 mph at Chart Siding, after two long stretches of gradually rising gradient. The next two runs, recorded by Mr D. W. Winkworth, showed almost identical times by a 'Schools,' and a 'West Country,' while the fourth run, recorded from the footplate by Mr Ronald Nelson, included some remarkable running by a 'Schools' retaining the original single blastpipe and chimney. Speed was worked up to no less than 80½ mph on the level at Headcorn and recovered after the permanent way check to 57½ mph at Chart and to 66 before slowing into

Ashford. The diesel got away from Tonbridge in great style, and was already doing 63 mph when the adverse signals of Paddock Wood were sighted. After that we ran well, and would have kept time to Ashford but for the concluding checks.

Next comes Table III, in which the excellent run I was privileged to make in the cab of the type '2' diesel on the 4.10 pm from Charing Cross is tabulated alongside two pre-war runs of my own on the Folkestone service behind 'Schools' class 4–4–0s. With No D5007 full power was used almost immediately from Charing Cross, and apart from an easing over the curve from St Johns to Parks Bridge Junction the controller was fully over from London Bridge throughout to Dunton Green. The working was easier thence to Tonbridge, but then full power was used throughout to Folkestone, except for the two permanent way checks. The first of the two comparative runs was what might be termed a normal 'Schools' performance on the pre-war 4.15 pm down, in which the overall time to

Victoria-Margate express, diverted via the Dartford Loop, hauled by 'D1' class Maunsell 4–4–0 No 31145. (Derek Cross)

TABLE III
SOUTHERN RAILWAY and SOUTHERN REGION: CHARING CROSS–FOLKESTONE

Run No		1		2		3	
Engine No		D5007		915		912	
Engine Name		—		Brighton		Downside	
Engine Class		'DE'		4-4-0 'S'		4-4-0 'S'	
Load, tons (E/F)		305/320		321/345		387/420	
Dist		Actual	Speeds	Actual	Speeds	Actual	Speeds
Miles		m s	mph	m s	mph	m s	mph
0.0	CHARING CROSS	0 00	—	0 00	—	0 00	—
0.7	Waterloo	2 25	—	2 43	—	3 20	—
		3 10	—	3 30	—	sigs	—
		sigs					
1.9	LONDON BRIDGE	7 20	—	6 40	—	6 35	—
		sigs	—	—	—	sigs	—
4.9	New Cross	11 35	51½	10 44	53½	11 40	48½
7.2	Hither Green	14 30	45	13 30	48	14 31	50
11.3	Chislehurst	20 31	37 (min)	19 27	33 (min)	20 20	39 (min)
13.8	Orpington	24 04	47½	22 49	51	23 37	54
16.6	Knockholt	27 42	40½	26 23	42½	27 00	44½
20.6	Dunton Green	31 53	75	30 36	69	31 05	70½
22.1	SEVENOAKS	33 13	58	32 01	55	32 29	55
27.0	Hildenborough	37 28	76	36 39	72	37 06	77
29.5	TONBRIDGE	39 45	50*	39 11	46*	39 55	38*
34.8	Paddock Wood	44 57	71	44 35	69½	46 02	67
39.4	Marden	48 53	65	48 34	65	50 14	62
41.9	Staplehurst	51 04	70	50 47	72½	52 35	69
45.2	Headcorn	53 57	70	53 36	70½	55 32	67
50.4	Pluckley	53 48	61½/67	58 27	62/66½	60 37	59/64
53.9	Chart Siding	62 07	61	61 46	61½	64 05	60
		pws	15	—	—	—	—
56.1	ASHFORD	65 35	—	63 44	67½	66 07	67
		—	57	pws	35	—	57/60
64.2	Westenhanger	75 02	54½	73 50	53	74 35	51½
65.4	Sandling	76 22	59/69	75 09	—	75 57	57
		pws					
69.2	Shorncliffe	80 18	—	78 48	67½	79 35	71½
69.9	FOLKESTONE CENTRAL ...	81 45	—	80 00	—	81 00	—
Schedule, min		85		80		80	
Net times, min		76½		77		78¼	

* Speed restrictions.   'DE' = Type '2' diesel-electric.   'S' = 'Schools' class

Folkestone was maintained despite a permanent way check that cost about 3 min in running.

The third run in Table III was a magnificent performance by the 'Schools' class engine No 912, *Downside*, on the Saturday 12.55 pm from Charing Cross, booked non-stop to Folkestone. Checks on either side of London Bridge nullified the advantage that might have been gained by the omission of the stop at Waterloo, so that the train passed New Cross 2¾ min late. Then the running to Tonbridge was the fastest of all three runs, despite the greatly increased load. Such minimum speeds as 39 mph at Elmstead Woods, and 44½ at Knockholt, were remarkable with such a load as 420 tons after the long stretches of 1 in 120 ascent. Had the driver not been so ultra-cautious in his approach and passage through Tonbridge we should have clocked in to Folkestone on time. He dropped a full minute on the times of the previous 'Schools' run between Hildenborough and Paddock Wood. By splendidly-sustained hard work east of the latter station an average of exactly 60 mph was made over the last 35 miles to the stop, and the arrival was no more than a minute late. For comparative purposes the net times in this table are calculated on the basis of the Waterloo stop constituting a check.

In the up direction we come next to four runs on the present 5.10 pm express from Ashford to Waterloo, in which the work of the rebuilt 'West Country' Pacifics is compared with that of a new type '3' diesel-electric. The diesel made the quickest start out of Ashford, but after that there is not a great deal to choose between any of the four runs until Tonbridge was passed. Then came the outstanding uphill performance of No D6509 up to Sevenoaks Tunnel, to which reference has already been made. The sustained minimum speed of 46 mph put this climb in a class apart, though of course it is evident from the results of the Interchange Trials of 1948, if

TABLE IV
SOUTHERN REGION: ASHFORD–WATERLOO

Run No			1		2		3		4	
Engine No			34004		34037		34027		D6509	
Engine Name			Yeovil		Clovelly		Taw Valley		—	
Engine Class			4-6-2 'WC'		4-6-2 'WC'		4-6-2 'WC'		Bo-Bo 'DE'	
Load, tons (E/F)			330/350		337/360		342/360		369/395	
Dist		Schd	Actual	Speeds	Actual	Speeds	Actual	Speeds	Actual	Speeds
Miles		min	m s	mph	m s	mph	m s	mph	m s	mph
0.0	ASHFORD	0	0 00	—	0 00	—	0 00	—	0 00	—
5.7	Pluckley	—	8 20	—	8 28	66	8 07	65½	7 21	72½
			pws	40	—	—	—	—	—	69
10.9	Headcorn	—	14 18	72	12 58	69	12 47	66½	11 45	73
14.2	Staplehurst	—	16 56	76	15 43	72	15 36	71	14 32	70
16.7	Marden	—	18 56	74	17 50	70	17 38	73	16 45	67/72
						74	pws	24*	pws	30
21.3	Paddock Wood	22	22 26	79	21 40	71	21 49	—	22 44	—
26.6	TONBRIDGE	27	27 13	32*	26 41	36*	28 52	49*	29 28	43*
							pws	31*	—	49
29.1	Hildenborough	—	31 37	36	30 43	38	32 15	—	32 46	46
31.0	Weald Box	—	34 46	38	33 51	36	—	39	35 22	46
34.0	SEVENOAKS	39	39 20	—	38 39	—	39 53	—	39 08	—
35.5	Dunton Green	—	40 54	60	40 17	62	41 28	64	40 36	66
39.5	Knockholt	—	45 19	52	45 00	54	45 35	54	44 47	50½
					sigs	—	—	—	—	—
42.3	Orpington	48½	47 51	74	49 10	40	48 05	68½	47 20	68
44.8	Chislehurst	51	50 01	65	52 23	62	50 32	66	49 45	—
47.1	Grove Park	—	sig stop	—	—	—	52 28	74	52 15	—
									pws	—
48.9	Hither Green	—	59 48	—	56 31	—	53 58	54	54 30	—
					sigs	—	—	—	—	—
51.2	New Cross	57½	63 13	—	61 18	—	56 49	51	58 00	—
			sigs	—	sigs	—	sigs	—	—	—
54.2	LONDON BRIDGE ...	62	72 38	—	67 00	—	62 26	—	63 08	—
55.4	WATERLOO	65	75 34	—	69 58	—	64 38	—	66 10	—
Net times, min			62½		64½		63		61¾	

* Speed restriction, temporary or permanent. 'WC' = 'West Country' class. 'DE' = Type '3' diesel-electric.

TABLE V
SECR, SOUTHERN RAILWAY AND SOUTHERN REGION:
FOLKESTONE–CANNON STREET–CHARING CROSS

Run No		1	2	3	4	5	6	7
Engine No		453	745	761	758	921	917	D5007
Engine Class		4-4-0	4-4-0	4-4-0	4-4-0	4-4-0	4-4-0	Bo + Bo
		'B'	'D'	'L'	'Ll'	'S'	'S'	'DE'
Load, tons /E/F)		187/200	187/200	197/215	308/340	224/235	356/390	337/355
Dist		Actual	Actual	Actual	Actual	Actual	Actual	Actual
Miles		m s	m s	m s	m s	m s	m s	m s
0.0	FOLKESTONE	0 00	0 00	0 00	0 00	0 00	0 00	0 00
5.7	Westenhanger	9 17	9 20	9 25	9 15	8 43	9 54	10 45
		pws	pws	—	—	—	—	pws
13.8	ASHFORD	18 24	18 44	16 45	16 20	15 25	17 00	19 15
								pws
19.5	Pluckley	24 12	24 26	21 50	21 10	19 54	21 47	27 58
24.7	Headcorn	29 09	29 08	26 20	25 30	23 52	25 59	32 37
28.0	Staplehurst	32 09	31 58	29 15	28 10	26 21	28 38	35 31
				pws	—	—	—	—
30.5	Marden	34 35	34 22	31 50	30 10	28 21	30 45	37 48
						pws	—	
35.1	Paddock Wood	38 58	38 30	36 25	34 10	32 55	34 30	41 43
40.4	TONBRIDGE	44 40	44 00	41 55	39 40	39 54	39 09	46 43
42.9	Hildenborough	48 40	48 03	45 45	43 45	43 28	42 18	50 25
47.8	SEVENOAKS	57 39	57 03	53 30	51 55	51 17	50 29	58 30
49.3	Dunton Green	59 32	58 53	55 05	53 35	53 18	52 09	60 10
53.3	Knockholt	64 58	64 24	59 40	58 25	57 55	56 51	64 47
		pws	pws	—	pws	—	—	—
56.1	Orpington	68 03	67 31	62 20	61 55	60 29	59 34	67 25
		pws	pws	—	—	—	—	—
58.6	Chislehurst	71 30	70 58	64 40	64 25	62 27	61 39	69 38
62.7	Hither Green	76 41	75 45	68 15	68 05	65 50	65 06	73 50
								sigs
65.0	New Cross	79 57	79 20	71 05	70 50	69 02	68 15	77 17
					sigs	pws	—	sigs
68.0	LONDON BRIDGE	sigs	sigs	75 20	75 00	74 07	72 36	82 00
68.7	CANNON STREET	86 24	84 11	—	—	sigs	—	—
69.2	Waterloo	—	—	—	—	77 32	74 49	85 00
						79 54	76 12	86 30
69.9	CHARING CROSS	—	—	80 10	79 10	82 45	79 27	89 57
Average speed:								
	Pluckley–Paddock Wood	63.5	66.5	70.8*	72.0	77.5*	73.8	68.2
Min speed:								
	Sevenoaks Tunnel	30	31½	37½	36	40½	34	34
Max speeds:								
	Headcorn	68	71	72½	76½	82	79	71½
	After Knockholt	60	60	71½	71½	79	75	71
Net times, min		82½‡	81½‡	78½	77¾	72¼†	74¾†	78½†

* Net average speed.   ‡ to Cannon Street.   † to Waterloo.
'B' = Stirling class 'B.'   'D' = Wainwright class 'D.'   'L' = Maunsell class 'L.'   'Ll' = Maunsell class 'Ll.'   'S' = 'Schools' class.
'DE' = Type '2' diesel-electric.

from nothing else, that the 'West Country' Pacifics were being worked a long way below their maximum capacity. Sevenoaks Tunnel is notoriously wet, and the drivers were most likely going easily to lessen the chance of slipping. On the other hand all three drivers went hard from Dunton Green up to Knockholt, and the excellent minimum speeds at the latter point ranging between 52 and 54 mph were all higher than that of the diesel in this instance.

The final collection of runs, in Table V, on non-stop expresses from Folkestone, does indeed span the years from the very early days of British Locomotive Practice and Performance. The first two were recorded by Charles Rous-Marten on the American car train long before the first world war; Runs 3 and 4 are interesting examples of Maunsell 4–4–0 performance recorded by Cecil J. Allen; while 5 and 6 are two of the best I noted personally with 'Schools' before the second world war. The last run is my own recent trip,

made in the cab of a type '2' diesel-electric. Runs 1 and 2 provide an interesting comparison in themselves, as the respective engines were a 4–4–0 of James Stirling's final SER design, the 'B' class, and a Wainwright class 'D'—one of the most beautiful 4–4–0 designs ever to run in this country. There was little to choose between these two engines uphill—in fact the Stirling, in accelerating from the minimum of 30 mph by Weald Signalbox to 35 mph at the north end of the tunnel, achieved by far the better performance on this critical length. The Wainwright held a steady 31½ mph through the tunnel. On these two early runs the speed downhill from Knockholt was very slow. Both engines were on time, and the bad old days of the chronic blocks outside London Bridge and Cannon Street had not entirely passed. Clearly there was no point in hurrying.

The third run was made in the early days of the 80-min service, when it was still South

One of the first of the 'Schools' class 4-4-0s No 902 Wellington, *in its original condition.* (W.J. Reynolds)

Charing Cross–Deal express near Weald signal box (at the south end of the Sevenoaks Tunnel) hauled by 'Schools' class 4-4-0 No 30927 Clifton. (Derek Cross)

Eastern & Chatham, and when the Managing Committee had the honour of operating the first express schedule anywhere in Britain at higher speed than the best offered in pre-war days. In certain quarters the 'L' class 4–4–0s had the reputation of being sluggish. I must admit I never had any evidence myself of any such trait, and the excellent run by No 761 detailed in the third column of Table V would seem to give the lie to it pretty effectively. West of Ashford the speed was sustained with little variation from the 70–72 level, until the underline bridge slack at Marden. Tonbridge was passed nearly a minute late, but with a good climb to Knockholt, and a clear road through the suburban area, Charing Cross was reached on time.

The next run, with one of the highly-efficient Maunsell 'L1' class 4–4–0 locomotives, makes the most direct comparison with the work of the

new type '2' diesel. I should explain at this stage that the large increases over the tare weight of the trains represented in the third and fourth columns are due to the use of non-corridor stock, in each case well filled. Despite the very much heavier load, the 'L1' engine on the fourth run got away from Folkestone very smartly, and some very fast running followed. Ashford was passed at 76½ mph and this maximum speed was renewed again at Headcorn. But perhaps the finest achievement on this run was the ascent to Sevenoaks Tunnel. Speed was reduced to 33 mph for Tonbridge curve, after which a sustained rate of 36 mph was made up the 1 in 122 to the south end of Sevenoaks Tunnel. This would have involved an equivalent drawbar horsepower of at least 900, and probably about 920—fully up to the standard of the new type '2' diesel-electrics when worked at full power.

During the years 1935 to 1939 I made many runs on the old 5.10 pm up from Folkestone with 'Schools' class engines. The usual load was of nine large corridor coaches, though during the

Charing Cross–Ramsgate express at Sandling Junction hauled by rebuilt Bulleid 'West Country' Pacific No 34003 Plymouth. (Derek Cross)

winter the minimum formation was sometimes down to seven. The fifth run, with engine No 921, *Shrewsbury*, was one of the fastest I recorded, though we ran into so many checks in the London area that in the end overall time was not maintained. This was unusual at that time, for this important train was usually given a good road inwards from New Cross. With two permanent way checks to come, we certainly started away from Folkestone in most thrilling style, and we had a maximum speed of 82 mph at both Ashford and Headcorn. Having made such good time to Tonbridge there was no need for any particular energy on the ascent to Knockholt, but a maximum of all but 80 mph was reached near Grove Park before speed was eased through Hither Green, and the series of checks began.

The sixth run tabulated was made on the corresponding express on Sunday evenings, and was completely unchecked. The load, too, was the heaviest I have ever personally experienced on one of the pre-war 80-min Folkestone trains in

the up direction. Appropriately to the occasion, the locomotive performance was also the finest I ever noted on this service. The immediate start was on the slow side, but from Westenhanger No 917, *Ardingly*, was taken along in grand style. The speed onwards to Tonbridge was second only to that of the lightly-loaded *Shrewsbury*, and reached a maximum of 79 mph at Headcorn. The engine was not unduly pressed up to Sevenoaks Tunnel, falling to 34 mph, but with a clear road, and fast running downhill from Knockholt, all was plain sailing, and we reached Waterloo 1¼ min early.

The performance of the diesel, as tabulated in Column 7, was extremely interesting. It will be appreciated that I could scarcely be other than mindful of past achievements on this service as we bowled along, and I could make my observations in the comfort and cleanliness of the diesel cab, with its clear and unrestricted outlook ahead. On previous occasions I have been privileged to ride on the footplate over this route on steam locomotives ranging from 'L1' 4-4-0s to 'Merchant Navy' and 'Britannia' 4-6-2s, and the contrast was a strong one, to say the least of it. Modernisation was in evidence at many points *en route*, and it was the remodelling of the west junction at Ashford that was responsible for the heaviest delay we experienced. There was a check at the very start through Shorncliffe Station, in course of rebuilding, but the driver was able to open up to full power at Milepost 69, and we accelerated to 47½ mph at the summit of the 1 in 264 gradient between Sandling Junction and Westenhanger. We were, however, not able to get above 70 mph before it was necessary to slow down for the Ashford restriction. These two initial checks cost us at least 5 min in running.

The locomotive was working at full power again from Milepost 55¼, and apart from the slowing through Tonbridge it was a case of 'all-out' the whole way to Knockholt. On the fast stretch to Paddock Wood the maximum speed was 71½ mph, but as will be seen from the data at the foot of Table V a fine average of 68.2 mph was maintained over the 15.6 miles from Pluckley to Paddock Wood. Speed was reduced to 41 mph through Tonbridge, and after a brief rise to 43 on the level beyond the pace fell off to a steady 34 mph on the 1 in 122 to Sevenoaks Tunnel. After Knockholt the working was eased considerably. The maximum speed permitted with these locomotives is 75 mph, and had full power been maintained we should undoubtedly have exceeded this. The concluding checks were not severe, and in the end we dropped only 4 min on the present working time of 81 min from Folkestone. The net time was not more than 78½ min. I found this particular variety of type '2' diesel a very pleasant one to ride on, and their use on this service provides an interesting intermediate stage between the passing of steam and the introduction of full electrification.

Settle and Carlisle — tests and coal consumption

In pre-Grouping days, locomotives of the Great Northern, Midland and London & North Western railways were ranked as dead rivals in the haulage of Anglo-Scottish express trains. Enthusiasts of those years would not, in their most fanciful dreams, have been likely to contemplate times when first LNWR 'Claughton' class 4-6-0s and then Gresley Pacifics would become the principal source of motive power over the historic Settle and Carlisle route. Yet so it transpired, and in the 1930s, with LNWR engines, and some 25 years later with LNER 'A3' Pacifics, I logged many interesting runs.

ONE of the most interesting recent developments in locomotive working arising from the dieselisation of the East Coast Route is the drafting of a number of Gresley 'A3' Pacifics to the Midland shed at Leeds, and the use of these famous engines on the Anglo-Scottish expresses over the Settle & Carlisle line. In itself there is nothing very significant about this move—merely a convenient way of utilising some first-class motive power displaced by new diesel-electrics at Gateshead shed. But over the past 36 years the Settle & Carlisle line has been a test route unequalled in the variety of power attached to succeeding generations of dynamometer cars: Midland, London & North Western, and Caledonian; LMSR, LNER, and Southern; British Railways' 'Standards'; and eventually, the 'Deltic.' Against such a pageant of power on parade the present working of the Gresley

Pacifics assumes an important place in locomotive history.

By the courtesy of Mr F. H. Petty, Motive Power Superintendent, North Eastern Region, I have had the privilege of making some runs on the footplate of 'A3s,' while through the kindness of Mr R. C. Bond, Technical Adviser, British Transport Commission, and of Mr A. E. Robson, Chief Mechanical & Electrical Engineer, London Midland Region, I have been able to study the results of dynamometer car test runs dating back to the historic trials of December, 1923, and January, 1924, when Midland engines were first pitted against their rivals from other constituent companies of the LMSR. One could discourse for whole issues of *The Railway Magazine* on these fascinating documents. The present article is, indeed, no more than a first instalment. I have chosen, therefore, 16 down journeys, shown in Tables I

TABLE I
MIDLAND LINE: SETTLE JUNCTION–CARLISLE
MR and LMSR Locomotives

Run No		1	2	3	4	5	6	7	8
Engine No		1000	1008	998	5535	5535	5660	5659	6108
Engine Class		4–4–0C	4–4–0C	4–4–0S	4–6–0P	4–6–0P	4–6–0J	4–6–0J	4–6–0R
Load, tons (E/F)		250/265	291/300	299/310	239/250	276/290	302/305	317/335	384/410
Dist		Actual	Actual	Actual	Actual	Actual	Actual	Actual	Actual
Miles		m s	m s	m s	m s	m s	m s	m s	m s
0.0	Settle Junction *	0 00	0 00	0 00	0 00	0 00	0 00	0 00	0 00
1.9	Settle	2 07	1 57	1 55	1 54	2 00	2 00	2 08	1 56
7.9	Horton	11 39	10 49	11 03	9 40	10 18	9 00	11 34	10 16
12.7	Ribblehead ...	20 38	18 32	19 37	16 10	17 05	14 43	20 09	18 00
14.0	Blea Moor ...	22 58	20 44	21 53	18 01	18 51	16 20	22 24	20 10
18.9	Dent	—	27 15	28 51	24 01	24 20	21 35	29 29	27 02
22.1	Garsdale	33 02	30 39	32 10	27 09	27 30	24 34	32 48	30 31
25.1	Aisgill	35 48	33 50	35 10	29 59	30 26	27 34	35 46	33 30
32.0	Kirkby Stephen	41 49	—	—	35 54	36 04	33 51	41 06	sig stop
42.7	APPLEBY	47 47	49 28	52 02	45 32	44 17	43 15	48 46	66 17
		pws	—	—	—	—	—	—	—
58.0	Lazonby	18 13	64 32	65 30	14 14	Many	55 48	61 26	
63.6	Armathwaite ...	23 13	—	—	18 42	signal	60 30	66 23	
70.8	Scotby	29 20	77 32	76 46	24 39	checks	66 53	72 26	
					sigs	—	—	sigs	—
73.5	CARLISLE ...	33 56	81 43	81 49	30 03	79 51	72 00	77 59	
		mph	mph	mph	mph	mph	mph	mph	mph
Average speed, Horton–Blea Moor		32.4	36.9	33.7	43.8	42.8	49.8	33.7	37.6
Min speed on ascent ...		30½	33¼	29	37½	41	46	31½	32
Max speed near Garsdale ...		66	65½	66¾	70	68	68	61	66
Min at Aisgill		60	52¼	56½	61	57	55	60	58½
Max to Carlisle ...		75	74½	76¼	86½	85	79	92	—

Engine Classes: C — Midland three-cylinder compound; S — Midland '990' class '4'; P — 'Patriot'; J — Stanier 'Jubilee'; R — Rebuilt 'Royal Scot.' * — Times from passing Settle Junction at 60–65 mph.

and II, to illustrate the work of no fewer than ten different types of locomotives. All except two were on service trains, some albeit with the dynamometer car attached; but all were made under service, rather than controlled test conditions. The tests made under the auspices of British Railways, at constant steam rates with special trains, must be held over until a further article.

Tables I and II should be considered together. In the former I have grouped together in columns 1 to 8 the runs with Midland and LMSR locomotives, and in Table II, runs 9 to 16, will be found the strangers. Because of the variation in service stops of the trains concerned, some

trains running non-stop from Leeds to Carlisle, and others calling at Hellifield, I have commenced the tabulation at Settle Junction, giving all engines a flying and roughly-equal start to the mountain section. Also the tabulation is confined to the down journey, which is the only one in which I have any details of Gresley Pacific performance. In addition to the official documents put at my disposal, and to my own recent recordings, I am much indebted to Mr G. J. Aston for putting at my disposal the voluminous records of the late R. E. Charlewood, who between the respective innings of Charles Rous-Marten and Cecil J. Allen, was responsible for these articles in *The Railway Magazine*.

TABLE II
MIDLAND LINE: SETTLE JUNCTION–CARLISLE
'Strangers'

Run No		9	10	11	12	13	14	15	16
Engine No		388	124	6005	2221	60069	60036	60022	60077
Engine Name		—	—	—	Sir Francis Dent	Sceptre	Colombo	Mallard	The White Knight
Engine Class		4-6-0P	4-4-0C	4-6-0L	4-6-0L	4-6-2 'A3'	4-6-2 'A3'	4-6-2 'A4'	4-6-2 'A3'
Railway		LNW	Cal	LNW	LNW	LNE	LNE	LNE	LNE
Load, tons (E/F)		291/300	301/310	304/320	349/365	272/285	317/335	340/365	390/420
Dist		Actual	Actual	Actual	Actual	Actual	Actual	Actual	Actual
Miles		m s	m s	m s	m s	m s	m s	m s	m s
0.0	Settle Junc*	0 00	0 00	0 00	0 00	0 00	0 00	0 00	0 00
1.9	Settle ...	2 10	—	2 10	2 10	2 00	1 59	2 07	1 50
7.9	Horton ...	12 02	—	12 35	11 55	9 27	9 25	9 52	10 52
12.7	Ribblehead	19 51	—	20 35	20 50	15 28	15 45	15 51	19 56
14.0	Blea Moor	21 59	24 55	22 45	23 15	17 15	17 32	17 22	22 26
18.9	Dent ...	28 23	—	29 05	31 10	23 48	23 53	22 51	30 21
22.1	Garsdale ...	31 47	—	32 40	34 50	27 32	27 23	26 13	33 46
25.1	Aisgill ...	34 55	41 00	36 15	38 10	31 18	30 30	29 50	38 17
32.0	Kirkby Stephen	—	—	42 25	44 25	39 24	36 51	36 18	Special stop
42.7	APPLEBY ...	51 20	—	51 20	54 10	52 27	46 33	48 13	64 25
							pws		pws
58.0	Lazonby ...	65 49	—	64 35	66 55	15 41	61 15	pws	78 06
63.6	Armathwaite	—	—	69 55	71 45	20 44	66 42	checks	82 39
70.8	Scotby ...	78 12	—	76 25	78 00	27 18	73 37	—	88 55
						sig stop	—	—	sig stop
73.5	CARLISLE	82 55	89 52	80 25	83 05	35 54	78 46	34 45	98 58
		mph	mph	mph	mph	mph	mph	mph	mph
Average speed, Horton– Blea Moor ...		35.9	—	35.4	32.3	46.9	45.2	48.8	31.6
Min speed on ascent		34	27¾	30	25	38½	38	43	26½
Max speed near Garsdale ...		64	—	60	61	55½	66	60	62½
Min at Aisgill ...		53½	—	45	51	45	54	45	—
Max to Carlisle ...		71½	71	78	80½	72	75	73	82

Engine Classes: P — 'Prince of Wales'; C — Caledonian Pickersgill; L — 'Claughton.' * — Times from passing Settle Junction at speeds of 60–65 mph.

The first run in Table I dates back to 1916, and was made with the original Midland compound, the Smith-Johnson no 2631, then recently superheated and renumbered 1000. Studying Mr Charlewood's notebooks I must confess to finding much of the performance over that route indifferent. The work of No 1000, and of No 1001, in a closely-similar run, was far above the general standards of the day. Although it was wartime, schedules in 1916 were still of pre-war

smartness, and the 10 am from Leeds on which this run was made was allowed 59 min for the 46 miles from Hellifield to Appleby. Over the 14 miles from Settle Junction to Blea Moor the ascent is at 1 in 100 continuously, save for two brief intermissions—past Helwith Bridge, and over Ribblehead viaduct. No 1000 passed Settle Junction at 64 mph, and thereafter the speeds were 34 and 36½ mph before and after Helwith Bridge; 30½ at Ribblehead, 33 over the via-

One of the ten Midland '999' class 4-4-0s used between Leeds and Carlisle, and classed '4', equal to the compounds. (F. Moore's Rail Photos)

duct, and 31½ mph at the summit. Time was kept exactly from Hellifield to Blea Moor.

Time was usually dropped on the stiff booking of 12 min from Blea Moor to Aisgill, and No 1000 was certainly no exception. All the same she must have been opened out with a vengeance at Hawes Junction (or Garsdale, as it is now known) to clear the final rise up to Aisgill without falling below 60 mph. Even Charlewood, who was not given to any excess of superlatives, concedes in his notes that this was very fine. Speed did not exceed 72 mph down to Appleby, where the arrival was in 56 min 46 sec from Hellifield. The run of 30.8 miles from Appleby to Carlisle was booked in 32 min start to stop, but a bad permanent way check prevented timekeeping. On the run with No 1001 previously mentioned a time of 32 min 16 sec was achieved, though generally speaking difficulty seems to have been experienced in maintaining that sharp time.

This run with No 1000 conveniently sets the stage, as it were, for consideration of runs 2, 3, 9

and 10, which were all made on the 4.8 pm express from Leeds, with the dynamometer car, and load augmented to give a nominal 300 tons tare. The compound No 1008, the '999' class '4' simple 4-4-0, and the North Western 'Prince of Wales' 4-6-0 were all running non-stop from Leeds to Carlisle, whereas at the time the second series of dynamometer car trials took place, in December, 1924, an intermediate stop had been inserted at Hellifield, and the departure from Leeds was at 4.3 pm. The test engines came south on the 12.10 pm express from Carlisle, and all were worked by Carlisle men. The North Western 'Prince' had been working over the route experimentally for some weeks previous to the tests, and her crew knew the road well. This engine, and the Midland simple 4-4-0 No 998, had both been out of the shops six months at the time of the tests. Both were in good condition, though one gathers that No 388 was a 'run-of-the-mill,' rather than a star engine. Against this, to represent the compounds, the Midland put forward 'the flower of the flock,' No 1008, which had just been nicely run-in after a general repairs at Derby.

One cannot help feeling, however, that mere figures—no matter how spectacular—cannot

LNWR 'Prince of Wales' class 4-6-0 of which No 388 (original renumbering) was used in the trials of 1923-4. (British Railways)

convey the thrill and excitement experienced by all taking part in these trials. Mr Bond, who was one of the engineers concerned, has told me of the intense partisanship shown by representatives of the different railways, and, perhaps, the author of these articles may, in an odd sentence or two, himself cast aside his traditional rôle of strict impartiality in referring to these railway battles of thirty to forty years ago. I have never attempted to disguise my admiration for the London & North Western Railway and its locomotives, but on the other hand, I yield to no one in my enthusiasm for the Midland compounds. On the footplate of these engines I had the pleasure of making journeys that are outstanding in my practical experience of locomotives at work; but even so, the compounds were not the marvels they were sometimes made out to be, any more than the Crewe engines were always as 'black' as they were painted. The test results speak for themselves, and serve to fan the fires of past controversies; in so doing, however, they enrich our knowledge of steam locomotive history.

The load for a superheater class '4' engine, simple or compound, was then 260 tons tare over this route on 'limited load' trains; yet in these tests there were two series, one with 300-ton trains, and one with 350-ton trains. I have no detailed logs on the northbound journey with loads of 350 tons, but some overall results are quoted later in this article. All three engines, Nos 388, 1008 and 998, did some magnificent hill-climbing between Settle Junction and Blea Moor, though difficulty was generally experienced in keeping the severe 13 min timing from Blea Moor to Aisgill. On one journey referred to in the official report the 'Prince' took only 11 min 53 sec, but the '999' on one occasion took as much as $16\frac{1}{4}$ min. The report also states that the usual working for the North Western engine was in 50 per cent cut-off, with regulator about three-quarters open. The cut-offs used on the '999' on the heaviest section were also around 50 per cent, whereas the compound was worked with full regulator, and cut-offs of 81 per cent high pressure, and 75 per cent low pressure. The equivalent cut-off in a simple engine would be about 40 per cent.

Anyway, it was all mighty hard work; an all-out slogging match between well-balanced opponents. As the data quoted later in this article shows, the compound had the best of it on coal consumption; but it was by no means a runaway victory, especially seeing that the North Western engine had amassed some 30,000 miles since last general repair. By contrast, the trials of November and December, 1924, were made on anything but level terms. The Pickersgill 4–4–0 of the Caledonian Railway, No 124, was severely handicapped in having no water pick-up on the tender. It is true that she had a water capacity of 4,200 gal, but in running between Carlisle and Leeds that would provide for an absolutely maximum usage of 36 gal a mile, in cold, wintry weather, when additional water would be required for train heating. One wonders indeed why one of the McIntosh 4–4–0s with the large bogie tenders was not used. There was little or nothing to choose between the road performance of the two types.

The Caledonian engine made only one round trip from Carlisle to Leeds and back. It was really more than could have been expected for an engine of class '3' capacity, with so relatively small a grate, to keep time, and although she steamed freely the power to pull was just not there. Her driver did extremely well to lose only 2¾ min on the southbound run, reaching Leeds in 145¾ min non-stop from Carlisle; but on the harder schedule of the northbound train 8½ min were lost. After this one experience no further tests were made with Caledonian engines. The coal consumption was extremely heavy, though how this was affected by the need to keep a very close watch on the water supply one cannot say. The times shown in Column 10 of Table II are taken from the official report.

Then, in December, 1924, the North Western 'Claughton' class engine No 2221, *Sir Francis Dent*, came on the scene. The history of this engine before the trials has some bearing on the results achieved. From Mr C. Williams, whose records of the goings and comings of Crewe locomotives have been a feature of *The Railway Magazine* for more than fifty years, I learn that No 2221 was out-shopped in July, 1924, and sent to Edge Hill. It was then worked hard, averaging over 6,000 miles a month until November 19, 1924, when it was transferred to Carlisle. In the following week two return trips were made to Leeds to enable the test driver and fireman to

LNWR 'Claughton' class 4-6-0 No 2221 Sir Francis Dent, *transferred from Edge Hill to Carlisle for the trials on the Midland line to Leeds.* (British Railways)

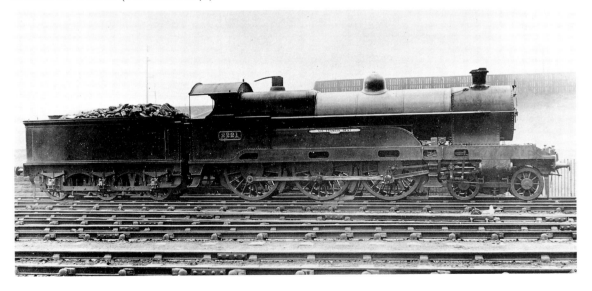

gain some familiarity with the engine, while burning hard Yorkshire coal, and on December 2 came the first of the dynamometer car trials. The Carlisle running sheds then obtained much of their coal from Tyneside, though in the previous trials best hard Yorkshire had been used by all the competitors.

Engine No 2221 worked the test trains to time, but the steaming was so poor that one feels it was a case of 1910 all over again, when Camden shed sent the engine they could best spare for the trials on the Great Western. In 1924 one could well suspect that Edge Hill were instructed to transfer a 'Claughton' to Carlisle, and they sent the one they were most anxious to be rid of! The result was a thoroughly unrepresentative performance—how unrepresentative was shown by the later 'Claughton' trials between Leeds and Carlisle in 1930. In December, 1924, No 2221 was persistently short of steam, and in the efforts of the enginemen to keep time the water was allowed to go very low in the gauge glass to try and conserve steam pressure. The log in Column 12, Table II, shows the running with a 350-ton train, on a very wild and windy night. Time was lost to Aisgill, but by some very fast

running downhill this was recovered, and Carlisle was reached a minute early.

Run No 11, together with Nos 4–7 in Table I, may next be considered. When the 'Claughtons' were put into regular service on the Settle & Carlisle line their maximum tare load was fixed at 350 tons—a big advance over the previous limit for Midland class '4' engines that obviated a good deal of piloting. No 11 is an excellent run, for details of which I am indebted to Mr G. J. Aston. Then, from 1931 onwards, the 'Baby Scots' came on to the scene. Unfortunately, I have not been able to find any runs with really heavy loads behind these engines. The two journeys with No 5535 include excellent hillclimbing, and fast work downhill. On No 4 run in particular, No 5535 passed Scotby, 28.1 miles, in 24 min 39 sec from the restart at Appleby, including in this length a maximum speed of 86½ mph.

No 6 run, in Table I, still remains the absolute record for the course. It was made in 1937 in a most remarkable four-day round trip from Bristol to Glasgow and back, with a special train including dynamometer car, to check the feasibility of the accelerated schedules proposed for

A Caledonian Pickersgill 4-4-0; one of the class was temporarily transferred to the Midland line for a return trip to Leeds.
(F. Moore's Rail Photos)

the summer service of 1938. Between Settle Junction and Aisgill, as on every other uphill section in the whole round trip, the going was as near to 'all-out' as makes no matter. For sheer hard slogging the 'Jubilees' would take some beating; when in good nick they seemed to revel in it, as I have seen from the footplate over this very route. No 5660, *Rooke*, certainly seems likely to hold the steam record for all time between Hellifield and Carlisle, in both directions of running.

The second 'Jubilee' run, shown in Column 7 of Table I, was clocked in 1936, by Mr R. Dyson on the 4.3 pm from Leeds. The train was running late, but the driver did not attempt any recovery of time on the uphill sections; in fact, he dropped 32 sec between Hellifield and Aisgill. Some very fast running followed down to Appleby with a maximum speed of 92 mph near

Crosby Garrett, and but for the check outside Carlisle fully 7 min would have been regained on the 89 min schedule from Hellifield to Carlisle. The last run in Table I, with the rebuilt 'Royal Scot' No 6108, *Seaforth Highlander*, was made not long after the introduction of those fine engines, while the second world war was still raging. It was an excellent piece of hillclimbing, made at a time when there was not a great deal of interest in locomotive performance to be noted in Great Britain as a whole.

And now we come to the Gresley Pacifics. All those with class 'A3' engines were recorded from the footplate. Mr Ronald Nelson rode *Sceptre*, in January, 1961, on the 10.35 am from Leeds, while on the two runs with the 'Thames-Clyde Express,' columns 14 and 16 of Table II, I was on the footplate myself. *Sceptre* gave an immaculate performance. Corkerhill men were in

In the beautiful scenery of the Lower Eden Valley near Armathwaite, the preserved 'Jubilee' class 4-6-0 No 5690 Leander *working the 'Cumbrian Mountain Pullman' in 1982.* (David Eatwell)

charge, and experts they both were. The engine was steaming very freely, yet Firemen McTiernon kept the needle around 210 to 220 lb per sq in without once allowing steam to go to waste by blowing off, until nearing Carlisle. Driver Reid handled the engine in the traditional Gresley style, with full regulator on all the adverse stretches. As to the cut-off figures, from 12 per cent passing Settle Junction, he increased to a maximum of 22 above Helwith Bridge; but the engine was going so well that the gear was gradually wound back to 18 per cent at Selside Box, 15 at Ribblehead, and 12½ per cent at Blea Moor Box. The load was, of course, light for so powerful an engine. On my two trips, like Mr Nelson, I had the pleasure of the company of Inspector A. E. Pullan, of Leeds, a man who has the most intimate knowledge of the route, extending back in his regular firing days to some of the early dynamometer car trials. He confessed to me that even in the greatest days of the LMSR, they were never entirely free from steaming trouble; nor were things better with the purely Midland engines. Not all the compounds were like No 1008! For that reason the Gresley Pacifics have been welcomed on all hands, for their consistently free steaming. In this respect my own first run, in Column 16, was unfortunate, not in the steaming itself but that we developed injector trouble and eventually had to make a special stop at Kirkby Stephen. This was a great pity, because *The White Knight* had done splendidly with this heavy train as far as Ribblehead.

My first trip, on a locomotive that I had last ridden on 'The North Briton' between Newcastle and Edinburgh, gave very similar times to those of *Sceptre* up to Blea Moor with a load heavier by 50 tons. The cut-off was unchanged at 25 per cent throughout from Settle Junction until we were inside Blea Moor Tunnel; the boiler pressure was mostly around 200 lb per sq in, sometimes falling to 195. That was not because the steaming was indifferent, but because the fireman regulated it at this figure. The safety valves never once lifted. Leeds men were in charge on this trip, Driver P. Chambers and

Fireman T. W. Gibbs, working through to Glasgow St Enoch, and by their good work, though leaving Leeds 6 min late we were 4 min early at Carlisle—an overall time of 126 min 28 sec, despite two moderate permanent way checks.

Run No 15 was made on a special excursion from Alford (Lincs) to Edinburgh, travelling *via* Doncaster and Carlisle, and worked throughout by the record-holding 'A4' No 60022, *Mallard*. She left Hellifield on time, at 9.15 am; by that time she had been at work since 5.34 am, at which hour Grimsby Town had been left. Between Leeds and Carlisle *Mallard* was in charge of Kingmoor men, and except for the LMSR 'Jubilee' No 5660, on a very special occasion, they stole the honours between Settle Junction and Blea Moor. I am very much indebted to Mr B. J. Hastings for details of this run. Speed fell to 43 mph on the first long stretch of 1 in 100 ending at Helwith Bridge, but then there was a remarkable recovery to 52 mph before Horton, while it cannot be very often that a train of 365 tons has crossed Ribblehead Viaduct at 50 mph going north. Bravo *Mallard*!

On the last run in Table II *The White Knight* had done well to Hellifield, and in thick drizzle we began the climb to Blea Moor working in 17 per cent cut-off with the regulator full open. We were running dead on time, and it was not until we were above Helwith Bridge that the driver advanced beyond 17 per cent. Speed had fallen to 33½ mph before Helwith Bridge and recovered to 37 beyond. At Horton the cut-off was advanced to 25 per cent, and in the prevailing weather the risk, with a Pacific, was of slipping on the wet rails. We did have one momentary slip, nearing Ribblehead, which brought speed down to 29 mph, but it was then that the injector trouble started, and this severely hampered our running to Aisgill and eventually compelled the stop at Kirkby Stephen. We had, however, kept time from Settle Junction to Blea Moor working under relatively easy steam.

To provide some basis of comparison between the 16 runs in Tables I and II, I have made an estimate of the equivalent drawbar horsepower

TABLE III
ESTIMATED AVERAGE POWER OUTPUT
HORTON-BLEA MOOR

Table	Run No	Engine No	Load, tons	Average Speed, mph	Estimated Equivalent dhp
I	1	1000	265	32.4	800
	2	1008	300	36.9	1,005
	3	998	310	33.7	934
	4	5535	250	43.8	1,115
	5	5535	290	42.8	1,200
	6	5660	305	49.8	1,495
	7	5659	335	33.7	1,035
	8	6108	410	37.6	1,375
II	9	388	300	35.9	985
	11	6005	320	35.4	1,065
	12	2221	365	32.3	1,040
	13	60069	285	46.9	1,380
	14	60036	335	45.2	1,485
	15	60022	365	48.8	1,815
	16	60077	420	31.6	1,190

based on the average speed between Horton and Blea Moor. This, of course, takes no account of the adverse weather conditions experienced, on run No 12, for example. These comparative figures are shown in Table III, and from this it will be seen that the work of *Mallard* stands head and shoulders over that of every other engine. Since the preparation of the tables I have seen details of another 'A3' performance, with engine No 60082, *Neil Gow*, and a load of 300 tons, on which the average speed from Horton to Blea Moor was 53 mph and the equivalent drawbar horsepower about 1,650.

We now come to the coal consumption figures for the engines engaged in the trials of 1923 to 1925. In Table IV I have shown representative performances of the Midland compounds, and this table reveals at once how exceptional the work of No 1008 was. In the trials of November and December, 1924, the new short-chimneyed engines 1065 and 1066 were involved and did well so far as weight pulling was concerned, though their basic coal consumptions of 4.33 to 4.68 lb per dhphr were much higher. No 1023, a standard Midland 7-ft compound, was also tried, with disastrous results. Her coal consumption figures were much the same as those of 1065 and 1066, but she lost time badly on all her runs.

The trials of February, 1925, were very interesting. Apparently Derby was not satisfied with the steaming of the new compounds. On engine No 1060 the blastpipe cap had been reduced from 4¾ in diameter to 4½ in, and a

TABLE IV
LMSR: LEEDS-CARLISLE DYNAMOMETER CAR TRIALS
COAL CONSUMPTION OF MIDLAND COMPOUNDS

Engine No	Date of Trial	Variety	Load, tons tare	Coal per Mile, lb	Coal per Dhp hr, lb	Evaporation lb water/ lb coal	Remarks
1008	17.12.23	Standard MR 7 ft	294*	38.1	3.64	6.88	Very fine run
1008	20.12.23	Standard MR 7 ft	226*	38.9	4.5	6.86	Light load
1008	18.12.23	Standard MR 7 ft	344*	44.1	3.73	6.51	Good run
1008	15.1.24	Standard MR 7 ft	353†	42.8	3.7	6.12	Exceptional run
1065	19.11.24	6 ft 9 in, 19¾/21¾ cyl	309‡	39.5	4.46	6.4	Good runs
1066	9.12.24	6 ft 9 in, 19¾/21¾ cyl	302‡	40.2	4.68	—	No water record
1065	20.11.24	6 ft 9 in, 19¾/21¾ cyl	358‡	44.5	4.33	6.49	—
1066	10.12.24	6 ft 9 in, 19¾/21¾ cyl	349‡	45.4	4.43	6.96	Very fine hillclimbing
1023	28.11.24	Standard MR 7 ft	354‡	43.3	4.42	—	Time lost heavily
1060	24.2.25	6 ft 9 in, 19¾/21¾ cyl	300‡	42.37	4.65	7.1	Timekeeping runs
1065	26.2.25	6 ft 9 in, 19/21 cyl	299‡	38.46	4.22	7.0	
1060	25.2.25	6 ft 9 in, 19¾/21¾ cyl	356‡	49.9	4.77	6.55	
1065	28.2.25	6 ft 9 in, 19/21 cyl	354‡	43.0	4.15	6.97	

* Leeds–Carlisle only. † Carlisle–Leeds only. ‡ Carlisle–Leeds and back

TABLE V
LMSR: LEEDS–CARLISLE DYNAMOMETER CAR TRIALS
COAL CONSUMPTION OF WEST COAST LOCOMOTIVES

Engine No	Date of Trial	Railway	Engine Type	Load, tons tare	Coal per Mile, lb	Coal per Dhp hr, lb	Evaporation, lb water/ lb coal	Remarks
388	11.12.23	LNW	'Prince of Wales'	301*	43.5	4.62	6.81 ⎫	Good
388	13.12.23	LNW	'Prince of Wales'	346*	53.9	4.96	5.91 ⎬	timekeeping
388	14.12.23	LNW	'Prince of Wales'	355†	54.5	4.39	6.43 ⎭	runs
124	26.11.24	Caledonian	Pickersgill 4–4–0	301‡	54.7	6.53	6.21	Time lost
2221	2.12.24	LNW	Std 'Claughton'	303‡	49.6	5.36	5.87 ⎫	Engine steaming
2221	5.12.24	LNW	Std 'Claughton'	355‡	58.5	4.91	5.96 ⎬	poorly
6001	13.5.30	LNW	Kylala blastpipe	309‡	38.1	3.79	7.53 ⎭	—
5973	14.5.30	LNW	Std 'Claughton'	310‡	45.5	4.64	7.57	—
6001	3.6.30	LNW	Std 'Claughton'	312‡	35.7	3.61	8.37	—
6001	4.6.30	LNW	Std 'Claughton'	316‡	35.5	3.64	8.16	—

* Leeds–Carlisle only. † Carlisle–Leeds only. ‡ Carlisle–Leeds and back

petticoat had been fitted to the underside of the chimney. This engine was put through a series of trials against No 1066, which had also been modified, by having the cylinders linered up from the standard 19¾ in and 21¾ in dia to 19 in and 21 in respectively. As will be seen from the table, No 1060 was relatively heavy on coal, though steaming very freely, while No 1065 was able to keep the schedule times of the usual two test trains even with a reduced size of cylinders. As a result of these trials it was decided to standardise on 19 in and 21 in as the cylinder diameter for the many new compounds built subsequently.

Table V gives the coal consumption figures for the engines of the West Coast companies. The North Western 'Prince,' although burning a lot of coal, had basic figures not greatly different from the compounds Nos 1060, 1065 and 1066, though it must be remembered she was judged by her performance against No 1008! The unfortunate Caledonian 4–4–0 was completely outclassed, as one would have expected it to be. A Midland class '3' engine would probably have been less effective still; yet there were engines within the LMSR group, nominally designated class '3,' of very different calibre. A North Western 'George the Fifth' in first-class condition, just out of the shops, like No 1008 was, might have produced results that would

have shaken Derby to their foundations.

Speaking of simple 4–4–0s, it is interesting to recall the very large number of runs made with the class '4' Midland engine, No 998. The 'Prince' was disposed of in a single week—December 10–14, 1923—making three return trips with 300-ton loads and two with 350 tons. The compound, No 1008, made two runs with 300-ton trains and four with 350-ton trains, but the '999' made no less than seven trips with 300-ton trains, and two with 350 tons. The coal consumption of this latter engine varied between 4.1 and 4.97 lb per dhphr, and on one occasion on the 12.10 pm up from Carlisle reached 61 lb per train mile. The official report states that this engine gave generally inferior results to those obtained with the 'Prince.'

Table V shows clearly the very poor results obtained from the 'Claughton' class 4–6–0 No 2221, *Sir Francis Dent*; but although steaming so badly there was sufficient reserve of power to run the heaviest of the test trains to time, in rough wintry weather. The trials carried out over this same route in May and June, 1930, are enough to show how unrepresentative were the results obtained from No 2221 in 1924. In 1930 the 'Claughtons' were coming into regular service on the Leeds-Carlisle route; the steaming of these engines was never as free as one could wish and No 6001 (LNWR No 23) was fitted experimentally with the 'Kylala' blastpipe, and an enlarged orifice of 6 in dia against the standard of 5 ½ in. This engine was tested against a standard 'Claughton' No 5973 (LNWR No 1741) on the same two trains used for all the previous trials. At the time of commencing the tests engine No 6001 had run 11,111 miles since last general repair, and No 5973 had run 35,894 miles. Since general repair, however, No 5973 had had a piston and valve examination, and the mileage since that was 14,713.

The series of tests began with No 6001, which steamed very freely, and gave generally an excellent performance. A coal rate of 3.79 lb per dhphr gave a very different picture from that of *Sir Francis Dent* some five years previously, when the rate was 5.36 lb. The standard engine No 5973 followed, and although she steamed well her general condition and performance was not of the best, though far superior to that shown in the 1924 trials. As the object of the trials was to assess the merits of the 'Kylala' blastpipe those responsible realised they were not comparing like for like. The condition of engine No 5973 was likely to overshadow any difference that might be attributed to the blastpipe. So the 'Kylala' apparatus was removed from No 6001; she was restored to standard condition, and a further series of trials was run. The result was an exposition of the 'Claughtons' at their best.

It will be seen from Table V that the coal consumption per dhphr was not only less than with the 'Kylala' arrangement, but equal to the very best registered with compound No 1008, in 1923–4. Note should be taken also of the high evaporation rates of 8.16 and 8.37 lb of water per lb of coal, which were better than any Midland engine produced. The compound had a considerably higher cylinder efficiency, however. These test results provide a classic example of the way in which trial runs, however comprehensive, with individual engines of a class, can give entirely misleading results. No 6001 was a superlative example of a 'Claughton,' just as No 1008 was an exceptionally good compound. On the other hand No 5973 was a run-of-the-mill engine in medium condition, and her work compares on equal terms with all compounds other than 1008 in Table IV. The Gresley Pacifics have a coal rate of about 3 lb per dhphr, and they are probably the most economical engines that have ever worked over the Settle & Carlisle road. While it would be extremely interesting to have some positive proof of this to set against all the other different locomotives featured in this article, it is extremely unlikely that any formal tests will be carried out at this late stage in the history of the steam locomotive.

West Coast Main Line — Preston to Glasgow

In my article in the March 1961 issue of *The Railway Magazine*, I appeared to have rather stirred things up a little with some comments on a somewhat controversial paper read by a distinguished American consulting engineer, H. F. Brown, at the Institution of Mechanical Engineers in London, in the previous November, on which occasion I was one of the audience. I had logged my first run with one of the class '40' diesels from Crewe to Glasgow at about the same time, and it was inevitable that I took an early opportunity to compare the results with what I had noted with steam.

I T is, perhaps, not altogether surprising that my article in the March issue of *The Railway Magazine* has brought forth an unusual amount of correspondence. A paper like that presented to the Institution of Mechanical Engineers, by Mr H. F. Brown, was bound to cause immense surprise, and consternation. The letters I have received on the subject, some from locomotive engineers of the highest standing, can be classified into three broad categories—two concerning the direct subject matter of the paper, namely, American conditions and results. The third category raises the far more vital question as to whether such a situation is likely to develop here in Great Britain. Several of my friends in the industry have met Mr Brown since the presentation of the paper, and have learnt a good deal more of the 'background' of this economic fiasco, but it is naturally the British case in which the greatest interest and concern is displayed.

In my original article referring to, and commenting on, Mr Brown's paper, I wrote, in the broadest terms, of the difference in conditions here and in America. Here, of course, the new locomotives are the outright property of British Railways and from the very outset of the modernisation plan the most careful attention has been given to the building up of a repair and maintenance organisation to ensure that every unit is kept in first-class order. I have been privileged to see something of the new repair shops at Crewe and Derby and can testify personally to the thoroughness of the new shop layouts.

At the moment, of course, there are failures both on the shed and on the road, and it is, perhaps, ironic that one of the most persistent sources of trouble on the diesel-electric main-line locomotives has been the steam-heating boiler. But to my mind the most reassuring point so far

Manchester–Glasgow express passing Tebay, hauled by 'Converted Scot' class 4-6-0 No 46145 The Duke of Wellington's Regiment (West Riding). (Derek Cross)

as British practice is concerned is the performance record of the oldest main-line diesel-electric locomotives in the country, the thirteen-year-old Nos 10000 and 10001, built for the LMSR under the direction of Mr H. G. Ivatt.

In America, as a result of Mr Brown's investigations, the New York, New Haven & Hartford Railroad applied to the High Court to amend its depreciation rates on main-line diesels to allow of an economic life of 12 to 14 years, according to type, instead of the previously-accepted 20 years. The case was very closely and severely contested, the Government of the USA opposing; but since the presentation of his paper in London, while Mr Brown was still in England, the court ruled in his favour. On the same basis the former LMSR locomotives Nos 10000 and 10001 should be just ready for scrapping; but on the contrary they are still doing excellent work and by the courtesy of Mr J. F. Harrison, Chief Mechanical Engineer of the

British Transport Commission, I am permitted to publish the economic history of these two locomotives. In so doing it should be emphasised that as prototypes they had many teething troubles to be ironed out, and that their repair costs have been considerably higher than would be experienced in a fully-developed production job like the type '4' of the 'D200' class. Despite this, however, the record of Nos 10000 and 10001 tells a very different story from that of the Americans.

Since the time of their construction—No 10000 in December, 1947, and No 10001 in July, 1948—both locomotives have run nearly 800,000 miles. Both have undergone no more than three general overhauls in that period, but what is far more important is to note the cost of repair. In both cases the cost during the incompleted fourth cycle is proving to be considerably less than during the third; this is remarkable bearing in mind that the locomotives have now run 254,605 and 301,216 miles since the third general overhaul. As these two locomotives get older the cost of overhaul, as measured in pence per mile, shows a fairly consistent trend. In the third cycle these figures were 23.5 and 24.9 pence per mile for No 10000 and 10001 respectively, while in the fourth cycle leading up to the fourth general overhaul which has yet to come, the corresponding figures are 21.9 and 20.6 pence per mile.

In the USA by the time a diesel-electric locomotive of a standard production model had been in service for ten years the aggregate cost of overhaul had usually equalled, or exceeded, the original cost of the locomotive; with Nos 10000 and 10001, despite all the initial troubles, the total amount so far spent on repairs, both classified repairs and shed maintenance, works out at 80 per cent of the original cost for No 10000 and 73 per cent for No 10001, after 13 to 14 years' service. Having regard to the fact that these locomotives were prototypes, these appear to be reassuring figures, and I am intending, in a future article, to give some performance data

showing how the diesel stud as a whole is shaping in terms of reliability in service.

In the meantime more and more express train services are being turned over to diesel haulage. At the time of writing the first of the new 'Deltics' have been running trials on the East Coast route between Kings Cross and Doncaster. No details of the trial runs have yet been made public, though with such a substantial increase in tractive power of the type '4' locomotives of the 'D200' series now in general use one can expect very fast hill climbing and some substantial acceleration of services when these locomotives are in general use. It has been announced that 22 new 'Deltics' will take the place of 55 steam Pacifics. It will need first-class

Birmingham–Glasgow express in the Lune Gorge near Tebay, hauled by 'Princess Royal' class 4-6-2 No 46210 Lady Patricia. *(Derek Cross)*

maintenance of the new power to give the availability that is required to secure such high utilisation.

From an observer who saw one of the trial trains pass through Grantham it would have seemed that the time for the 105.5 miles from Kings Cross had been 85 min at most, with a load of eleven coaches. The 'Silver Jubilee' on its first introduction in 1935 was booked to pass Grantham in 87½ min, and this timing was maintained in 1937 with the 'Coronation,' even though the tare load was increased, in the latter case, to 312 tons against 220 tons with the original streamlined train of the LNER.

At the present time the type '4' diesel-electrics are completely master of any train on the East Coast Route on present schedules, but on the West Coast, the alteration in working of the 'Midday Scot,' whereby it ceases to be a train of limited formation, has provided an extremely interesting example of diesel working. Travelling from Bristol to Glasgow in mid-February the steam workings south of Crewe provided a curious contrast to the sustained hard work that was needed once we were attached to the 'Midday Scot.' From the start a 'Castle' in excellent nick, working through from Newton Abbot to Shrewsbury, had time to kill on very leisurely schedules throughout the West to North route *via* the Severn Tunnel. The scheduled average speed over the 119.8 miles from Bristol to Shrewsbury is no more than 36 mph, and includes station stops of 3 min at Pontypool Road and 5 min at Hereford.

By far the liveliest work was done between Shrewsbury and Crewe after an unrebuilt 'Patriot' had taken over, and her 'wild-cat' scream of a whistle, in the best North Western style, was certainly a reminder of old days. The engine was No 45543 *Home Guard*, hauling a load of 390 tons gross behind the tender. We were practically stopped by signal shortly after starting, at Crewe Bank Box, and after climbing the bank at slow speed the 23.6 miles from Hadnall to Nantwich were covered in 26¼ min, with a maximum of 72 mph down the Wrenbury bank. We were stopped outside Crewe and took

no less than 13 min over the last 4½ miles in from Nantwich, but it served to brighten things up after the long dawdle from Bristol up to Shrewsbury. Even so, there was nothing startling about this 'Patriot' run in itself. As long ago as May, 1929, I clocked a Midland compound, No 1132, with 385 tons on the late evening mail leaving Shrewsbury at 10.30 pm to cover the 23.6 miles from Hadnall to Nantwich in 23¾ min. The minimum speed up the long rise to Milepost 12 was 53 mph, against 43 by the 'Patriot,' and the maximum before Nantwich was 75 mph.

At Crewe, on this recent run, diesels were changed on the 'Midday Scot,' and we went forward with a load of twelve coaches, 414 tons tare. Throughout to Glasgow this proved to be a most interesting run, and to bring out some of the more salient features I have tabulated it alongside a number of steam-hauled runs in Table I. The run with the type '4' diesel, No D268, is shown in column 6. The point for immediate notice is the relatively slow speed made up the Grayrigg and Shap inclines—slow that is in relation to the fast work that had been done between Preston and Milnthorpe. The schedule has been eased out a good deal, to permit of the heavier loading, now allowing 96 min for the 90 miles from passing Preston to the stop at Carlisle. On this trip we passed Preston 5 min late, and were slightly ahead of time on arrival.

Observance of the sectional times is shown in Table II. Time was regained between Carnforth and Oxenholme by an 'all-out' dash at the Grayrigg bank, and afterwards exact time was kept from Oxenholme to Shap Summit, although from a careful estimation of the horsepower developed it was clear that the locomotive was being worked at high power all the way, probably 'all-out,' though the drawbar horsepower figures I have calculated are a little on the low side compared with the designed power output of these locomotives. The present schedule is admirably arranged for modern power.

In North Western days the Glasgow portion of the 10 am from Euston was allowed 69 min

TABLE I
WEST COAST ROUTE: PRESTON–CARLISLE

Run No		1	2	3	4	5	6	7
Engine No		1159	6154	46241	71000	46228	D268	10001
Engine Name		Ralph Brockle-bank	The Hussar	City of Edinburgh	Duke of Gloucester	Duchess of Rutland	—	—
Engine Type		4–6–0C	4–6–0R	4–6–2D	4–6–2B	4–6–2D	DE4	DE4
Load, tons (E/F)		343/360	371/400	382/405	437/465	524/570	414/430	498/525
Dist		Actual	Actual	Actual	Actual	Actual	Actual	Actual
Miles		m s	m s	m s	m s	m s	m s	m s
0.0	PRESTON	0 00§	0 00§	0 00§	0 00§	0 00§ sig stop	0 00§ —	0 00§ sigs
4.7	Barton	6 15	7 05	6 38	7 35	—	6 26	10 37
9.5	Garstang	10 30	11 32	10 39	11 43	15 35	10 35	15 17
16.6	Galgate	16 45	18 00	16 57	17 55	22 07	16 32	—
21.0	LANCASTER	20 45	21 55	21 02	21 53	26 00 sigs	20 19 —	25 55
27.3	CARNFORTH	26 15	27 47	26 40	27 10	33 05	25 17	31 25
31.8	Burton	30 15	32 42	30 49	31 18	—	29 10	35 42
34.6	Milnthorpe	32 45	35 35	33 03	33 45	39 33	31 30	38 17
40.1	OXENHOLME	39 00 pws	42 35 —	37 59 —	39 32 —	45 35 —	37 03 —	44 44 —
47.2	Grayrigg	48 15	52 50	45 46	48 35 pws	56 21 —	46 47 —	57 25 —
53.2	Tebay	54 30	59 10	51 08	55 15	63 00	53 13	68 50 70 00
58.7	Shap Summit	61 00	68 07	57 30	67 06	70 37	62 01	84 37
72.3	PENRITH	75 15	81 47	70 24 pws	79 23 —	84 00 —	74 05 —	97 50 —
85.2	Wreay	87 15	94 13	84 13	90 43	—	84 02	sig stop
90.1	CARLISLE	93 15	100 50	89 55	96 30	100 45	90 33	119 20‡
Max speed before Lancaster, mph		71	67½	74	72	70	72½	67
Speeds at:								
Carnforth	... ...	71	63	72	72	61	78	71
Milepost 9½	... ...	60	47½	58½	57	52	60½	53
Milnthorpe	... ...	71	60	76	68	68	72	66
Oxenholme	... ...	55	43	62	54	48	51½	41
Grayrigg	... ...	checked†	37½	48½	41	34	37	29
Tebay	... ...	71	66	77	65*	64	68	—
Shap Summit	... ...	37½	24½	37	28*	30	25	23
Calculated edhp on Grayrigg Bank	... ...	1,260	1,200	1,750	1,600	1,640	1,300	1,150

* Before and after check at Tebay. † mph sustained on 1 in 131 gradient. ‡ Passing time at 15 mph
§ Times from passing Preston at 15 mph.
Engine classes: C—LNWR 'Claughton'; R—'Royal Scot' unrebuilt; D—'Duchess' class 4–6–2; B—BR 3 cyl 4–6–2 class 'B';
DE4—Diesel-electric type '4'

TABLE II
LONDON MIDLAND REGION:
PRESTON–CARLISLE
THE 'MID-DAY SCOT'

Dist			Sch	Actual	
Miles			min	m	s
0.0	PRESTON	... ...	0*	0	00*
1.3	Oxheys Box	... ...	3	2	27
9.5	Garstang	... ...	11	10	35
21.0	LANCASTER	... ...	21	20	19
27.3	CARNFORTH	... ...	26	25	17
40.1	Oxenholme	... ...	40	37	03
53.2	Tebay	... ...	56	53	13
58.7	Shap Summit	... ...	65	62	01
72.3	PENRITH	... ...	78	74	05
77.1	Plumpton	... ...	82	77	49
			†		
90.1	CARLISLE	... ...	96	90	33

* Times from passing Preston at 15 mph
† 1 min recovery time Plumpton to Carlisle

from Preston to Shap Summit, but the difference from the present 65 min was made up entirely between Preston and Carnforth. The uphill times showed one minute less than today between Carnforth and Oxenholme, the same allowance up to Tebay, and a minute more on the final pull to Shap Summit. Drivers were thus encouraged to nurse their engines on the easier stretches, and then go really hard uphill. This practice became thoroughly characteristic of LNWR working over Shap, and on run after run every effort was made to keep strict sectional time over the mountain section.

The diesel, No D268, in keeping the fast sectional time from Oxheys to Carnforth sustained a maximum speed of 72½ mph on the level between Garstang and the approach to Lancaster. Taking a coach resistance of 11 lb per ton, this would be equal to a drawbar horsepower of about 920. On the last stages of the Shap incline, and again up Beattock, the equivalent dhp at 27 mph comes out at about 1,300.

Contrasting with this, one of the most striking examples of the old traditions that I can find is a run on the 10 am from Euston in the autumn of 1915. The schedule then in operation, of 159 min from Crewe to Carlisle, had persisted

from the days when the usual load of the train was about 200 tons, and the engine a non-superheater 4-6-0 of the 'Experiment' class. It remained unchanged in the early years of the war even after the Glasgow and Edinburgh sections of the train had been combined, and the load was over 400 tons tare daily! On this schedule the load for the 'Claughtons' was 420 tons as far as Tebay, and it was apparently left to the driver's discretion afterwards whether he tackled Shap unassisted, or not.

On this particular journey the tare load was 416 tons, and, with a crowded passenger complement, about 440 tons full. In the early stages of the run delays were experienced from wartime traffic, but north of Preston the road was clear, and despite bad weather conditions the driver kept the sectional times comfortably to Carnforth. Speed was sustained at 60 mph on the level north of Garstang, this representing an output of about 650 dhp. Then, for the mountain section, came the most astonishing opening out, and between Oxenholme and Grayrigg the edhp was between 1,150 and 1,250 continuously. Speed was sustained at 37½ mph on the 1 in 131 stretch of the bank, and at 34 over Grayrigg Summit. With the weather continuing adverse, however, the driver judged it wise to stop for rear-end banking assistance from Tebay to Shap Summit.

Run No 1, in Table I, is the very fast dynamometer car trial run made on this same train in November, 1913, with engine No 1159, *Ralph Brocklebank*. Even on this run the power output on the Grayrigg bank was no greater than on the wartime run just mentioned. On the test run the going had been a good deal harder from Preston and the values of indicated horsepower varying between 992 and 1,206 had been recorded before Carnforth. Then the effort was stepped up with a vengeance and the eight sets of indicator diagrams taken between there and Shap Summit gave values, successively, of 1,504, 1,407, 1,494, 1,526, 1,669, 1,606, 1,593 and 1,496. The last named was taken just before Shap Summit, at the remarkable minimum speed of 37½ mph. The second run in Table I shows the same characteristic, in a quieter and more normal form. This was a trip of my own on the 'Royal Scot,' in 1933, when on a good time-keeping run a most vigorous climb was made of the upper part of Grayrigg bank. The speed was no more than 60 mph at Milnthorpe, and was down to 43 mph as early as Oxenholme, yet the fall in speed afterwards was only 5½ mph by *The Hussar*, against 14½ mph by the type '4' diesel in column 6.

Run No 3 is the magnificent run of the *City of Edinburgh* on the 'Birmingham Scotch' that I discussed at some length in the September, 1960, article, when the edhp on Grayrigg bank was 1,750. Even so, this engine did no more than equal the record assault upon Shap made by *Ralph Brocklebank*, in column 1. The fourth journey was an interesting example of the work of the one and only 'BR8' Pacific No 71000, *Duke of Gloucester*, on the 'Midday Scot' at a period when the schedule allowed 99 min from passing Preston to the stop at Carlisle. The recovery from the Preston slack was slower than that of the diesel, and the engine was eased considerably after a maximum speed of 72 mph had been attained at Brock troughs. But after Lancaster some excellent work was done, gaining on the diesel considerably with a minimum speed of 41 mph over Grayrigg. The permanent way restriction checked speed down to 25 mph at Tebay, but up Shap the engine recovered in fine style to a sustained 28 mph, putting forth an edhp of 1,550 in the process. I am indebted to Mr W. Robertson, of Glasgow, for details of this run.

I now come to the fine run detailed in column 5, which was recorded from the footplate by Baron Vuillet on one of his ever-welcome visits to this country. The load was exceptionally heavy for this road, but it was tackled with supreme confidence by Driver Pape and Fireman Gillespie of Polmadie. After the signal

Birmingham–Glasgow express just north of Tebay hauled by 'Princess Royal' class 4-6-2 No 46210 Lady Patricia. (Rail Archive Stephenson, D.M.C. Hepburne-Scott)

Anglo–Scottish express climbing Beattock Bank with engine No 46226 Duchess of Norfolk *and a bank engine in the rear.* (Rail Archive Stephenson, D.M.C. Hepburne-Scott)

stop just north of Preston, speed rose to 70 mph on the level after Garstang, but the approach to the mountain section was hindered by a check before Carnforth, which prevented any higher speed than 61 mph before tackling the rise to Burton. Fine work was done up Grayrigg bank, with cut-off advanced from 25 per cent on passing Oxenholme to 30 per cent near Hay Fell, and finally to 32 per cent to sustain 34 mph over the summit. Boiler pressure at no time fell below 225 lb per sq in and the water level was maintained high in the glass. As usual with the 'Duchesses' the fire was maintained thick at the back, and fed 'little and often.'

Good though the work was up the Grayrigg bank it was put completely in the shade by a terrific attack upon Shap. Tebay was passed at 64 mph, and then, while the speed was still 60 mph on the 1 in 146 approach grade, the reverser was put into 32 per cent with full regulator. Over the four miles of 1 in 75 gradient the average values of edhp work out at 2,305, 2,360, 2,065 and 1,800, and the five miles bet-

ween Mileposts 32¼ and 37¼ were covered in the astonishing time—with a 570-ton load (!)—of 6 min 47 sec. The time of 7 min 42 sec from Tebay to Shap Summit was extraordinary, but was achieved without any appreciable mortgaging of the boiler. Baron Vuillet was most careful to note the water level during the ascent, which remained practically constant, and boiler pressure fell slightly from 220 at Tebay to 215 lb per sq in at the summit. Cut-off was advanced finally to 43 per cent.

Just at the time I was completing this article I enjoyed another fine trip over this route, on the 11 am from Birmingham, and the running on the mountain section was strikingly similar. With engine No 46235, *City of Birmingham*, and a load of 530 tons gross we took 11 min from Oxenholme to Grayrigg, against 10 min 46 sec on Baron Vuillet's run, and charged Shap in much the same style. From Milepost 32¼ to 37¼ our time was 7 min 8 sec, and our average edhp figures over the four miles previously quoted were 2,165, 2,075, 1,670, and 1,595. Although not quite so meritorious as the run recorded by Baron Vuillet it was an exhilarating experience, especially as we had left Crewe 10 min late, and reached Carlisle 2 min early. It was in any case another example of 'Duchess' performance far in excess of anything that could be obtained with the type '4' diesel-electrics. The similarity of the running to that in Baron Vuillet's journey suggested to me that we might have had the same driver; but I ascertained from the guard that this was not so.

In view of the earlier discussion about the deterioration of diesel-electric locomotives the last run in the table is of particular interest with engine No 10001. It was made in 1951, it is true, but shows how a heavy, moderately-timed train can be worked by a diesel, driven all-out. This run was made on the 9.10 pm Glasgow 'sleeper' calling only at Kingmoor No 1 Box to re-man. The booked point-to-point time from Preston to Carlisle was 114 min, with 32 min to Carnforth, and 49 min from this latter point up to Shap Summit. The train passed Preston only 1¾ min late, and then after a signal check costing about 3 min No 10001 did some excellent work with this 525-ton train, sustaining 67 mph on the level north of Garstang, and passing Oxenholme 2½ min early. It was, of course, no more than natural that Grayrigg should take its toll, and the minimum was 29 mph. The speed was still slightly falling at the summit, which indicates that the edhp was something under 1,200. Whether an attempt would have been made to take Shap unassisted I do not know, but the train was brought to a dead stand by signals south of Tebay, and in such conditions it was imperative to take the bank engine. In any case the locomotive had been working all-out the whole way from Preston to Grayrigg Summit.

Passing now to the Caledonian part of the journey, the continuation from Carlisle of No D268's run of the 'Midday Scot' is shown in Table III. The initial allowance of 10 min to pass Gretna Junction, 8.6 miles, is very sharp, and we lost nearly a minute here. Then the sectional times were closely observed to Beattock Summit, with the locomotive working at full

TABLE III
SCOTTISH REGION: 6.40 pm
CARLISLE–GLASGOW
THE 'MIDDAY SCOT'

Load: 12 coaches, 414 tons tare, 430 tons full
Engine: Type '4' diesel-electric No D268

Dist			Sch	Actual		Speeds
Miles			min	m	s	mph
0.0	CARLISLE ...	...	0	0	00	—
4.1	*Rockcliffe*	...		6	12	—
8.6	Gretna Junc	...	10	10	50	63
13.1	Kirkpatrick	...		15	41	50*
16.7	Kirtlebridge	...		19	30	65
20.1	Ecclefechan...	...		22	55	58
22.7	*Castlemilk* ...	...		25	45	52
25.8	LOCKERBIE	...	27	28	35	72
28.7	Nethercleugh	...		30	57	75
31.7	Dinwoodie ...	...		33	21	75/72
34.5	Wamphray ...	...		35	38	75
39.7	BEATTOCK	...	39	40	05	60
45.4	*Greskine Box* ...	...		48	44	28
49.7	*Beattock Summit* ...		57	58	00	27
52.6	Elvanfoot ...	...		61	04	73
57.8	Abington ...	...		65	21	75
63.2	Lamington ...	...		69	28	82
66.9	SYMINGTON ...	...		72	17	—
73.5	CARSTAIRS ...	...	78	77	45	55
—	*Craigenhill Box* ...	...	—			51 min
84.0	Law Junc ...	...	89	89	30	slack
89.4	MOTHERWELL ...		96	97	02	—
				pws		
93.9	Uddingston ...	...	100	102	07	—
—				pws		
98.3	*Rutherglen Junc* ...		106	107	15	—
—				sigs		
102.3	GLASGOW CENT		115	117	15	—

*Min speed above Kirkpatrick

power. Again one notes the fast running over the easier stretches of line, with a fall to a relatively low minimum speed on Beattock bank. The speed was sustained at 27 to 28 mph over the 4¼ miles from Greskine Box to the summit, and this shows an edhp of about 1,330. With a load of 414 tons, however, there seemed to be nothing in reserve on this booking, and I understand that the use of two type '4' diesels in multiple-unit is not unusual on this train. Downhill speeds were brisk but the 2-min recovery time between Rutherglen Junction and Eglinton Street was insufficient to offset the checks that were experienced north of Motherwell and 2¼ min was dropped on the overall time from Carlisle.

TABLE IV
SCOTTISH REGION: GLASGOW–CARLISLE
THE 'MIDDAY SCOT'

Load: 13 coaches, 444 tons tare, 465 tons full
Engine: 4-6-2 No 46251, *City of Nottingham*

Dist		Sch	Actual		Speeds
Miles		min.	m	s	mph
0.0	GLASGOW CENT	0	0	00	—
3.1	Rutherglen		6	31	47
—			pws		—
6.6	Newton	10	11	03	—
8.4	Uddingston ...	13	13	44	43
—			sigs		—
12.9	MOTHERWELL ...	18	20	32	sig
			21	29	stop
14.0	Flemington		25	01	38
15.9	Wisham South ...		28	22	34
18.3	Law Junc	26	32	20	36
20.4	Carluke		35	45	42/35
23.8	*Craigenhill Box* ...		41	08	41
26.5	*Lanark Junc* ...	36	44	08	60
28.8	CARSTAIRS ...	39	46	49	46
32.3	*Leggatfoot Box* ...		50	54	56/53
33.8	Thankerton ...		52	29	62
35.4	SYMINGTON ...		54	09	56
39.1	Lamington		57	40	69
41.9	*Wandelmill Box* ...		60	08	70/67
44.5	Abington		62	20	74
47.0	Crawford		64	28	68
49.7	Elvanfoot		66	45	73
52.6	*Beattock Summit* ...	63	69	18	64
56.9	*Greskine Box* ...		72	28	91
62.6	BEATTOCK ...	73	75	54	105
67.8	Wamphray		79	07	93
70.6	Dinwoodie		80	57	88
73.6	Nethercleugh ...		83	09	77
76.5	LOCKERBIE ...	85	85	25	77
79.6	*Castlemilk Sdgs* ...		88	04	64
—			pws		52
82.2	Ecclefechan ...		90	24	—
85.6	Kirtlebridge ...		93	38	71/68
89.2	Kirkpatrick ...		96	49	70
92.1	*Quintinshill Box* ...		99	18	70
93.7	Gretna Junc ...	99	100	38	70
—			pws		40
98.2	*Rockcliffe* ...		105	47	—
102.3	CARLISLE	111	112	10	—

Net time about 105 min

Since I took over the authorship of these articles I have had the pleasure, on numerous occasions, of publishing details of very fine work by Sir William Stanier's 'Duchess' class 4-6-2s; but I do not think there has been anything so brilliant, or outrightly thrilling, as the trip I am about to describe now. It was made in January, 1959, on the up 'Midday Scot,' and with the lapse of time, and with the agreement of the young Scottish friend who recorded the details so carefully what happened may now be revealed. The 'Midday Scot' then had the sharp timing of 111 min non-stop for the 102.3 miles from Glasgow Central to Carlisle—sharp, that is, seeing that then the train regularly loaded to over 400 tons tare. On this occasion the load was 'thirteen,' 444 tons tare, behind engine No 46251, *City of Nottingham*.

The run began normally, with no more than a moderate slack over the Newton 'pitfall' that has been such a nuisance in recent years. Then, however, came a dead stand for signals at Motherwell, on the heaviest part of the long ascent to Craigenhill Box. Although the train stood for less than a minute a stop in such a locality must have cost at least 3½ min, probably more. On getting the road this heavy load was lifted off the mark in great style on the 1 in 116 gradient, passing Flemington, 1.1 miles, in 3 min 32 sec, and accelerating rapidly to 38 mph on the subsequent stretch of 1 in 137. As usual, however, the long and relatively-sharp curve at Garriongill Junction lowered the speed somewhat, and averaging 37½ mph over the rest of the climb from Law Junction to Craigenhill the train was 8 min late past Lanark Junction. The booked time of 10 min for the 8.2 miles from Law Junction to the former point is exceptionally severe, and 1¾ min were dropped by the engine over this section.

It was after Symington that a really phenomenal effort to recover the lost time began in earnest. On the descent to the Clyde viaduct near Lamington, speed rose to 69 mph and it was about this point that the engine was evidently opened out. Over the remaining 13.5 miles to Beattock Summit the gradient averages 1 in 215,

On the Three Summits railtour in June 1963, 'Duchess' class 4-6-2 No 46255 City of Hereford *near Lamington in the Clyde Valley.* (Derek Cross)

yet such was the effort put forth that speed averaged 69.5 mph over this length. There was an uphill acceleration at one point to 74 mph at Abington, and after a fall to nothing less than 68 mph on the 1½ miles at 1 in 142–152 after Crawford speed rose again to 73 mph at Elvanfoot. The last 2¼ miles up to Beattock Summit, inclined at 1 in 99, were cleared at a minimum speed of 64 mph. This tremendous running involved a continuous output of between 2,100 and 2,200 edhp and a firing rate well above the 3,000 lb per hr regarded as the maximum to be expected for any appreciable time from a single fireman. Yet so far barely 2 min had been won back—such were the demands of the 'Midday Scot' schedule.

On passing Beattock Summit barely 42 min remained in which to cover the 49.7 miles to Carlisle, that is if a punctual arrival was to be made. There were two moderate permanent way checks to be observed, and a stretch of downhill road where speed was then temporarily limited to 70 mph, so that altogether the prospect was not very favourable. Believe it or not, however, the train was practically on time *by Lockerbie*! In my article for March, 1960, I wrote of the traditionally 'canny' descents of the Beattock Bank made by Caledonian drivers; the details of this astonishing run certainly make me eat my words, for it was the work of a Polmadie driver. By Greskine, the speed was 91 mph, and thenceforward, without the slightest hesitancy or easing, the *City of Nottingham* was allowed to sweep downhill till a maximum of 105 mph was reached near Beattock Station.

The factors that make possible such high-speed running are worth careful consideration. On such a steep descent as the Beattock bank the power required from the locomotive would be very small indeed, in fact, it would be a measure of the ability of the engine itself to attain such a speed. Internal resistances would predominate over any matters of power output. Then again the riding qualities of the particular engine would contribute in no small measure. No driver, however keen he may have been to make up time, would have allowed a rolling, lurching engine to attain such a speed; and it is, of course, a magnificent tribute to the standards of permanent way maintenance. From the way the speed fell away once the easier gradients were reached I would hazard a guess that the controls were untouched; that the bank was descended in light steaming conditions, without any hindrance, and that things continued thus until the brakes were applied for the Ecclefechan slack.

From the foot of the incline at the crossing of Annan, the speed gradually fell away to 88 mph at Dinwoodie, 77 at Lockerbie, and 64 at Castlemilk automatic signals. Some of the averages make exciting reading, such as 98 mph from Greskine Box to Wamphray; 89 mph from Beattock Summit to Lockerbie; or still more extraordinary 81 mph throughout from Lamington to Lockerbie including the climb over Beattock Summit! As a result of this thrilling exposition of the speedworthiness of these engines the train was less than half a minute late through Lockerbie. It was certainly unfortunate after such an exhibition of superb uphill effort, and fast running downhill, that the run could not be rounded off with an on-time arrival in Carlisle; but the speed restrictions at the southern end of the line were all carefully observed, and with this restraint the train was 1¼ min late in. My correspondent alighted at Carlisle, otherwise it would have been interesting to see how this very keen driver and fireman dealt with Shap.

When I was in the north in April this year another Scottish friend handed me details of yet another magnificent performance over the Caledonian line, this time on the up 'Royal Scot,' with engine No 46239, *City of Chester*, and the usual eight-coach train of 274 tons tare. There was no need for any exceptional downhill speed on this trip, for after a series of permanent way checks in the early stages the driver got such an effort from the engine as to pass Beattock Summit 4 min early, having averaged 77.6 mph up the 13½ miles of ascent from Lamington, and cleared the summit at exactly 75 mph! Steam may be on the way out on the West Coast Route, but the 'Duchesses' seem to be doing finer work than ever before.

'9F' tests, including the Somerset & Dorset

The British standard heavy freight engines of the 2–10–0 type were one of the only instances of the councils of the mechanical engineering department of the Railway Executive being seriously divided. Bond and Cox wanted the engine to be a 2–8–2, to use a maximum of parts, including the boiler, interchangeable with the 'Britannia' Pacifics. But Riddles, having designed a 2–10–0 for wartime service with the 'WD', favoured that wheel arrangement, and his view prevailed. The 'BR9s' were remarkable engines, though why the continued building of them once the 'Modernisation Plan' was launched is indeed a mystery.

IN March, 1960, at Swindon Works, the completion of the last steam locomotive to be built for British Railways was signalised by a ceremony that must have been saddening to the majority present, and no less to railway enthusiasts all over the world. The end of the line had long been foreseen, and accepted as inevitable, but the occasion was none the less moving when it actually arrived. Since then several readers have asked whether it would be possible to present, in these columns, a kind of Alpha and Omega of British steam locomotive performance, extending from *Locomotion* to *Evening Star*. Even if one could unearth enough information about Stockton & Darlington running in its early days, the latter end of the story would not be entirely representative, for the '9Fs,' despite their occasional flights at 90 mph, do not lie in the very top class of express passenger service—nor could one expect them to do so! Nevertheless the '9Fs' can, without hesitation, be set down as an outstandingly successful class.

For some time past I have been endeavouring to collect details of a series of performances from them in various classes of service, passenger and freight; and although I have not obtained so far quite such a variety as I had hoped for, the results are enough to show very clearly what manner of engine the '9F' is. It was designed primarily as a freight engine. For some time there was considerable discussion in the higher engineering councils of the British Transport Commission as to whether the wheel arrangement should be 2–8–2 or 2–10–0. In support of the 2–8–2 was argued the increased flexibility of wheelbase. On the other hand the very successful 'WD' 2–10–0s had not suffered from any trouble in this respect. So 2–10–0 it became, and there can have been little cause for regrets ever since.

It is interesting to compare the basic dimensions of the '9F' with those of the 'WD' 2-10-0, as Mr R. A. Riddles was responsible for both designs:

	'WD' 2-10-0	'BR9' 2-10-0
Cylinder, dia stroke (in)	19×28	20×28
Coupled wheels, dia (ft in)	4–8½	5–0
Heating surface (sq ft)		
tubes	1,759	1,836
firebox	192	179
superheater ...	423	535
total	2,374	2,550
Grate area (sq ft)	40	40.2
Boiler pressure (psi)	225	250
Nom te, at 85% bp (lb)	34,215	39,667
Max axle load (tons)	13.45	15.5
Adhesion weight (tons)	67.15	77.5
Total engine weight (tons)	78.3	86.7

As originally built, the British Railways '9F' had a single orifice blastpipe, and although some slight adjustments were made to the diameter of the orifice to secure improved draughting it was as a single-chimneyed design that three locomotives of the class were tested, partly on the stationary plant at Rugby and partly on controlled road tests from Carlisle. Some of these latter tests were carried out with the mobile test units built by the former London, Midland & Scottish Railway, at constant speeds, and others with trains of ordinary stock at constant steaming rates. In view of what happened on the line when some of these engines were used in ordinary passenger service it was amusing to read in the official bulletin: 'During the tests on the line, although no controlled tests were carried out at more than 55 mph, speeds of 60 mph were attained and the riding of the locomotive up to that speed was found to be excellent.'

Although the performance was amply adequate for the freight service in which the locomotives were originally engaged, it cannot be said that the power outputs attained were anything out of the ordinary—compared in particular with those obtained with the 'Britannia' class Pacifics. Working right up to the front-end limit of the boiler the maximum drawbar horsepower established in this series of tests was 1,780, at a speed of 35 mph working in 45 per cent cut-off with full regulator. At 55 mph the dhp had fallen away to 1,675, requiring a cut-off of 32 per cent. The corresponding figures for indicated horsepower at 35 and 55 mph were 1,970 and 2,060 respectively. These figures were obtained

One of the War Department 2-10-0s built by the North British Locomotive Co, No 73798, named North British, *with R.A. Riddles and A. Black of NBL standing in front.* (NB Loco Co)

with a steam rate of 30,000 lb per hr and a coal consumption of 4,530 lb per hr or 82.5 lb per train mile at 55 mph. To sustain such an output required two firemen. At the maximum coal rate for one fireman, namely 3,000 lb per hr, the maximum drawbar horsepower of 1,355 occurred at 30–35 mph, and at this same firing rate the dhp at 55 mph was 1,220. All these figures were obtained with Blidworth coal.

Some of the constant speed tests were carried out on the Glasgow & South Western main line between Carlisle and Hurlford, while others were run southwards from Carlisle to Skipton. One of the controlled road tests at the maximum coal rate for one fireman was made with a trailing load of 642 tons, consisting of dynamometer car, passenger brake van, two 20-ton brake vans, and 25 loaded 16-ton fitted mineral wagons. The test began 1½ miles south of Appleby, where the train was travelling at 50 mph. From there, the 16.3 miles to Aisgill summit took exactly 30 min. The log of this interesting test is shown in Table I:

TABLE I

Dist		Time from start of test		Speeds
Miles		m	s	mph
0.0	Milepost 276 (pass)	0	00	50
1.3	Ormside ...	1	25	55
4.3	Milepost 271¾	6	15	29
6.3	Crosby Garrett	9	55	40
9.5	Kirkby Stephen	15	15	28/30
12.0	Milepost 264	20	40	25
13.0	Milepost 263	22	45	33
16.3	Aisgill Box (pass)	30	00	23

The drawbar horsepower was at its maximum near Crosby Garrett, at about 1,300, while on the long final pull at 1 in 100 up to Aisgill summit it was steady at 1,100. This was the actual pull registered in the dynamometer car. Correcting this for gradient the edhp would be approximately 1,300. Although this run was made with a train of freight vehicles these were all vacuum fitted with couplings screwed tight. The figure of 642 tons quoted is the gross load behind the tender.

Arising from the comprehensive tests carried out, the bulletin includes examples of the performance to be expected with various loadings of freight trains. As the sustained speeds on various gradients that are predicted are of special interest, I have picked out some typical examples for tabulation herewith. All the examples quoted in the bulletin are related to trains of loaded 16-ton mineral wagons, and the table shows the predicted performance in three conditions of engine working: (a) at front-end limit of boiler; (b) at maximum firing rate for one fireman

600-TON TRAIN
Speeds (mph) on various gradients

Gradient 1 in	Steaming conditions		
	Max efficiency	Max firing rate for one man	At front-end limit
80	15	21½	27½
100	18	26	32½
150	27	34	41
200	32	39	46

800-TON TRAIN
Speeds (mph) on various gradients

Gradient 1 in	Steaming conditions		
	Max efficiency	Max firing rate for one man	At front-end limit
120	15	23½	30
200	25	32½	39½
300	32	38	45
Level	47	53	57

1,000-TON TRAIN
Speeds (mph) on various gradients

Gradient 1 in	Steaming conditions		
	Max efficiency	Max firing rate for one man	At front-end limit
150	15	23	29
200	20	28	34
300	27	33½	40
Level	42½	47	53

(3,000 lb of coal per hr); and (c) at minimum coal consumption per dhph.

Condition (c) lies about mid-way between maximum and low rates for firing, and corresponds to running on cut-offs of about 20 per cent at 50 mph down to 30 per cent at 20 mph. Like all the BR standard locomotives the coal rate per dhph is quite low, showing, at the most economical rates, a value of about 2.4 lb per dhph. The three accompanying tables relate to trailing loads of 600, 800 and 1,000 tons—all made up of 16-ton mineral wagons.

One last point of interest to be mentioned in connection with the published bulletin is the running resistance of the 16-ton loaded mineral wagons as compared with that of passenger stock. The following table shows the relative figures when running into a 7½ mph head-wind blowing at 45 deg to the line of railway:

Speed (mph)	Resistance (lb per ton)	
	16-ton loaded mineral wagons	Bogie passenger stock
20	4.2	4.1
30	6.0	5.2
40	8.4	6.5
50	11.0	8.0

Following these tests engine No 92178 was fitted with a double blastpipe and chimney, and some trials were carried out with the Western Region dynamometer car and trains of empty coaching stock between Reading and Stoke Gifford. By the courtesy of Mr R. A. Smeddle, Chief Mechanical & Electrical Engineer, Western Region, I was privileged to accompany one of these tests, travelling in the dynamometer car on a day when a huge load of 19 vehicles was conveyed, 632 tons tare behind the tender. I was not able to travel on the outward journey, and instead joined the train at Stoke Gifford sidings some little time before it was scheduled to start on the return trip.

It was evident that the test staff had had something of a rough trip on the way down. The engine was being fired with Blidworth coal of rather poor quality, and a layer of clinker about 1½ in thick was forming over the fire. While the engine was being steamed hard this blanket of clinker was carried in suspension, but, to quote one of the engineers concerned, 'it knocked the steaming for six.' They had not a single bag of coal left on arrival at Stoke Gifford, and they then proceeded to heave what seemed *tons* of clinker out of the firebox before the return journey.

The steam rate on the run back to Reading was to be 22,000 lb per hr, and starting away with a bright, clean fire the going at first was very good. Up the continuous 1 in 300 to Badminton speed rose to a sustained 45 mph, giving a drawbar horsepower, uncorrected, of 1,150 to 1,170. Badminton, 11.5 miles, was passed in 20 min 10 sec—a precisely similar start to that of the GWR 4-6-0 No 6001, *King Edward VII*, when that engine was steamed at 30,000 lb per hr to haul a tremendous train of 796 tons. On the latter occasion the time to Badminton was 20 min 6 sec, and the intermediate times showed correspondence to within a few odd seconds at each timing point. After Badminton, however, the 2-10-0 was not allowed to attain any high speeds—more's the pity! Sixty miles per hour was laid down as the maximum for this particular run, and once this was being approached the brakes were gradually applied, and the cut-off increased accordingly so as to keep the rate of steaming constant throughout. As to maximum speeds my friends in the dynamometer car told me that during some of the trial runs speeds up to nearly 75 mph had been attained, and that No 92178 had ridden well at such speeds.

On this trip, after reaching 60 mph at Alderton Tunnel, about mid-way between Badminton and Hullavington, the brakes were applied, and speed brought down to 21 mph while steaming hard on a descending 1 in 300 gradient. There were self-imposed checks afterwards to 31 mph at Wootton Bassett, to 22 at Shrivenham, to 32 at Wantage Road, and to 29 before Didcot, from each of which the engine accelerated very freely and easily. Even before Swindon, however, the poor coal was once again

Last of the British Railways '9F' 2-10-0s No 92250. (British Railways)

having its effect, and from Shrivenham to the end of the test at Milepost 45½ we never had more than 175 lb per sq in in the boiler. To keep the steaming rate constant, longer cut-offs had to be used, and just before the conclusion of the test it was requiring 30 per cent cut-off to keep this 632-ton train running at 62 mph on level track. The boiler pressure was then no more than 165 lb per sq in. We finished in rather better form than on the outward trip, having four bags left; but the approximate coal consumption had been 4,200 lb per hr—a very big increase over the 3,000 lb per hr established in the earlier tests for one of these engines steamed at 22,000 lb per hr. This journey was a most illuminating experience for me, as showing what an enormous increase in the physical labour of firing can be caused by indifferent fuel and rapidly deteriorating conditions in the firebox. With such coal there is no doubt we should have been in far worse straits but for the double blastpipe fitted to engine No 92178. The log of this interesting journey is shown in Table II.

One of the most interesting regular passenger workings set to these locomotives has come during the period of the summer service on the Somerset & Dorset Joint line between Bath and

TABLE II
WESTERN REGION:
STOKE GIFFORD–READING
Dynamometer Car Test Run
Load: 19 vehicles, 632 tons tare, 635 tons full
Engine: Class '9F' 2–10–0, No 92178

Dist		Actual	Speeds
Miles		m s	mph
0.0	*Stoke Gifford East Box*	0 00	—
1.6	Winterbourne ...	5 29	31
6.9	Chipping Sodbury	14 04	42
11.5	Badminton	20 10	45
—		brakes	60 (max)
17.3	Hullavington ...	26 49	37
—		brakes	21
21.8	Little Somerford	34 12	60 (max)
—		brakes	—
28.6	Wootton Bassett	41 55	31
34.2	SWINDON ...	49 14	53
—		brakes	60 (max)
40.0	Shrivenham ...	57 02	22
42.5	*Knighton Crossing*	61 16	49
47.6	Challow ...	66 44	63
—		brakes	32
51.1	Wantage Road ...	71 45	41
—		brakes	29
58.4	DIDCOT ...	82 09	50½
63.0	*Milepost 48½* ...	87 00	62
72.8	Tilehurst ...	97 49	—
75.5	READING (Goods Line)	106 17	—

A '9F' 2-10-0 No 92078 on a train of coal empties near Bushey. (British Railways)

Bournemouth. The very severe gradients of this route, combined with curvature, and the incidence of tunnels in awkward places, has provided a serious motive power problem for many years. Until quite recently every train of more than eight coaches required double-heading between Bath and Evercreech Junction, and on summer Saturdays there were times when the resources of the line, both in locomotives and in crews, were strained to the utmost. It was hoped that use of the Bulleid 'West Country' Pacifics would enable loads up to ten coaches to be taken without assistance; but these engines proved so prone to slipping on the heavy gradients that their load was finally fixed at 'eight,' the same as that of the class '5' 4-6-0s of Stanier and BR design. At times of the heaviest traffic the old Somerset & Dorset 2-8-0 freight engines were used in passenger service. These stalwarts could be relied on to take ten coaches up the banks without assistance, and their use eased the position on Saturdays in the height of the summer.

But as regular passenger locomotives this could not be regarded as satisfactory, and in any case they were required for freight service during the week.

During the past summer four of the '9F' 2-10-0s have been allocated to Bath Midland shed, and they have done much good work. I do not think, however, that there can have been a finer performance than that of Friday, July 14, with the southbound 'Pines Express.' The physical conditions could scarcely have been worse, with a high westerly wind and heavy rain. Furthermore, while previous regular engines have been limited to eight coaches on the service, the 2-10-0s are rostered to take no less than 410 tons tare. The train was wired on this occasion as 'twelve' for 416 tons. In every other respect, however, the circumstances could not have been more propitious. That most experienced of observers, Baron G. Vuillet, had a footplate pass, and in Driver Donald Beale and Fireman Peter Smith of Branksome shed he had a crew of exceptional keenness and ability. It only needed the cheerful presence of Headquarters Locomotive Inspector Darrell Smith to

Dynamometer car trials with a '9F' 2-10-0 working from Swindon: an eastbound trial trip shortly after leaving Stoke Gifford yard. (Ivo Peters)

complete a notable party on the footplate. I am only sorry that other matters prevented me from witnessing anything more than the start out of Bath. Baron Vuillet has been kind enough to send me very complete details of what proved to be a most remarkable trip.

To appreciate what is entailed in the working of a 450-ton train over the Somerset & Dorset line, considerably more than a mere study of the gradient profile is needed. The very start from Bath is exceptionally difficult, climbing at 1 in 50 at once from Bath Junction, round what Driver Beale had aptly described to his guests as 'a hairpin bend.' Then comes the villainous single-line bore of Devonshire Tunnel on the continuation of the 1 in 50; to sample the joys of this inferno to the full, however, one must ride on the second engine of a double-header! Fortunately the summit of the 1 in 50 is reached at the entrance to the much longer tunnel under Combe Down. Then, what appears to be a stretch of 'give and take' on to Radstock is for the most part so sharply curved as to permit of no fast running, and the severe speed restriction over the curve through Radstock itself comes precisely at the foot of the

main climb, where the gradient is 1 in 50–53 with only the slightest intermissions for the four miles. It is small wonder that the haulage of southbound trains out of Bath has always been treated with the greatest respect, although the load limits so far as the class '5' 4–6–0s are concerned are no more severe than those laid down for the same engines on the worst stretches of the Highland main line, or over the Callander & Oban line. It is the Bulleid Pacifics that succumbed to the local conditions more seriously.

In a storm of wind and rain, the 'Pines Express' got away from Bath 12½ min late. After saying farewell to my friends on the footplate I stayed on the platform for a few minutes chatting to Mr Morris, the Shedmaster, and we heard the exhaust of No 92000 sharp and clear as she rounded the 'hairpin-bend' and headed southeastwards for Devonshire Tunnel. She sounded in good fettle, and not many days were to pass before I learned how exceedingly good she had been. On that first length of 1 in 50 she had been worked with regulator full open, and cut-off gradually increased from 35 to 42 per cent; speed was sustained at 24 mph, and in this first spell of hard pounding the boiler pressure was nicely maintained at 235–245 lb per sq in. Incidentally the engine was being fired with ovoids. One knows only too well how a spell of very hard working at the immediate start of a run can knock the fire 'for six' if it is indulged in carelessly, and I have seen some of the most expert of enginemen severely handicapped for half an hour, or more, through a bad spell in starting up a steep bank. No such trouble occurred on the footplate of No 92000, and Radstock was approached in great form for the climb over the Mendips.

As the log detailed in Table III shows, there was a loss of 30 sec on the point-to-point time from Midford to Radstock, but then came a remarkable climb to Masbury summit. The really severe length is contained in the four miles between Mileposts 10¾ and 14¾, where the gradient is almost continuously at 1 in 50–53; but above Midsomer Norton the track enters upon a positively serpentine course, climbing up the exposed hillside, and on this day catching the full force of the wind broadside on. Baron Vuillet has calculated that the effect of the curves is to increase the severity of the actual average inclination of 1 in 56 to one of 1 in 52½ for the whole four miles. From the speed of 37 mph just after Radstock speed at first fell off very slowly. Cut-off was increased to 35 per cent approaching Midsomer Norton, and nearing the end of the straight length beyond that station, while the speed was still 28½ mph, cut-off was further increased to 40 per cent. Boiler pressure was held rock-steady at 240 lb per sq in, and the water level was maintained right at the top of the glass. There was no question of a brief mortgaging of the boiler; steaming conditions were quite steady.

The incidence of the curves brought an immediate fall in the speed, and the quarter-mile timings which had hitherto shown 30.7, 31.0, 29.7 and 28.5 mph now dropped to 24.7, 22,

TABLE III
SOMERSET & DORSET LINE: BATH–BOURNEMOUTH

The 'Pines Express'
Load: 12 coaches, 416 tons tare, 450 tons full
Engine: Class '9F' 2–10–0 No 92000 (double chimney)
Driver: D. Beale; Fireman: P. Smith (of Branksome)

Dist		Sch	Actual	Speeds
Miles		min	m s	mph
0.0	BATH (GREEN PARK)	0	0 00	—
—	Combe Down Tunnel (in)		—	24
4.3	Midford	10	10 10	—
10.7	RADSTOCK ...	19	19 40	37
12.0	Midsomer Norton		21 50	31
13.5	Milepost 13* ...		25 23	22
14.5	Chilcompton ...		27 52	25¼
15.2	Milepost 14¾* ...		29 11	36/33
17.5	Binegar		32 25	36
18.2	Milepost 17¾ (Masbury)*	41	34 43	30
26.4	EVERCREECH JUNC	56	46 00	—
3.8	Cole		4 55	—
7.1	Wincanton ...		10 55	—
			3 tablet slacks	
20.9	Shillingstone ...	31	31 45	—
5.5	BLANDFORD ...	9	9 00	—
6.1	Bailey Gate ...		7 40	64½
—	Corfe Mullen Junc		—	50
—	Top of 1 in 80 ...		—	43
10.9	BROADSTONE ...	16	14 10	—
			sigs	—
3.4	POOLE	8	7 05	—
			—	47 (max)
1.8	Parkstone ...		3 20	41 (min)
3.1	Branksome ...		5 10	—
4.4	BOURNEMOUTH WEST	10	8 00	—

Total time on trip: 2 hr 10 min 50 sec
Time lost by signals: 1 min
Overtime at stations: 1 min 50 secs
Schedule time: 2 hr 23 min
Gain to locomotive: 15 min

*Mileposts are measured from Bath Junction, 0.5 miles from Bath Green Park

23.7 and 23.2, despite the fact that the driver had been increasing the cut-off step by step after threading the short tunnel near Milepost 13¼. No 92000 approached Chilcompton working in 48 per cent; the slight easing of the grade through the station brought a rapid acceleration to 30¾ mph, and a further rise to 36 beyond, and it was at this most unusual speed that the last length of 1 in 50 gradient was mounted. Thus the average speed over the four miles from Milepost 10¾ to 14¾ was 27.7 mph on a gradient which, compensated for curvature, averages 1 in 52½. Baron Vuillet calculates that the average edhp during this ascent was no less than 2,000, and that the indicated horsepower was at least 2,240. I am fully in agreement with his calculations. Over the remaining three miles of the climb to Masbury summit, on easier gradients, the cut-off was shortened, step by step, to no more than 23 per cent on passing Binegar. Nevertheless the last mile, at 1 in 63-73, was cleared at 30 mph, and the average edhp for the entire climb from Radstock works out at 1,840.

By this superb hillclimbing the lateness on leaving Bath had been exactly halved on passing Masbury summit, and before examining another aspect of this performance the unusual timing will be better appreciated by comparison with two runs of my own, both double-headed. On the first, with a class '2' 4-4-0 and a class '4' 2-6-0, No 43017, hauling 330 tons between them, the time from Radstock to Masbury was 19 min 44 sec against the brilliant 15 min 3 sec by No 92000 unassisted. On the 'Pines Express' itself, another class '2' 4-4-0 and a Stanier class '5' 4-6-0 took 20 min 10 sec to climb the bank from Radstock, but this time with a much heavier train of 415 tons. On the first of my two runs the speed fell to as low as 15½ mph on the worst part of the bank, while the double-headed 'Pines Express' fell at one stage still lower, to 14½ mph. The total times from Bath to Masbury summit were 38 min 55 sec and 40 min 2 sec, against the 34 min 43 sec of No 92000. The very steep descent to Evercreech Junction was taken cautiously, and whereas the times on my two previous runs for the 7.7 miles

were 11 min 4 sec and 9 min 50 sec respectively, No 92000 took 11 min 17 sec. The schedule here is very liberal, however, and Evercreech Junction was reached only 2¾ min late.

This substantial regaining of lost time, entirely by the good hillclimbing, was most satisfying in itself, but when it comes to comparing the horsepower figures with those quoted in the bulletin issued by the British Transport Commission it would seem that the performance of these engines has been considerably enhanced by fitting of the double blastpipe and chimney. Originally the limiting factor in the performance of these engines was the front-end, which precluded anything in the way of steady continuous steaming above 30,000 lb per hr, on Blidworth coal. At a speed of 28 mph—the average of No 92000 on the Radstock-Chilcompton bank—the maximum edhp quoted in the bulletin was 1,750, and this required a cut-off of 50 per cent. Yet No 92000 developed over 2,000 edhp for 8¾ min on end, and it was only when she got on to the sharply-curved section that the cut-off had to be increased much above 40 per cent. The firing, it is true, was frequent, with four or five shovelfuls at a time, but in response the steaming was very free. Baron Vuillet comments that the draught was spread evenly over a fairly thin fire.

Evercreech Junction has a reputation for smart working, and running true to form on this occasion the staff there cut their allowance by two minutes and saw the train away less than a minute late. With the assistance of half a mile down at 1 in 116, the start was extremely rapid, and Cole, 3.8 miles, was passed in 4 min 55 sec. The rising length to Wincanton was taken in good style, on no more than 20 per cent cut-off; but between Wincanton and Shillingstone there are three slacks for single-line tablet exchange, which precludes any appreciable fast running. Furthermore the scheduled stop at Shillingstone for crossing a northbound train was extended from the booked 3 min to 5½, and the 'Pines Express' was thus 3 min late into Blandford. Here water was taken, and a check on the tender gauge showed the consumption from Bath to be

On the Somerset & Dorset Joint Line north of Radstock; a northbound express hauled by '9F' 2-10-0 No 92245. (Ivo Peters)

3,500 gal, an average of 66 gal per mile, and an approximate evaporation of 23,000 lb per hr. The bulk of this would have been used between Bath and Masbury summit. Between the severe slacks for negotiating the crossing loops some brisk running was performed, and for the first time since Bath a maximum speed of 60 mph was attained at Henstridge, between the Templecombe junctions and Stalbridge. At this speed, Baron Vuillet tells me, the engine rode as smoothly as a coach.

It is perhaps characteristic of the Somerset & Dorset line to have a couple of vicious 'stings in the tail,' when having reached the broad smiling vale of the Stour there are still two very stiff gradients to be climbed. From Blandford the line undulates on sharp gradients, though at first their extent is short, and the aggregate effect is level. Bailey Gate, 6.1 miles from the restart, was passed in the fast time of 7 min 40 sec at 64 mph. Speed was then eased to 50 mph for mechanical tablet exchange at Corfe Mullen Junction and with nearly two miles of 1 in 80 ascent coming immediately beyond the junction the reverser was put into 45 per cent cut-off and regulator opened to the full. The drop in speed was relatively slight and Baron Vuillet records that speed was sustained at 43 mph up the 1 in 80 gradient. It is unlikely that such a tremendous effort could have been maintained for very long, as it involved a cylinder horsepower estimated at 2,700; but the capacity to produce a burst of such exceptional power when required is invaluable over a route of this character, and it regained 2 min between Blandford and Broadstone.

But Driver Beale and Fireman Smith still had the greatest thrill in store for their distinguished guest. Because of a signal check from a Southern Region train the departure from Poole was still 2½ min late. Ahead of them was the Parkstone-Branksome bank, beginning with 1½ miles at 1 in 60, and easing to a quarter-mile of level and a half-mile of 1 in 130. From Poole there is just a mile of level to get a run at this final 'stinger,' and No 92000 was driven away on full regulator and 49 per cent cut-off. There was no linking up as the engine roared with speed, and at the foot of the bank where speed had risen to 47 mph the cut-off was *increased*, to 52 per cent. The 1 in 60 gradient was thereafter stormed with no lower speed than 41 mph, and at the top boiler pressure was still 225 lb per sq in. Baron Vuillet writes: 'It is difficult to assess the horsepower output because of the shortness of the run and the helping wind; but calculations point to a cylinder horsepower in the region of 2,800–3,000 during one minute.' With regard to the wind, I should add that on the Parkstone bank the line is running due east, whereas for the bulk of the journey the wind had been directly athwart the course. Extrapolating on the graphs

of indicated horsepower published in the BTC bulletin for the single-chimneyed version of these engines shows a value of about 2,700 for 52 per cent cut-off and a speed of 45 to 47 mph. Technicalities apart it was certainly a grand conclusion to a splendid run, and it regained all but 30 sec of the lost time still outstanding when Poole was left.

Before I quote Baron Vuillet's concluding comments on this performance, I feel it is only right to say that he is probably the most experienced observer of locomotive performance anywhere in the world at the present time. His footplate journeys have covered most countries in Europe, and an extensive mileage in the United States of America. Praise of the kind he has lavished on No 92000 and her crew is therefore praise indeed. He sums up the run as 'a magnificent example of skilled driving and firing, with high sustained capacity and remarkable outbursts of exceptional power showing the flexibility of the steam locomotive.' Those of us who may be at times saddened by the striking progress of railways overseas, compared with the relative slowness of our own progress in modernisation, may be heartened by Baron Vuillet's final comment in his letter to me: 'This is one of the most remarkable trips I have made on a locomotive, and the class '9' engines are certainly among the very best.'

Great Western — steam finale on 'The Limited'

The introduction of the 'Warship' diesel-hydraulic locomotives on the Western Region, and a Train Timing Computer for them produced by the Testing Section of the Chief Mechanical Department at Swindon, naturally aroused thought as to how the new power compared with the old. By the kindness of Mr R. A. Smeddle, I was kept in close touch with what was then going on, visiting the Testing Plant and accompanying experimental runs, as well as making many footplate trips on ordinary service trains. From these associations I wrote 'Steam Finale on "The Limited" '.

THE remodelling of the Western Region passenger train services to Devon and Cornwall, and the acceleration at the same time of the Southern Region 'Atlantic Coast Express' to an overall time of less than three hours from Waterloo to Exeter, naturally tends to focus some attention on West of England matters this autumn. After getting over the inevitable disappointment at the passing of much of the old-time glamour of the 'Cornish Riviera Express' it will at once be realised that the new service, to Taunton and Exeter at any rate, will be an excellent one, with an overall time from Paddington to St Davids of 172 min, not only by the 10.30 am but by the 2.30 pm down as well.

The new schedules of 137 min from Paddington to Taunton, and of 32 min from Taunton to Exeter, will require some smart work, particularly the latter, with the 10.9 miles of as-cent to Whiteball Tunnel coming immediately from the Taunton start. I have not personally clocked any diesel runs, start to stop, from Taunton to Exeter, but over many years of travelling the best I have had with steam have all given passing times of about 14 to 14½ min at Whiteball summit with loads of 350 to 380 tons. The Brown-Boveri gas-turbine No 18000 at the very top of its form, hauling 380 tons, did not better this time either.

The train timing computer for the diesel locomotives, produced by the Testing Section at Swindon, shows a theoretical time of 13.6 min from Taunton start to Whiteball, with a 400-ton train, using maximum power throughout, and with a continuance of maximum power, and observing all permanent speed restrictions, the 19.9 miles from Whiteball to Exeter stop are shown to be covered in 17.1 min, thus giving a total of 30.7 min from Taunton to Exeter. According to the computer, a time of 29 min start to stop should be possible with a 300-ton train, if maximum power is used wherever possible.

In view of the oft-quoted fallacy that 'diesels can accelerate quicker than steam' it is interesting to see that the calculated all-out performance of the 'Warships' between Taunton and Whiteball is so little faster than that of steam locomotives that were certainly not being driven to anything approaching their limit. Here are four examples:

Engine		Load	Time from Taunton start to passing Whiteball
No	Name	(tons)	Box
			m s
2923	Saint George	320	14 27
1015	County of Gloucester	380	14 24
6022	King Edward III	375	14 30
18000	(Gas Turbine)	375	14 28

I was on the footplate of the 'King' during this ascent, and although the working was very good the steaming and firing rates were nothing approaching the maximum of which these locomotives were capable in their original form.

In these changing times it is just as well to recall something of what has been done in the past over this route, and from my own notebooks I have prepared a symposium of journeys on the down 'Cornish Riviera Express.' With two exceptions, every journey I have personally recorded on this train is included; they show some of the variations in working at different phases in its history, and show the running of 'King' class locomotives in four stages of their evolution. On many of these journeys I was privileged to ride on the footplate and on at least one occasion had a first-hand view of the kind of difficulties that are sometimes encountered in the operation of a long turn such as this.

The up 'Limited' in the first months of 'King' haulage, August 1927. Engine No 6002 King William IV *east of Reading.* (M.W. Earley)

The 'Castles' do not figure at all in my own records of the train in its normal working. Their innings was relatively short. From the autumn of 1923 they began working from the London end, but my own notes show that it was not until 1925 that engines of this class were stationed at Laira, and even in that summer 'Stars' were still frequently on the job. What 'stars' they were too! *Knight of the Thistle, Queen Adelaide, Queen Berengaria, Malvern Abbey* and *Llanthony Abbey* were all in magnificent form, and in that summer *Queen Adelaide* in particular must have been amassing a tremendous mileage on the Plymouth-London trains.

The traffic department had not waited for the advent of the 'Kings' to load the train up to 500 tons or more, on leaving Paddington. At the time the 'Castle' class locomotives 'hit the headlines' in these articles a train of 14 coaches was nothing unusual on 'The Limited.' 'Castles' and 'Stars' alike were expected to take such loads without assistance—in fact the idea of taking assistance would probably never have entered the head of any driver or fireman in the link. On its normal winter working the load got progressively lighter as the journey proceeded. Two coaches were slipped at Westbury, another two at Taunton, and two or three at Exeter; but as the load is lightened so the gradients become progressively worse until the South Devon line was entered upon. Long before the 'Castles' came on the scene, however, Great Western drivers had had some experience of working gargantuan loads; for the old non-stop schedule

TABLE I
GWR AND WESTERN REGION: 'CORNISH RIVIERA EXPRESS'

Run No		1	2	3	4	5	6	7	8	9
Engine No		4036	4018	6016	6008	6029	6007	6013	6015	D601
Engine Name		Queen Elizabeth	Knight of the Grand Cross	King Edward V	King James II	King Edward VIII	King William III	King Henry VIII	King Richard III	Ark Royal
Load: to Westbury, tons (e/f)		401/435	457/490	410/440	397/425	371/400	465/500	460/490	365/390	351/375
to Taunton, tons (e/f)		329/360	373/400	410/440	330/355	335/360	465/500	393/420	327/350	351/375
to Exeter, tons (e/f)		329/360	301/320	410/440	330/355	335/360	465/500	393/420	327/350	351/375
to Plymouth, tons (e/f)		329/360	—	376/405	330/355	335/360	465/500	393/420	327/350	351/375
Dist		Actual	Actual	Actual	Actual	Actual	Actual	Actual	Actual	Actual
Miles		m s	m s	m s	m s	m s	m s	m s	m s	m s
0.0	PADDINGTON ...	0 00	0 00	0 00	0 00	0 00	0 00	0 00	0 00	0 00
		—	—	—	—	—	—	—	sigs	—
9.1	Southall	13 05	12 49	11 41	11 50	13 32	14 30	12 20	12 21	12 36
16.2	Langley	20 00	19 53	17 46	18 19	19 43	21 37	19 04	18 34	19 28
		—	sigs	—	—	—	sigs	—	—	—
18.5	SLOUGH	22 05	22 41	19 35	20 29	22 50	23 39	21 00	20 23	21 30
24.2	Maidenhead	27 25	30 32	24 12	26 13	28 24	29 21	25 51	25 00	26 30
		—	—	—	pws	—	—	—	—	—
31.0	Twyford	33 45	37 24	30 10	33 17	35 19	35 44	31 31	30 34	32 10
		—	—	—	pws	—	—	—	—	sigs
36.0	READING	38 45	42 17	35 28	41 39	40 58	40 48	35 58	35 01	37 07
		—	—	—	—	—	—	pws	—	—
44.8	Aldermaston	48 25	52 29	44 25	51 47	50 44	50 25	46 37	44 11	46 42
		—	—	—	—	sigs	—	—	—	—
53.1	NEWBURY	57 00	61 21	52 02	60 00	60 28	58 58	54 10	51 43	54 37
61.5	Hungerford	65 50	70 28	59 42	68 07	69 15	67 43	61 49	59 05	62 24
70.1	SAVERNAKE	75 50	80 20	68 01	77 17	78 31	77 11	70 04	67 19	70 45
		pws	—	—	sigs	—	—	—	—	—

Dist	Engine Name	Queen Elizabeth	Knight of the Grand Cross	King Edward V	King James II	King Edward VIII	King William VIII	King Henry VIII	King Richard III	Ark Royal
		Actual	Actual	Actual	Actual	Actual	Actual	Actual	Actual	Actual
81.1	Patney	89 10	90 38	77 32	87 07	88 52	87 20	79 14	76 29	80 27
		—	—	—	pws	—	—	pws	fog stop	—
91.4	Edington	98 30	98 42	85 51	100 22	97 37	95 38	88 20	89 48	89 24
94.6	Heywood Rd Junc	—	—	88 42	103 17	100 30	98 17	91 08	—	92 05
95.6*	WESTBURY	102 40	102 39	—	—	—	—	—	95 03a	—
									96 53d	
101.3*	Frome	110 10	110 32	—	—	—	—	—	—	—
102.3	Blatchbridge Junc	—	—	97 44	110 35	107 50	105 42	97 48	—	99 07
108.3	Brewham Box	119 30	—	104 46	116 13	114 36	111 56	103 11	110 35	105 15
115.1	CASTLE CARY	125 30	125 42	111 42	122 28	121 20	119 40	108 49	116 28	111 37
							pws			
125.5	Somerton	135 00	134 17	121 31	131 12	130 52	134 46	117 00	127 51	120 17
						pws			pws	
138.0	Cogload Junc	146 35	144 29	132 17	141 30	144 08	145 57	126 25	137 32	129 36
142.7	TAUNTON	151 50	149 14	136 32	145 56	148 40	150 24	130 18	143 54	133 26
									pws	
149.8	Wellington	159 15	156 43	143 25	152 32	156 17	157 38	136 45	153 23	139 47
					pws					
153.6	Whiteball Box	165 55	161 54	149 00	157 42	161 39	165 01	141 37	157 39	144 42
158.6	Tiverton Junc	171 25	166 33	154 22	162 30	166 38	170 18	146 18	162 03	149 26
166.3	Silverton	177 40	172 52	161 18	169 05	173 38	177 19	153 01	168 16	156 05
173.5	EXETER	183 40	179 29	168 50	176 05	180 40	184 30	159 14	174 41	163 21
		—	—	—	—	—	—	pws	—	sig stop
182.0	Starcross	193 25		10 29	184 55	189 17	193 26	170 50	183 11	178 00
		—			pws	sigs		—	—	—
185.7	Dawlish	197 10		14 30	188 57	193 28	200 02	175 08	187 26	182 15
							sigs			
188.5	Teignmouth	200 00		17 49	192 34	197 15	207 28	178 44	191 06	185 47
		—		sigs stop						
193.7	NEWTON ABBOT	206 00		23 48	199 25	203 45	216 13	186 15	196 40	191 57
		—†			200 05			190 25‡		
194.8	Aller Junc			25 42	202 49	205 20		192 58	198 09	193 33
197.5	Dainton Box	7 25		30 57	207 58	210 55		197 32	203 20	198 18
202.3	TOTNES	13 05		36 43	215 50	218 00		207 20	209 31	205 09
205.1	Tigley Box	17 00		41 23	221 21	223 53		213 18	214 50	209 55
206.9	Rattery Box	20 20		45 17	225 43	228 30		216 24	217 39	213 48
209.2	Brent	23 35		48 42	229 25	232 09		219 13	220 49	217 05
211.4	Wrangaton	5 25		51 28	232 23	235 16		221 44	223 29	219 37
		—		—	—	sigs		—	—	—
214.7	Ivybridge	9 10		55 29	236 22	240 20		225 33	227 16	223 25
		—		—	—	—		—	—	pws
218.8	Hemerdon Box	13 05		60 07	240 55	246 08		230 26	231 47	228 50
221.5	Plympton	15 30		62 40	243 32	249 03		233 07	234 09	232 15
		sigs		sigs	—	sigs		—	—	sigs
225.5	PLYMOUTH (N ROAD)	24 55		69 25	251 25	256 30		239 55	239 50	239 27

* Mileage *via* Westbury and Frome stations (0.2 miles greater than *via* by-pass lines)
† Piloted by '43XX' class 2-6-0 from Newton Abbot to Brent
‡ Piloted by No 5000, *Launceston Castle*, from Newton Abbot to Plymouth

of 4 hr 7 min was maintained during the first world war until the autumn of 1916, and there is at least one recorded occasion when a load of 535 tons was taken unassisted out of Paddington, and Plymouth was reached a minute early!

It would be expecting too much of machinery, and of human nature, to imagine that performance on the 'Limited' could always be set in so grandly heroic a mould, and my first experience on the train was a disappointment. It is worth recalling, however, what manner of running constituted a disappointment on the Great Western, in 1924, and this is the first run detailed in Table I. It was made at mid-week, in the height of the summer season, with only the Weymouth slip portion, so that there was no relief in the loading at any point after Westbury.

The engine had been out of the shops for more than a year since last overhaul, and looked drab in the plain unlined green of wartime amid the many more-recently overhauled engines that were then brilliant in their flashing array of polished brass and copperwork. The weather, also, turned sour as we made our way westward, and from Castle Cary onwards we were running through thick driving rain. It was typical of travel at that time that the train left Paddington with every seat taken, save for a very few in the first class compartments, and in view of the high seating capacity of the stock in relation to its tare weight the gross load would have been at least 435 tons, if not more.

The start was quite brisk, with speed rising to 66 mph at Slough, and although one could hardly expect the severe sectional time of 37 min to Reading to be kept we were going well enough to be no more than a minute late at Newbury. The engine was not unduly pressed on the last stage of the climb to Savernake however, and on the last three-quarters of a mile at 1 in 154–106 from Wolfhall Junction speed fell to 40¼ mph. Then, as if to anticipate a long relaying slack that was to come, the driver went very easily to Pewsey, and recovery from the check itself had not the 'dash' usually associated with the working of the 'Limited.' Speed did not exceed 74 mph at Lav-

ington, and we passed Westbury 5¼ min late.

With the reduced load of 360 tons engine and crew did no more than hold their own onwards to Exeter, though to be sure the weather across the exposed country from Castle Cary to Taunton was not exactly helpful. Speed did not exceed 69 mph anywhere on the Langport cut-off line, and the minimum on the Whiteball ascent was 29 mph. There was some brisk running downhill, with a maximum of 76½ mph, but for all that Exeter was passed 4¾ min late. The net time was about 180 min, showing a loss of one minute to engine.

Run No 2 is an example of 'Star' performance with a heavy wartime load and was recorded by the late R. E. Charlewood. With so great a load as 490 tons the start out of Paddington was very fine with speed rising to 64 mph at Langley. Then came the check at Slough, which was a very severe one, costing about 4¼ min in running, and with this discouragement added to the exceptional loading, one might have expected the crew to give up any ideas of timekeeping. The train was 5¼ min late through Reading and making due allowance for the difference in load *Knight of the Grand Cross* was doing no better than *Queen Elizabeth* on the ascent to Savernake. But the former engine was driven like the wind down to Westbury, reaching a top speed of 83 mph at Lavington.

The train was still running just over 5 min late at both Westbury and Castle Cary, and then again the driver of *Knight of the Grand Cross* made such excellent use of the favourable stretches across the Langport cut-off line that he passed Taunton practically on time. Maximum speed on this stretch was 80 mph at Curry Rivel Junction. With two more coaches slipped, and load now reduced to 320 tons, the ascent to Whiteball was very fine, and with the minimum speed of 37 mph this engine had gained 4 min on *Queen Elizabeth* from Castle Cary. Mr Charlewood was travelling in the Exeter slip portion, and this arrived ½ min early.

On another occasion, of which only the journal times are available, *Knight of the Grand Cross* took a gross load of 535 tons out of Paddington.

Above *The down train emerging from Sonning Cutting with engine No 6024* King Edward I. (M.W. Earley)

Below *The down 'Limited' near Reading West in 1955 with engine No 6026* King John. (M.W. Earley)

This was reduced to 435 tons at Westbury, and 340 tons at Taunton. There was a permanent way slack between Reading and Newbury costing about 2 min, but despite this the train passed Westbury in 104 min, Taunton in 151 min, and Exeter in exactly three hours, with net times about 2 min less in each case. The sectional average speeds of 56 mph from Paddington to Westbury, 60½ mph from Westbury to Taunton and a most remarkable 63½ mph from Taunton to Exeter, may nowadays seem almost unbelievable from so relatively small an engine, with loads of 535, 435 and 340 tons respectively over the three successive stages. Furthermore, in those days the train ran through Westbury and Frome stations with severe slacks at each place. Such a double-barrelled hindrance is worth 4 to 5 min compared with fast unchecked running over the two by-pass lines today.

Run No 3 brings the saga forward to the year 1935, to the Saturday before Easter, with the train divided, and carrying no slip portions. Then the 'Kings' needed no such modern aids to performance as improved draughting, and double chimneys, and No 6016 dashed away from Paddington in a style that made 440 tons seem like a mere featherweight. A maximum speed of 75 mph was sustained for mile after mile from Langley; the average for 25 miles up the Kennet Valley was 66 mph and Savernake summit was topped at 53 mph. After that it was simply a case of spinning out time, as minimum speeds of 45 mph at Brewham and 29 mph at Whiteball bore witness. The non-stop run to Plymouth had been abandoned some years earlier, and this engine had to work really hard over the South Devon line. With a tare load of 376 tons the driver would have been entitled to a bank engine from Newton Abbot, but all assistance was disdained. However, I will defer reference to the conclusion of the run to later in this article.

We now come forward to more recent times. In June, 1952, after a long spell in the doldrums, the 'Limited' was accelerated to a 4¼-hour run from Paddington to Plymouth, and I was privileged to ride on the footplate on the first day of the speed-up. On reaching Paddington I was concerned to find that the train was running in three portions, and that the main train was to be preceded by a relief leaving at 10.20 am and also running non-stop to Plymouth in 4¼ hr. I was somewhat reassured, however, to find that the relief was loaded to no more than nine coaches, and because of an unbalanced engine working was double-headed with a 'King' and a 'County.'

I was hoping for a high-superheat engine on our own train, but instead we had No 6008 in original condition, with low superheat and jumper top to the blastpipe. At that time, also, the engine was painted blue. On the footplate with me came Chief Locomotive Running Inspector C. J. Pullen, who, in his retirement, has recently been honoured by the award of the British Empire Medal. I always enjoy recalling the many trips Charlie Pullen and I have made together on the footplate, which over the years have taken me over most of the Western Region main-line network. On this trip Driver Kent and Fireman Courtney, of Laira shed, were on the job.

Engine No 6008 was in grand form, and the start out to Langley was little slower than that of the fire-eating No 6016, on the run No 3. At that time however there was a 60 mph slack through Slough, and we had to ease up. The two permanent way checks before Reading set us well back, and two further checks before Westbury led to our being 14½ min behind No 6016 when we entered the Westbury by-pass line. Some grand running followed. Up the stiff gradients to Brewham summit speed at no time fell below 58½ mph, with cut-off all the time in 15 per cent, and a maximum of 82 was reached at Curry Rivel Junction, where the Langport cut-off line descends to the Athelney marshes. It is true that the load had been reduced to 355 tons by slipping the Weymouth portion at Heywood Road, but even so the ascent of Wellington bank was unusually fast, with a speed of 64 mph through Wellington Station. Unfortunately a permanent way check in Whiteball Tunnel prevented a really record minimum speed at the

The 1.20 pm Penzance to Paddington express after leaving Parsons Tunnel near Dawlish with engine No 6017 King Edward IV. *(Peter W. Gray)*

summit. Despite all checks Exeter was passed comfortably within three hours, and the net time was no more than 166 min.

Had I experienced no other footplate journeys on the 'Limited' I could have been seriously misled as to the problems of working the train in present-day conditions. On No 6008 it all looked just too easy. The steaming was perfect; the engine was very strong at the front-end, and responded readily to every demand. But when I made No 5 run, later that same year, things were very different. Engine No 6029, again one of those in original standard condition, was very strong and free running, but we had the four-pronged handicap of a brake tending to leak on somewhere down the train, much poor coal, a strong southwesterly wind, and a fireman who was not quite up to the job. The big ejector was on for quite one-third of the journey. With Inspector Pullen's aid the fireman was able to mix the coal successfully after Castle Cary so that the steaming was much better from that point onwards, but the performance all round was much below the best 'King' standards. I venture to suggest that had there not been an inspector on the footplate on this trip time would have been lost heavily. As it was, but for the succession of

signal checks at the very finish we should have been on time at Plymouth.

Run No 6 was made on a Saturday in the height of the summer, when the full load is carried through to Truro, the first passenger stop. Double heading is necessary from Newton Abbot westward and the interesting arrangement was made of changing engines on the through road at Newton Abbot. The 'King' came off, and was replaced by two smaller 4–6–0s, in various combinations of 'Manors,' 'Granges,' 'Halls,' 'Counties' and 'Castles,' and a non-stop run made from Newton Abbot to Truro. In view of the congestion that sometimes occurs on Saturdays in the height of the summer we got a remarkably good road. The 10.20 am *ex*-Paddington, for the Torquay line, was loaded to 'eleven,' and worked by a 'Hall' class engine, and until traffic began to pile up west of Starcross we never sighted her signals. The slight check at Slough was quite local. On No 6007 Driver Emery and Fireman Hexte, of Laira, gave us an immaculate example of 'King' performance. Except in recovery from speed restrictions the engine was worked in 15 per cent cut-off until after Taunton, save for a brief increase to 18 per cent for the final mile up to

Savernake, and 16 per cent for the last two miles up to Brewham.

The leisurely start out of Paddington was deliberate, because we had seen that the 10.20 am had been checked in getting away; but from Southall onwards the work with this 500-ton train was absolutely first class. Especially fine was the work up the Kennet Valley, with an average speed of 58 mph from Theale to Bedwyn, 25.1 miles. Savernake was topped at 44½ mph and a maximum of 80½ mph was reached at Lavington. Beyond the Westbury by-pass line the work was particularly interesting, as we were continuing with the heaviest load of the whole series, and in these conditions, on 16 per cent cut-off, the minimum speed of exactly 50 mph at Brewham was notable.

Two severe permanent way checks then came in rapid succession, one at Castle Cary and one at Keinton Mandeville, and these cost us 7 min between them. Speed was quickly regained; a maximum of 73 mph was touched at Curry Rivel Junction, and Taunton was passed only 1½ min late on the Saturday schedule. Throughout the run, so far, the engine had been steaming freely, but by this time the fireman had dug down to some very poor stuff on the tender. Engine No 6007 then had the modified draughting, with jumper cap removed and a liner fitted in the chimney, and with this un-doubted aid in adversity pressure was held at 220 to 235 lb per sq in during the ascent to Whiteball.

We passed Taunton at 59 mph working in 15 per cent cut-off with regulator full open. There was a recovery to 61 at Norton Fitzwarren, and then Driver Emery began to open out, first to 18 per cent at Victory Siding, then to 19 a mile

The Up 'Limited' in 1958, with a 14-coach load, climbing Hemerdon Bank with engine No 6026 King John *assisted as far as Newton Abbot by No 7916* Mobberley Hall. *(Peter W. Gray)*

short of Wellington, and next to 20 per cent just as we came on to the really steep part of the bank. The speed through Wellington was 50½ mph, but then it naturally fell off rapidly, to 26½ mph at the tunnel entrance, and to 23 at the summit. Cut-off had been increased to a maximum of 24 per cent, and this very easy working had secured a *gain* of nearly ½ min on the sectional time from Taunton to Whiteball. Easy running downhill followed, not exceeding 75 mph anywhere, and with clear signals we ran through Exeter in 184½ min from Paddington at a little under 60 mph. Net time to this point was 177 min, showing an average speed of 58.8 mph with a 500-ton load throughout.

This run required an evaporation of approximately 23,000 lb of water per hour, which makes an interesting comparison with the dynamometer car test run that follows. Because of the signal checks west of Starcross we were 6¼ min late in reaching Newton Abbot. There, Inspector Pullen and I transferred from No 6007 to a 'Grange,' No 6873, which was the leading engine of the pair to which the non-stop run to Truro was entrusted. Summer Saturday or not, we got an absolutely clear road to the Truro home signal, but the fine work of *Caradoc Grange* and *Wolseley Hall* in partnership must wait for some future occasion.

Run No 7 was the dynamometer car test run made on March 10, 1955, before the restoration of the four-hour non-stop schedule to Plymouth. I have discussed this run at considerable length in the May, 1959, issue of *The Railway Magazine*, but the details are tabulated once more, for reference. It is certainly one of the hardest runs on record over the West of England line. The most spectacular work was done after the Weymouth portion had been slipped at Heywood Road, and the principal maximum and minimum speeds were 60 mph at Brewham, 84 at Curry Rivel Junction, 37 at Whiteball, and 80 descending to Exeter.

The individual items are not in themselves very exceptional; it was the sustaining of the effort throughout from Paddington to Newton Abbot that made possible such a notable overall

time. If, for example, No 6016 on run No 3 had been steamed equally hard from Savernake westwards as it had been from Paddington to Savernake there is no knowing what time might not have been achieved. On the dynamometer car test run engine No 6013 had the improved draughting and high superheat, but although a good engine was not in absolutely first-class condition. With a 420-ton load assistance was necessary from Newton Abbot to Plymouth. No 6013 was worked by Driver Shave and Fireman Mitchell of Old Oak, with Inspector Pullen riding with them on the footplate.

The eighth run introduces the fourth variation in the 'King' design, in which a twin-orifice blastpipe and chimney has been added to the other post-war modifications. This, my last steam run on the 'Limited,' proved to be a most exciting and rewarding experience. Engine No 6015 was worked by Driver Newcombe and Fireman Hawkes of Laira, and my own guide and philosopher was Inspector W. Andress, who has now succeeded Pullen, as Chief Running Inspector of the Western Region. I had been staying at Oxford overnight, and when I awoke to find a thick fog my first concern was at catching the 'Limited' at all. The 8.35 am up gave me a turn-round time of little more than half an hour in London, and on a bad morning this could easily be lost. Despite weather that was quite thick in places No 7005, *Lamphey Castle*, was splendidly driven, and although leaving Oxford 8 min late she reached Paddington at 9.56 am, having run the 58.3 miles up from Radley in 62 min 24 sec start to stop. This enterprise augured well for the rest of the day, though we had several more alarms before we reached the West Country.

Engine No 6015, *King Richard III*, was a very fast and powerful unit, and with the fog dispersing we raced out to Reading in brilliant style, sustaining 73–75 mph throughout from Iver to Sonning. From Reading we were gradually drawing ahead of the fiery 6016, in column 3, with speeds of 62 to 68 mph all the way up the Kennet Valley, and Savernake was passed just over 4 min early on the schedule then in force.

Then we struck it! Dense fog prevailed around Westbury.

We were stopped at Lavington to be told it was too thick for us to slip the Weymouth portion at Heywood Road. We must go into Westbury and stop, and the outcome of these checks was that while we had passed Savernake 4 min early, we passed Clink Road Junction 6½ min late. It was still very thick, and in the murk I completely missed the signalbox at Blatchbridge Junction. Then almost as suddenly we ran out into the joy of a still and cloudless November day. Though the weather no longer troubled us there were three permanent way checks to come, and the time our driver had been getting in hand was more than lost. By dint of some magnificent running, however, all the time was won back, and we stopped at Plymouth just ten seconds inside the even four hours.

There was a fine burst of speed between the Castle Cary and the Creech Junction checks, with a top speed of 82 mph at Curry Rivel Junction. Here the engine was working in 12 or 13 per cent cut-off. Then came a vigorous acceleration to 63 mph at Norton Fitzwarren, before check number three, near Victory Siding. Because of this latter we began the climb to Whiteball at no more than 15 mph. Driver Newcombe then put the engine to it with great gusto, working at first in 30 per cent and gradually linking up to 25 per cent by Poole Siding, by which time speed had risen to 53½ mph.

Wellington Station was passed at 60, after which, without any advance beyond 25 per cent, Whiteball summit was cleared at the exceptional minimum speed of 47 mph. Even with the incidence of a bad permanent way check the total time from Taunton to Whiteball was only 13¾ min. A fast run down to Exeter with a maximum speed of 80 mph near Stoke Canon, took us through St Davids in 174 min 41 sec from Paddington, after a series of checks that had cost us 21 min in running. The net time of 153¾ min showed an average speed of 67.7 mph. The train was nevertheless still running 10 min late, and on passing Exeter I was

still doubtful if we should recover much more time.

Last in the table comes the work of the North British-built diesel-hydraulic locomotive *Ark Royal*, driven by C. Mapstone of Laira shed, with whom I was again privileged to ride in the cab. We had a load of ten coaches throughout to Plymouth, and while this made for easier working east of Exeter the diesel had one of the toughest tasks after Newton Abbot. We made good time out to Savernake, working very carefully to the various minor speed restrictions, such as Midgham and Hungerford, to observe them precisely. The speed limit at Grafton Junction has now been raised to 60 mph on the down road, however, and this enabled us to clear Savernake summit at 54½ mph. For the most part the engine had been working in the 6th notch, out of a maximum of seven, but for the downhill run to Heywood Road notches 4 and 5 were used. Castle Cary was passed dead on time, and then some really fast running was made over the Langport cut-off. The controller was in the 6th notch, and speed rose to 85 mph on the descent past Langport to Curry Rivel Junction.

The controller remained in the 6th notch for the ascent to Whiteball. Taunton was passed at 71½ mph, Wellington at 60, and the tunnel was entered at 39½ mph. Just before going in the controller was eased back to the 5th notch to lessen the chance of wheel-slip inside, and speed fell to 36½ mph at the summit. Here the train was running 2¼ min early. The time from Taunton to Whiteball was 11 min 16 sec, whereas the computer gives 10 min 6 sec for one of these locomotives worked at full power and hauling 375 tons. It is interesting to note that *King Richard III* was 40 sec faster than the *Ark Royal* from Wellington to Whiteball, even though the steam locomotive had been heavily checked at the foot of the bank. With the diesel Exeter was passed 1¾ min early, but then came a severe delay at Exminster because of a point failure. As a result Newton Abbot was passed 3 min late.

Over the heavily-graded section from Newton

Abbot to Plymouth interest is centred principally on runs 3, 4, 8 and 9. On my earliest run, with *Queen Elizabeth*, we took a Mogul of the '43XX' class as pilot, and the only unusual feature of the running was the very high speeds run downhill by No 4036 after the pilot had been put off at Brent. I have never since travelled over Ivybridge Viaduct at well over 60 mph—nor do I wish to! Table II sets out the speeds at the principal points run on the four most interesting journeys.

TABLE II
NEWTON ABBOT-WRANGATON

Engine No.	6016	6008	6015	D601
Load, tons (full)	405	355	350	375
Location	Speeds			
	mph	mph	mph	mph
Max. after Aller Junc.	48	47	56	53
Dainton Summit	21½	20	26	22
Passing Totnes	56	47	54	51
Passing Tigley Box	23¼	18½	26½	22½
Rattery Summit	31	30	34½	34½
Passing Brent	50	46	50	53
Wrangaton Summit	46	45	47	50
	m s	m s	m s	m s
Time, Aller-Wrangaton ...	25 46	29 34	24 20	27 18

The performance of No 6016 with 405 tons was magnificent, especially as the greatest restraint was shown on the descent from Dainton to Totnes. No 6008 had plenty of time in hand and had no need to hurry, whereas No 6015 continued to make a superb effort to regain lost time. On this run the maximum cut-off used up Dainton bank was 32 per cent, and 35 per cent on Rattery—a long way below the maximum capacity of the locomotive. By contrast the *Ark Royal* was 'flat-out' from Aller Junction up to Dainton, and from Totnes to Rattery. On this occasion it would seem that D601 was not running up to the standard expected by the com-

puter. Against the predicted times of 5.3 min from Aller up to Dainton, and 7 min from Totnes to Rattery, our times were 6 min 0 sec and 8 min 39 sec, even though full power was being used throughout both ascents.

Technicalities apart, after more than a dozen trips on the footplates of steam locomotives over the South Devon line it was a novel experience to ride through to Plymouth in a cab of a diesel from which one could appreciate, more than ever, the extraordinarily severe curvature of the route. But more than any scenic or civil engineering interests, there was—to me at any rate—the odd sensation of seeing the locomotive put into full power at Aller Junction, and again at Totnes, and of seeing the fearsome gradients gradually wear down the speed, with the knowledge that no one on the locomotive could do anything about it. There was no extra turn on the reverser that could be given; no boiler capacity that could be briefly mortgaged. If the full power given to the *Ark Royal* at Aller Junction had not been enough we should, in the modern vernacular, have 'had it.' Actually we climbed both major banks very well, albeit with absolutely nothing in reserve.

There must have been times, in the past, when drivers of the 'Stars' must have thrown in very nearly all they had on the last mile up to Dainton, and I remember a hair-raising occasion when No 4054, *Princess Charlotte*, started slipping on Hemerdon while hauling a 320-ton load on the Penzance-Wolverhampton express. Once the engine had regained her feet it needed 73 per cent cut-off and full regulator to get that load fairly on the move again. One wonders, no less, what cut-offs were needed when No 4042, *Prince Albert*, worked a 310-ton train from Newton Abbot to Brent in 20 min pass to pass—nearly 2 min faster than the all-out performance of the *Ark Royal*!

East Coast route — 'Deltics' and steam compared

By the time the following article was written, some notably sharp timings had been introduced to the East Coast route, primarily as a result of the 'Deltic' locomotives and the special measures that had been set up for their well-nigh immaculate maintenance. At that time it was by no means the same with all the most recently introduced of the new power then running on British Railways. The 'Deltics' did excellently from the very start of their career; but what of the outstanding performance of some of the Gresley Pacifics that were still called on to do first class work?

THE extent to which diesel traction has now taken hold of the main-line express workings in this country is exemplified by my own travelling experience since the beginning of the year 1961. Up to the time of proof correction for this particular article, out of 118 long-distance journeys no fewer than 88 have been diesel-hauled. Taken all round the punctuality record has been quite good, with drivers doing all they can to regain time lost from causes outside their control. The easy schedules on the London Midland main line south of Crewe have permitted some spectacular recoveries; at the same time I must add that some of the worst delays should never have been permitted to occur, so elementary and obvious were the operating errors that led up to them.

On the reorganised Western Region services put into effect last September, my own travelling experiences have not been too good. On the Bath and Bristol trains the arrivals have been, successively, the following number of minutes late: 7, 0, 3, 0, 2 early, 2, 17, 21, 15, 15, 3, 0, 10, 5, 7, 5 and 0. The first up business express, due in Paddington at 9.35 am, has been a particularly bad offender, with successive arrivals of 17, 15, 15, and 5 min late. At the same time, even though the loads are mostly light the drivers of the diesels have their work cut out to keep some of the smart bookings seeing that the 'Warship' class locomotives are still limited to a maximum speed of 80 mph.

On one journey with the up evening express that used to be known as 'The Merchant Venturer' we left Chippenham 10 min late, and although we had a perfectly clear road from Swindon we were still 3 min late on arrival, with a nine-coach train. On both stages the speed was held very closely to the 80 mph limit, yet this did not permit of faster start-to-stop times

than 35½ min from Swindon to Reading, 41.3 miles, and 33¾ min from Reading to Paddington.

Even with heavier trains there is ample power available, and if the locomotives could be permitted to run at the 'nineties' they attained easily in their earlier days there is no doubt the standard of punctuality would be a great deal higher. As yet, however, the authorities are not sufficiently satisfied with their riding qualities to agree to any relaxation. On one of my most recent journeys I must admit to being caught napping—literally! It was convenient to me to travel on the 12.54 pm from Chippenham to Paddington, and when the train came in from Bristol loaded to no more than six coaches and headed by a diesel, I took no detailed notes of the running. After lunch I went back to my compartment and must confess to dozing off into a 'cat-nap'.

I awoke just after Didcot, and noticed that exhaust steam was drifting past the windows. I imagined that we were overtaking a train running on the relief line; but we continued merrily at

At the beginning of the 'A4' saga, in 1935, engine No 2512 Silver Fox in the original silver livery at King's Cross. (W.J. Reynolds)

70 mph, and I was to discover that on this service portions from Weston-super-Mare and Cheltenham are combined at Swindon, and that a Gloucester engine works through to Paddington. Our engine turned out to be No 5064, *Bishops Castle*, and with a load of 405 tons she did well, running the 77.3 miles up from Swindon in 80¼ min start to stop, or about 77 min net, bringing us in a minute early.

This month I am mainly concerned with the East Coast Route, and readers will naturally be interested to know how the new 'Deltics' are running on the fastest train in Great Britain, the 8.19 am from Hitchin to Retford. Despite the historic reputation for speed enjoyed by the Great Northern it is perhaps not generally known that there are numerous restrictions in the way of uninterrupted fast running, and while experience with the diesel-electric locomotives is being gained, both from the motive power and the track points of view, it is most important that the stipulated restrictions be carefully observed. I well remember the early days of Sir Nigel Gresley's streamlined trains, and with what meticulous care the charts from the mechanical speed recorders on the 'A4' engines were scrutinised to see that none of the prescribed speed restrictions had been exceeded. Having regard to the limits of speed laid down, the schedule of the 7.50 am express from Kings Cross appears to be a hard one.

By the kindness of the Eastern Region authorities I was recently privileged to ride in the cab of one of the 'Deltics' on the new service, and this journey, which is shown in Table I, makes a most interesting comparison with a footplate journey I made on this same train in 1955, when the start-to-stop time from Hitchin to Retford was 96½ min, against the 89 min of today. At the present time the maximum line speed on the

down road is 60 mph out to New Barnet, and 70 onwards to Woolmer Green. Northwards the limit is 90 mph to the commencement of the Offord curves, and 90 again from Werrington Junction to the outskirts of Grantham.

Apart from Peterborough Station the most hampering restriction is a stretch limited to 65 mph across the Fens from Holme almost to Yaxley, and there are limits of 70 mph over Langley troughs and 60 mph over Werrington troughs. There is also a limit of 70 mph through Grantham Station. The line maximum is 85 mph between Offord and Peterborough and again between Grantham and Newark, while after a 60 mph limit over Muskham troughs the line maximum is 80 mph onwards to Retford. In addition to the above there is a short length of about 1¼ miles past Abbots Ripton where the limit is 80 mph.

In running a fast train like the down 'West

TABLE I
EASTERN REGION: KINGS CROSS–RETFORD
'THE WEST RIDING'

Run No									1			2	
Engine No									D9009			60117	
Engine Name									*Alycidon*			*Bois Roussel*	
Load, tons (E/F)									386/405			339/360	
Driver									Arrand			Wallace	
Depot									Kings Cross			Copley Hill	
Dist								Sch*	Actual		Speeds	Actual		Speeds
Miles								min	m	s	mph	m	s	mph
0.0	KINGS CROSS	...	...	...	...	...		0	0	00	—	0	00	—
2.6	Finsbury Park	...	...	...	...	...			4	50	—	6	35	—
5.0	Wood Green	...	...	...	...	...			7	14	62	9	43	56
9.2	New Barnet	...	...	...	...	...			11	25	58	14	17	55
									—		70	sigs		—
12.7	Potters Bar	...	...	...	...	...		15	14	30	69	18	37	25
17.7	HATFIELD	...	...	...	...	...		19	18	35	72	24	35	66/60
23.5	*Woolmer Green*	...	...	...	...	...			23	24	69/86	30	10	62/76
28.6	Stevenage	...	...	...	...	...			27	20	69	34	34	74
									—		82	—		82
31.9	HITCHIN	...	...	...	...	...		32	31	11	—	38	21	—
3.8	*Three Counties*	...	...	...	...	...			4	35	84	5	06	68
9.2	Biggleswade	...	...	...	...	...			8	17	90	9	35	80
12.2	Sandy	...	...	...	...	...		9½	10	15	91	11	50	79/82
19.8	St Neots	...	...	...	...	...			15	18	89	17	29	79
									pws		—	—		85

Engine Name							Sch*	Alycidon		Bois Roussel	
Dist								Actual	Speeds	Actual	Speeds
24.0	Offord Box	...	...	...	...	...		18 55	40	20 35	70
27.0	HUNTINGDON	...	...	...	...	...	20	21 58	72	22 49	74
30.1	Milepost 62	...	...	...	...	...		24 22	80	25 25	70
35.5	Connington South	...	...	...	...	...		28 07	87	29 37	85
43.1	Fletton Junc	...	...	...	...	...		34 23	—	35 17	—
								sigs	—	—	—
44.5	PETERBOROUGH	...	...	...	...	...	38	37 13	10	37 27	—
47.6	Werrington Junc	...	...	...	...	...	42	41 25	64½	41 51	62
52.9	Tallington	...	...	...	...	...		45 38	82	46 27	73
56.7	Essendine	...	...	...	...	...	48½	48 25	80	49 35	72
60.3	Little Bytham	...	...	...	...	...		51 07	80	52 34	68
								pws	20	—	66½
65.2	Corby Glen	...	...	...	...	...		57 29	71½	56 50	69
68.2	Stoke	...	...	...	...	...	56½	59 52	76	59 34	65
								—	89	pws	15
73.6	GRANTHAM	...	...	...	...	...	60½	63 48	68	66 31	68
								sigs	—	—	—
77.8	Barkston S Junc	...	...	...	...	...	63½	67 23	—	69 58	76
								sig stop	—	—	—
83.5	Claypole	...	...	...	...	...		82 44	87	73 58	86
88.2	NEWARK	...	...	...	...	...	73½	85 05	—	77 37	82
	Muskham troughs	...	...	...	...	...		—	60	—	70
95.5	Crow Park	...	...	...	...	...		91 50	82	83 39	72½
								—	75	sigs	30
102.1	Milepost 34	...	...	...	...	...		96 54	76½	90 55	52
								—	84	sigs	—
106.7	RETFORD	...	...	...	...	...	89	101 33	—	99 17	—
Net times, min								86		92½	

*No 1 run only. Schedules on No 2 run: Hitchin 39½, Peterborough 38½, Grantham 66, and Retford 96½ min.

Riding' it is largely a case of driving up the maximum speed permitted over each succeeding stretch of line. How skilfully the driver did this will be seen from the average speeds of 60.2 mph from Finsbury Park to New Barnet, 71 from Hadley Wood to Woolmer Green, and exactly 90 mph from Arlesey to St Neots. Before coming to the really fast stage of the journey, however, some mention may be made of the comparison run with the 'A1' Pacific engine No 60117, *Bois Roussel*. It was made on a cold and blustering March day when we were running through snow showers for much of the distance. With no more than 360 tons behind the tender it was an easy task, and no difficulty would have been experienced in running to the present schedule, if necessary. Until the signal check

before Potters Bar the engine was working in 23 to 24 per cent cut-off, with a partly-opened regulator, and making light work of it.

No 60117 was taken quite easily out of Hitchin, and by Three Counties the gear had been linked up to 17 per cent. After that she ran at a continuous 79 to 85 mph from Biggleswade to the approach to Offord. There were no restrictions over the Fenland stretch in those days, and *Bois Roussel* ran at 84–85 mph continuously from the foot of Abbots Ripton bank almost to Yaxley. In starting from Hitchin the diesel was quickly opened up to full power, but despite this it was not possible to observe strictly the very fast sectional time of 9½ min to Sandy.

Peterborough was passed on time, and I was looking forward to an interesting exhibition of

At the end of the Second World War at Edinburgh Waverley after the re-numbering: engine No 19 Empire of India *on the 5.25 pm Glasgow–Leeds express.* (O.S. Nock)

'Deltic' capacity on the climb to Stoke. Unfortunately the weather conditions were far from good. We had climbed out of London in mist, with the rain clouds exceptionally low, and when the driver attempted to put the engine to it in full vigour north of Werrington Junction she began slipping at any speed above 80 mph. From the long and severe permanent way check north of Little Bytham a fine recovery was made, working throughout on full power, to 76 mph over Stoke summit.

The steam locomotive did well up the bank on relatively short cut-offs. The percentages were 17 from Werrington, 20 from Essendine, and 25 from Little Bytham to the summit. This gave us a sustained minimum speed of 66½ mph on the 1 in 200 gradient. Because of the relaying slack through Stoke Tunnel *Bois Roussel* was fractionally behind time at Grantham, whereas the 'Deltic' was 4½ min late. Even with 3 min recovery time in the schedule between Grantham and Newark I was now beginning to doubt if we should maintain our end-to-end time. As it turned out both runs were spoiled in conclusion

by operating delays. The Pacific ran freely to Crow Park, and even after a signal check at Tuxford there was still time in hand. In the approach to Retford, however, we were twice all but stopped, and so came in 2¾ min late.

On my trip with the 'Deltic' we became involved with an extraordinary operating 'tangle.' Drawing to a stand at Barkston North advanced starting signal we could see some prolonged shunting operations in progress with a down freight train, at Hougham, in which not only ourselves, but a southbound passenger train were also involved. We stood for a solid 7 min, and, with all the preliminary slowings, we took 15¾ min to cover the six miles from Grantham to Hougham. After such a delay it was not surprising that we arrived at Retford 12½ min late. The net time was 86 min, and with the engine being driven up to the maximum permissible speeds of the road for most of the journey it does not appear that there is much time in hand on this schedule. So far as the Stoke bank is concerned I have received from an old friend details of a run on which some very much faster climbing was made. There was a permanent way check to 20 mph at Helpston, after which speed was worked up to 90 mph at Essendine, and averaged 87.7 mph from there to the summit.

From various correspondents I have received details of 'Deltic' runs on a variety of trains. Mr J. F. Speakman, of Harrogate, has sent me logs of two runs on the up 'West Riding,' booked non-stop over the 175.9 miles from Wakefield to Kings Cross in 164 min. The load is the same as that of the 7.45 am down, namely eleven coaches, and recovering time lost by signal and permanent way checks, engine No D9003, *Meld*, first of all pulled off a net time of 141 min for the run—an average speed of exactly 75 mph—while on his second experience with the train my friend recorded an actual time of 153 min 54 sec, and a net time of 142¾ min, with engine No D9007, *Pinza*. Both these journeys displayed the capacity of these locomotives to haul an eleven-coach train up the long 1 in 200 gradients at 84–85 mph.

I have shown in Table II a further run of Mr Speakman's recording, on which No D9007 made almost as good running with the much-heavier load of the down 'Yorkshire Pullman,' and some 460 tons gross behind the locomotive. The climb from Peterborough to Stoke was exceptionally fine on this trip, with its average of 85.8 mph from Tallington to the summit, and its minimum speed of 84½ mph after a full three miles at 1 in 178 up from Corby Glen. The net time of 130 min from Kings Cross to Doncaster, with its net average speed of 72 mph, was made with the most careful observance of the many slight speed restrictions enforced over lengths of this main line.

By contrast, a run on the 'Queen of Scots' Pullman, with one of the type '4' English Electric diesels, No D345, involved comparatively leisurely work. This train is allowed 164 min to pass Doncaster, and with a load of only eight cars, as against the eleven conveyed on the 'Yorkshire Pullman,' Grantham was passed in 107½ min after several signal checks. The train was ahead of time at every check point north of Huntingdon, and although the overall net time

TABLE II
EASTERN REGION: KINGS CROSS-DONCASTER 'THE YORKSHIRE PULLMAN'

Load: 11 Pullmans, 440 tons tare, 460 tons full
Engine: Type '5' Diesel-electric No D9007, *Pinza*

Dist		Sch	Actual		Speeds
Miles		min	m	s	mph
0.0	KINGS CROSS	0	0	00	—
2.6	Finsbury Park		5	36	53
5.0	Wood Green		7	52	65½
9.2	New Barnet		11	50	61
12.7	Potters Bar	16	15	11	64
17.7	HATFIELD	21	19	21	74
			sigs		45
23.5	*Woolmer Green* ...		24	49	60½
28.6	Stevenage		29	13	73
			sigs		—
31.9	HITCHIN	34	31	43	40
37.0	Arlesey		37	12	83
			sigs		—
41.1	Biggleswade		42	20	5
44.1	Sandy	42	47	10	67
51.7	St Neots		52	39	88
55.9	*Offord Box*		55	42	66
58.9	HUNTINGDON N ...	53½	58	08	71½/79
63.5	*Abbots Ripton*		61	35	82/88
67.4	*Connington South* ...		64	17	83
69.4	Holme		65	46	71
					(slack)
72.6	*Yaxley*		68	48	61/72
76.4	PETERBOROUGH N ...	73	72	53	25
84.8	*Tallington*		81	38	86
88.6	*Essendine*	84	84	24	84
92.2	*Little Bytham*		86	52	85½
97.1	*Corby Glen*		90	17	87
100.1	*Stoke*	92½	92	21	84½/88
105.5	GRANTHAM	97	96	08	66
109.7	*Barkston South Junc* ...	100½	99	45	71
115.4	*Claypole*		103	54	83
120.1	NEWARK	112	107	26	76/64
127.4	*Crow Park*		113	36	82
131.7	*Tuxford North Junc* ...		116	49	79/80½
			sigs		—
138.6	RETFORD	127	124	34	25
144.0	Ranskill		130	18	75
			pws		—
147.7	Bawtry		136	06	15
151.3	Rossington		140	16	76
			sigs		—
156.0	DONCASTER	145	146	40	—

TABLE III
EASTERN AND NORTH EASTERN
REGIONS: KINGS CROSS-NEWCASTLE
THE AFTERNOON 'TALISMAN'

Load: 9 coaches, 312 tons tare, 330 tons full
Engine: Type '5' Diesel-electric No D9011

Dist		Sch	Actual		Av Speeds
Miles		min	m	s	mph
0.0	KINGS CROSS	0	0	00	—
			engine and sig delays		
17.7	Hatfield	22	49	26	—
28.6	Stevenage		59	05	67.2
			pws		
31.9	HITCHIN	35	63	43	—
35.7	Three Counties ...		67	15	64.7
51.7	St Neots		77	41	91.6
			pws		
58.9	HUNTINGDON ...	55	85	14	—
75.0	Fletton Junc		96	24	86.5
76.4	PETERBOROUGH ...	75	98	12	—
79.5	Werrington Junc ...	80	101	33	—
92.2	Little Bytham ...		109	54	91.2
			pws		
100.1	Stoke Box	96	117	20	—
105.5	GRANTHAM	103	121	14	83.0
138.6	RETFORD	134	144	18	86.0
			sigs pws		—
156.0	DONCASTER	154	166	52	—
160.2	Shaftholme Junc ..	161	170	42	65.8
169.8	Templehirst		176	56	92.3
			sigs		
174.4	SELBY	173½	184	04	—
186.2	Chaloners Whin Junc		193	58	71.5
			sigs		
188.2	YORK	188½	197	39	—
			sigs		
197.9	Tollerton	199	208	05	—
218.2	NORTHALLERTON ...	215	221	19	91.8
			pws		
227.1	Eryholme Junc	224½	229	44	—
232.3	DARLINGTON ...	229	233	54	75.0
253.3	Relly Mill Junc		250	46	74.7
			sigs		—
254.3	DURHAM	250½	252	45	—
			sigs		—
268.3	NEWCASTLE	270	270	51	—

Traffic and pw delays: 34 min
Delay due to engine trouble: 25 min

of 197 min from Kings Cross to Leeds Central showed a gain of 10 min on schedule, the net average speed of 57.5 mph is slow compared with the new standards of running over this route.

What can be done in the way of time recovery, in emergency, is shown by a log sent to me by Mr Ronald Nelson, and reproduced in abridged form in Table III. For one of the 'Deltics' a load of 'nine' would be a mere featherweight in the ordinary way, even on a schedule of almost 60 mph non-stop from Kings Cross to Newcastle, but after a fast start up the Holloway bank a defect developed in the locomotive, and a stop was made at Milepost 2¾, just north of Finsbury Park. The train stood there for 22 min, and then being completely out of its proper path suffered a series of signal checks until Hatfield was passed—by that time 29 min late, after leaving Kings Cross 1½ min late. With no more than 33 min allowed for the 41.2 miles on to Huntingdon, it was not surprising that further time was lost because of two severe relaying checks intervening. On passing Huntingdon the train was at its maximum lateness, of 31¾ min.

However, already some very fast running had been made between the checks, and despite the incidence of many more time was now steadily won back. The lateness was reduced to 24¾ min at Peterborough, 19¾ at Grantham, 11¾ at Retford, and 10½ at York. Up to this point three permanent way checks, and six signal checks, had been experienced. But there was no discouraging this very determined driver, and on passing Durham only 3¾ min late there were justifiable hopes of a punctual arrival in Newcastle. This was unfortunately not to be, and bad signal checks at Chester-le-Street and Bensham prevented the recovery of more than 1½ min on this easily-timed final stretch. The traffic and engineering slacks accounted for 34 min in running, leaving a net time of 236¾ min for the 268.3 miles. Strictly speaking one cannot deduct the time lost by the Finsbury Park check, as this was due to engine trouble; but if one does so, to arrive at the potentialities of these 'Deltics,' we come down to the remarkable net time of 211¾ min—an average speed of 76.2 mph throughout.

I have not tabulated this most exciting journey in any but the most summary detail, because of its length. There were some slight excesses over the maximum line speeds laid down, but only in the most favourable conditions, and it is notable that the maximum speed of the whole journey, namely 96 mph, took place on a slight rising gradient, up the 1 in 626 from Thirsk to Northallerton. The same permanent way check that was experienced on my run with the 'West Riding' spoiled the ascent from Peterborough to Stoke. It would otherwise have been interesting to see whether the bank could have been cleared at a full 90 mph. A maximum of 95¼ mph had been attained near Essendine, and the train was still travelling at 94 well up the 1 in 200 above Little Bytham when it was necessary for it to shut off for the slack. Seeing that the 460-ton 'Yorkshire Pullman' had been taken over Stoke at a minimum speed of

84½ mph, a full 90 with the 330-ton 'Talisman' should have been quite a reasonable possibility.

And now to turn from diesel to steam once more, I have in my files some truly magnificent examples of 'A4' performance that have been collected over the years, mostly by Mr P. J. Coster. In Table IV are shown two runs from Kings Cross to York, the first on the 'Elizabethan,' with engine No 60013, *Dominion of New Zealand*, and the second on the summer 9.40 am with *Mallard*. The first of the two runs includes some of the fastest running between Kings Cross and Peterborough that I have ever seen with a 400-ton train. The engine was certainly not pressed in the immediate start out to Holloway, and I have personally recorded some much faster climbing to Potters Bar by the engine *Seagull* and a load of 475 tons. But after Stevenage *Dominion of New Zealand* was given her head; she reached a level 100 mph at Arlesey and averaged 87.1 mph over the 27 miles from Hitchin to Huntingdon. There was no restriction across the Fens at the time this run was

The up 'Elizabethan' south of York hauled by 4-6-2 No 60017 Silver Fox. (C. Ord)

TABLE IV
EASTERN REGION: KINGS CROSS–YORK

Run No Engine No Engine Name Load, tons (E/F)		1 60013 *Dominion of New Zealand* 406/425		2 60022 *Mallard* 454/490	
Dist		Actual	Speeds	Actual	Speeds
Miles		m s	mph	m s	mph
0.0	KINGS CROSS	0 00	—	0 00	—
		—	—	sig stops	—
5.0	Wood Green	10 27	48	17 27	—
12.7	Potters Bar	19 20	52	29 20	40
17.7	HATFIELD	23 57	76	36 31	65
23.5	*Woolmer Green*	29 00	62	42 29	52
28.6	Stevenage	33 25	—	47 19	—
31.9	HITCHIN	35 57	85	50 00	86
37.1	*Arlesey*	39 18	100	53 19	96
41.1	Biggleswade	42 05	87	55 55	92
44.1	Sandy	44 04	94	57 49	95
51.7	St Neots	49 17	84	62 42	91
	Offord	—	95/70	—	94/70
58.9	HUNTINGDON	54 33	72	67 56	83
62.0	*Milepost 62*	57 03	—	70 37	61
		—	—	pws	20
69.4	*Holme*	62 21	90 (max)	77 21	92 (max)
		—	—	sigs	—
76.4	PETERBOROUGH	69 42	—	84 35	—
79.5	*Werrington Junc*	75 43	60	89 24	60
84.8	*Tallington*	80 33	70	94 24	72
88.6	*Essendine*	84 00	70	97 27	77
92.2	*Little Bytham*	87 33	65	100 28	70
97.1	*Corby Glen*	92 29	60	105 07	65
100.1	*Stoke Box*	95 47	57	108 00	61
105.5	GRANTHAM	100 21	80/70	112 41	75
115.4	Claypole	107 47	95	121 58	70
120.1	NEWARK	111 16	77	126 17	65
		sigs		—	—
131.9	Tuxford	123 08	60	137 18	60
		sigs	10	sigs	—
138.6	RETFORD	129 18	—	144 38	35
		sigs	—	sigs	—
156.0	DONCASTER	145 25	—	165 48	—
169.8	Templehirst	158 13	75	184 09	70
174.4	SELBY	162 05	(slack)	186 59	—
184.0	Naburn	170 17	72	—	—
188.2	YORK	175 12	PASS	205 01	—

made, and a maximum of 90 mph at Connington South was followed by very little falling off in speed until Peterborough was neared. Passing this station nearly 5 min early things were taken relatively easily up to Stoke, and with numerous restrictions and checks north of

Newark there was no opportunity for further fireworks. Even so, York was passed 6¾ min early.

On the second run *Mallard*, with her 490-ton train, was very badly delayed out to Wood Green, to such an extent indeed as to make the

A 'Deltic' on the up 'Flying Scotsman' at Monktonhall Junction: engine No 9018 Ballymoss. (Derek Cross)

time through Hatfield as much as 36½ min. By this time the engine was going splendidly, and the high-speed section from Hitchin to Huntingdon produced an amazing average of 90.2 mph—faster by 40 sec than the previous run with the 'Elizabethan.' This time there was a superb ascent to Stoke, especially as the driver got a bad start to it through signal checks between Peterborough and Werrington Junction. Such speeds as 77 mph before Essendine and 61 over Stoke Summit were outstanding, even for an 'A4,' with a load of all but 500 tons. There was no need to hurry afterwards, and on a schedule of 210 min the arrival in York was 5 min early. The net time to passing Grantham was less than 100 min.

So far as a passing time through Grantham was concerned, both these fine runs were substantially beaten by the run of the 'Plant Centenarian' express, in 1953, chiefly by reason of a magnificent climb to Stoke. On that occasion No 60014, *Silver Link,* was the engine, with a

gross load of 400 tons, and Peterborough was passed in 70 min 37 sec. Then Driver Hailstone opened out, and over the 15.3 miles from Tallington to the summit box we averaged 74.7 mph, with a 69 mph minimum. The maximum at Arlesey might have been higher, and today I may tell of an amusing occurrence on the run. When we passed Hitchin at 90 mph, and were still accelerating fast, a certain senior locomotive man decided this was nearly enough and went through the corridor tender on to the footplate. When he arrived the speed was 98 mph, and having come down the bank with a partly-opened regulator Hailstone was just in the act of opening out to absolutely full regulator—at 98 mph! Much to the driver's disgust a restraining hand was laid on his shoulder, and he was not allowed to make a faster average than 86.9 mph from Hitchin to Huntingdon.

In the days when the Kings Cross Pacifics were single-manned, the combination of Ted Hailstone and *Silver Link* became almost legen-

TABLE V
EASTERN REGION:
GRANTHAM–KINGS CROSS

Load: 13 coaches, 452 tons tare, 500 tons full
Engine: Class 'A4' 4-6-2 No 60014, *Silver Link*
Driver: E. Hailstone, Kings Cross shed

Dist		Actual	Speeds
Miles		m s	mph
0.0	GRANTHAM	0 00	—
3.5	*Great Ponton*	6 30	46
5.4	*Stoke Box*	8 56	52
8.4	*Corby Glen*	11 52	73
13.3	*Little Bytham*	15 27	90
16.9	*Essendine*	17 51	90
20.7	*Tallington*	20 26	88
26.0	*Werrington Junc*	24 36	—
		sigs	—
29.1	PETERBOROUGH ...	28 06	—
		sigs	—
36.1	Holme	38 42	69
42.0	*Abbots Ripton*	45 51	—
		sigs	50
46.6	HUNTINGDON	49 48	82
49.5	*Offord*	51 58	(slack)
53.8	St Neots	55 12	78
58.0	*Tempsford*	58 12	86
61.4	Sandy	60 35	85
64.4	Biggleswade	62 40	81
68.4	Arlesey	65 36	84
73.6	HITCHIN	69 21	77
76.9	Stevenage	71 57	74
82.0	Woolmer Green	76 00	73
85.2	Welwyn Garden City ...	78 23	87
87.8	HATFIELD	80 09	85
		sigs	—
92.8	Potters Bar	85 20	—
		sigs	—
100.5	Wood Green	95 23	—
		sigs	—
102.9	Finsbury Park	97 51	—
105.5	KINGS CROSS	101 41	—

celerating like lightning afterwards, *Silver Link* reached the usual 90 mph on the descent to Tallington, and the checks around Peterborough were not an unduly serious hindrance. They cost about 3 min between them.

Then came an exhibition without parallel, even for Hailstone and *Silver Link*. Not only were the 27 miles from Huntingdon to Hitchin covered at the extraordinary average—uphill!—of 82.8 mph, but the entire bank to Stevenage was cleared at a minimum speed of 74 mph. A maximum speed of 87 mph at Welwyn Garden City put the finishing touch on a time of 30 min 21 sec over the 41.2 miles from Huntingdon to Hatfield—an average speed of 81.2 mph.

This astonishing piece of load haulage can best be analysed by comparing the average speeds over the generally-rising gradients from Offord to Woolmer Green—32½ miles in 24 min. This itself can be divided into the easier and harder length at Biggleswade. The average gradient throughout from Offord is 1 in 625, and taking the train resistance as that for calm weather the average equivalent drawbar horsepower sustained for half an hour works out at 1,920. From Biggleswade onwards the average edhp was 2,020, but the engine was considerably eased after passing Stevenage, and it is clear that a most exceptional effort was being made up the 1 in 200 bank from Hitchin. Mr Coster recorded a minimum speed of 74 mph at the summit, a drop of only 3 mph in the last 3¼ miles of 1 in 200. Over this section the output appears to have been at least 2,300 edhp.

After such running another 17 min from Hatfield should have seen the train comfortably into Kings Cross; but this was long before the quadrupling of the line south of Potters Bar, and a succession of delays from a goods train caused the 15.1 miles from Hatfield to Finsbury Park to take 17¾ min. Even so the journey eventually took no more than 101¾ min, and the net time of about 92½ or 93 min was a performance of the very greatest merit. In the years 1932–5 we used to think that the running of the so-called Leeds 'Breakfast Flyer' was a great feat, with its

dary, and in Table V I have set out details of a run on the up 'Flying Scotsman' which was then allowed 122 min from Grantham to Kings Cross. After relieving the Gateshead engine, *Silver Link*, coming on fresh, was 29 min late away, and Hailstone set out systematically and deliberately to arrive in Kings Cross on time. With a packed train of 13 coaches this would have seemed as near impossible as makes no matter. Going hard up to Stoke, and ac-

A 'Deltic' on the down 'Yorkshire Pullman' near Potters Bar. (English Electric Co)

schedule time of 100 min from Grantham to Kings Cross. With the non-streamlined Pacifics the load used to be limited to a maximum of about 400 tons; yet here was the old schedule being bettered by 7 or 8 min with a load of 500 tons!

Mr Coster has sent me details of a run on the up 'Elizabethan' on which some even faster running was made over certain stretches, this time with engine No 60032, *Gannet*, the usual load of 425 tons gross, and Driver W. Hoole, who is now enjoying his retirement driving on the Festiniog Railway. Because of checks further north the train had passed Grantham 3 min late, and nothing was regained by Peterborough despite a maximum speed of 100 mph down the bank. Worse still, practically no water was picked up from Werrington troughs because of another train no more than a block ahead, and Hoole stopped at Huntingdon for water.

On getting away again he had 55 min left in which to reach Kings Cross on time, and with an amazing time of 35 min 25 sec from the dead start to passing Hatfield, 41.2 miles, the job might well have seemed 'in the bag.' But for

TABLE VI
EASTERN REGION:
HUNTINGDON–KINGS CROSS
'THE ELIZABETHAN' (from water stop)

Load: 11 coaches, 408 tons tare, 425 tons full
Engine: Class 'A4' 4-6-2 No 60032, *Gannet*
Driver: W. Hoole, Kings Cross shed

Dist		Sch	Actual		Speeds
Miles		min	m	s	mph
0.0	HUNTINGDON ...	0*	0	00	—
2.9	*Offord*		5	12	60
7.2	St Neots		9	28	67/62
11.4	*Tempsford*		13	05	73
14.8	Sandy...		15	38	90
17.8	Biggleswade ...		17	37	92
21.8	*Arlesey*		20	28	83/85
				sigs	66
27.0	HITCHIN	23	24	42	—
30.3	Stevenage ...		27	25	76
35.4	*Woolmer Green* ...		31	21	72 (min)
38.6	Welwyn Garden City		33	37	90
41.2	HATFIELD	36½	35	25	85
				sigs	—
46.2	Potters Bar ...	44½	42	55	—
				sigs	—
56.3	Finsbury Park ...	59½	56	25	—
				sigs	—
58.9	KINGS CROSS ...	64½	63	35	—

*From passing Huntingdon

once the road for the 'Elizabethan' was not clear, so much so that the last 17.7 miles in from Hatfield took as much as 28¼ min. The work between Huntingdon and Hatfield is detailed in Table VI, and it certainly forms a fitting counterpart to that of *Silver Link* in Table V. I have not got the names of the firemen who were playing such a vital part in the making of these fine runs; but Hailstone and Hoole were typical of the kind of drivers who encouraged and inspired their mates.

In recent months I have been riding on diesels in many parts of the country, and I have been interested to hear from many of the men that they don't seem to get the same satisfaction out of diesels that they did out of steam. This has applied particularly on some of the heavily-graded routes in the north where the top-link men have always seemed to take banks like Shap, Beattock and their like as a challenge to their skill. Now, as one of them put it to me, 'there's nothing you can do about it except put the handle hard over and hope for the best.'

Midland Line: Settle and Carlisle test runs

This very famous mountain route has already featured in this collection of articles from my own contributions to *The Railway Magazine*; but the continuance of the route as a major testing ground for some of the latest and most powerful British express passenger locomotives and the privilege accorded to me of having some of the dynamometer rolls for study in the comfort and privacy of my own home afforded me further opportunities of studying some of these great runs. Furthermore, the introduction of the powerful 'Peak' class diesel-electric locomotives on that route made some interesting comparisons of performance to be made.

NOT many months ago one might have said that the overall pattern of British railway motive power in the diesel age was settling down into something stable. The several varieties of type '2,' type '3,' and type '4' locomotives were becoming familiar sights in most parts of the country, and the enthusiasts were becoming sufficiently aware of the 'look' of 'Warships,' English Electric 'D200s,' and BR Sulzer type '4s' of the 'Peak' class to debate their external styling. Now, within the space of a very few months, the familiar and hard-working type '4s' have been joined by a group of new designs—mostly in the prototype stage, including the 'D1000' class on the Western Region, the *Falcon*, and latest of all the white *Lion*. These new locomotives are all in the 2,700-hp group and their performances will be watched with much interest.

At the same time notes on my own experiences on the 'footplates' of the BR/Sulzer type '4s' are overdue. Some of my own most interesting runs with these fine locomotives, and those of correspondents, have been over the Settle and Carlisle line; and the work of the diesels over this most fascinating route makes an interesting comparison with the maximum efforts of steam locomotives in the controlled road tests with the dynamometer car conducted with many famous designs since nationalisation. In the May, 1961, issue of *The Railway Magazine* I gave details of some of the test runs carried out by the LMSR, after grouping; the present notes bring the story of testing to the end of the steam era. By the kindness of Mr A. E. Robson, Chief Mechanical & Electrical Engineer, London Midland Region, I have had the loan of many of the original dynamometer car rolls.

Stanier 'Black Five' 4-6-0 No 4866 attached to the Mobile Testing Unit. By means on the structure on the front of the locomotive, the speed and direction of the wind is electrically recorded on the dynamometer car chart. (British Railways)

To anyone who has witnessed or taken part in steam locomotive testing these records, made while engines were being worked practically to their limit for an hour on end, or more, are most revealing documents. It is not so much the factual records of drawbar pull, boiler pressures, cut-offs, and so on, as the odd jottings, the violent slip that sometimes took place when a tunnel was entered, showing how near to the limits of adhesion the engines were worked at times, or the fact that 'John Blank' had been relieved by 'George So and So' in the firing. Sometimes the locomotives were being pounded to such an extent that the drivers found difficulty in keeping the steaming rate constant; there was fluctuation in the boiler pressure, and when one reads of 'Britannias' and 'Duchesses' worked in 50 per cent cut-off, with full regulator, it does not need much imagination to guess at the pandemonium let loose in that wild countryside over Aisgill when *John Milton* or *Duchess of Gloucester* climbed to Blea Moor or Birkett Tunnel under maximum loading conditions.

In this article I have chosen the up journeys for detailed reference, partly because the nature of the road produces some fast running in-

termediately, by Lazonby and Ormside, as well as the tremendous pounding from Ormside Viaduct right up to Aisgill, and partly because the best of the new diesel runs I have in my files are also in this direction. It is not possible to set out all these runs for direct comparison. The controlled road tests with the steam locomotives all began from the sidings adjacent to the old Durran Hill engine sheds of the Midland Railway; but even with these runs there is a lack of uniformity. On some the footplate and test crews took longer to get the working conditions stabilised at the pre-arranged steaming rate than on others. On one run in particular all seemed to be settling down nicely by Armathwaite when the engine slipped violently in the tunnel just beyond, and kept on slipping right through Baron's Wood Tunnel.

With Pacific-type locomotives, on two of the most severe tests when coal was being shovelled at the rate of almost equal to one hundredweight per minute (!), the tests were stopped some way short of Aisgill summit—not because the locomotives themselves could not sustain it, but because the effort was beginning to tell on all concerned. Because of the different starting points of the runs at constant steaming rates the details are presented in a number of different tables. Thus, in Table I there are three runs with 4-6-0 locomotives of class '5' capacity over the section between Appleby and Garsdale, two with the 'B1' class engine No 61353, using the dynamometer car of the former Lancashire & Yorkshire Railway, and one with a new British Railways class '5' 4-6-0, No 73008. This latter engine was brand new at the time of testing; it was prepared for testing at the time it was built, and it had run no more than 880 miles in traffic before it was sent to Rugby for the tests on the stationary plant.

TABLE I
TEST RUNS: APPLEBY–GARSDALE

Engine No 4-6-0 class Load, tons		61353 'B1' 343		61353 'B1' 405		73008 'BR5' 560	
Dist		Actual		Actual		Actual	
Miles		m	s	m	s	m	s
0.0	APPLEBY	0	00	0	00	0	00
2.4	Ormside ...	3	25	2	30	2	50
7.5	Crosby Garrett ...	10	30	9	10	10	00
10.7	Kirkby Stephen ...	15	00	13	55	14	30
17.5	*Aisgill*	26	30	26	10	26	55
20.6	Garsdale	30	10	29	40	30	25

Note: Times from passing Appleby to passing Garsdale

Run No 1, with the 'B1' engine No 61353, was made at a steaming rate giving a minimum rate of coal consumption. This test is thus particularly interesting as showing the kind of work in which a 'B1' is at its best. From the tabulated details it will be seen that, in making an average speed of 39.6 mph from Appleby to Aisgill with a load of 343 tons, the coal rate was 2,160 lb per hour. In quoting speeds and performance generally over this route I ought to mention that from Ormside the ascent is continuous to Aisgill, and mostly at 1 in 100. There is an easing for three miles past Crosby Garrett, beginning at 1 in 162, then 215 and finally a quarter of a mile of dead level over Smardale Viaduct. The only other respite is one mile at 1 in 302 past Mallerstang Box.

The loads were so fixed in relation to the pre-

arranged steam rate that all the test trains ran approximately to the same times, and on the three runs tabulated not merely the point-to-point times, but the actual hour of the day, varied by no more than 4 min at Aisgill Summit. On the run with the new class '5' 4-6-0 No 73008, the actual weight of the empty coaching stock being hauled was augmented by electrical braking from two of the former LMSR mobile testing units. The actual times and speeds corresponded very closely to the normal working of the 'Thames-Clyde Express' in LMSR days, and against the times of 26 min 30 sec, 26 min 10 sec, and 26 min 55 sec from Appleby to Aisgill on the three runs tabulated I have one of 26 min 57 sec by the *ex*-LNWR 4-6-0 *Sir Gilbert Claughton*, made in 1931, with a load of 335 tons. The latter engine appeared to be working quite easily and economically judging by the relative quietness of the exhaust.

I have previously commented in these articles on the way in which good drivers will naturally work at an approximately constant steam rate over a difficult section, without any guidance from a steam-flow indicator such as that fitted for these controlled road tests, and it is interesting to compare the fluctuation of speed on this ordinary service run with the 'Claughton' class engine to that of the 'B1' with a roughly equal load under controlled test conditions. This particular 'Claughton' had the original-type boiler, though by that time it had probably been fitted with solid valve heads and narrow rings, instead of the original Schmidt type rings. The following were the comparative speeds between Appleby and Aisgill:

TABLE II

Engine No	5900	61353
Load, tons	335	343
Location	Speeds, mph	
Ormside Viaduct	63½	60
Griseburn Box	35¼	38
Smardale Viaduct	46	46
Leaving Birkett Tunnel	31¼	32
Passing Mallerstang	39	41
Aisgill Summit	34	32

These figures indicate that *Sir Gilbert Claughton* was given a little 'extra' for the last miles up to Aisgill.

On the three test journeys the locomotives were fired with Grade 1A hard coal, and the class '5' 4-6-0 No 73008 was working practically at its limit. The actual firing rate was 3,360 lb per hr and over the 17½ miles from Appleby up to Aisgill this would correspond to 83 lb per train mile. Very complete details of the performance of the 'B1' and the 'BR5' have been given in bulletins published by the British Transport Commission, and it is interesting to compare the results from the two classes when working at a steam rate equivalent to the heavier of the two runs with No 61353 detailed in Table I. The values of equivalent drawbar-horsepower and coal consumption are given in Table III. From this table it would seem that the 'B1' gives slightly higher power outputs in the speed range from 40 to 60 mph, but at a higher coal consumption. A 'B1' at its best is certainly a most formidable engine, and during the Interchange Trials of 1948 I must say that one of my own most impressive personal experiences was the working of the 'B1' between Exeter and Bristol. I shall never forget the sureness and vigour with which she took hold of a train of all but 500 tons and tore along the level of the Somerset coast.

TABLE III
4-6-0 Locomotives: 18,000 lb of feed water per hr

Engine class				'B1'	'BR5'
Coal rate, lb/hr ...	...	...	...	2,500	2,380
Equivalent dhp at 20 mph		...	...	960	950
" 30 "		...	...	1,075	1,075
" 40 "		...	...	1,120	1,090
" 50 "		...	...	1,110	1,060
" 60 "		...	...	1,060	1,000
" 70 "		...	...	955	935

Next we come to the 'Merchant Navy' class. If ever a testing crew—footplate and dynamometer car alike—had the task of producing order out of chaos it was in running engine No 35022 *Holland Amerika Line* between Carlisle and Skipton. The engine was immensely strong, free in

steaming, and game to run at any kind of speed; but to get any logical performance data was rather like trying to run a stage coach of old with a wild, undisciplined horse in the team. She slipped so badly that no one dared attempt to run over Aisgill at the maximum steaming rate the boiler could produce, and while a constant steam rate could be maintained without difficulty the test engineers found there were many quite unaccountable variations in the performance that could not be related to the point of cut-off. The run tabulated herewith (Table IV) was no mean effort with a load of 597 tons over such a route; but if the engine could have 'kept her feet' much finer work could have been got out of her. The 'Merchant Navy' class in its original state was well suited to its own road, and particularly to the sweeping ups and downs of the Salisbury-Exeter section. Where one could go unrestrainedly downhill, and dash up the next bank using impetus to the full, they did very well, at times with exceedingly heavy trains. But they never seemed to be at home in sustained hard slogging.

TABLE IV
TEST RUN: CARLISLE–AISGILL
Load: 597 tons, dynamometer car and empty stock
Engine: 'Merchant Navy' class 4-6-2
No 35022, *Holland Amerika Line*

Dist				Actual*		Speeds
Miles				m	s	mph
0.0	Cumwhinton ...	...PASS		0	00	—
2.9	Cotehill	...	...	5	37	33½
6.1	Armathwaite ...		...	10	13	61/56
11.3	LAZONBY	...	...	15	47	73½
14.4	Little Salkeld	...	...	18	14	67½
19.5	Culgaith	...	...	22	51	61
				pws		30
24.0	Long Marton ...		...	28	00	—
26.9	APPLEBY	...	...	32	15	—
29.3	Ormside	...	...	34	55	65
—	*Griseburn*	...	...	—		40
34.4	Crosby Garrett	...	...	41	26	48
37.6	Kirkby Stephen	...	...	45	52	37
—	*Leaving Birkett Tunnel*	...		—		29
—	*Mallerstang*	...	...	—		38
44.4	*Aisgill*	...	...PASS	58	25	28

*From passing Cumwhinton.

Above *LNER Class 'B1' 4-6-0 No 1040. A later engine of this class performed splendidly on the Settle and Carlisle route.* (British Railways)

Below *Dynamometer trial runs in 'zero weather'. A 'Britannia' class 4-6-2 No 70005* John Milton *taking water at Blea Moor after a maximum output run up from Carlisle.* (W.H. King)

Diesels on the Midland route: a 'Peak' class '4', No D176, on the up 'Thames–Clyde Express' working through from Glasgow to Leeds, here seen near Garrochburn on the Nith Valley section. (Derek Cross)

It is true that there were some fine individual feats in the Interchange Trials of 1948, but I can recall many personal experiences on the footplate when they slipped uncontrolledly and could be given nothing but the lightest of reins. It is rather amusing to recall that they were originally described as mixed-traffic engines. Now if there is one quality above all others that is essential in a mixed-traffic unit it is a capacity for being pounded away from a slack, or up a gradient. This could not be done with the 'Merchant Navy' class. They were high-speed express engines of remarkable capacity, but generally you had to let them accelerate in their own time. They did not like being hustled from rest.

The accompanying log shows the work of *Holland Amerika Line* on a test at the maximum steam rate used for the engine on the Settle and Carlisle line, namely 28,000 lb per hr. Conditions were stabilised nearing Cotehill, and after

passing the summit point near Low House box the engine dashed away in characteristic style, and touched 73½ mph near Lazonby. This is an unusual speed at this point going south; but between Langwathby and Culgaith she also ran true to form, with a tremendous slip at 60 mph on practically level track! There was an awkward hindrance in the permanent way slack near Long Marton, which had affected running over this route for some years; but No 35022 got going well after Appleby, touching 65 mph at Ormside Viaduct, and going up the long stretches of 1 in 100 without any further slipping. The minimum speeds of 29 mph leaving Birkett Tunnel, and 28 at Aisgill, were both good in such loading and steaming conditions.

The dynamometer car chart shows that the engine was being worked with full regulator from Appleby, and the maximum cut-offs noted were 30 per cent, towards the end of the longest stretches of 1 in 100. Too much notice should not be taken of these cut-offs, because even in controlled test conditions there were times when considerable doubt was existing as to whether the actual admission agreed with the cut-off indicator. The steaming was very free and between Kirkby Stephen and Aisgill the pressure was kept steadily at 280 lb per sq in. The coal consumption was fairly heavy, though not outrageously so. The firing rate between Cotehill and Aisgill was 3,400 lb per hr; the average speed between these two points was 47 mph and this gives a consumption of 72 lb per train mile. The maximum equivalent drawbar-horsepower was about 1,500.

Those who defend the 'Merchant Navy' class may feel that I ought to have chosen for comparison other Pacific performances at the same steam rates and loadings. Because of the planning of the schedules, runs with the 'Britannia' and the 'Duchess' would have shown very similar logs, with a difference only in the coal rates. I have put in, instead, details of two astonishing performances when these Crewe-built engines were worked practically to their respective limits. With the 'Britannia,' indeed, the maximum sustained steam rate on Rugby testing plant was a little under 32,000 lb per hr.

On the tabulated run with *John Milton* (Table V) over the Settle and Carlisle line the steam rate

for half an hour on end was the very high figure of 36,000 lb per hr. The train hauled included two of the mobile test units, and was equivalent to a trailing load of ordinary stock of 850 tons. With this tremendous load the engine was driven and fired with such skill as to make times roughly equal to those of the 'B1' and 'BR5' 4-6-0 locomotives. Even with two firemen it was a remarkable achievement to keep the box fed at such a rate as 5,600 lb per hr, and with well-nigh perfect steaming the engine put forth a sustained output of roughly 2,000 drawbar-horsepower. It should be emphasised, however, that this was the performance of a lifetime, and one that it would be difficult to equal once in a hundred runs.

Much the same can be said about the equally gargantuan effort of No 46225, *Duchess of Gloucester*, which the testing staff succeeded in steaming at the phenomenal rate of 40,000 lb per hr for 43 min on end. To average 48.4 mph from Lazonby to Crosby Garrett, with a test load equivalent to 900 tons of ordinary stock, inclusive of a bad permanent way check near Long Marton, leaves one rather bereft of words. This engine slipped heavily in the tunnels just south of

TABLE V
TEST RUN: CARLISLE–CROSBY GARRETT
Load: equal to 850 tons trailing load
Engine: 'Britannia' class 4-6-2 No 70005, *John Milton*

Dist				Actual*	Average Speeds
Miles				m s	mph
0.0	LAZONBY	...	...PASS	0 00	—
3.1	Little Salkeld	...	...	2 40	69.8
4.5	Langwathby	...	...	4 00	63.0
8.2	Culgaith	...	...	7 50	57.9
9.5	New Biggin	...	...	9 35	44.5
				pws	(15 slack)
12.7	Long Marton	...	...	14 55	36.2
15.6	Appleby	...	...	18 55	43.5
18.0	Ormside	...	...	21 50	49.5
23.1	Crosby Garrett		...PASS	29 15	41.3

*Times from passing Lazonby.

TABLE VI
TEST RUN: CARLISLE–KIRKBY STEPHEN
Load: 442 tons, dynamometer car and mobile test units: equal to 900 tons
Engine: 'Coronation' class 4-6-2 No 46225, *Duchess of Gloucester*

Dist				Actual*	Speeds
Miles				m s	mph
0.0	Cumwhinton	...	...PASS	0 00	—
2.9	Cotehill	...	...	5 54	30
6.1	Armathwaite	...	...	11 12	—
				slipping	—
11.3	LAZONBY	...	...	17 21	70
14.4	Little Salkeld	...	...	19 53	74/55
19.5	Culgaith	...	...	25 00	60
				pws	30
24.0	Long Marton	...	...	29 45	—
26.9	APPLEBY	...	...	34 50	—
29.3	Ormside	...	...	37 46	54
34.4	Crosby Garrett	...	...	46 00	37
37.6	Kirkby Stephen	...PASS		52 06	31½

*Times from passing Cumwhinton.

The 'Cumbrian Mountain Pullman' crossing Arten Gill viaduct hauled by Bulleid 'West Country' class 4-6-2 No 34092 City of Wells. *(David Eatwell)*

Armathwaite, and again in Helm Tunnel on the 1 in 100 gradient between Ormside and Crosby Garrett. Even so, in this latter case the speed did not fall below 37 mph near Griseburn, and the sustained minimum on the 1 in 100 past Kirkby Stephen was 30 mph. This needed the use of 48 per cent cut-off, and gave an output of 2,200 equivalent dhp. As with the 'Britannia' the steaming was perfect, and boiler pressure was steady at 250 lb per sq in from Ormside right up to the point of conclusion of the test, just above Kirkby Stephen. The coal rate was 5,700 lb per hr, or 118 lb per mile.

This is probably the biggest sustained effort that has ever been made by a British steam locomotive for so long a duration. But so far as tests on the Settle and Carlisle line are concerned I always feel that it was a pity these controlled-road tests at high steaming rates could not have been made in the conditions in which locomotives like the 'Merchant Navy's' and the 'Duchesses' were at their best and most spectacular, namely in sustained high-speed running. Bulleid may have classified his Pacifics as mixed-traffic, but there were no such delusions over the 'Duchesses.' They were designed primarily for high-speed work, and as such they have been outstandingly good. In this connection it is a great pity for the sake of future records that no full-dress dynamometer car trials were ever conducted with the Gresley 'A4' Pacifics. It is not, alas, likely to be done now!

Last of all among the special test runs over Aisgill comes the prototype 'Deltic,' with a trailing load of 642 tons, and working at full power throughout from Durran Hill Junction to the summit. It would have been extremely interesting to see what a 'Duchess' could have done if worked at 40,000 lb of steam per hour with a similar load. The 'Deltic' was developing an actual drawbar-horsepower of approximately 2,200 between Lazonby and Aisgill, whereas the *Duchess of Gloucester* achieved about 1,900. From

TABLE VII
TEST RUN: CARLISLE–AISGILL
Load: 642 tons (empty stock)
Engine: The prototype 'Deltic'

Dist			Actual*		Speeds
Miles			m	s	mph
0.0	Durran Hill Junc	...START	0	00	—
1.3	Scotby ...	... ...	5	00	38
2.5	Cumwhinton ...	... ...	6	40	45
7.0	Low House Box	... ...	11	35	53
8.6	Armathwaite	... ...	13	00	74
			pws		15
13.8	LAZONBY ...	... ...	17	10	—
16.9	Little Salkeld ...	... ...	24	15	53½
22.0	Culgaith ...	... ...	29	10	70
			pws		25
26.5	Long Marton ...	... ...	34	45	—
28.4	APPLEBY ...	... ...	38	10	58
31.8	Ormside ...	... ...	40	25	73
34.7	Griseburn ...	... ...	43	10	56
36.9	Crosby Garrett ...	... ...	45	25	64
40.1	Kirkby Stephen ...	... ...	48	35	55/50
43.4	Mallerstang ...	... ...	52	20	55
46.9	Aisgill ...	... ...	56	20	50

*Times from dead start at Durran Hill.

the full-dress trials carried out, the edhp figures for the 'Deltic' were:

Speed, mph	edhp
30	2,530
40	2,590
50	2,570
60	2,500
70	2,400

Figures apart, however, it must have been an unusual and thrilling experience to travel the 17.5 miles from Appleby up to Aisgill in 18 min 10 sec with a 642–ton load, and to pass Aisgill summit at 50 mph. Today, with the ordinary express trains, uphill speeds of 50 to 60 mph on the long gradients of the Settle and Carlisle line have become a commonplace with the BR/Sulzer type '4' diesels. These latter locomotives can develop an equivalent dhp of about 2,100 at 60 mph, and I understand they are considered capable of working the new high-speed 'Deltic' turns, if necessary on the East Coast route.

To conclude these notes of running on the Settle and Carlisle line I have tabulated details of two interesting runs on the 4.5 pm from Glasgow St Enoch to Leeds, as between Carlisle and Settle. Both were logged by Mr M. Derenberg, and he was fortunate in travelling on at least one occasion when there were severe delays to provide a reason for much faster running than usual over the mountain section. On the first of the two runs tabulated the train was punctual from Carlisle, and with a load of no more than 320 tons, such schedules as 42 min for the 30.8 miles to Appleby, and 32 min from the restart there up to Aisgill, provided no more than a trifling task. In the early stages, indeed, speed *fell* on the downhill sections approaching Armathwaite and Lazonby, and then accelerated rapidly up the rise from Little Salkeld to Langwathby. From Appleby, although gaining 8½ min up to Aisgill, it is evident that the

TABLE VIII
LONDON MIDLAND REGION:
CARLISLE–SETTLE

Engine, BR/Sulzer type '4' Load, tons (e/f) Driver (Corkerhill shed)				D23 304/320 Reid		D17 341/370 Mac-Donald	
Dist			Sch	Actual		Actual	
Miles			min	m	s	m	s
0.0	CARLISLE ...	...	0	0	00	0	00
3.9	Cumwhinton ...	...		7	48	7	29
6.8	Cotehill ...	...		10	58	11	27
10.0	Armathwaite ...	...		14	07	14	40
15.2	LAZONBY ...	...	21	20	57	19	02
18.3	Little Salkeld ...	...		23	49	21	32
23.4	Culgaith ...	...		28	37	26	12
				pws		pws	
27.9	Long Marton ...	...		33	14	30	41
30.8	APPLEBY ...	...	42	38	21	34	07
2.4	Ormside ...	...		4	09	4	02
7.5	Crosby Garrett ...	...		10	45	10	16
10.7	Kirkby Stephen ...	...	18	14	11	13	42
17.5	Aisgill ...	...	32	23	17	23	14
20.6	Garsdale ...	...		27	08	26	03
28.7	Blea Moor ...	...	44	36	19	35	01
				sigs		pws	
34.7	Horton ...	...		43	17	43	02
				sigs		—	
40.8	SETTLE ...	...	55	51	19	48	04

locomotive was being worked a long way inside full power. In these days one can expect 60 mph up a 1 in 100 with a load of 300 to 320 tons.

The second run was much more interesting. Delays at Carlisle resulted in a start 18 min late; but Driver MacDonald of Corkerhill made full use of the power at his command, and Aisgill was passed 1½ min early. Some of the intermediate speeds quoted by my correspondent are not fully borne out by the point-to-point times he recorded, but the average speeds of 47 mph in each case from Ormside to Aisgill give evidence of very good work, especially on the second journey, with its load of 370 tons. On this second journey too some fast running was made through Lazonby with a maximum speed of 77 mph.

Finally, to make a sudden transition from the extreme north to the south-western extremity of the old Midland Railway system, I am glad to be able to give details of my first unassisted run up the Lickey Incline. Since my June article was written the maximum tare load for a BR/Sulzer type '4' diesel has been fixed at the remarkably high figure of 465 tons tare, which means that practically any passenger train load likely to be experienced over the West of England main line of the Midland will be taken up unassisted. My own first run under the new arrangements was made on the 7.40 am from Bristol with a tare load of 312 tons. What with station stops and checks there was nothing of interest to record until after leaving Ashchurch, and even then we experienced a long permanent way slowing on the rise from Defford to Abbots Wood Junction. Then we went like the wind, reaching 80 mph on the slightly rising stretch beyond, and averaging all but 75 mph throughout from Spetchley to Stoke Works Junction.

There was no suspicion of taking a run at the Lickey Incline. Speed was allowed to drift down as we approached Bromsgrove, and it was only when we were through the station and on to the actual bank that the engine was opened out. Then we settled down to a steady 26 mph, and held this comfortably to the top. The equivalent-drawbar-horsepower was 2,070, thus indicating that the locomotive was working at full power. A study of the power capacity of these very capable locomotives suggests that with the full load of 465 tons they ought to be able to climb the bank at about 19 to 20 mph. From the tabulated log it will be seen that on this run of mine we took only 6 min 47 sec for the 4.3 miles from Stoke Works Junction to Blackwell, compared with 10 min 47 sec on one of the best runs I have ever timed with steam haulage, and three engines to get the train up the bank. On the diesel run with a brisk and unchecked run into Birmingham, we completed the 38.2 miles from Ashchurch to New Street in exactly 48 min, or 44 min net, allowing for the Wadborough check. Now all we need over this route are some schedules worthy of the new locomotives!

TABLE IX
LONDON MIDLAND REGION: ASHCHURCH–BIRMINGHAM

Load: 9 cars; 312 tons tare, 325 tons full
Engine: BR/Sulzer type '4' diesel No D33

Dist		Actual		Speeds
Miles		m	s	mph
0.0	ASHCHURCH	0	00	—
2.1	Bredon	3	26	—
4.8	Eckington	6	20	60
5.9	Defford	7	32	easing
		pws		20
9.4	Wadborough	13	38	52
10.7	Abbots Wood Junc ...	14	58	63
13.2	Spetchley	17	11	76
17.3	Dunhampstead	20	20	80
19.2	Droitwich Road	21	50	75
21.9	Stoke Works Junc	24	10	—
24.0	BROMSGROVE	26	25	40 (slack)
26.2	Blackwell	30	57	26
31.3	Northfield	36	14	69 (slack)
32.7	Kings Norton	37	35	40 (slack)
34.9	Selly Oak	40	47	—
38.2	BIRMINGHAM NEW ST ...	48	00	—

Net time: 44 min

Southern: timings on the ex-LSWR line

The electrification of the former SE & CR lines into Thanet made possible some notable accelerations of the boat train services, and I was favoured with a cab pass for the locomotive working the 'Golden Arrow'. At that time, partisanship between steam and non-steam enthusiasts was still very keen, and in the preamble to an account of the run I made I referred to the often derogatory remarks made by steam buffs at the expense of the electrics. There was certainly plenty of steam about then on the Southern; in fact, the famous Salisbury-Exeter route, scene of so many brilliant runs extending back even to the days of Dugald Drummond, was one of the last in Great Britain to be worked exclusively by steam.

MY first task this month is to refer once again to 'The Flying Scotsman,' and to the memorable run with 'A4' Pacific engine No 4491, *Empire of India*, to which I made reference in my article in the September issue of *The Railway Magazine*. No later than September 3, I received from that doyen of East Coast enthusiasts, Mr R. A. H. Weight, a letter which gives the entire circumstances in which that run was made, and corrects one mistaken impression of mine. The journey was logged not by Mr Cecil J. Allen but by Mr G. W. Field. It was made in September, 1938, at the height of the Munich crisis when many people were hurrying home from holidays in the face of the threat of war. Extra coaches had been put on to the train at very short notice, and the train was packed to its limit from York northwards. The engine was working out of the normal course of double-home running between London and Newcastle, and was a Haymarket engine working home after the conclusion of the non-stop Kings Cross-Waverley run at the end of the summer service. The fireman's name—very appropriately!—was Armstrong.

And now for my main subject this month, current affairs on the Southern Region. By the kindness of the authorities I was favoured with an invitation for the inaugural runs of the accelerated electric service to Folkestone and Dover, and I have since had the privilege of making a number of trips in the cab of a variety of electrically worked services in Kent. From diehards among the steam 'fans' one sometimes hears the craft of driving electric trains tossed aside as 'a boy's job,' 'mere tram-driving,' and

Above *Flashback to LSWR days: a Drummond 'Paddleboat' four-cylinder 4-6-0 as modified by Urie with a superheater.* (W.J. Reynolds)

Below *Maunsell's four-cylinder 4-6-0* Lord Nelson, *fitted with shelters at the front end for taking indicator diagrams on a high-power test run to Exeter.* (W.J. Reynolds)

by other depreciatory remarks. Equally it is sometimes imagined that handling the multiple-unit diesel railcar sets used on so many express and local services elsewhere in the country is so standardised as to take all the individuality and skill out of the driver's job. Making an isolated trip here and there one could well form the impression that this is actually so. But travel on the same service for several days or weeks in succession, and note carefully the methods of, say, half a dozen different drivers, and the experienced observer will appreciate how great is the difference in the methods used. There may be no more than seconds in it, when it comes to overall times from station to station, but while one driver gives his passengers a beautifully steady and even run, another, by lack either of experience or *finesse*, may overdo speed restrictions, make heavy brake applications, and have to run at higher speed intermediately to maintain schedule times.

These thoughts were brought to mind recently by the experiences of two of my friends travelling by trains at the opposite ends of the country. On the one hand Mr Ronald Nelson told me personally of a series of runs he had made recently on the fast railcar services between Huntly and Inverness, when some considerable variations in driving techniques were apparent, while on the other, an old friend extolled the electrically-hauled 'Golden Arrow' as the finest train he had ever travelled in, praising to the skies the extreme smoothness of the travelling. This latter comment was extremely interesting to me, because it is not by any means an easy train to work. In this instance I do not mean 'easy' in the sense of power output required to run the train to time. The tare load of 366 tons conveyed on the day I rode in the cab provided no tax whatever upon the powerful and efficient electric locomotives drafted to this duty. But it is far from a simple or straightforward task if one is to secure that smoothness of travel in the coaches which is desirable in any train, but which is a *sine qua non* on a De Luxe service of this kind.

When writing of the 'Night Ferry' train in *The Railway Magazine* for August, 1960, I referred to

the numerous gaps in the conductor rails encountered on the run from Dover to Victoria, via Chatham. They are no less frequent on the old South Eastern main line, via Tonbridge. The need to have complete gaps in the conductor rails is of course one of the disadvantages of the third rail system of electric traction; but the number of locomotive hauled trains is so very few in comparison with the swarms of multiple-unit expresses and locals as to make the inconveniences of the gaps of no real consequence—except, of course, as a challenge to the skill of the top link drivers who work the 'Golden Arrow' and the 'Night Ferry.' The gaps were a problem to the locomotive designers; but that problem was most successfully overcome by the arrangement of booster sets that are incorporated in the 'E5000' class. In running expresses like the 'Golden Arrow' and the 'Night Ferry' it is the driver's aim so to regulate the speed as to avoid those surges that can sometimes be felt when passing over the gaps.

Dover men now work these two famous trains in both directions, one duty covering the up 'Night Ferry' and the down 'Golden Arrow,' and the evening turn including the reverse workings of both trains. On my run with the 'Golden Arrow,' detailed in Table I, Driver W. Mills had worked to London on the 'Night Ferry' train earlier that morning. The load of 366 tons tare was relatively light compared with the tonnages that are regularly worked on the 'Night Ferry,' but because of the need to ease off over the gaps in the conductor rails in making our way across the many points leaving Victoria, the multiple-unit 'Brighton Belle,' leaving from the 'Central' side of the station, showed us a very clean pair of heels climbing the 1 in 64 bank up to Grosvenor Road bridge. This is not to say we did not get away very smartly, and incomparably faster than in steam days; but if we had been able to take a real 'bite' at the bank the capacity of these fine locomotives would have been shown off to still greater advantage.

There are some close timetable paths through the suburban area, and we were checked by signal at Brixton, down to 20 mph. With other

TABLE I
SOUTHERN REGION:
VICTORIA–DOVER
MARINE
'The Golden Arrow'

Load: 366 tons tare, 380 tons full
Engine: 2,500-hp electric No 5015
Driver: W. Mills (Dover)

Dist			Sch	Actual		Speeds
Miles			min	m	s	mph
0.0	VICTORIA	...	0	0	00	—
	Factory Junc	...		3	43	—
—				sigs		—
4.0	HERNE HILL	...	6½	7	15	—
5.7	Sydenham Hill	...		9	32	54
7.8	Kent House	...		11	47	66
8.7	Beckenham	...	12	12	37	—
10.0	Shortlands ...	...	13½	13	50	60
10.9	Bromley South	...		14	37	64½ (max)
—				sigs		20
12.6	*Bickley Jc* ...	...	16½	17	00	—
14.9	Orpington ...	...	19	20	10	53
17.7	Knockholt ...	...		23	08	58½
21.7	Dunton Green	...		26	35	77½
23.2	SEVENOAKS	...	27	28	01	60 (slack)
28.1	Hildenborough	...		32	20	75
30.6	TONBRIDGE	...	34	34	43	50 (slack)
35.9	Paddock Wood	...	39½	39	54	69
				pws		20
40.5	Marden	...	...		45	31	70
43.0	Staplehurst	...		47	30	70/80½
46.3	Headcorn	...		50	06	76/72
51.5	Pluckley	...	...		54	17	78
				sigs		50
57.2	ASHFORD	...	59½	59	25	64
61.5	Smeeth	...	...		63	14	78
65.3	Westenhanger	...		66	15	72
72.0	Folkestone Jc	...	73	72	00	eased
—				sigs		—
78.0	DOVER MARINE		82	81	10	—

Net time 76 min

forms of power this would have made a very bad start to the climb up to Penge Tunnel, continuously at 1 in 102 for nearly 3 miles, save for a brief 'level' through Herne Hill; but we sailed up the bank, accelerating swiftly to 54 mph at Sydenham Hill. From the eastern end of the tunnel one cannot make any real speed over the broken gradients to Bromley South, because the curves and junctions entail moderate reductions of speed at Kent House, Beckenham and Shortlands. But despite the check at Brixton,

and the relative tightness of the schedule in these opening stages of the run, we were practically on time at Shortlands. Then came a second bad check down to 20 mph at Bickley. The necessity for easing prior to the gaps in the conductor rails through the yard at Orpington made the recovery in speed slower than might have been expected. It is, of course, possible to keep full power on over the gaps; the booster set will ensure continuity of supply to the traction motors, but usually a surge can be felt in the train, and this our driver was avoiding by easing a little prior to passing over the gap.

Working on practically full power speed rose to 58 mph up the 1 in 120 from Orpington to Knockholt, and we did some free running down to Tonbridge—easing intermediately for the 60 mph slack through Sevenoaks. The locomotive rode very smoothly throughout, particularly in rounding curves at 60 mph or so. There was, of course, no need for any undue haste. The most difficult part of the new 'Golden Arrow' schedule is on the London side of Tonbridge, and on passing Paddock Wood we were practically on time. A third hindrance came in the permanent way check to 20 mph immediately beyond Paddock Wood Station. The termination post was adjacent to Milepost 36½, and from this point we got the fastest sustained running of the journey.

Speed rose to 80½ mph on the level nearing Headcorn, and although there were still more slight easings, to pass over gaps, a fine speed was maintained up the rise towards Ashford. The long stretches of 1 in 287–277 might not have existed for all the effect they had on the speed, and nearing the site of the former Chart Intermediate signal box, where the incline was usually beginning to make itself felt with steam locomotives, we were sustaining 78 mph. There was a slight signal check to 50 mph nearing Ashford, but recovery was immediate, and speed was held comfortably above 70 mph throughout the final ascent to Westenhanger, on a gradient of 1 in 266–286. Very easy running concluded the run. We got a 'single yellow' entering Shakespeare's Cliff Tunnel, but the

Right *Up West of England express climbing to Honiton tunnel hauled by 'King Arthur' class 4-6-0 No 449* Sir Torre *in August 1928.* (H.C. Casserley)

Below *The same engine still on the same work 30 years later, and only modified by having a Maunsell instead of a Drummond 'watercart' tender. No 30449 is seen here on a heavy up West of England express nearing Semley.* (K.H. Leech)

The 14-coach 'Devon Belle' climbing Honiton bank, hauled by Bulleid Pacific No 21C8 Orient Line *in original Southern Railway livery.* (W.N. Lockett)

road was cleared in time and we finished almost a minute early.

Later that same day I made an interesting circular trip in East Kent on multiple-unit trains to see for myself the very smart workings demanded on services calling at all stations. These runs gave the following results:

Guston Tunnel. Unfortunately a permanent way check to 20 mph was in force right in the middle of the bank; we nevertheless attained 50 mph on the gradient afterwards. Except at Deal, where the Saturday traffic was heavy, the station stops were smartly made and rarely exceeded 30 or 35 sec duration.

3.4 pm DOVER PRIORY–MINSTER

Dist					Actual	
Miles					m	s
0.0	Dover Priory ...	...	...	...	0	00
1.1	*Buckland Junc* ...	...	...	...	2	42
—					pws	
4.0	Martin Mill	...	...	...	8	35
2.7	Walmer	...	...	...	3	32
					sigs	
1.6	Deal ...	...	...	...	3	09
4.1	Sandwich	...	...	...	5	17
					sigs	
4.8	Minster ...	...	...	...	7	13

Overall schedule time for 17.2 miles, 33 min
Actual overall time, 32 min 58 sec

3.53 pm MINSTER–ASHFORD

Dist					Actual	
Miles					m	s
0.0	Minster ...	...	...	...	0	00
5.0	Grove Ferry	...	...	...	6	30
2.1	Chislet ...	...	...	...	3	16
2.0	Sturry ...	...	...	...	3	18
2.4	Canterbury West	...	...	...	3	55
3.0	Chartham	...	...	...	4	40
2.2	Chilham	...	...	...	3	47
4.7	Wye ...	...	...	...	6	12
					sigs	
4.3	Ashford	...	...	...	6	27

On this run I had looked forward to seeing how the electric train would climb the 1 in 70 ascent from Buckland Junction to the eastern end of

Again the run was made almost exactly to time throughout, with speed rising to 60 mph or slightly over between stations. The overall allowance of 43 min for the distance of 25.7 miles represents excellent travelling for an 'all-stations' train, inclusive of the stopping time at seven intermediate stations. The actual running time totals up to 38 min 5 sec giving a running average speed of 40.6 mph. The schedules of these local trains are an impressive example of the service an electrified line can give in rural parts. A time of 24 min from Canterbury to Ashford (14.2 miles) would take some beating on a crowded highroad with any form of vehicle, let alone public transport.

Turning now from electric traction to steam, I have next, in Table II, a splendid run with a

TABLE II
SOUTHERN REGION: 6.22 pm
WATERLOO–SOUTHAMPTON
Load: 10 cars, 336 tons tare, 350 tons full
Engine: 4-6-0 No 30850, *Lord Nelson*

Dist			Sch	Actual		Speeds
Miles			min	m	s	mph
0.0	WATERLOO	...	0	0	00	—
				sigs		
3.9	Clapham Junc	...	7	8	25	—
7.3	Wimbledon	...		12	45	54
				sig stop		—
9.8	Malden	...		19	29	40
				sigs		—
12.0	Surbiton	...		22	51	35
17.1	Walton	...		28	45	60
19.1	Weybridge	...		30	42	68
21.7	West Byfleet	...		32	58	66
24.4	WOKING	...	29	35	25	64/66
28.0	Brookwood	...		38	51	64
31.0	*Milepost 31*	...		41	45	62
33.2	Farnborough	...		43	47	68
36.5	Fleet	...		46	39	72
42.2	Hook	...		51	50	64/67
47.8	BASINGSTOKE	...		56	56	62
50.3	*Worting Junc*	...	55	59	25	60
58.1	Micheldever	...		66	27	74
61.8	*Wallers Ash*	...		69	15	82
64.4	*Winchester Junc*	...	69	71	16	79
66.6	WINCHESTER	...		72	59	72
				sigs		—
73.6	EASTLEIGH	...	81	81	12	62
				sigs		—
78.2	*Northam Junc*	...	86	88	19	—
79.3	SOUTHAMPTON		89	93	12	—

Net time 79½ min

'Nelson'—*Lord Nelson* himself—on the 6.22 pm Friday relief to the 6.30 pm Bournemouth express. For details of this run I am indebted to Mr D. W. Winkworth. Out to Surbiton the train was dogged by signal checks, including a diversion to the slow line at Raynes Park, and a crossover back to the fast line at Surbiton. But having passed Hampton Court Junction nearly 7 min late, *Lord Nelson* ran splendidly to Winchester after which more checks intervened. Excellent features of this journey were the minimum speeds of 62 mph at Milepost 31 (after 10½ miles at 1 in 387–326–314–300) and 60 mph at Milepost 52, after many miles rising at 1 in 249. The uphill average speed of 64.7 mph over the 33.2 miles from Walton to Worting Junction shows a finely sustained effort throughout. Despite a bad signal check at Shawford Junction the train was practically on time in Eastleigh, but the subsequent checks were more than could be recovered. Engine No 30850 has proved to be one of the last survivors of this small, but distinguished class of locomotives. I am much indebted to Mr Winkworth for this example of their performance at its best.

Next, through the kindness of Mr B. L. Smith, there is a fine run with one of the 'BR5' standard mixed traffic 4-6-0s, on the 8.35 am from Waterloo to Salisbury. This, like the run with *Lord Nelson*, was made in 1961, at the height of the summer holiday season, on a Saturday. The 12-coach train was heavily loaded with passengers, but although the gross trailing load of 430 tons could be considered a heavy one for the type of locomotive, the Saturday schedule is not difficult in itself. Fortunately, from the viewpoint of displaying the capacity of the locomotive, there were several delays, which the enterprising crew of No 73113 were keen to recover. Starting from Waterloo 1¼ min late the train was stopped by signal no farther out of the terminus than Loco. Junction, and passed Clapham Junction 4¾ min late in consequence. After getting away from Surbiton, however, the road was clear, and some fine running was made on to Basingstoke.

After the immediate start the engine was a lit-

TABLE III
SOUTHERN REGION: 8.35 am (SAT)
WATERLOO–SALISBURY

Load: 12 cars, 398 tons tare, 430 tons full
Engine: 'BR5' 4-6-0 No 73113

Dist		Sch	Actual		Speeds
Miles		min	m	s	mph
0.0	WATERLOO ...	0	0	00	—
1.3	Vauxhall		4	10	—
			sig stop		—
3.9	Clapham Junc ...	7	10	30	39
7.3	Wimbledon ...		15	05	51
8.7	Raynes Park ...		16	45	56
9.8	Malden		18	00	59½
12.0	Surbiton	18	21	16	—
1.3	Hampton Court Jc	3	3	12	38½
2.4	Esher		4	37	47
5.1	Walton		7	39	56½
7.1	Weybridge ...		9	50	57½/65½
9.7	West Byfleet ...		12	16	63
12.4	WOKING ...	15	15	02	—
			pws		18
16.0	Brookwood ...		21	17	45
19.0	Milepost 31 ...		26	07	50
21.2	Farnborough ...		28	28	60
24.5	Fleet		31	31	69
27.7	Winchfield ...		34	25	67
30.2	Hook		36	42	68½/75
35.8	BASINGSTOKE ...	43	41	45	—
2.5	Worting Junc ...	5½	5	37	39
4.6	Oakley		8	26	54
7.8	Overton		11	14	64½
11.4	Whitchurch ...		14	48	73
13.3	Hurstbourne ...		16	22	75
18.6	ANDOVER ...		20	30	83
25.0	Grateley		26	03	56
30.5	Porton		31	07	73/79
—			sig stop		—
34.9	Tunnel Junction ...	44	39	49	—
36.0	SALISBURY ...	47	43	09	—

tle slow in getting into speed; but a maximum of 65½ mph was touched near Weybridge, and this was being finely held up the first part of the long rise to Milepost 31, until the bad permanent way check after Woking. On the continuous rise of 1 in 326–314–300 the recovery was excellent, to 50 mph at the summit, and some fast running on the level from Farnborough was rounded off by a maximum of no less than 75 mph in the very slight dip after

Hook. Thus time was more than kept on this stage despite the permanent way check. The net time of 37½ min, from Surbiton to Basingstoke, was a fine piece of work with a 430-ton train over a stretch with a markedly adverse tendency.

After Basingstoke, although the start is a difficult one, up the continuous 1 in 249 gradient to the parting of the West of England and Bournemouth roads at Battledown 'flyover,' there is plenty of opportunity for fast running afterwards. The BR Class '5' 4-6-0s are as free-running as the Stanier engines from which they were so closely derived, and No 73113 got away in great style from Oakley, reaching 75 mph at Hurstbourne, and 83 mph at Andover. The steep rise from Red Post Junction to Grateley was rushed, at a minimum speed of 56 mph, and with time now well in hand the engine was run less vigorously down the final descent into Salisbury. Even so the speed was close upon 80 mph below Porton, when adverse signals twice brought the train to a stand. On the easy schedule of this train however there was plenty in hand to secure a punctual arrival, and this excellent run finished 1½ min early. The net time of 37¾ min from Basingstoke to Salisbury was again an impressive commentary upon the capacity of the locomotive. The aggregate net gain of 15¼ min was however a reflection upon the liberality of the schedule.

The accelerated schedule of the 'Atlantic Coast Express' continues to provide opportunities for the rebuilt 'Merchant Navy' class 4-6-2s to display their prowess, though space precludes more than a brief mention of some excellent runs logged by Mr B. L. Smith. Three runs between Waterloo and Salisbury, and a further three between Salisbury and Sidmouth Junction are tabulated herewith in summary form. They show that despite the fast schedules the locomotives seem to have a comfortable margin in hand. It is another matter on the corresponding up journey, at any rate between Sidmouth Junction and Salisbury, and the three runs detailed in Table VI will repay close study. All these were logged by Mr D. W. Winkworth, and although they were made on three suc-

TABLE IV
SOUTHERN REGION: WATERLOO–SALISBURY

Run No Engine No Load, tons (e/f)			1 35020 399/430		2 35029 427/465		3 35028 427/460	
Dist		Sch	Actual		Actual		Actual	
Miles		min	m	s	m	s	m	s
0.0	WATERLOO	0	0	00	0	00	0	00
3.9	Clapham Jc	7	7	22	6	42	7	25
—			pws		—		—	
13.3	Hampton Court Jc	17	20	04	16	14	17	11
24.4	WOKING	27	30	11	25	20	26	17
31.0	Milepost 31		35	50	31	09	32	31
47.8	BASINGSTOKE		48	38	45	45	46	23
50.3	Worting Jc	50	50	57	48	13	48	41
66.4	ANDOVER		63	20	61	57	61	58
82.7	Tunnel Jc	77	76	22	75	45	75	55
83.8	SALISBURY	80	79	05	78	37	78	22
Net time, min			76		$78\frac{1}{2}$		$78\frac{1}{4}$	
Speeds, mph								
Milepost 31 (min)			69		$68\frac{1}{2}$		61	
Hook (max)			83		72		$75\frac{1}{2}$	
Worting			65		59		$63\frac{1}{2}$	
Andover			85		$78\frac{1}{2}$		$80\frac{1}{2}$	
Grateley			70		63		62	
Porton			$83\frac{1}{2}$		79		78	

Engine names: 35020, *Bibby Line*; 35028, *Clan Line*; 35029, *Ellerman Lines*

TABLE V
SOUTHERN REGION: SALISBURY–SIDMOUTH JUNCTION

Run No Engine No Load, tons (e/f)			1 35020 367/395		2 35030 368/400		3 35015 368/400	
Dist		Sch	Actual		Actual		Actual	
Miles		min	m	s	m	s	m	s
0.0	SALISBURY	0	0	00	0	00	0	00
17.5	Semley		19	24	19	36	20	23
28.4	TEMPLECOMBE		27	42	27	38	29	15
39.1	YEOVIL JUNC	40	36	13	36	07	37	39
49.7	Milepost 133¼		45	06	45	38	47	01
			pws		—		—	
64.3	SEATON JUNC		59	30	56	51	58	43
70.0	Milepost 153½		66	30	64	11	66	43
75.8	SIDMOUTH JC	75	72	28	70	24	72	40
Speeds, mph								
Semley (min)			$64\frac{1}{2}$		66		55	
Templecombe (max)			$83\frac{1}{2}$		90		82	
Sherborne (max)			86		87		$92\frac{1}{2}$	
Milepost 133¼ (min)			62		54		50	
Axminster (max)			81		86		82	
Honiton bank (min)			39		33		33	

Engine names: 35015, *Rotterdam Lloyd*; 35020, *Bibby Line*; 35030, *Elder Dempster Lines*

TABLE VI
SOUTHERN REGION: EXETER–SALISBURY

Run No			1		2		3	
Engine No ('MN' class)			35014		35018		35014	
Load, tons (e/f)			364/390		363/390		363/390	
Dist		Sch	Actual	Speeds	Actual	Speeds	Actual	Speeds
Miles		min	m s	mph	m s	mph	m s	mph
0.0	EXETER CENTRAL	0	0 00	—	0 00	—	0 00	—
1.1	*Exmouth Junc*		3 05	30	4 07	25	4 19	25
4.8	BROAD CLYST		7 00	76	8 18	70	8 36	74
8.5	Whimple		10 11	63	12 04	40/48	11 56	48
10.3	*Milepost 161¼*		11 56	56	14 22	42	13 51	51
12.2	SIDMOUTH JUNC	17	14 16		16 52		16 38	
		0	0 00		0 00		0 00	
1.3	*Milepost 158*		2 55	50	3 07	45	3 01	48
4.6	Honiton		7 11	45	7 56	38/42	7 12	45
5.8	*Milepost 153½*		8 47	46	9 43	40	8 49	46
6.8	*Milepost 152½*		10 08	52	11 01	52	10 07	55
11.5	SEATON JUNCTION ...		14 21	72/84	15 13	62/78	14 10	70/78
14.8	Axminster		16 55	75	17 56	74	16 49	72
19.9	Chard Junction		21 12	70	22 35	66	21 31	66
26.1	*Milepost 133¼*		27 03	60	28 31	57	27 22	60
27.9	Crewkerne		28 47	77	30 09	84	29 01	78
29.1	*Milepost 130¼*		29 43	80	31 00	88	29 58	82
			pws		pws		pws	
33.1	*Milepost 126¼*		38 25	28	36 24	40	35 24	41
34.5	Sutton Bingham		40 09	61	37 49	66	36 51	65
36.7	YEOVIL JUNCTION ...	37	42 10	75/80	39 36	80	38 40	78
41.3	Sherborne		45 56	72	43 15	76/54	42 32	72/54
45.9	*Milepost 113½*		50 37	55	47 41	62	47 02	60
47.4	TEMPLECOMBE		52 01	70/85	48 58	78/85	48 21	75/85
51.9	*Milepost 107½*		55 28	68	52 21	68	51 57	62
54.2	Gillingham		57 20	78	54 08	81	53 57	72
58.3	Semley		61 02	62	57 38	65	57 58	55
63.3	Tisbury		65 19	72	61 34	78	62 18	74
67.6	Dinton		68 56	74	64 55	78/82	65 55	72/74
73.3	Wilton		73 51		69 37		71 08	
75.8	SALISBURY	74	78 12		73 53		75 08	
Net times (min)			71¾		71¼		72½	

Engine names: 35014, *Nederland Line*; 35018, *British India Line*

cessive days in May, 1962, three different crews were concerned. They emphasise that the up journey is much the harder of the two directions of running, largely because it is not possible to indulge in unrestrained high speed on two of the principal descents, namely from Honiton Tunnel down to Seaton Junction, and again from Semley down to Salisbury.

The differing techniques of crews is apparent in the first few miles out of Exeter. On the first run there was an unusually vigorous start up the 1 in 100 to Exmouth Junction, a dash down to Broad Clyst, and a minimum speed of 56 mph up the 5 miles of 1 in 170–135–100 to Milepost 161¼. The start from Exeter had been 6½ min late, and by this energy nearly half of the lateness had been recovered by Sidmouth Junction. Neither of the other drivers came anywhere near this performance. There is a mile downhill at 1 in 100 after the Sidmouth Junction start, and this gives some useful impetus for the stiff climb up to Honiton Tunnel. The latter bank is 4¾ miles long, 1 in 100 at first and steepening to 1 in 90 for the last mile. Engine No 35014, on runs 1 and 3, was driven in closely similar style, with excellent speeds of 46 mph in each case on entering the tunnel. All three engines were taken very easily down most of the bank to Seaton Junction, and the maximum speeds of 78 to 84 mph noted in the table were attained right at the foot of the

TABLE VII
SOUTHERN REGION: 2.45 pm SALISBURY–EXETER

Load, to Templecombe: 399 tons tare, 430 tons full
" , to Exeter: 302 tons tare, 325 tons full
Engine: 4-6-2 No 34052, *Lord Dowding*
Driver G. Spray; Fireman Webb; Inspector S. Smith

Dist		Sch	Actual	Speeds	Regulator opening	Cut-off	Steam-chest	Boiler
Miles		min	m s	mph		per cent	psi	psi
0.0	SALISBURY	0	0 00		$\frac{1}{2}$	55/40	180	240
2.5	Wilton		5 49	—	$\frac{1}{2}$	25	180	240
8.2	Dinton		12 19	58	$\frac{1}{2}$	20	180	200
12.5	Tisbury		16 42	66	F	20	180	200
17.5	Semley		21 50	—	$\frac{1}{2}$	20	120	190
21.6	Gillingham		25 32	78	$\frac{1}{2}$	20	100	220
23.9	*Milepost 107$\frac{1}{2}$*		27 28	66	$\frac{1}{2}$	20	120	220
26.2	*Milepost 109$\frac{3}{4}$*		29 27	75	C	20	0	220
28.4	TEMPLECOMBE	34	32 06	—	—	—	—	—
		0	0 00	—	$\frac{1}{2}$F	60/30	180/220	240
2.4	Milborne Port		5 53	—	$\frac{1}{2}$	20	160	210
6.1	Sherborne	11	10 08	—	—	—	—	—
			sigs					
4.6	YEOVIL JUNCTION	8	7 17	—	—	—	—	—
2.2	Sutton Bingham		5 00	45	F	20	220	240
7.6	*Milepost 130$\frac{1}{4}$*		—	68/70	$\frac{1}{2}$	20	140	215
8.8	Crewkerne		11 50	60	F	20	200	210
10.6	*Milepost 133$\frac{1}{4}$*		13 57	54	F	20	220	230
16.8	Chard Junc		19 23	76	$\frac{1}{2}$	20	85	190
21.9	Axminster		23 21	78	$\frac{1}{2}$	20	120	185
23.6	*Milepost 146$\frac{1}{4}$*		—	80	$\frac{1}{2}$	20	100	200
25.2	SEATON JUNCTION		25 59	67	F	20	180	210
27.9	*Milepost 150$\frac{1}{2}$*		28 47	49	F	30	190	200
28.9	*Milepost 151$\frac{1}{2}$*		30 04	45	$\frac{1}{2}$/F/$\frac{1}{2}$/F	30	180	190
29.9	*Milepost 152$\frac{1}{2}$*		31 28	41	$\frac{1}{2}$/F/$\frac{1}{2}$/F	30	180	190
30.9	*Milepost 153$\frac{1}{2}$*		32 59	45	—	—	—	—
			sigs					
32.1	Honiton		35 26	15/76	$\frac{1}{2}$	20	160	200
36.7	SIDMOUTH JUNCTION		40 26	70	St open	18	130	200
40.4	Whimple		43 39	75	" "	18	20	190
44.1	Broad Clyst		46 32	77	" "	18	70	200
			sigs					
46.0	Pinhoe		48 11	54	$\frac{1}{2}$	18	180	195
			sigs					
47.8	*Exmouth Junc*	52	50 50	30	C	—	0	200
			sigs					
48.9	EXETER CENTRAL	55	53 50	—	—	—	—	—

incline. Excellent work followed up to Milepost 133¼ on all trips, though No 35018 (Run 2), which had been the slowest from the Exeter start, was again falling behind until her driver indulged in a great sprint up to 88 mph past Crewkerne.

The permanent way check near Hardington Siding was much more severe on the first day, with the result that engine No 35014, which had done the finest all-round work up to this point, was well behind the other two engines passing Yeovil Junction. The three trains had lost 5¼, 2½, and 1¾ min on schedule at this stage. Continuing to Salisbury there is little time to spare on a timing of 37 min pass to stop over 39.1 miles of a road so awkwardly graded as this, and on runs 1 and 3 the drivers did little better than keep the point to point times—despite excellent work. But on the second run a truly magnificent effort was made. Sherborne was passed at 76 mph; speed fell to 54 up the 1¾ miles of 1 in 100–80 that follows, and touched 85 mph below Templecombe. Then came 68 mph at Buckhorn Weston Tunnel, 81 through Gillingham, and a most unusual minimum of 65 mph at Semley, after 4 miles climbing at 1 in 130–114–100. A fast run down to Wilton brought the train into Salisbury on time—a sterling effort. That the hard running on these three journeys yielded net gains on schedule of no more than 2¼, 2¾, and 1½ min tells its own tale.

Lastly, I am again indebted to Mr Winkworth for putting at my disposal details of a journey which, by kind permission of Mr P. M. Haydon, Motive Power Officer, Southern Region, he was privileged to make on the footplate of a rebuilt Pacific of the 'Battle of Britain' class, on the 2.45 pm from Salisbury to Exeter. It is a run in which I too have a personal interest, in that the driver, G. Spray, is an engineman with whom I rode 28 years ago, when he was firing an 'S.15' mixed-traffic 4–6–0 on the up night fitted goods from Exeter to Salisbury.

In the case of this recent run Mr Winkworth has recorded details of the engine working very carefully and successfully, and they are included in Table VII. The chief point of interest in an excellent run is the ascent of Honiton bank. It will be seen that with no longer cut-off than 30 per cent, the minimum speed at the entrance to the tunnel was 41 mph. Mr Winkworth remarks that when fully opened the regulator handle tended to work back to a position about half way over on the sector and required frequent pulling out to the 'full.' This is covered in the table by the note ½/F½/F against the regulator position when climbing Honiton bank. From these notes, for which I am much indebted to Messrs Smith and Winkworth, it is evident that the standard of steam locomotive performance on the Southern Region remains very high.

West Coast Main Line: Preston–Carlisle dynamometer car runs, 1925–6

Whenever the subject was raised of locomotive testing at one or other of the learned Institutions in this country, inevitably, it seemed, thoughts and reminiscences used to go back to one of the gladiatorial contests of steam days. The occasion that touched off my article of May 1963 was a paper read by an engineer of long experience of steam locomotive testing emphasising the difference involved when testing diesels. Having referred to some aspects of that paper, I switched to some fascinating details of the little known trials conducted by the LMS in 1925 between Preston and Carlisle, which continued the following year, involving locomotives of the 'Prince of Wales' and 'Claughton' classes of the LNWR, a Midland compound, an LYR rebuilt four-cylinder 4–6–0, and a Caledonian 'Pickersgill' 4–6–0. It was small wonder that those North Country trials attracted little or no public attention, even though they were run in broad daylight, because they came at the very time when most enthusiasts were absorbed with the famous 'Castle' versus 'Gresley Pacific' trials in the South.

THE prowess of diesel traction on British Railways naturally continues to be the main subject of many letters reaching me at the present time; but so far as the locomotives themselves are concerned, I am giving it a break this month so that I may touch briefly on one aspect of the transition period that I do not think is fully appreciated. I have frequently mentioned the problems of getting locomotive enginemen used to the new power; but no more than a passing thought, if that, has been given to the technical and executive officers who have had to sponsor the new machines, and to nurse them through the difficult period of teething troubles. Almost without exception the senior men have been trained and grown up in steam. That might seem a disadvantage, and lie at the root of the undoubted troubles that have been experienced: but I am certain this is not so. On the contrary I would suggest that it is *because* of that early training of the men most deeply concerned that the troubles have been *so few*.

Over the years it has been my privilege to know many British locomotive engineers personally, and whatever their particular talents and responsibilities they are, one and all,

LNWR 'Prince of Wales' class 4-6-0 No 5834 in the Midland red livery. (British Railways)

railwaymen above all else. I always chuckle over the story told of one of them, with whom I was closely associated for a time, who was having a good deal of trouble with a new and most ingenious device fitted to many of the new non-steam locomotives. Troubles were causing total failures of engines in express passenger service, and a conference was called with technical experts of the manufacturers. My friend was presiding, and for some time he listened to much talk of efficiencies, high performance ratings, and so on, and then he said drily: 'Gentlemen, you know we've been having to take these locomotives off after less than half the journey. Do you think we could have a little less "efficiency", and get the whole way?'

It is not only in running, but in every aspect of railway locomotive engineering, that the men technically concerned have been involved. This was aptly summarised in the concluding paragraphs of a Paper read before the Midland Centre of the Institution of Locomotive Engineers at Derby, some two years ago, by Mr E. Sharp, an engineer who for many years was connected with dynamometer-car testing of steam locomotives, and who played a leading part in the memorable tests of the 'Britannia' and 'Duchess' class 4-6-2s between Skipton and Carlisle. Sharp was discussing the testing of diesel-electric locomotives, and he concluded thus: 'The transition from steam to diesel has created a minor revolution on British Railways, which has to some extent affected all departments.

'This is especially true in the CM & EE Department with which the author is associated, and in spite of the advantages at Derby of an early lead in the field of diesel practice, the acquisition of necessary technical knowledge is a process which must continue for some time to come. In common with many of his colleagues, the author is a steam locomotive engineer who has been compelled by the course of events to make a complete revision of former practice, in the particular sphere of locomotive performance testing. In five short years, it has been necessary to put aside over 20 years of work connected with boiler efficiencies, a/s ratios, valve lap and lead,

LNWR 'Claughton' class 4-6-0 No 171 on a down West Coast express near Hest Bank. (Real Photos)

etc, in favour of motor currents, excitation, torque regulation, field weakening and the like. Even the language has changed.

'No apology is therefore necessary for the many obvious omissions in the Paper, which is intended as a record of the progress in testing which has been made to date, rather than a complete treatise on the behaviour of a diesel-electric locomotive. It will be remembered that some aspects of steam locomotive performance remained scientifically unexplained after 100 years of experience, and empirical rules were in general use. While the diesel locomotive is inherently a machine which lends itself more readily to calculation, railway engineers still have much to learn, and the necessity for testing and adding to the fund of technical knowledge is one which continues.'

Having brought in the subject of testing with the dynamometer car, I am going to switch right off diesels for the rest of this article, and go back to a fascinating piece of steam locomotive history that fills in a few of the gaps in our knowledge of individual designs and of their relative effec-

tiveness and economy. It is no exaggeration to say that the various series of trials carried out by the LMSR on the Midland main line between Leeds and Carlisle have become world famous, but so far little is known of the two sets of trials conducted over Shap in May 1925 and June 1926. These were in some ways a sequel to the Midland trials, because the *ex*-Lancashire & Yorkshire four-cylinder 4-6-0s were precluded from running over Aisgill. Why this was so I have no idea, for these latter engines had a slightly lighter maximum axle-loading than the North Western 'Claughtons'. The difference between the two designs lay in the drive, which was divided in the case of the LYR engine, and entirely on to the leading coupled axle in the 'Claughtons'. The latter engines had no hammer blow at all, and could presumably be accepted on the Midland line while the L & Y engines could not.

Be that as it may, a series of trials was conducted between Preston and Carlisle in May 1925, in which the following engines were involved: Midland Compound No 1065; LNWR

'Prince of Wales' No 90, *Kestrel*; LYR 4-6-0 No 10460; and LNWR 'Claughton' No 30, *Thalaba*.

In June 1926, an entirely comparable series of trials was carried out with a Pickersgill '60' class 4-6-0 of Caledonian design, No 14630, the first of a new batch of those engines built under the auspices of the LMSR and at first painted in Derby red. By the courtesy of Mr A. E. Robson, Chief Mechanical and Electrical Engineer, London Midland Region, I have been able to study the reports of these two groups of tests, and all the data quoted subsequently in the article is taken from these reports. The 1925 trials were carried out while Mr George Hughes was Chief Mechanical Engineer of the LMSR, and the report was issued from Horwich. The report on the Caledonian 4-6-0 was issued from Derby. The Midland Compound, the North Western 'Prince', and the Caledonian 4-6-0 were all in 'No 4' class, and were tested with loads of 300 and 350 tons; the 'Claughton' and the Horwich 4-6-0 were both in 'No 5' class, and were tested with loads of 350 and 400 tons.

The tests, using the Horwich dynamometer car, were made on special trains of empty coaching stock, and were timed at the fastest schedules then worked between Carlisle and Preston, namely 114 min for the 90 miles southbound, and 103 min northbound. This latter was a tough proposition for the class '4' engines with 350 tons, and no less for the class '5' 4-6-0s with 400 tons. The latter trains were the heaviest of which I have ever seen a record, taken unassisted from Tebay up to Shap, until the 'Royal Scots' came on the scene in 1927. In North Western days the 'Claughton' load was 420 tons as far as Tebay, and I have records of loads of 415 and 419 tons being taken successfully up to Grayrigg; but in each case a stop was made at Tebay for rear-end banking assistance. In LMSR days the load for an unassisted class '5' engine of LNWR or LYR design was 320 tons from Tebay up to Shap Summit. In the 1925 trials each engine was based at Carlisle, and made one return trip to Preston with each of the specified loads. In 1926 the Caledonian engine

TABLE I

Engine class	Mileage since last shopping	Detail of engine
LNWR 'Prince of Wales'	6,529	Standard representative of class
Midland Compound	28,063 (10,000 miles since piston and valve examination, when liners were fitted)	Short-chimneyed type with cylinders lined up to 19 in (hp) and 21 in (hp)
LYR 4-6-0	20,783 (since new)	Long-lap valves, $6\frac{7}{16}$ in travel in full gear
LNWR 'Claughton'	22,977	Double-cowl chimney, shortened blast-pipe

made two return trips with each specified load.

The four engines concerned in the 1925 trials had the mileages and characteristics shown in Table I. From this it will be seen that only the North Western 'Prince' was a standard representative of its class. The Horwich 4-6-0 had long-lap valves, and a large grate, the former tried no doubt after the profound impression created at Horwich by publication of the test results on the Great Western 4-6-0 No 4074, *Caldicot Castle*, in Mr Collett's Paper to the World Power Conference in 1924. The 'Claughton' had some alterations to its draughting, and certain Horwich details incorporated. The Midland Compound was of the new short-chimney series, but with lined-up cylinders. No attempt seems to have been made to secure uniformity in running times, so that comparisons of coal, water, and oil consumption could be made on the closest possible basis. The drivers of the two competing North Western engines ran fairly closely to schedule times, whereas on the Midland Compound and on the LYR 4-6-0 both crews attempted spectacular ascents of Grayrigg Bank on their northbound trips.

Tables II and III give details of the 12 southbound runs from Carlisle to Preston, and on these of course it is the ascent to Shap, from a cold start, that provides the greatest interest. I have put the runs with 300-ton and 400-ton trains in Table II, and grouped all the runs with 350-ton trains into Table III for more direct comparison. It will be seen that with the exception of the Pickersgill 4-6-0 on her first run with a 300-ton train, run No 2, when there was a dead stand for signals at Penrith, every engine passed Shap Summit on or before time. The fastest climb of the whole series was made by the Pickersgill 4-6-0, on her second 300-ton trip, but in actual merit this was surpassed by the Midland Compound (run No 10) when Shap

TABLE II
LMSR DYNAMOMETER CAR TESTS: CARLISLE–PRESTON
300-ton and 400-ton trains

Run No				1	2	3	4	5	6
Engine No				90	14630	14630	1065	10460	30
Engine Name				*Kestrel*	—	—	—	—	*Thalaba*
Railway				LNWR	CR	CR	MR	LYR	LNWR
Load, tons tare				299.3	301.6	301.6	304.9	397	393.6

Dist			Sch	Actual	Actual	Actual	Actual	Actual	Actual
Miles			min	m s	m s	m s	m s	m s	m s
0.0	CARLISLE ...	...	0	0 00	0 00	0 00	0 00	0 00	0 00
—				—	sig stop	—	—	pws	pws
17.9	Penrith ...	...	27	28 11	30 58	26 25	28 01	28 55	28 30
31.4	*Shap Summit*	...	50	48 07	56 53	45 43	46 28	49 51	50 07
—				—	pws	pws	sigs	—	sigs
69.1	LANCASTER	...	90	86 22	98 23	87 10	83 06	85 49	88 20
—				—	sig stop	—	—	—	—
90.1	PRESTON ...	...	114	112 01	131 32	114 30	109 08	107 23	113 04

Net times		min 112	—	min 112	min 108	min 105½	min 109

	Reg	Cut-off %	Reg	Cut-off %	Reg	Cut-off %	Reg	Cut-off *	Reg	Cut-off %	Reg	Cut-off %
Engine working:												
Carlisle	0.1	Full	—	—	—	—	Full	12	0.4	50	Full	Full
Calthwaite	0.3	30	0.3	35	Full	35	0.6	6	0.4	30	Full	30
Penrith	0.3	25	—	—	0.2	35	0.4	6	0.4	40	Full	20
Milepost 44	0.4	36	0.4	39	Full	35	0.6	7	0.4	40	Full	38
Shap Summit	0.4	30	0.3	39	0.3	35	0.4	5	0.2	33	Full	35

	Bp psi	Water level	Bp psi	Water level	Bp psi	Water level	Bp psi	Water level	Bp psi	Water level	Bp psi	Water level
Boiler performance:												
Carlisle	175	1	180	0.8	180	0.8	200	1	180	1	166	0.9
Calthwaite	170	0.9	181	0.6	174	0.5	197	1	175	1	174	0.9
Penrith	175	0.9	184	0.7	175	0.5	205	1	180	1	164	1
Milepost 44	173	0.9	180	0.6	176	0.4	195	0.95	175	0.87	169	1
Shap Summit	170	0.9	177	0.5	174	0.3	205	0.95	165	0.62	175	1

	tons	tons	tons	tons	tons	tons
Max drawbar pull	3.8	3.9	3.7	3.5	4.5	4.6
	mph	mph	mph	mph	mph	mph
Corresponding speed	30	32	26	26	29	34
Min speed on Shap Bank	35	37	37.5	38	35	33

* Notch on reverser; for cut-offs corresponding see separate table

TABLE III
LMSR DYNAMOMETER CAR TESTS: CARLISLE–PRESTON
350-ton trains

Run No				7		8		9		10		11		12	
Engine No				90		14630		14630		1065		10460		30	
Engine Name				*Kestrel*		—		—		—		—		*Thalaba*	
Railway				LNWR		CR		CR		MR		LYR		LNWR	
Load, tons tare				345.9		350.6		350.6		347.9		342.6		347.9	
Dist			Sch	Actual		Actual		Actual		Actual		Actual		Actual	
Miles			min	m s		m s		m s		m s		m s		m s	
0.0	CARLISLE	... ...	0	0 00		0 00		0 00		0 00		0 00		0 00	
17.9	Penrith	... ...	27	27 31		27 32		28 00		27 55		27 30		27 10	
—				—		—		—		—		psw		psw	
31.4	Shap Summit	... ...	50	47 33		47 19		48 00		45 55		48 28		48 40	
—				—		—		sigs		pws		sigs		—	
69.1	LANCASTER	... ...	90	84 33		86 30		90 42		84 28		89 02		85 23	
—				—		pws		psw		—		—		—	
90.1	PRESTON	... ...	114	109 07		112 17		114 54		109 58		110 26		110 57	
Net times				min 109		min 110½		min 111		min 109		min 107½		min 108½	
				Reg	Cut-off %	Reg	Cut-off %	Reg	Cut-off %	Reg	Cut-off *	Reg	Cut-off %	Reg	Cut-off %
Engine working:															
Carlisle	...	... ...		0.1	Full	—	—	—	—	Full	12	0.4	50	Full	Full
Calthwaite	...	... ...		0.4	35	0.5	39	0.4	39	0.6	8	0.4	30	Full	30
Penrith	...	... ...		0.5	32	0.3	35	0.4	35	0.5	7	0.4	40	0.25	20
Milepost 44	...	... ...		0.5	—	0.5	35	Full	35	0.5	8.5	0.4	40	Full	30
Shap Summit	...	... ...		0.5	—	Full	35	Full	35	0.4	8	0.2	38	Full	25
				Bp psi	Water level	Bp psi	Water level	Bp psi	Water level	Bp psi	Water level	Bp psi	Water level	Bp psi	Water level
Boiler performance:															
Carlisle	...	... ...		174	0.95	180	0.9	182	0.8	190	1	180	0.87	170	0.8
Calthwaite	...	... ...		154	0.5	178	0.5	176	0.4	200	1	180	0.75	170	0.9
Penrith	...	... ...		170	0.7	182	0.5	173	0.4	200	0.95	165	0.87	170	1
Milepost 44	...	... ...		176	0.8	178	0.4	179	0.4	200	1	180	0.87	173	1
Shap Summit	...	... ...		164	0.5	175	0.3	176	0.3	200	0.95	160	0.5	175	0.8
				tons		tons		tons		tons		tons		tons	
Max drawbar pull	...	... ...		4.0		3.6		4.0		3.5		4.2		4.3	
				mph		mph		mph		mph		mph		mph	
Corresponding speed	...	...		32		35		33		28		31		35	
Min speed on Shap Bank	...	...		33		33		34		37		33.5		35	

* Notch on reverser; for cut-offs corresponding see separate table

Summit was passed 4 min early with the 350-ton train. From the point of view of climbing speeds it was unfortunate that during the week the big 4–6–0s were on test there was a heavy permanent way slack in operation at Penrith, costing about 2–2½ min in running. In view of all this the times of 49 min 51 sec and 50 min 7 sec by the LYR 4–6–0 and by the 'Claughton' were excellent with 400-ton trains (see runs 5 and 6).

Apart from timekeeping, the engine working details are in some cases revealing. The North Western 'Prince', No 90, *Kestrel*, was in excellent condition throughout, and although she had to be worked hard she steamed well, and

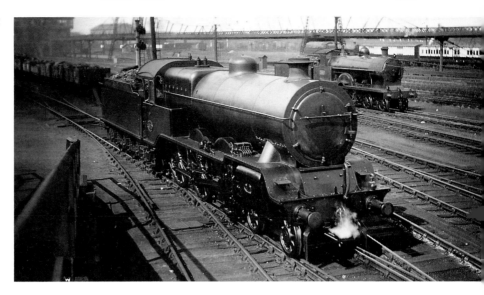

LYR four-cylinder 4-6-0 rebuilt with a superheater at Crewe. (Real Photos)

maintained water level consistently during the heavy hill climbing. The Caledonian engine pulled and steamed well, though at the expense of a falling water level. It was surprising however to read, especially in a report from Horwich, that the LYR engine tended to get 'winded' on the banks. Certainly she dropped both pressure and water level, and although she was fitted with long-lap valves it will be seen that her driver worked with a narrow regulator opening, and relatively long cut-offs. With regard to the readings of water level given in the table these relate to the proportion of a full glass prevailing at the points specified. Thus '1' indicates a full glass, '0.5' half a glass, and so on. The 'Claughton', about which class so much misleading surmise has been written in the past, steamed well and maintained water level consistently. The uphill performance from Penrith in column 6 was altogether admirable. But it will also be noted that this driver, alone among all the competitors, was consistently using a full open regulator, and cut-offs that were comparatively short in relation to the load and the gradients being mounted.

The driver of the Midland Compound was obviously out to show his rivals a thing or two, and he certainly got some magnificent work out of No 1065. She steamed very freely throughout, and the driver was able to extend her in full confidence on the banks. The regulator openings quoted in the reports are doubtless taken from the position of the handle on the quadrant, but on the Compounds the regulator needed to be opened to its fullest extent to bring compound working into operation; after, some easing back was customary. The fixed relation between the cut-offs in the high and low pressure cylinders was in some ways a handicap to the free working of the engine. If the gear was wound up too short the exhaust port openings on the low pressure side became restricted and the engine was sluggish in consequence. If they had retained the original Johnson controls, and the driver had been able to keep going with full regulator, notch up the high pressure cylinder, and leave the low pressure cutting off at 60 per cent, or even more, the Midland Compounds in their final superheated form would have been amazing engines. They were good enough as it was, but as I shall show later in this article they could develop a healthy appetite for coal—again contrary to popular surmise!

Lastly, in referring to Tables II and III, a word is necessary about the figures of drawbar pull quoted. The report does not state where these maximum figures were recorded, but in the majority of instances I imagine they came in accelerating up the 1 in 132 gradient out of Carlisle, to Wreay. I am sorry that I cannot quote the coal consumption figures separately for the Carlisle-Preston runs, which is rather a pity. The method of recording coal consumption was that six hours before each trip the engine was fired up from a separate supply of coal, 7 cwt in the case of the 'Prince', the Compound, and the Pickersgill 4–6–0, and 8 cwt in the case of the LYR 4–6–0 and the 'Claughton', with their much larger fireboxes. The coal for running purposes was of uniform quality throughout the trials, from Kingshill Colliery (Lanark), and was such as was regularly used for LNWR express engines working from Upperby shed, Carlisle. Enough was weighed on to the tenders for the double trip to Preston and back, and the amount left at the end of a day's duty was removed and carefully weighed.

The northbound runs provided a much more severe test of capacity, because the ascent to Shap was prefaced by half an hour's fast work on level track. On the southbound run only the LYR 4–6–0 had done any substantially fast running on the level stretch between Lancaster and Preston, and the times of 21 min 34 sec (run 5) and 21 min 24 sec (run 11) resulted in arrivals in Preston well before time. On the northbound runs there was no time to spare. Again, I have grouped the 300-ton and 400-ton trips into Table IV, and set all the 350-ton journeys in Table V. The report unfortunately gives no details of the speeds attained on the level between Preston and Lancaster, but from the engine working at Scorton only the Pickersgill 4–6–0 on her second 350-ton trip seems to have been going really hard, with full regulator and 30 per cent cut-off. Even with her 400-ton train the 'Claughton' was being handled on a fairly light rein. On only one trip of the whole series, that of the LYR 4–6–0 with the 350-ton train (run 23), was Carnforth passed on time, though the lateness on other occasions was almost entirely due to permanent way checks experienced

TABLE IV
LMSR DYNAMOMETER CAR TESTS: PRESTON–CARLISLE
300-ton and 400-ton trains

Run No			13	14	15	16	17	18
Engine No			90	14630	14630	1065	10460	30
Engine Name			*Kestrel*	—	—	—	—	*Thalaba*
Railway			LNWR	CR	CR	MR	LYR	LNWR
Load, tons tare			299.3	301.6	301.6	304.7	397	393.6
Dist		Sch	Actual	Actual	Actual	Actual	Actual	Actual
Miles		min	m s	m s	m s	m s	m s	m s
0.0	PRESTON	0	0 00	0 00	0 00	0 00	0 00	0 00
1.3	*Oxheys Box*	3	3 48	3 58	3 41	4 17	4 09	4 05
—			sigs	pws	pws	—	pws	pws
21.0	LANCASTER	23	24 56	24 50	23 37	24 54	25 48	25 53
—			—	—	pws	—	—	—
27.3	CARNFORTH ...	29	31 15	32 54	31 32	31 00	32 17	32 10
—			—	pws	sigs	—	—	—
40.1	Oxenholme	43	45 19	49 22	49 00	45 03	46 00	46 28
47.2	Grayrigg	55	56 11	59 55	61 35	55 06	55 41	57 49
53.2	Tebay	61	62 41	66 30	68 10	62 21	61 45	64 42
—			—	—	sigs	—	—	—
58.7	Shap Summit ...	71	71 14	76 25	80 31	71 49	70 27	73 39
—			—	—	—	sigs	—	—
90.1	CARLISLE	103	102 43	107 51	113 50	104 43	101 04	102 16
Net times			min 100¾	min 103½	—	min 103½	min 98	min 99½

Engine No	90		14630		14630		1065		10460		30	
	Reg	Cut-off %	Reg	Cut-off %	Reg	Cut-off %	Reg	Cut-off *	Reg	Cut-off %	Reg	Cut-off %
Engine working:												
Scorton	0.2	24	0.4	30	0.3	30	0.5	5	0.4	25	0.2	22
Carnforth	0.7	25	0.3	35	0.5	30	0.3	6	0.4	30	0.2	22
Milnthorpe	0.7	30	0.4	35	Full	30	0.6	6.5	0.4	30	0.2	22
Oxenholme	0.7	32	0.6	35	0.4	39	0.7	7.5	0.5	40	Full	35
Grayrigg	0.8	38	0.5	39	0.5	39	0.6	8	0.4	38	Full	30
Tebay	0.8	30	Full	30	0.6	30	0.6	6.7	0.4	37	0.2	22
Milepost 36	Full	45	Full	48	Full	48	Full	8	0.4	40	Full	40
Shap Summit	Full	48	Full	48	Full	48	Full	9	0.4	40	Full	60
	Bp psi	Water level	Bp psi	Water level	Bp psi	Water level	Bp psi	Water level	Bp psi	Water level	Bp psi	Water level
Boiler performance:												
Scorton	168	0.9	182	0.4	175	0.6	200	1	180	1	166	0.9
Carnforth	175	0.9	180	0.7	183	0.6	203	0.95	180	1	168	1
Milnthorpe	170	0.9	180	0.8	180	0.7	200	1	180	1	175	1
Oxenholme	175	0.9	178	0.7	182	0.8	200	1	175	1	166	1
Grayrigg	162	0.8	177	0.7	181	0.7	205	0.85	165	0.62	162	0.9
Tebay	175	0.8	175	0.4	180	0.5	195	1	165	0.75	160	0.9
Milepost 36	168	0.8	176	0.6	175	0.8	205	1	170	0.75	170	0.9
Shap Summit	166	0.5	175	0.3	177	0.7	205	1	160	0.62	165	0.6
Average speed	mph		mph		mph		mph		mph		mph	
Oxenholme–Grayrigg	39.3		40.3		checked		42.4		44.0		37.5	
Min speed on Shap	27		24		24		24.5		24		28.5	
Max spd descending to Carlisle ...	74		72		71		71		74		79	
Max drawbar pull	tons 4.3		tons 4.85		tons 5.7		tons 4.4		tons 5.3		tons 5.8	
Corresponding speed	mph 27		mph 23		mph 21		mph 24.5		mph 24		mph 28.5	

* Notch on reverser; for cut-offs corresponding see separate table

Caledonian Pickersgill two-cylinder 4-6-0 No 63 on an Aberdeen–Glasgow express south of Perth. (Author's collection)

TABLE V
LMSR DYNAMOMETER CAR TESTS: PRESTON–CARLISLE
350-ton trains

Run No					19		20		21		22		23		24	
Engine No					90		14630		14630		1065		10460		30	
Engine Name					Kestrel		—		—		—		—		Thalaba	
Railway					LNWR		CR		CR		MR		LYR		LNWR	
Load, tons tare					345.9		350.6		350.6		347.9		342.6		347.9	
Dist				Sch	Actual		Actual		Actual		Actual		Actual		Actual	
Miles				min	m s		m s		m s		m s		m s		m s	
0.0	PRESTON	...	...	0	0 00		0 00		0 00		0 00		0 00		0 00	
1.3	Oxheys Box	...	...	3	3 47		3 57		3 53		4 24		3 53		3 39	
—					sigs		pws		pws		pws		—		pws	
21.0	LANCASTER	...		23	23 44		25 06		24 40		24 35		23 07		25 07	
—							pws		pws				—		—	
27.3	CARNFORTH	...		29	31 12		33 08		33 04		30 49		28 58		31 18	
40.1	Oxenholme	...		43	46 25		48 53		48 03		43 40		41 19		45 39	
47.2	Grayrigg	...		55	58 00		60 23		59 26		53 27		50 00		56 26	
—					—		—		sigs		—		—		—	
53.2	Tebay	...	...	61	64 41		67 08		68 58		59 48		55 46		62 49	
58.7	Shap Summit	...		71	73 11		76 50		79 48		68 14		63 29		71 16	
90.1	CARLISLE	...	...	103	103 33		108 58		111 33		100 00		95 19		101 57	
Net times					min 101½		min 104		min 103		min 98		min 95¼		min 100	

					Reg	Cut-off %	Reg	Cut-off %	Reg	Cut-off %	Reg	Cut-off *	Reg	Cut-off %	Reg	Cut-off %
Engine working:																
Scorton	...	...	...	...	0.5	28	0.6	30	Full	30	0.2	7	0.2	20	0.3	22
Carnforth	...	...	...	...	Full	32	0.4	30	0.9	30	0.4	6.7	0.2	20	0.5	22
Milnthorpe	...	...	...	...	Full	35	Full	30	0.5	35	0.6	7.2	0.4	30	0.5	25
Oxenholme	...	...	...	...	Full	35	Full	35	Full	35	Full	7.5	0.2	42	Full	25
Grayrigg	...	...	...	...	0.6	44	Full	45	0.5	45	Full	9	0.2	30	Full	35
Tebay	...	...	...	...	0.7	34	Full	30	Full	30	Full	7	0.5	40	0.7	22
Milepost 36	...	...	...	...	Full	52	Full	48	Full	60	Full	9	0.5	48	Full	40
Shap Summit	...	...	...	...	0.7	52	Full	60	Full	60	Full	10	0.5	38	Full	58

					Bp psi	Water level	Bp psi	Water level	Bp psi	Water level	Bp psi	Water level	Bp psi	Water level	Bp psi	Water level
Boiler performance:																
Scorton	...	...	...	...	166	0.9	176	0.6	173	0.5	205	1	180	0.87	173	0.9
Carnforth	...	...	...	...	170	0.9	180	0.6	177	0.6	192	1	175	1	164	1
Milnthorpe	...	...	...	...	172	0.9	180	0.7	176	0.5	200	0.95	180	1	170	1
Oxenholme	...	...	...	...	175	0.9	179	0.6	175	0.6	200	0.95	175	0.87	175	1
Grayrigg	...	...	...	...	178	0.8	177	0.6	175	0.5	195	0.9	170	0.62	170	1
Tebay	...	...	...	...	170	0.8	180	0.5	174	0.5	202	0.9	175	0.62	174	1
Milepost 36	...	...	...	...	175	0.8	178	0.7	172	0.6	202	0.95	170	0.62	175	1
Shap Summit	...	...	...	...	164	0.5	177	0.7	172	0.4	207	0.95	160	0.62	175	0.9

					mph		mph		mph		mph		mph		mph	
Average speed																
Oxenholme–Grayrigg		...		...	36.6		37.0		37.5		43.5		48.9		39.5	
Min speed on Shap		...		...	26.5		25		23		25.5		32		31	
Max spd descending to Carlisle				...	74		73		73		70		71		73.5	

Engine No			90	14630	14630	1065	10460	30
Max drawbar pull	...	...	tons 4.7	tons 5.3	tons 5.3	tons 4.75	tons 5.2	tons 5.1
Corresponding speed	...	...	mph 26.5	mph 25	mph 23	mph 25.5	mph 32	mph 31

* Notch on reverser; for cut-offs corresponding see separate table

in the neighbourhood of Lancaster.

Without exception the climbing to Shap was very good. The North Western engines *Kestrel* and *Thalaba* were handled with care and skill. No attempt was made to rush either Grayrigg or Shap inclines; the opening out was gradual, to a big concluding effort in each case, and the climb from Tebay to Shap Summit by No 30, *Thalaba*, with the 400-ton train (run 18) produced the biggest recorded drawbar pull of the entire series. So far as actual pull was concerned it beat that of the Pickersgill 4-6-0 (run 15) no more than fractionally; but the 'Claughton's' 5.8 tons was at

28.5 mph, against the 5.7 tons at 21 mph by the Caledonian engine—a far bigger effort. As on the southbound runs the driver of the 'Claughton' was using a fully opened regulator on all the main climbs, and note will be taken of the steady steaming and well maintained water level in the boiler. Some relaxation was to be noted on nearly all the runs at Shap Summit; but it was no more than natural with so long a stretch of very light steaming to follow.

Scottish enthusiasts may well be delighted with the performance of the Pickersgill 4-6-0. This engine did some stalwart work on the

LYR four-cylinder 4-6-0 in the LMS style of painting. (British Railways)

banks, and steamed well. It is a great pity that so many checks were experienced, resulting in late arrivals in Carlisle on every journey. What one does note however is that no fast running was made with this engine between Shap Summit and Carlisle. The Pickersgill '60' class could not, by any stretch of the imagination, be called free-running engines, and even with the test train passing Shap Summit behind time the downhill allowance of 32 min for the 31.4 miles to Carlisle was taken up fully on practically every trip.

The only occasion during the entire series when some really fast downhill running was made came on the 400-ton 'Claughton' test (run 18), and Shap Summit had been passed 2¾ min late because of the check at Lancaster. On that trip the time down to Carlisle was only 28 min 37 sec, with a maximum speed of 79 mph, and an arrival ¾ min early. The 'Claughtons', of course, were very smooth and free-running engines, and this fine sprint would not have involved any appreciable coal consumption. This driver was clearly out to secure timekeeping on a minimum of coal, and while he carefully fulfilled test requirements by keeping the uphill schedule of 42 min from Carnforth to Shap Summit he left the regaining of the time lost by the Lancaster permanent way check to the downhill stretch.

The driver of the Lancashire & Yorkshire 4–6–0 did some most spectacular work uphill, with results that were reflected in the mortgaging of steam supply in the boiler, and on his coal consumption. As the final table shows, the engine came off badly in comparison with the 'Claughton' in coal consumption. One could have understood it, from studying the logs of the runs, if the actual consumption per train mile had been heavier; but it was also considerably heavier in relation to the work performed, by the vital ratio of coal burned per drawbar horse-power hour.

There are several points that caused some surprise about the working of this engine. The use of long-lap, long-travel valves did not appear to make any appreciable difference. Studying the details of the engine working the driver might be criticised, on grounds of economy, for using relatively narrow regulator opening, and long cut-offs, in contrast to the methods of the 'Claughton's' driver. But with a good valve gear, there have been many locomotives that have responded equally well to the full regulator method of working and to a partial opening with longer cut-offs. The Southern 'Schools' were an outstanding example of this, while the Stanier 'Black Fives' were definitely better on a narrow regulator, and a cut-off of 25 to 30 per cent.

Driving methods and coal consumption apart, however, the Lancashire & Yorkshire engine 'stole the show' in climbing Grayrigg Bank, and on No 23 run, it was a remarkable achievement to pass Shap Summit in 63½ min from Preston, with a 350-ton train. Again on the 400-ton trip (run 17) it was excellent work to regain the 3¼ min of arrears on passing Carnforth *before* Shap Summit was passed, though with this heavy train there was some noticeable flagging in the effort towards the end of the Grayrigg and Shap inclines, and on Shap in particular the 'Claughton' handsomely surpassed her rival on the last few miles up to the summit, where the minimum speed was 28½ mph and the drawbar pull 5.8 tons, against 24 mph and

TABLE VI
COAL CONSUMPTION
CARLISLE-PRESTON AND RETURN

Engine No	90		14630				1065		10460		30	
Railway	LNWR		CR				MR		LYR		LNWR	
Load, tons nominal	300	350	300	300	350	350	300	350	350	400	350	400
Coal, lb/mile	40.1	48.3	52.6	48.7	51.5	51.6	38.1	43.4	51.3	58.1	42.4	52.7
Coal, lb/dhp hr ...	5.1	5.05	—	5.18	4.95	4.73	4.29	4.25	5.07	5.13	4.78	4.75

Midland type three-cylinder 'Compound' 4-4-0 No 1111, in the later black livery. (British Railways)

5.3 tons pull by the LYR engine. As previously mentioned, the report was issued from Horwich and signed by George Hughes; and while showing evident pleasure at the uphill performance of the LYR 4-6-0, it quite frankly concedes the superiority to the North Western engine on grounds of fuel economy.

The North Western 'Prince of Wales' class 4-6-0 *Kestrel* seems to have done a particularly fine job of work having regard to its limited size and relatively small boiler and firebox. The run with the 350-ton train (column 19) shows that some very hard work was needed on the climb from Carnforth to Shap. Exact sectional time was kept over this stage, and the minimum speed of 26.5 mph on Shap itself was excellent. The 'Princes', despite their small coupled wheels, of 6 ft 3 in diameter, were always fast and free-running engines, and *Kestrel* went briskly down to Carlisle, on run 19, with a time of 30 min 22 sec pass to stop for the 31.4 miles, and a maximum speed of 74 mph. The coal consumption of 48.3 lb per mile on this round trip

with the 350-ton train was by no means inordinately heavy for an engine of such moderate size and vintage.

However unpalatable the facts may be for enthusiasts of the North Western, the Caledonian and of the Lancashire & Yorkshire, it is the Midland Compound that stands out in this fascinating comparison. One has only to glance at the details of boiler performance to see the quality of her steaming, and so far as actual performance the ascents of Grayrigg Bank, both with 300-ton and 350-ton trains, are among the finest among the whole collection. Added to this it must not be forgotten that she was the *only* 4-4-0 engine in the party. On No 16 run the arrears at Carnforth had been fully recovered by Grayrigg Summit, though for some reason the engine was markedly eased after that point, and lost 1¼ min on to Tebay. Whatever the reason it was *not* shortage of steam, or low water in the boiler, as the details of boiler performance show. Whether the driver misjudged things on the first trip we are not to know; but he certainly did not mince matters with the 350-ton train. After going still faster up Grayrigg Bank, and producing the remarkable average speed of 43.5 mph between Oxenholme and the summit, he tore on to Tebay, and then made the astonishing time, for a 4–4–0 engine hauling 350 tons, of 8 min 36 sec from Tebay up to Shap Summit. The latter point was passed nearly 3 min early.

Some very hard pounding was needed to achieve this, with the reverser advanced to the ninth notch out of 12 on Grayrigg Bank, and the tenth for the last mile up Shap. The actual cut-offs corresponding to the notches of the reverser are as follows:

Notch number	Cut-off (per cent)	
	Hp cylinders	Lp cylinders
6	67	55
7	71	61
8	75	67
9	79	72
10	83	77

The range of expansion of the steam would be equivalent, in a simple engine, to a cut-off of 27 per cent in notch 6, and to 35 per cent in notch 10. Thus when slogging up the last mile of Shap, in notch 10, the Compound was not being worked anything like so hard as the North Western engines. Despite the hard work done on the banks, and the fast uphill times made, the Midland Compound stood out easily first so far as coal consumption per drawbar horsepower hour, though in the comparison with 350-ton trains the careful work of the 'Claughton' driver, on run 24, resulted in the lowest actual consumption of coal. In view of the assumed extravagance of Crewe engines the comparison is indeed revealing, thus:

350-TON TRAINS

'Claughton'	42.4	lb per mile
Midland Compound	43.4	lb per mile
'Prince of Wales'	48.3	lb per mile
LYR 4-6-0	51.3	lb per mile
Caledonian 4-6-0	51.55	lb per mile

The basic coal consumption of the 'Claughton', namely, 4.75 lb per dhp, was typical of the class at that period, though as I have related in connection with the trials over the Midland line in 1930 the fitting of solid valve heads and narrow piston rings brought the consumption down to 3.6 lb per dhp, and equal to the best Midland Compound figures.

Western Region: Paddington–Exeter historic runs, and elsewhere

The mere suggestion that Swindon might be surpassed in locomotive design or efficiency was as a 'red rag to a bull' to certain correspondents in *The Railway Magazine* in that era. Indeed, I got myself into serious trouble with some of them by hinting at certain shortcomings that were then looming up. By way of appeasement I recalled some very fine runs on the West of England road, but also gave some test results in which the overall performances of 'Kings' and also the Hawksworth variation of the 'Halls' were compared to those of other British standard designs, and did not come out too favourably!

IT is one of the phenomena of the present railway age that, while events are moving towards the ultimate standardisation of all fixed equipment and rolling stock on British Railways, enthusiasm and partisanship for the old companies is growing stronger than ever. Ties and car badges bearing the insignia of the pre-grouping era, let alone the 'Big Four' of 1923–47, are being sold in quantity, and enthusiasts are being exhorted to display their favours in one or another of these ways. In such an atmosphere it is not surprising that I receive many letters expressing interest in steam locomotive performance of old, and occasionally, as I mentioned briefly last month, irate comments if I happen to make an appraisal of certain designs that does not measure up to the views of their staunchest admirers.

The Great Western in particular has a very large and loyal band of supporters, and one of the most fervid of these took me to task, in a long letter to the Editor, for a remark I made in the June issue of *The Railway Magazine*: 'The Great Western, under Churchward, had made tremendous strides in stepping up thermal efficiency, and the Grouping Era saw the other railways beginning to follow suit, and eventually surpassing Swindon achievements.'

The mere suggestion that Swindon might be surpassed in any matter of locomotive practice or performance was like the proverbial 'red rag to a bull' to this particular correspondent. In his letter to the Editor he quoted a number of individual engine performances—some well-known and fully authenticated, and others not authenticated, of which the details have unfortunately been exaggerated as the story has been passed from mouth to mouth. But the gradual overhauling of the one-time supremacy of Swindon in terms of power output and basic coal consumption is a fact that has been established by careful and sustained testing, and these articles have many times included feats of performance elsewhere in Great Britain which no Great Western engine of equivalent power rating, whether class '8', class '7', or class '5', could equal, let alone surpass. This is not to write deprecatingly of 'Kings', 'Castles' and 'Halls'. No one has a greater admiration than I for all three classes; but it is important to regard them in true perspective, and not to surround them with an aura of omnipotence which they do not possess.

The design of the three classes dates back to 1927 in the case of the 'Kings', to 1923 for the 'Castles' and to 1903 for the 'Halls'. No one has followed with greater interest and enthusiasm than I the recent developments carried out on all three classes, in the form of modified draughting, and double blastpipes and chimneys. All these changes were devised to make the locomotives steam freely on a gradual worsening quality of fuel, but even so I very much doubt if the resulting performance very greatly surpassed

the finest work done in the years 1927–39.

The really significant point is that the cylinder design remained unchanged. No matter how freely the boiler is steaming there is a limit to the volume of steam that can be put through the cylinders. At the time they were first introduced the cylinder designs of all three classes were admirable—that of the 'Halls' in particular, developed on Churchward's 4–6–0s No 98 and 171, *Albion*, of 1903 was quite outstanding. But the cylinder designs of the 'Kings', 'Castles' and 'Halls' belong to the pre-Chapelon era, and the engineers of other railways, noting the phenomenon of the rebuilt Pacifics on the Paris-Orleans Railway, applied the principles embodied in those remarkable engines with the result that we had in this country, to take a few random examples, the Gresley 'A4' Pacifics, the Stanier 'Coronations', 'Duchesses' and rebuilt 'Scots', and the Bulleid rebuild of the 'Lord Nelsons' on the Southern. The astonishing improvement in the last named engines came not

Engine No 6014 King Henry VII, *when partially streamlined, hauling the down 'Cornish Riviera Express' on the Frome bypass line.* (Author's collection)

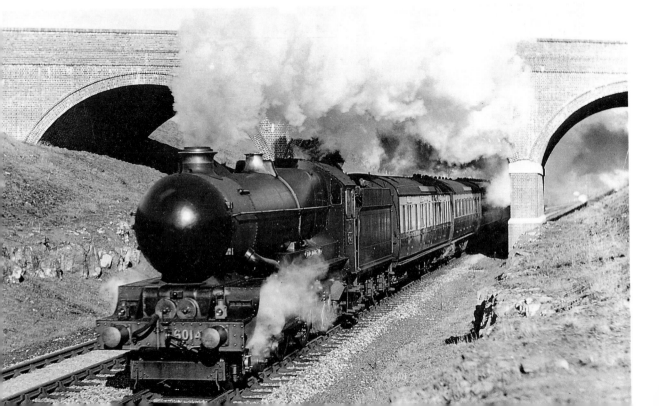

Engine No 6013 King Henry VIII *on a dynamometer car trial run on 10 March 1955 near Reading West. The author was in the dynamometer car.* (M.W. Earley)

so much from the re-arrangement of the blastpipe and chimney, but from the fact that Mr Bulleid fitted them with *new cylinders.*

Now I am quite aware that one can turn through the pages of *The Railway Magazine*, extending back to the volumes of the 1930s, and find occasion after occasion when Great Western locomotives have put up superb performance. In those pre-war years, indeed, the sustained excellence of it could be positively monotonous. But the mere mention of Great Western running in the 1930s brings in two factors not always appreciated by those who are today surprised, dismayed, or indignant at the suggestion that Swindon practice has come to be surpassed. In

two respects the Great Western maintained a substantial lead over their northern confrères right up to the outbreak of war, namely in the quality and precision of the repair work put into locomotives passing through Swindon Works, and the care—nay devotion!—with which they were fired on the road. The quality of the coal, though far better than the stuff we have been used to in post-war years, was variable, even in those days; but every fireman made it almost a point of honour to keep the needle practically a fixture on the red line.

Another factor that I feel was of the utmost importance in maintaining the high standards of all-round performance on the Great Western —high power output, reliability, and low running costs—was that the entire organisation, from the men who worked out the designs in the Swindon drawing office to the men who drove

The 'Cornish Riviera Express', also on 10 March 1955, approaching Heywood Road Junction near Westbury at high speed. (K.H. Leech)

and fired the finished or repaired product, was under the Chief Mechanical Engineer. One man was ultimately responsible for designing and building the locomotives, maintaining them at the sheds from end to end of the line, and for running the trains. The advantages of such organisation, of which that of the Great Western was the last survival of a system that was at one time universal in Great Britain, have been strongly disputed by the advocates of the divided responsibility used on the Midland in pre-grouping days, and later extended to the LMSR, and in a modified form to the LNER. But in a closely knit entity like the GWR it worked extremely well. The out-stations of the loco-motive department were part and parcel of the central organisation, and the line of promotion for men destined for high responsibility lay, variously, from the drawing office, through the out-stations of the Running Department, and through the locomotive and carriage works at

Swindon.

With locomotives used as they were intended to be used, and superintended, often at the far-thest end of the line, by men who had close familiarity with the inner workings of Swindon, it was no surprise that a first-class basic design, like the Churchward two-cylinder 'family', ser-ved the Great Western magnificently; and there was no need to change from the precepts of 1903, despite what Chapelon and others were doing elsewhere. It was the same with the four-cylinder engines. 'Stars', 'Kings' and 'Castles' sped their quiet way on low repair costs and a moderate coal consumption, while maintaining an express train service which, in relation to the overall mileage run, remained one of the fastest in the country. There was no need for any dissatisfaction with individual performance on the road. Swindon locomotives, with their moderate degree of superheat, hydrostatic sight-feed lubricators, and jumper rings on the blastpipes, could, in all-round performance, equal the more modern developments on the northern lines because of the almost perfect consistency of their steaming.

I have been recently examining a number of old records of the 1930s and three runs on the 'Cornish Riviera Express', as far as Westbury, show the quality of performance that was then just taken for granted with the 'Kings', thus:

Engine No		6020		6000		6024	
Load, tons, full		505		510		535	
Dist		Actual		Actual		Actual	
Miles		m	s	m	s	m	s
0.0	Paddington	0	00	0	00	0	00
9.1	Southall ...	11	36	12	00	12	05
36.0	Reading ...	34	15	35	15	36	20
53.1	Newbury ...	50	58	51	35	53	32
70.1	Savernake...	67	19	68	00	70	48
—		—		pws		—	
95.6	Westbury...	89	24	92	40	92	05

The schedule time was then 36 min to Reading, and 94 min to passing through Westbury Station at reduced speed of 30 mph. With engines that could do that kind of thing as a matter of course, why change!

The third run of the three, with engine No 6024, *King Edward I*, was clocked from the footplate by Mr A. V. Goodyear, and in a most comprehensive record that he has put at my disposal, including 120 passing times between Paddington and Exeter, some 50 records of individual speeds and full details of the engine working, there is this most significant note: 'Steam pressures not included, as except for a slight drop to 245 lb at Whiteball the needle might have been fixed at 250 lb throughout.' Therein, of course, lies the 'secret' of Great Western performance in the 1930s. This splendid run was made on Whit-Tuesday 1932, and on arrival at Exeter Mr Goodyear, accompanied by Chief Inspector Davies, crossed over to the up side of St Davids Station, and in a quarter of an hour was away again on the footplate of the up 'Cornish Riviera Express', to record another fine example of 'King' performance.

The logs of these two runs, which are typical

of these famous engines at the zenith of their achievement, are set out in very full detail in Tables I and II. On the down journey they had what was then quite a normal load for 'The Limited', with 15 to Westbury, 13 to Taunton, and 11 on to Exeter. Mr Goodyear does not mention what load was taken forward from the latter point; but if it was unchanged I have no doubt that the eleven coaches, with their tare weight of 372 tons, were taken unassisted from Newton Abbot over the exceedingly heavy gradients of the South Devon line. In the brief notes of the three runs between Paddington and Westbury details were given of a run with No 6000. On this occasion, dating back to 1929, the load was reduced, by slipping, to 405 tons gross from Westbury, but no other slip portions were carried. The engine ran through non-stop to Plymouth, taking 378 tons tare unassisted from Newton Abbot, and arriving at North Road 3 min early. The driver would have been entitled to stop for a bank engine, because the load limit was then 360 tons tare; but in those days the idea of taking assistance was scorned, with so 'slight' an excess over the limit!

Writing of past achievements on the 'Limited', and before coming to a detail reference to Mr Goodyear's footplate journeys, I must mention a trip made before the first world war on which a two-cylinder 4-6-0, No 2943, *Hampton Court*, had a load of 500 tons tare to Westbury, and of 467 tons tare onwards to Taunton. This was on the original schedule of 4 hr 7 min to Plymouth, when the booked passing time to Taunton was 149 min. With this somewhat staggering load *Hampton Court* equalled the 'Kings' out to Southall, by taking no more than 12 min 9 sec from Paddington; passed Reading in 37 min 12 sec; Savernake in 74 min 17 sec; Westbury in 98 min 10 sec; and Castle Cary—dead on time—in exactly 121 min. After a succession of signal checks they stopped at Taunton in exactly 150 min, to take a bank engine up to Whiteball. This magnificent run was logged by a very experienced recorder, the late Rev Hilary Dunn, one time of Bathwick, Bath, and is contained in a notebook kind-

TABLE I
GWR: 10.30 am PADDINGTON–EXETER

Load, ton (e/f) to Westbury: 498/530
to Taunton: 434/460
to Exeter: 372/395
Engine: Four-cyl 4–6–0 No 6024, *King Edward I*

Dist		Sch	Actual		Speeds
Miles		min	m	s	mph
0.0	PADDINGTON	0	0	00	—
1.3	Westbourne Park		3	00	—
5.7	Ealing Broadway		8	45	57
9.1	Southall ...	11	12	05	62½
13.2	West Drayton		16	03	68
18.5	SLOUGH	20	20	40	70½
24.2	Maidenhead		25	47	67
31.0	Twyford ...		31	52	66½
34.0	*Milepost 34*		34	35	
36.0	READING	36	36	20	(slack)
37.8	*Southcote Junc*		38	30	—
44.8	Aldermaston		45	16	62
53.1	NEWBURY	54	53	32	60/61
58.5	Kintbury		58	52	61
61.5	Hungerford		61	55	59
66.4	Bedwyn ...	67	66	48	60
70.1	Savernake	71	70	48	51¾
75.3	Pewsey ...		75	45	75
86.9	Lavington		84	46	82½
95.6	WESTBURY	94	92	05	(slack)
101.3	FROME ...		99	00	(slack)
106.6	Witham ...		105	17	54½
108.5	*Milepost 122¾*		107	29	51½
			Sig		35
115.3	Castle Cary	116	114	55	—
120.2	Keinton Mandeville		119	10	—
125.7	Somerton		123	55	—
129.9	Langport ...		127	34	76
137.9	*Cogload Junc*	137	134	35	55
			pws		—
142.9	TAUNTON	141½	140	12	—
144.9	Norton Fitzwarren		142	30	57
150.0	Wellington		148	08	54½
152.8	*Milepost 173*		151	37	44
153.8	*Whiteball Box*		153	10	39½
			pws		5
158.8	Tiverton Junc		161	30	—
165.3	Hele ...		169	18	72
170.2	Stoke Canon		173	20	—
173.7	EXETER ...	175	177	12	—

Net time 167½ min

ly made available to me by his son, the Rev H. A. Dunn.

Turning to the first of Mr Goodyear's trips, engine No 6024 was started vigorously out of Paddington, using full forward gear for a short time, with a narrow regulator opening; but by Westbourne Park the gear was linked up to 25 per cent and regulator opened full. Cut-off was further reduced to 20 per cent at Old Oak Common, and to 16 per cent at Hanwell. By the latter point speed had just topped 60 mph. There was no attempt to break records for the benefit of this privileged observer. With an absolutely constant boiler pressure the engine was driven in perfect 'copy book' style with a wide-open regulator, and short cut-offs. There was no change from 16 per cent between Hanwell and Reading, to produce some fine running between West Drayton and Sonning, and on the rising gradients up the first part of the Kennet Valley no more than a modest increase, to 17 per cent, sufficed. Passing Newbury fractionally ahead of schedule time, the driver reverted to 16 per cent as far as Bedwyn, increasing there to 17, and finally to 18 per cent for the last 1½ miles up to Savernake. The first valve of the regulator, with 15 per cent cut-off, was enough to produce the fast downhill running necessary to take the train through Westbury 2 min early.

There were no cut-off lines in those days, and the 'Limited' had to slacken speed to 30 mph through both Westbury and Frome Stations, with the need to recover speed subsequently up still rising gradients. The effect of these slacks, as compared with modern conditions, can be seen by comparing the times of this run, as between Lavington and Milepost 122¾, with a run of my own, in more recent times on the 3.30 pm with a 'Castle' class engine. Between these two points, 19.4 miles apart by the cut-off lines, and 0.2 miles further through Westbury and Frome Stations, the respective times were 22 min 43 sec on Mr Goodyear's run, and 19 min 54 sec on mine. This latter was not a particularly fast run. I have details of a still more recent journey on the 'Torbay Express' on which No 5033, *Broughton Castle*, took no more than 18 min

36 sec between the same two points, with a 425-ton train. One can say that the construction of the cut-off lines saved 4 min on the down West of England journey.

Once Milepost 122¾ was passed the task of No 6024 became relatively easy to Taunton, and despite some slow running over the widening works north of Taunton the Minehead and Ilfracombe slip coaches were detached just over a minute early. Excellent work was done up to Whiteball. The cut-off was advanced from 20 to 25 per cent at Wellington Station, and this was enough to give the fine minimum speed of 39½ mph through the tunnel. There was, however, insufficient time in hand to offset the effect of the very bad permanent slowings at Sampford Peverell Halt and Tiverton Junction, where subways were under construction, and Exeter was reached 2¼ min late. Some drivers I have known would have gone a good deal harder between Tiverton Junction and Exeter in the circumstances, to have recovered the lost time; but this point about Mr Goodyear's run serves to emphasise its 'ordinary' rather than exceptional character. The net time of 167½ min, with its start-to-stop average of 62.2 mph from Paddington to Exeter, nevertheless gives a good idea of what an 'ordinary' run with the 'Kings' was like in the year 1932!

Despite the returning holiday traffic of Whit-Tuesday, the up 'Limited' got away from Exeter only 2 min late; but with the Tiverton Junction and Sampford Peverell slacks, each, once again, to 5 mph, and the slow running at little more than 50 mph throughout from Norton Fitzwarren to Cogload Junction, the latter point was passed a little over 8 min late. In studying the very fine work by which the arrears were wiped out between Cogload and Slough, note should be taken of the very moderate speeds run downhill, and once again of the hampering effect of the Frome and Westbury slacks as compared with conditions that became normal in later years. Especially fine was the climb to Savernake, with the 22 miles between Posts 92 and 70 covered in 20 min 40 sec, and a minimum speed of 57 mph up the 1 in 222 between Lavington

TABLE II
GWR: 1.46 pm EXETER–PADDINGTON

Load: 399 tons tare, 430 tons full
Engine: Four-cyl 4–6–0 No 6010, *King Charles I*

Dist		Sch	Actual	Speeds
Miles		min	m　　s	mph
0.0	EXETER	0	0　00	—
3.5	Stoke Canon		5　52	—
12.6	Cullompton　...		16　22	55½
			pws	5
14.9	Tiverton Junc		19　32	5
17.9	*Milepost 176*		25　13	43½
19.9	*Whiteball Box*		28　03	41½
23.7	Wellington		31　49	70½
			pws	50
30.8	TAUNTON	33	38　45	50
35.8	*Cogload Junc*	38	44　16	—
38.8	Athelney		47　37	63
43.8	Langport		52　25	60
48.0	Somerton		56　55	60
53.5	Keinton Mandeville		62　10	67½
				(max)
58.4	Castle Cary	61	66　40	59
61.8	Bruton　...		70　18	51
65.2	*Milepost 122¾*		74　17	45
67.1	Witham　...		76　28	72
72.4	FROME		81　00	(slack)
78.1	WESTBURY　...	83	87　10	(slack)
82.3	Edington　...		91　53	62
86.8	Lavington　...		96　04	66½
92.6	Patney　...		101　51	57
98.4	Pewsey　...		107　10	68½
103.6	Savernake　...		111　52	64½
107.3	Bedwyn　...	112	115　08	easy
120.6	NEWBURY　...		126　32	70½
				(max)
135.9	*Southcote Junc*		140　05	—
137.7	READING　...	142	142　10	45
142.7	Twyford　...	147	147　00	66½
149.5	Maidenhead	153½	152　38	75
155.2	SLOUGH　...	159	157　15	76½
160.5	West Drayton		161　38	68
			Sig	—
164.6	Southall　...	168	165　35	—
169.4	Acton　...		170　45	54
			Sig	—
172.4	Westbourne Park		174　20	—
173.7	PADDINGTON	179	177　40	—

Net time 170¼ min

'Duchess' class LMR Pacific No 46237 City of Bristol *when on loan to Western Region in 1955 approaching Chippenham with 'The Merchant Venturer'.* (K.H. Leech)

and Patney, on 22 per cent cut-off and full regulator. Quite a leisurely descent followed, to Reading; but a grand finish was developed from Twyford onwards, working in 16 per cent cut-off and regulator no more than two-fifths open, and speed rising to 76½ mph on the level near Taplow. Things were all set for an 'on-time' arrival in Paddington, but the checks at Southall and Royal Oak made them one minute late in.

These runs are typical of the immaculate standards of performance put up by the 'Kings' when all the conditions corresponded to those for which they were designed. The net times of 167½ min going down, and 170¼ min coming up, with their gains of 7½ min and 8¾ min on the fast schedule times, showed a handsome margin in reserve. Mr Goodyear records the names of the drivers responsible, but not those of the firemen. In this, I feel, his otherwise supremely competent record missed the point, for it was above all by the quality of the firing that such performances were made possible. In those days, when the standards were so good, the work of the firemen was all too often taken for granted. When the quality of fuel began to vary, and when engines were sometimes sent out with blocked tubes, then not even the traditional

competence of Great Western firemen could cope with the deficiencies. It was in an attempt to compensate for these increasing difficulties in working that Swindon men of post-nationalisation days carried out some changes to the basic Churchward locomotive, and the modified draughting applied to 'Halls', 'Castles', 'Kings', and to some of the lesser lights, proved very effective, up to a point.

The scientific trials of various 4–6–0 locomotives showed some interesting results. In Table III I have shown the results from the modified 'Hall', the LNER 'B1', and the British Railways standard class '4' 4–6–0 which was tested at Swindon, thus:

TABLE III
STEAM RATE, 18,000 lb per hr

Speed, mph	Drawbar horsepower		
	'Hall'	'B1'	'BR4'
20	890	875	960
30	950	985	1,020
40	930	1,020	1,020
50	880	1,000	980
60	750	950	880
70	530	850	730

The above figures relate to Blidworth coal, which was a fuel common to all locomotive tests under the auspices of British Railways. With this grade 2 'hard', the 'Hall' barely reached Churchward's famous target of performance, namely a two-ton drawbar pull at 70 mph. With high quality South Wales soft coal the engine naturally produced a higher optimum steaming rate; but it is in the utilisation of the steam that the above table reveals the extent to which later designs have surpassed the Swindon layout of sixty years ago. It would have been very surprising if they had not done so. I must say I was tremendously impressed with the performance of the LNER 'B1' when she ran between Bristol and Plymouth in the Interchange Trials of 1948, and her vast superiority over the 'Hall' at speeds of 50 mph and over, revealed in Table III, was borne out in some brilliant running with 500-ton loads on the level line between Taunton and Bristol.

With further reference to Table III it is important to emphasise that each engine was being steamed at an absolutely constant rate of 18,000 lb per hour, steam to cylinders. Fed thus with the same amount of steam the 'B1' at 70 mph was producing 60 per cent more power at the drawbar. The 'BR4' 4-6-0, tested at Swindon, also at 70 mph, produced 38 per cent more power at the drawbar than the 'Hall'. This latter, be it noted, was a class '4' engine, whereas the 'Hall' is rated class '5'. There is another method of comparing these results—namely, to take Churchward's performance target, and set down the steaming and firing conditions in which the three engines achieved it. These figures are set out in Table IV. The 'Hall' needed 22,000 lb of steam per hour to reach the target, and on Blidworth coal, fired up to the tremendous rate of 4,250 lb per hour, for such a grate she barely attained it. The 'BR4', fired on Blidworth, was developing a fairly healthy appetite by the time this performance target was reached, but she had plenty in hand; but it was the 'B1' that shows up so well in the comparisons.

Too much notice should not be taken of the

TABLE IV
TWO-TON DRAWBAR PULL AT 70 MPH

Engine	'Hall'		'B1'		'BR4'	
Fuel	B	M	B	SK	B	BW
Steam, lb/hr	21,690*	22,000	18,000	18,000	19,600	19,600
Coal, lb/hr	4,260	2,680	2,450	2,000	3,250	2,835
Cut-off	18	18	23	23	27	27

B-Blidworth. M-Markham. SK-South Kirkby. BW-Bedwas.
* Maximum steam rate achieved with Blidworth coal.

actual cut-offs used, which are relative to the cylinder characteristics of the engine. Table IV shows that a short nominal cut-off does not necessarily mean efficient working. So far as other Great Western locomotives are concerned, I gave figures comparing the 'Kings' against the 'Duchesses' and the 'BR8' Pacific No 71000, in *The Railway Magazine* for May, 1959, and against the rebuilt 'Merchant Navy' 4-6-2s of the Southern in August, 1960; but in view of the present discussion I have set them out again together in Table V, in relation to high performance rates at 30,000 lb of steam per hour.

In connection with test results on British locomotives, another reader has asked whether I could give a complete list of results that have been published from time to time, not necessarily in these articles but in railway literature generally. Now that the days of steam locomotive, in express passenger service, are coming to an end I agree it would be a most

TABLE V
CLASS '8' ENGINES: 30,000 lb OF STEAM PER HR

Speed, mph	Drawbar horsepower			
	'King'*	'Merchant Navy' (Rebuilt)	'Duchess'	'BR8' 71000
30	1,640	1,600	1,735	1,870
50	1,450	1,660	1,765	2,010
70	1,190	1,480	1,570	1,980

* Single chimney, high superheat and improved draughting.

worth-while task to summarise these results. It will also take some doing! Possibly a list, in the form of a bibliography stating where the results have been published, will be a start. True comparisons will never really be possible, because of the different circumstances in which tests have been conducted in the past. In this connection it is extremely unfortunate that one of the most interesting and famous locomotive 'families' in British railway history—the Gresley Pacifics—has never been put through a series of full-dress trials, in the same way that the engines concerned in Table V in this article have been treated.

To return, finally, to Great Western steam locomotives, I have set out three runs from Oxford to Paddington, all made quite recently, which show that with properly maintained engines the old quality of performance could still be achieved. The run of *Donnington Castle*, on the

5.30 pm up, was clocked in February, 1962, by Mr F. G. Cockman, while the other two runs were clocked on successive days, in July, 1963, by Mr D. W. Tuck. *Donnington Castle*, with a moderate load, was running splendidly up to Slough, but a whole succession of checks spoiled the end of the run. *Eshton Hall* on the 8.52 am up got a bad start to Radley, but ran well after Didcot, with a sustained maximum speed of 76 mph on little easier than dead level track between Twyford and Maidenhead. This run was beset by permanent way checks, though the net time was not more than 63 min—a fine effort for a 'Hall', with a load of 325 tons. On the following day *Sudeley Castle* had a clear run to Ealing Broadway, and in passing that station, 56.7 miles, in 53 min 41 sec, was in measurable distance of a 61 min run. *Eshton Hall* and *Sudeley Castle* were manned by the same crew—Driver

TABLE VI
WESTERN REGION: OXFORD—PADDINGTON

Run No		1		2		3	
Engine No		4089		6942		7025	
Engine Name		Donnington Castle		Eshton Hall		Sudeley Castle	
Load, tons (e/f)		205/215		311/325		311/325	
Dist		Actual	Speeds	Actual	Speeds	Actual	Speeds
Miles		m s	mph	m s	mph	m s	mph
0.0	OXFORD	0 00	—	0 00	—	0 00	—
		—	—	pws	20	—	—
5.1	Radley	7 14	69	11 25	50½	7 16	58½
7.3	Culham	9 14	73	13 50	60	9 21	65
10.6	Didcot East Junc	12 29	38 (slack)	17 22	40 (slack)	12 35	40 (slack)
14.9	Cholsey	17 34	67	22 19	63½	17 15	66½
18.6	Goring	20 48	78	25 42	65	20 22	73½
21.9	Pangbourne	23 26	79	28 38	69	22 58	76
27.4	READING	27 52	80/68	33 25	71/68	27 26	72½
32.4	Twyford	32 00	79	37 42	69	31 36	75/68
39.2	Maidenhead	37 09	80	43 13	76	37 02	79½
44.9	SLOUGH	41 32	81	48 02	75	41 39	68
		Sig	38	pws	—	—	—
50.2	West Drayton	46 16	50	54 33	60½	46 09	73
54.3	Southall	50 19	75	58 25	67½	49 28	74
—		Sig stop	—	—	73	—	69½
57.7	Ealing	58 13	—	61 15	70	52 09	72½
		Sig	—	pws	20	pws	20
62.1	Westbourne Park ...	—	—	67 52	—	59 48	—
63.4	PADDINGTON ...	68 45	—	71 13	—	63 38	—
	Net time, min	60		63		61	

Woodburn and Fireman Yates—and their enterprising work in the last days of Great Western steam is a pleasure to set on record.

Last of all comes the special trip organised by the Stephenson Locomotive Society on April 28, 1963, when engine No 6018, *King Henry VI*, worked an excursion on a round trip from Birmingham to Swindon and back: outward via Greenford and the West Ealing loop, and returning via Oxford. As was to be expected on a Sunday many checks for permanent way were experienced, but on certain sections of the route some very fine and spectacular work was done, and in Table VII I have set out details of the running between Leamington and Southall. But

TABLE VII
WESTERN REGION:
LEAMINGTON–SOUTHALL
SLS SPECIAL
Load: 396 tons tare, 440 tons full
Engine: Four-cyl 4–6–0 No 6018, *King Henry VI*

Dist		Actual		Speeds
Miles		m	s	mph
0.0	LEAMINGTON	0	00	—
3.7	*Fosse Road*	6	17	50
6.1	Southam Road	9	05	55
11.1	Fenny Compton	14	04	63/65
		slow		—
19.8	BANBURY	36	25	48
24.9	*Aynho Junc*	41	29	67
30.1	Ardley	46	26	60
33.9	BICESTER	49	29	81
36.9	Blackthorn	51	33	88
39.9	Brill	53	42	82
43.2	*Ashendon Junc*	56	55	57 (slack)
47.2	Haddenham	60	44	68
52.6	Princes Risborough ...	65	45	62
55.8	Saunderton	69	00	55
		Sig stop		—
60.8	HIGH WYCOMBE ...	81	35	—
4.8	Beaconsfield	7	05	52
9.1	Gerrards Cross	11	05	76
11.7	Denham	12	57	91
14.4	West Ruislip	14	51	83
16.2	Northolt Junc	16	32	64
18.7	Greenford	20	02	—
		via		—
		Castlebar		
		loop		
—	SOUTHALL	30	22	—

before discussing the performance I should explain that there were no fewer than 650 passengers on board, and this accounted for the unusually large increment of 'gross' over 'tare' load of the train. The opening run from Birmingham to Leamington had been badly delayed, but on restarting the engine went splendidly up to Southam Road, accelerating to 50 mph on the 1 in 187 gradient, and still further to 55 before the crest of the bank passed. Then came some slow running on the relief line between Fenny Compton and Banbury.

Once clear of this hindrance *King Henry VI* was opened out with a vengeance. Speed was worked up to 67 mph at Aynho Junction, and the four miles rising at 1 in 200 to Ardley Tunnel were cleared at a minimum of exactly 60 mph. Then came a real old-time descent to Blackthorn, with speed rising to 88 mph, and after the slack at Ashendon Junction there came a fine climb over the Chilterns. Here, after six miles rising at 1 in 176–200–167, the minimum speed was 55 mph. Further very fast running followed the water stop at High Wycombe, with a top speed of 91 mph near Denham. In earlier days the up Birmingham express used to sustain a very high rate of speed almost to the point of shutting off steam for Old Oak Common. The line is magnificently straight throughout this length, and it was nothing unusual to clock up average speeds of 80 mph or more over the 12.8 miles from Gerrards Cross to Park Royal. On this run, however, easing began soon after West Ruislip, as the train was diverging from the main line at Greenford, and taking the loop line to West Ealing.

There were many slacks between Southall and Reading, but afterwards it was very good work to run from the latter station to Swindon, 41.3 miles, in 48¼ min with two heavy slacks, and then to cross back again on to the main at Moreton Cutting. The return journey, via Didcot west curve and Oxford, was a succession of fits and starts, with the engine frequently giving evidence of its tremendous capacity for rapid acceleration. But the final demonstration came at

the finish, when a most vigorous ascent was made of the Hatton bank. It is usually possible to make a very brisk start from Leamington, and on this occasion the two miles to Warwick took no more than 3 min 38 sec. But the chances of making an absolutely record ascent of Hatton bank were spoiled by a check to 37 mph through Warwick. After this, however, the engine must have been driven absolutely all-out. Speed rose to 48 mph on the mile of easier gradient after Warwick, and following this the three miles of continuous 1 in 108–103–110 to Hatton Station were climbed without speed falling below 42 mph. This latter speed was practically sustained on the 1 in 110 gradient.

Comparisons are always interesting, and not necessarily odious, and on gradients of 1 in 100, or thereabouts, one inevitably thinks of the record Pacific ascents from Settle Junction to Blea Moor recently discussed in these articles. The performances of *Mallard* and *City of Liverpool* make an interesting comparison with that of *King Henry VI* up to Hatton bank thus:

BR three-cylinder Pacific No 71000 Duke of Gloucester *on a dynamometer car test run from Swindon to Westbury via Reading West Junctions, at Southcote Junction.* (Author's collection)

The 'King' was putting forth an exceptional effort. It was, in fact, greater than the maximum sustained efforts at comparable speeds of No 6001, *King Edward VII*, in the memorable trials of 1953 that preceded the re-introduction of the high-speed 'Bristolian' schedule. Then, when running practically at the maximum capacity of the boiler, and with two firemen, the maximum sustained output was a little under 1,600 equivalent dhp. The effort of *King Henry VI* up Hatton bank could be no more than transitory, and the result was a drop in boiler pressure and water level. The Pacifics, with their more modern cylinder designs, were able to make better use of the steam generated in their boilers and were able to sustain their high outputs of power, without any drop in either boiler pressure or water level. This is not to denigrate the last glorious 'fling' of *King Henry VI*, and indeed the last bow of the class as a whole. The 'Kings' will go down in history as one of the greatest and most successful of all British steam locomotives, but in praising them it is important to regard their achievements in true perspective.

Engine	Load, tons, full	Sustained speed, mph	Equivalent dhp
Mallard	365	48½	1815
City of Liverpool ...	355	57½	2210
King Henry VI ...	440	42	1615

JUNE 1964

Red 'Duchess' to the rescue at Crewe

It was in the volume commencing in 1964 that the editoral department of *The Railway Magazine* began sub-titling the 'British Locomotive Practice and Performance' articles for the first time since their inauguration by Rous-Marten in 1901. It was a sign of the journalistic times, since I had followed in the traditions set by my predecessors and not consciously abided by one set theme throughout. I was horrified at the June 1964 sub-title, and 'blew my top' with the editor, as it seemed a blatant case of steam crowing over a diesel failure. The article itself included some excellent examples of English Electric Type '4' diesel performance on the West Coast expresses, including that on the down 'Midday Scot' which ended prematurely at Crewe with a leaking water tank. How a 'Red Duchess' was provided as a substitute in record time, and how she and her crew gave me the finest run I had yet timed from Crewe to Carlisle, was a rousing story, yet not so as to justify that sub-title.

STEAM, even in these days, still provides the 'first reserve' form of motive power in many parts of the country; but the occasions on which it can rise to the retrieving of a difficult situation are inevitably becoming rare. It is not merely a case of the mechanical condition of locomotives. It is only when steam has reached its last years that the outsider begins to realise something of the elaborate organisation that existed for watering steam locomotives. Now, in areas where dieselisation is complete, many water columns are being removed. On the Highland main line, for example, there are now only two intermediate stations between Perth and Aviemore where water can be obtained for locomotive purposes. There are other places where water supply could be the governing factor in the running, if steam had to be substituted for diesel in emergency.

Great disappointment has more than once been expressed to me that some of the serviceable preserved engines, such as the Midland compound No 1000, could not be retained longer as working units, available for working special trains. As such they would remain so very much more vivid memorials than in the guise of so many museum pieces. But the servicing facilities that steam locomotives need are

Diesel-electric Type '4' No D219 on a Manchester–Glasgow express climbing Beattock Bank. (Derek Cross)

gradually being withdrawn, and the time cannot be so very far away when the routes possible for steam-hauled enthusiasts' specials will be noticeably fewer.

Incidentally, while on the subject of museum pieces, I understand that discussions are now in progress towards the transferring of responsibility for the three Railway Museums, and their wonderful collection of relics, from the Railways Board to the Ministry of Education. If this arrangement is successfully concluded it will ensure the continuance of these collections, under national ownership, on the same basis as the exhibits in the Science Museum, the Natural History Museum and the great national art galleries, and other priceless collections.

Last month I referred to the transition stages on the London Midland main line south of Crewe. Quite apart from the gradual change in motive power there are a number of incidental works in progress which can at times have quite a serious effect on punctuality. For this reason

the express train schedules of today mostly include lavish amounts of recovery margin. When this is not needed, for making up time lost through permanent way slacks and diversions, drivers obviously have a good deal of time on their hands. Hardly a day passes without some expresses arriving in Euston considerably ahead of time. There are other times when, despite the most enterprising and determined efforts in the cab, long-distance trains arrive substantially behind time. I had a very interesting example of this recently on the up 'Royal Scot', when I had the privilege of an engine pass, and so saw the whole affair at first hand.

I was travelling through from Glasgow to Euston, and we had an English Electric type '4' diesel, No D292, throughout, with a load of 348 tons tare, 370 tons full. I logged the Scottish part of the journey from the train, and we made a very steady and uneventful run. There was no check of any kind from start to finish. We climbed the 52.6 miles from Glasgow Central to Beattock Summit in 61½ min, passing Summit at 50½ mph, and then ran the remaining 49.7 miles down to Carlisle in 43 min 48 sec,

without exceeding 77 mph at any point. The overall time was thus 105 min 18 sec. The load was, of course, not a heavy one, and the locomotive had things very comfortably in hand the whole way. On Polmadie shed, however, it was interesting to see no fewer than three red 'Duchesses' in steam—an increasingly rare sight these days. The hardest piece of climbing on this part of the run is between Motherwell and Law Junction, and on the 1 in 100 gradient here, between Wishaw South and Garriongill Junction, the speed was steadily maintained at 43½ mph.

At Carlisle the engine was remanned, and Driver Shepherd and Passed-Fireman C. Ireson took over for the non-stop run to Euston. With them also in the cab was Locomotive Inspector H. Phillipson. The Scottish crew reported that all was well, and we set off with Ireson doing the driving on the first stage of this long non-stop run. We were checked in getting away from Carlisle, and so made relatively slow time to passing No 13 signalbox; but after that the locomotive climbed the 1 in 132 gradient to Wreay in excellent style, topping this first bank at 45 mph. The controller was kept in the fully

'Duchess' class 4-6-2 No 46250 City of Lichfield *climbing Shap with an eight-coach West Coast express.* (Rail Archive Stephenson, T.G. Hepburn)

open position until we reached the level stretch past Plumpton, and then, although the handle was brought well back, a speed of 65 mph was attained before Penrith.

Ireson reverted to full power soon after Eamont Junction, and we made an excellent climb to Shap, with speed averaging 51½ mph over the 9.2 miles between Milepost 47 and Shap Summit. The minimum speed on the long 1 in 125 gradient between Eden Valley Junction and Shap Station was 48 mph, although it was still inclined to fall a little before the easing in the gradient was reached after Thrimby Grange Signalbox.

We had gained substantially on time during the ascent, passing Shap Summit in 37 min 12 sec from Carlisle. With the line south of Crewe subject to a variety of checks, because of the electrification work, it is certainly advisable to get a little time in hand where this can be done without difficulty. Although the English Electric

TABLE I
LONDON MIDLAND REGION: 11.51 am
CARLISLE–EUSTON

The 'Royal Scot'
Load: 10 coaches, 348 tons tare, 365 tons full
Engine: English Electric type '4' diesel D292

Dist		Sch	Actual	Speeds
Miles		min	m s	mph
0	CARLISLE ...	0	0 00	—
			sigs	—
4.9	*Wreay* ...		8 54	45
13.1	*Plumpton* ...		18 01	—
17.9	PENRITH ...		22 34	65 (max)
29.4	Shap ...		35 02	48/56
31.4	*Shap Summit*	43½	37 10	50
36.9	Tebay ...		41 59	80 (max)
43.0	*Grayrigg* ...		47 07	67
50.0	OXENHOLME	59	52 52	78/70
62.8	CARNFORTH		62 56	82 (max)
			sigs	50
69.1	LANCASTER	73½	68 51	—
80.6	Garstang ...		79 01	75
90.1	PRESTON ...	96½	88 24	10
99.5	Coppull ...		99 24	65/57
105.3	WIGAN ...	115	104 59	45/66
117.0	WARRINGTON	126½	117 04	—
			sigs	15
124.8	*Weaver Junc*		126 09	—
			sigs pws	—
141.1	CREWE ...	154	153 29	—
151.6	*Whitmore* ...		166 42	60
160.3	Norton Bridge		174 01	75
			sigs	—
165.6	STAFFORD ...	180	178 59	—
174.9	Rugeley ...	189	187 20	75/69
189.1	TAMWORTH		199 22	75
202.0	NUNEATON	212	210 09	66/78
216.5	RUGBY ...	224½	223 19	40
223.5	*Watford Lodge*		230 47	60
232.7	Church Brampton		238 37	72
			sigs	—
235.7	NORTHAMPTON		244 24	—
			sig stop	—
241.6	ROADE ...	245	260 21	—
249.1	Wolverton ...		268 35	75
			sigs.	5
254.8	BLETCHLEY	255½	276 35	—
			sigs	—
261.3	Leighton Buzzard		293 14	10
269.8	Tring ...	269	303 06	64
277.0	Hemel Hempstead		308 55	80
284.0	WATFORD JUNC	285	314 23	72
291.1	Harrow ...		319 11	80
			pws	20
296.1	WILLESDEN JUNC ...		326 44	64
			pws	—
301.5	EUSTON ...	314	337 49	—

type '4' locomotives are a little less powerful by comparison with some later designs introduced, they are doing excellent work, and their riding is always very smooth and comfortable.

The descent to Carnforth was a beautifully judged piece of work on the part of Passed-Fireman Ireson. With a free running locomotive, and a long stretch of favourable road on which the gradients vary, and where there are many slight restrictions for curves, it is all too easy for the running to partake of a series of fits and starts, with spells of high speed interspersed with heavy brake applications. But Ireson kept the train running at a beautifully even speed. On the steeper descents engine and train were coasting, with an occasional but very gradual brake application; while along the level stretch in the gorge of the River Lune and over Grayrigg Summit, and again between Milnthorpe and Burton, he made judicious use of the throttle.

As the log shows we just touched 80 mph descending Shap itself, and again when nearing Carnforth; but otherwise speed was kept between the relatively narrow limits of 67 and 78 mph and the average between Scout Green box and Carnforth was 74.2 mph. So we passed Carnforth in the fine time of 62 min 56 sec for the 62.8 miles from Carlisle, despite the initial check in starting. There was a 'distant' on, momentarily, nearing Hest Bank, but notwithstanding this slight hindrance we were through Lancaster in less than 'even' time.

In climbing the sharp bank at 1 in 98 up to Lancaster Old Junction, as it used to be known, full power was used, and the driver kept the controller fully open for the fast-running, almost level stretch to Preston. Here, constructional work on the new motorway, closely adjacent to the railway on some stretches, was a reminder of

The up 'Mid-Day Scot' near Gretna Junction hauled by 4-6-2 No 46210 Lady Patricia. (Rail Archive Stephenson, D.M.C. Hepburne-Scott)

competition to come. Our locomotive ran well here, working up to 75 mph at Garstang, and with a clear road in from Barton we were able to pass Preston, 90 miles, in 89 min 24 sec from Carlisle—8½ min early.

We continued to get a remarkably good road, and although things were being taken quite easily we passed both Wigan and Warrington comfortably ahead of time. We needed this time in hand, for a whole series of checks now beset us. There was a long permanent way slowing in force between Winsford and Coppenhall Junction, for which we had several minutes in reserve. But on this busily-worked section of line reaction from several preceding trains spread backwards, as it were, and we began to sight double-yellows as far back as Hartford. Nevertheless we had enough time in hand to offset these checks, and passed Crewe exactly on time.

Through the Midlands we ran very closely to the booked point-to-point times. There was a slight signal check approaching Stafford, but we ran the 75.5 miles from Crewe to Rugby in

69 min 50 sec, against the sharp allowance of 70½ min for this section. It was interesting to see that the all-out performance of this locomotive up the 1 in 177 gradient of Madeley Bank was a sustained 54 mph. At Rugby, however, to my considerable interest, we were diverted to the Northampton loop line, over which I had not previously ridden on the footplate. South of Rugby there are now many places where the cable trains are at work, installing the overhead wires. That, of course, means absolute possession of the line in question. The Northampton line includes some considerably harder gradients than the main line, via Weedon, though the climb out of Rugby is only a little steeper—1 in 300, against 1 in 370. The summit comes at Watford Lodge, and here speed had just reached 60 mph. From there it is a continuous descent at 1 in 230 into Northampton, and speed was restrained to a maximum of 72 mph.

There is a severe speed restriction through the Castle Station, but we were checked additionally by signal, to 10 mph. From Northampton there is a continuous ascent of 1 in 200 to the point of rejoining the main line, at Roade. Up this we were going well, and had already attained

50 mph when adverse signals brought us to a stand at the intermediate colour-light signals between Middleton Box and Roade. Having passed Northampton at 3.55 pm, and with 70 min left for the remaining 65.8 miles to Euston, I was quite hopeful that we should keep time, despite the divergence. But there was a goods ahead of us, and we were kept standing for a full 5 min. We were checked to walking pace before crossing on to the fast line at Roade, and passed that junction 16 min late, with 53 min left for the 59.9 miles to Euston.

We soon got going, passing over Castlethorpe troughs at 75 mph; but then, after a long preliminary slowing, we were turned on to the slow line at Denbigh Hall Box, just north of Bletchley. There was a cable train at work on the up fast line near Linslade Tunnel, and everything on this busy quadruple-tracked main line was being funnelled through a veritable bottleneck, on the up slow line between Denbigh Hall and Leighton Buzzard. We were unlucky enough to take our place in the queue immediately behind the heavy goods, and somewhat naturally we had a rather slow passage—to say the least of it. When a new railway is being built on top of an existing one it is not reasonable to expect that traffic will always flow without delay, and in actual fact we took 15½ min to cover the 6½ miles from Bletchley to Leighton Buzzard.

Once back on the fast line we ran merrily enough, though a long permanent way check at Kenton robbed us of some further time. But despite this, and a final heavy check for engineering work at Camden, we covered the last 36 miles, from Cheddington into Euston, in a shade over 39 min. So far as the non-stop running of the 'Royal Scot' is concerned, between Carlisle and Euston, I shall always regard as a personal yardstick the schedule in force when I made my first footplate journey on the train, in 1934, when the Stanier Pacifics were first on the job. The allowance was then 334 min. On this recent trip of mine, with such a succession of delays, the total time was 337 min 49 sec. The net time is difficult to estimate, but I do not think that a figure of 296 or 297 min is far out, for the com-

plete 301.4 miles from Carlisle to Euston, via Northampton. This shows a net gain of 17 or 18 min on the present schedule of 314 min. This latter, of course, provides for a normal run via Weedon. The allowance of 20½ min for the 22.7 miles from Rugby to Roade is distinctly sharp.

TABLE II
LONDON MIDLAND REGION: 1.15 pm EUSTON–CREWE
The 'Midday Scot'
Load: 10 coaches, 355 tons tare, 370 tons full
Engine: English Electric type '4' diesel D322

Dist		Sch	Actual		Speeds
Miles		min	m	s	mph
0.0	EUSTON ...	0	0	00	—
1.0	Milepost 1 ...		2	41	—
5.4	WILLESDEN JUNC	14	7	55	67
			pws		15
11.4	Harrow ...		17	05	—
16.0	Bushey ...		23	22	—
			pws		15
17.5	WATFORD JUNC	31	25	55	—
24.5	Hemel Hempstead		34	37	64
			pws		20
31.7	Tring ...	44½	44	31	62
36.1	Cheddington		48	05	77
			sigs		20
40.2	Leighton Buzzard		51	17	—
46.7	BLETCHLEY	56½	58	26	75
52.4	Wolverton ...		62	54	80
59.9	ROADE ...	67½	69	01	68
			pws slight		45
69.7	Weedon ...	76½	77	33	75
			pws		20
78.8	Kilsby Tunnel				
	North ...		88	06	68
82.6	RUGBY ...	93	91	50	—
			sig stop		—
91.3	Shilton ...		102	40	71
97.2	NUNEATON ...	106½	107	15	80
110.1	TAMWORTH ...	116½	117	25	70/82
116.3	Lichfield ...	121½	121	59	72/78
			pws		20
124.3	Rugeley ...	128	128	25	—
133.6	STAFFORD ...	136½	140	28	58/60
138.9	Norton Bridge	141½	145	00	72
147.6	Whitmore ...		152	12	72
150.2	Madeley ...	152	154	10	77
			sig stop		—
158.1	CREWE ...	159	166	25	—

'Duchess' class 4-6-2 No 46251 City of Nottingham *at Nottingham Victoria with an RCTS special on 9 May 1964.* (Rail Archive Stephenson, T.G. Hepburn)

Another very interesting experience was on the down 'Midday Scot', on which we had a very similar load, and engine No D332. This time we were turned on to the slow line at Harrow because there was a cable train at work near Bushey. This express has quite a fast booking, of 159 min for the 158.1 miles from Euston to Crewe, and with the numerous hindrances we could not keep strict time. In addition to the diversion to the slow line we had permanent way checks at Hemel Hempstead, Blisworth, Welton, and Rugeley, and there were signal checks at Leighton Buzzard and Rugby. In addition to the cable train that necessitated our diversion to the slow line between Harrow and Watford, I noted other cable trains at work at Berkhamsted, north of Linslade Tunnel, and at Rugby.

The locomotive was being worked in full power wherever possible, but the succession of checks was too much for timekeeping, added to a late start of 2¼ min from Euston. We passed Madeley 4¼ min late; but the locomotive had been putting up an excellent performance, and I was looking forward to recording the work from Crewe to Carlisle, with an increased load, because of the addition of the through carriages from Plymouth.

We were brought to a stand by adverse signals outside Crewe, and then our fireman, on climbing down to go to the telephone, noticed something amiss under the locomotive. The water tank was leaking, and he shouted across to us 'fresh engine from Crewe'! Inspector Evans, who had been riding with me, immediately climbed down, and at once confirmed that the engine had become a failure, and we ran into Crewe Station with him leaning out of the cab to advise the controller as soon as possible.

Crewe is deservedly famed for getting things done quickly, but even at such a large locomotive centre substitute engines suitable to make a 245-mile run can scarcely be produced at a moment's notice; and while D322 was coupling off someone on the platform said 'he's giving you 6228.' The fresh driver laughed and commented that it was a leg-pull. Obviously D228 was coming down for us. But even while we thus joked, a red 'Duchess' came backing down from the shed. It was now my turn to be taken aback, for I was by no means prepared, clothing wise, to ride steam! Fortunately not the least of the emergency arrangements had been to find an inspector's overall 'slop' for me, and with Driver Purcell, Fireman Keen, and Inspector Kirk I climbed aboard No 46228, *Duchess of Rutland*.

To say that the new driver and fireman were put out by this contretemps would be an understatement. The *Duchess of Rutland* was certainly a prepared engine, fully coaled and watered; in fact she was booked for the succeeding Perth express, a considerably less onerous task than the 'Midday Scot'. But she was the first engine Crewe North shed could give us, and I learned afterwards that a type '4' English Electric diesel was hurriedly got ready for the Perth.

In these days steam, taken on at a moment's notice, can land one in for a very rough trip, and for our fireman in particular, who had come on duty prepared for nothing more strenuous than the tending of a steam-heating boiler, there was now the task of shovelling some six tons of coal in the space of 4½ hours! But it was very soon evident that no half-hearted attempt was to be made to deal with the emergency. A knotted handkerchief replaced his uniform cap, and he commenced vigorously to dig. By the time all was ready we were 18 min late away, with a load of 12 coaches, 423 tons tare, 455 tons full.

Driver Purcell started very gently over the maze of points at the north end of Crewe Station, and acceleration was moderate as he took the measure of the engine. But by the time we passed the site of Minshull Vernon Station we were doing 61 mph and we were soon getting well into the 'seventies'. Several things became apparent: notably that the engine seemed in good nick at the front end; she rode as though a considerable mileage had been worked since last general overhaul, but no one minds a bit of hard riding if the engine will go, and from Winsford Junction to Moore we averaged 76 mph for 12½ miles on end.

This was an exhilarating start, but I must say I watched the boiler pressure gauge with some anxiety at first. I need have had no fears. Our young fireman fairly lived up to his name, and

TABLE III
LONDON MIDLAND REGION: 4.4 pm CREWE–CARLISLE
Load: 12 coaches, 423 tons tare, 455 tons full
Engine: 4-cyl 4–6–2 No 46228, *Duchess of Rutland*

Dist		Sch	Actual	Speeds
Miles		min	m s	mph
0.0	CREWE ...	0	0 00	—
2.7	*Coppenhall Junc*		4 35	—
4.9	*Minshull Vernon*		7 17	61
8.9	*Winsford Junc*		10 45	70
11.8	Hartford ...		13 06	76
16.3	*Weaver Junc*	16½	16 52	77½/75
21.2	*Moore* ...		20 45	77½
24.1	WARRINGTON	23½	23 05	62
				(eased)
27.5	*Winwick Junc*		26 20	66
29.8	*Golberne Junc*		28 44	56
33.2	Bamfurlong		32 05	68½
35.8	WIGAN ...	35½	34 32	(eased)
38.1	*Boars Head*		37 12	46
39.1	*Standish* ...		38 30	50
41.7	Coppull ...		41 29	49½ (min)
45.5	*Buxton Junc*	48½	44 46	76/70
48.7	*Farington* ...		47 17	75 (max)
51.0	PRESTON ...	53½	50 46	10
55.7	*Barton* ...		58 05	64
60.5	Garstang ...	65½	62 10	74/72
66.2	*Bay Horse* ...		66 54	75
	Oubeck Box		—	77
72.0	LANCASTER	75½	71 31	eased
75.1	Hest Bank ...		74 08	75½
78.3	CARNFORTH	81	76 40	74/77
	Milepost 9½ ...		—	61
85.6	Milnthorpe ...		83 05	69
87.5	*Hincaster Junc*		83 00	56
91.1	OXENHOLME	94	89 05	48
96.0	*Milepost 24* ...		95 28	44
98.2	*Grayrigg* ...		98 40	40
104.2	Tebay ...	111½	104 30	71
106.0	*Milepost 34* ...		106 13	56
107.0	*Milepost 35* ...		107 23	44
108.0	*Milepost 36* ...		108 49	37
109.0	*Milepost 37* ...		110 38	—
109.7	*Shap Summit*	120	111 59	30
111.7	Shap ...		114 35	60
119.0	Clifton ...		121 14	73 (max)
123.2	PENRITH ...	133	125 00	eased
128.0	*Plumpton* ...		129 15	77/75
133.7	*Southwaite* ...		133 42	80
136.2	*Wreay* ...		135 47	72
139.7	*Carlisle No 13*		138 48	—
			sigs	—
141.1	CARLISLE ...	151	141 30	—

Three preserved 'Black Five' 4-6-0s, Nos 44871, 45407 and 44932, at Carnforth in August 1974, with Hardwicke *in the background.* (Derek Cross)

worked with energy and skill. The other point that struck me *after* the run was the familiarity of steam conditions. I had not ridden a steam locomotive for over two years, and yet one felt immediately at home once again among all the incidental effects of steam footplate work—coal dust, the water spray, the 'sing' of the injector, the smell of warm oil and that compelling rhythmic beat of the exhaust.

We began to hear the exhaust in earnest after Warrington; for the driver put the engine to it hard up the sharp rise to Golborne Junction, and from passing Winwick Junction at 65 mph we did not fall below 56 in the next 2¼ miles, at 1 in 132-470-255-156. We got away splendidly to 68½ mph past Bamfurlong, and when we eased through Wigan we had already won back a minute on the very sharp allowance of 35½ min for the 35.8 miles from Crewe to this point. We

passed through Wigan at 55 mph, and then the exhaust really sharpened as we mounted the 1¾ miles of 1 in 104 to Boars Head. Here cut-off was advanced to 30 per cent with the regulator opened well out on to the second valve, and this stiff rise was cleared at 46 mph.

This was excellent work in every way, and by this time—so rapid was our progress, and so wonderfully clear the road—that the situation of an emergency was receding, so far as I was concerned, and I realised I was clocking some of the fastest running I have *ever* recorded over this route. The last mile up to Coppull Summit, at 1 in 242-119, was cleared at 49 mph, and we ran swiftly down to Preston. We passed the site of Farington Station, 48.7 miles from Crewe, in 47 min 17 sec and then for the first time got signals on slightly in the approach to Preston. Nevertheless we were through this station in

50¾ min with a gain already of 2¼ min to engine and crew.

To give the fireman a breather, Inspector Kirk took the shovel for a spell after Preston. The engine got away well, to run freely at 75 to 77 mph on level track; indeed, the average speed over the 19.8 miles from Brock to Carnforth was 73.3 mph inclusive of the usual slack at Lancaster No 1 Junction. The engine was steaming well, and there were smiles all round now as we passed Carnforth with 4¼ min of lost time regained, and with speed rising to 77 mph as we entered upon the ascent to Shap. To Carnforth we had taken only one minute more from Crewe than on the fire-eating dynamometer-car test trip of November, 1913, with the 'Claughton' 4-6-0 No 1159, *Ralph Brocklebank*.

The 2¼-mile rise at 1 in 134 to Milepost 9½ was cleared at 61 mph, and speed rose again to almost 70 mph before we reached the foot of the Grayrigg bank, just south of Milnthorpe Station. We made an excellent climb. Purcell started lengthening the cut-off as soon as we got on to the grade, and by Oxenholme, passed at 48 mph, we were working in 30 per cent. For the steeper gradients beyond he advanced to 35 per cent. We sustained 44 mph on the 1 in 131, which then extends to Lambrigg Viaduct, and the last two miles at 1 in 106 to Grayrigg brought us down to exactly 40 mph.

It had been noticeable at every point in the journey how swiftly the engine worked into speed after each summit point was passed, and here, with the regulator eased back, and cut-off in 20 per cent, No 46228 got quickly up to 71 mph at Tebay troughs. Shap was then taken in grand style. As the speed fell off so the cut-off was lengthened: to 29 per cent, at 56 mph; to 34 per cent at 44 mph; and finally to 40 per cent just after Scout Green Box, when the speed had dropped to 37 mph.

In drizzling rain we went steadily up to the last miles, with successive average speeds—over full miles—of 51½, 41¾, and 33 mph, to Milepost 37, and a sustained 30 over the last half mile. Here the engine was inclined to slip, in conditions that were distinctly unfavourable.

But although this final ascent was not spectacular, we had climbed the full 31.4 miles from Carnforth to Shap Summit in 35 min 19 sec, an average speed of 53.4 mph, and a further gain of 3¾ min on schedule. We had now won back *eight minutes*, and had made the really splendid time of 111 min 59 sec over the 109.6 miles from Crewe to Summit.

No exceptional high speed was run down to Carlisle. For the greater part of the distance the engine was coasting, while some respite was being taken before the very hard work required north of the Border. We just reached 80 mph at Southwaite, and were inside even time once more on passing Wreay—136.2 miles in 135 min 47 sec. Signals checked us slightly in the approach to Carlisle, but we stopped, after a slow draw-in to 'spot' the tender to the water column, in 141½ min from Crewe—a gain of 9½ min on schedule. When I donned that overall 'slop' on Crewe platform, if anyone had told me then I was about to log the fastest run I had ever experienced personally from Crewe to Carlisle I am afraid I should have told him not to be silly! Yet so it turned out.

The work of Messrs Purcell and Keen and Kirk was just beyond praise. Quite apart from the tremendous personal thrill the run gave me it was, beyond all else, an outstanding piece of railway working. The train had arrived in Crewe 9¼ min late—not, I hasten to add, through any fault of the diesel or its enginemen—and yet despite the sudden emergency and change of engine we were only 8½ min late into Carlisle. In achieving such a result the promptitude of the locomotive control at Crewe also played a notable part.

Unfortunately such spectacular progress could not be continued. One cannot now be sure of getting water at the troughs in Scotland, and although the train had a booked stop of only 2 min at Carlisle, a full 6 min was spent topping up the tank of No 46228. My footplate pass did not extend beyond Carlisle, and by the time I had washed and tidied up my friends were going for it with renewed vigour. Speed had risen very rapidly from the Carlisle start to 75 mph at the

Solway Firth, and after six miles of 1 in 200 speed had not fallen below 58 when there came a bad, though short, permanent way check, to 15 mph. Again, as at point south of Carlisle, the recovery was extremely rapid; Kirtlebridge was passed at 64 mph and the second long piece of 1 in 200 ascent, 4¼ miles of it, was cleared at a minimum speed of 57 mph.

TABLE IV
SCOTTISH REGION: 6.37pm
CARLISLE–GLASGOW
Load: 12 coaches, 423 tons tare, 455 tons full
Engine: 4-cyl 4-6-2 No 46228, *Duchess of Rutland*

Dist		Sch	Actual	Speeds
Miles		min	m s	mph
0.0	CARLISLE	0	0 00	—
			—	75
8.6	Gretna Junc ...	10	9 55	—
10.2	*Quintinshill* ...		11 17	63
13.1	Kirkpatrick ...		14 10	58
			pws	15
16.7	Kirtlebridge		19 45	64
20.1	Ecclefechan ...		23 04	61
22.7	*Castlemilk* ...		25 40	57
25.8	LOCKERBIE	27	28 23	72
28.7	*Nethercleugh*		30 46	eased
34.5	*Wamphray* ...		36 07	67
39.7	BEATTOCK	39	41 10	—
45.3	*Greskine Box*		49 39	32
49.7	Summit	57	58 40	28 (min)
55.3	Crawford		63 48	71
63.2	Lamington ...		70 57	70
66.9	SYMINGTON ...		74 28	58
68.5	Thankerton ...		76 00	72
70.0	*Leggatfoot Box* ...		77 18	67
			—	75
73.5	CARSTAIRS	78	81 35	—
			86 05	—
76.3	Cleghorn		91 25	—
78.5	*Craigenhill Box* ...		94 02	53
80.7	Braidwood ...		95 56	72
81.9	Carluke		96 54	76 (max)
84.0	LAW JUNC	89	98 43	eased
86.4	*Wishaw South*		101 07	67
			pws	—
89.4	MOTHERWELL ...	96	104 30	—
			sig stop	—
93.9	Uddingston	100	113 20	—
			sigs	—
101.2	Eglinton Street ...	110	123 38	—
102.3	GLASGOW CENT	113	126 20	—

Gathering speed again we passed Lockerbie at 72 mph, having lost barely 1½ min on this fast schedule, despite the permanent way check; but it then became apparent that the engine was being nursed a little in readiness for the ascent of Beattock bank. Normally the acceleration continues north of Lockerbie, whereas on this trip speed fell slightly, and at the crossing of the Annan, which is virtually the foot of the bank, the speed was no more than 67 mph.

Nevertheless a fine ascent was made of the bank itself. Beattock Station was passed at a shade under 60 mph, and the ten miles to Summit took 17½ min, with a sustained minimum speed of 28 to 29 mph. As at Shap, conditions were not favourable to good climbing, and one could feel that the engine was slipping very slightly during the last mile or so of the bank. The net time of 56 min to Beattock Summit was again a splendid piece of work in the circumstances. I should add that Inspector Kirk, who rode with me, had left the train at Carlisle, so that there was no relief 'fireman' available to take an occasional spell north of the Border.

Down the Clyde valley the running was no more than brisk, and sure enough a special stop had to be made at Carstairs for water. While the stop, like the prolonged station stop at Carlisle, could be debited to the locomotive, it was, more strictly, a debit to the transition period on British Railways. Such a stop would not have been needed in normal steam days. As a result of these hindrances our lateness had increased to 22½ min at Law Junction.

By this time our luck seemed to be out. We were stopped by signal at Douglas Park Box, between Motherwell and Uddingston, and were checked to 15 mph by adverse signals at Rutherglen Junction. As a result of these delays we arrived just over 26 min late in Glasgow. But there had been a loss of only 8½ min since we got the right away from Crewe, and if one relates the work north of Carlisle to normal steam days, and treats the Carstairs stop as an out-of-course check, then the net time for Carlisle to Glasgow works out at 110½ min, another gain of 2½ min in running time to engine and crew.

On arrival in Glasgow it was a pleasure once again to congratulate and thank Driver Purcell and Fireman Keen on their work. A net running time of 252 min over the 243.3 miles from Crewe to Glasgow, with its average speed of 58 mph over Shap and Beattock, was a grand piece of work, seeing in what circumstances it commenced. In years to come, when I look back on the many journeys I have made over the West Coast Route, and on the times when I have been privileged to ride on the footplate, I feel sure that this run on the 'Midday Scot' will take its place as one of the most memorable of all.

AUGUST 1964

Southern electric and steam

After the row over the 'Red Duchess' it was agreed that I should provide my own sub-titles, and the present one, it will be agreed, was innocuous enough! In this article I certainly ranged far and wide, from the South Eastern suburban to the Salisbury-Exeter racing ground, and an interesting comparison of past and present logs under steam traction over the Portsmouth line, when certain of the Bournemouth expresses were diverted that way. Then there was a comparison between multiple-unit electric trains and a Saturdays-only steam express on the main Brighton line.

WHEN there is much that is new to record in railway engineering and traffic working it is perhaps inevitable that parts of a railway system that are giving steady and reliable service, and are not 'hitting the headlines' with any sensational developments, or mishaps, tend to get ignored. There is more natural joy over 'the sinner that has repented', than over he who has been pursuing a steady, even, and reliable course for many years. This can well be the case for the Southern Region of British Railways, and it is very evident from the number of logs that reach me of steam perfor-mance between Waterloo, Bournemouth and Exeter, that the Western Division, at any rate, is still very popular with the compilers of logs.

These logs are however confined to a very small proportion of Southern operating in general; they are, indeed, confined, with very few exceptions, to no more than a single train in each direction—the 'Atlantic Coast Express'. The fact that this is one of the last crack expresses out of London to be regularly hauled by steam invests it with a particular interest; but in this ar-ticle I wish to refer to Southern operating in a broader sense than the details of running by in-dividual trains.

It is safe to say that nowhere else in the world is there, in the aggregate, a service of the density and speed operated regularly from the London terminal stations of Cannon Street, Charing Cross, London Bridge, Victoria, and Waterloo. There may be individual stations elsewhere, like Liverpool Street, which can equal or surpass in-dividual Southern stations. But taking the five termini together (and not forgetting Holborn Viaduct either!), the volume of traffic, and the speed with which it is conveyed to the outskirts of London and the south coast, is unsurpassed.

To say that a wealth of experience has been

packed into the organisation and running of the service would be such an understatement as to be a mere platitude. And yet it is a fact that is apt to be forgotten or overlooked. That experience is not one that is confined to the working of multiple-unit electric trains. The London & South Western Railway, the Brighton, and the South Eastern & Chatham in days just before the grouping were all three masters of suburban traffic operation, and all three contrived to work in a remarkable number of fast residential trains in the height of the peak hours. The Brighton, for example, despatched two of its most famous expresses from London Bridge in the midst of the evening 'rush'.

Traffic concentration

The South Eastern & Chatham, in particular, achieved a remarkable degree of co-ordination in the working of suburban and long-distance trains in its celebrated 'parallel' traffic working west of London Bridge. Then, as now, the problem was to squeeze a few more trains into the rush hours, and a most intense study of the

available track capacity at Borough Market Junction revealed that the line capacity, measured in trains per hour, could be increased if all four tracks between London Bridge and Cannon Street were used so that two ingoing and two outgoing trains were passing Borough Market Junction simultaneously. The movements were entirely 'parallel' at that moment; no train had to wait to cross a conflicting path. The entire service was then worked by steam, and the parallel movements might include an incoming express from the coast, inward and outward suburban movements, and an outward empty stock train.

Of course the realisation of such a project depended on strict punctuality. If an express from Hastings or Ramsgate arrived 5 min late it would defeat the whole object of the scheme. By that time it would be necessary to make some movement to or from Charing Cross; there

'Merchant Navy' class 4-6-2 No 35005 Canadian Pacific at Clapham Junction before a trial run to Salisbury with the Mobile Test Unit. (W.J. Reynolds)

would be a demand for conflicting routes; and one or other of the trains would be stopped. The late running of an oncoming coast train would already be having its reaction on succeeding trains, and a signal stop at Borough Market Junction would put the entire service that much later. It is astonishing to recall that in 1922, between 9 am and 10 am, *forty* westbound trains were scheduled to leave London Bridge. The usual arrangement was to despatch two simultaneously for Cannon Street, and then 2 min later one train for Charing Cross. By this method it was possible to increase the number of trains from the previous 36 to a maximum of 40 per hour.

The introduction of electric traction and multiple-aspect colour-light signalling, in 1926, enabled a still further improvement in service to be carried out, while the gradual elimination of steam from the coast trains, with the consequent

reduction in light engine movements at the termini, has resulted in yet more increase in line capacity. Experience has gradually built up in the working of an exceedingly intense service, not only in timetable planning, but in the actual operation and signalling. Borough Market Junction is likely to remain a classic example of an operating keypoint, where scientific planning, long experience, and all those unique qualities that go to make up a good railwayman, are combined in getting optimum utilisation of the track capacity available.

In these days of automation I suppose it is not unnatural that scientific men have been attracted by the complexities of Borough Market Junction, and have fallen to wondering if the regulation of traffic there could not be more effectively arranged by a computer, than by the two signalmen who between them operate the 35-lever all-electric interlocking frame already in service. This suggestion came into the open at a meeting of the Institution of Railway Signal Engineers in December, 1962. While Southern men of long experience were inclined to be sceptical, any proposal that offered the prospect of

A multiple-jet 'Lord Nelson' class 4-6-0, No 860 Lord Hawke, *on the up 'Atlantic Coast Express' near Winchfield* (M.W. Earley)

getting more trains through Borough Market Junction in the rush hours was worth examining, and the research staff of the British Railways Board carried out an investigation on site. It is generally understood, however, that the improvements offered over the working of two experienced signalmen were so slight as not to justify any further investigation.

Borough Market Junction is an example of the accumulated traffic experience of the Southern Region; the system of electric traction provides a parallel experience in motive power. Today, of course, the use of a third-rail, low-voltage traction system is considered out of date except for anything but purely urban railways; but the simplicity of the Southern system, and the speed with which it can be installed, is an important factor when extensions are planned, and a quick return on capital expenditure and a rapid increase in traffic is needed. There are times when its drawbacks are apt to be highlighted, as in extreme winter conditions when ice forms on the conductor rails. But taken all round the standard of reliability is very high, and the regularity in running is such as to divest day-to-day performance of any individual interest.

It is, however, not only on the electric services that Southern Region operating can claim a very high degree of reliability. At this late hour in the history of the steam locomotive its critics are apt to talk glibly of its foibles and uncertainties; but while I would not for one moment suggest that the maintenance of steam power is being deliberately neglected, so that its successors can have an easier 'walk-in' when the time comes, it is nevertheless apparent that no technical attention is now being given to steam matters, and the job of carrying on rests almost entirely in the hands of local superintendents and shed foremen.

It is all the more interesting therefore to study reports of train running on the steam-worked services of the Southern Region. I am constantly receiving logs of the running of the 'Atlantic Coast Express'. Most of these are isolated experiences of various readers, sent to me when there is something out of the ordinary, either in

the circumstances or in the locomotive performance. But quite recently I received from Mr D. W. Winkworth an extremely interesting document in the form of a complete week's working of this up train.

My friend spent a week's leave travelling on this train every day, from Exeter through to Waterloo, and the results of his observations are contained in Tables I and II herewith. Before commenting on the runs themselves there are a few preliminary points to be emphasised. Between Exeter and Salisbury there was a different driver every day, whereas the same driver worked the train all the week between Salisbury and Waterloo. Four different engines were concerned, and curiously enough the one most frequently used was a high-mileage unit in run-down condition, that was 'stopped' after the second day and placed under repair at Nine Elms shed. After three days it was returned to Exmouth Junction to be put back on to the up 'Atlantic Coast Express' on the very next day!

The analysis of the factors contributing to the 'end product'—namely, the arrival time at Waterloo—make interesting reading, thus:

Day of week	Time		Delays en route	Regained by engine
	Leaving Exeter	Arriving Waterloo		
	min	min	min	min
Monday	RT	8½ late	14	5½
Tuesday	2¾ late	1½ late	3½	2¾
Wednesday	4 late	1 early	1	5
Thursday	½ late	8½ late	11½	3½
Friday	5 late	2½ late	5½	8
Saturday	6 late	1 late	4	9

First of all there was no time to be booked against any engine, and the tables of running I and II show that this record was maintained on both stages of the journey, with all the seven drivers concerned. So far as traffic delays went, on the Monday the stopping train that feeds into the 'Atlantic Coast Express' at Salisbury was running late and blocked the express from Gillingham onwards. On the Thursday, the only other day on which the arrival was appreciably late, the relaying slack at Hurstbourne had come into operation, and the effects of this were followed by a dead stand for signals at Pirbright Junction. All the engines were in good mechanical condition except No 35025, which was used on Monday, Tuesday and Saturday.

So far as the engine performance was concerned, the net average speeds on the six successive days work out at 64.5, 63.9, 63.1, 62.0, 65.5 and 66.8 mph from Sidmouth Junction to Salisbury, and at 64.5, 65.2, 66.7, 65.8, 64.9

TABLE I
SOUTHERN REGION: EXETER–SALISBURY

Run No		1		2		3		4		5		6	
Engine No		35025		35025		35024		34002		35013		35025	
Engine Name		Brocklebank Line		Brocklebank Line		East Asiatic Company		Salisbury		Blue Funnel		Brocklebank Line	
Load, tons (e/f)		368/390		368/390		368/385		368/390		370/390		368/390	
Driver (Exmouth Junc shed)		Denman		Watts		Pessley		Davey		F. Turner		Gidley	
Dist		Sch	Actual	Speeds	Actual	Speeds	Actual	Speeds	Actual	Speeds	Actual	Speeds	Actual	Speeds
Miles		min	m s	mph	m s	mph	m s	mph	m s	mph	m s	mph	m s	mph
0.0	EXETER CENTRAL	0	0 00		0 00		0 00		0 00		0 00		0 00	
1.1	Exmouth Junc		3 56		3 52		4 05		3 40		3 47		4 08	
2.9	Pinhoe ...		6 32	60	6 31	50	6 51	48	6 14	50	6 13	52	6 49	50
4.8	Broad Clyst		8 10	74	8 15	68	8 34	70	7 53	75	7 51	74	8 28	74
8.5	Whimple		11 33	53	11 55	59	12 10	44	11 36	52	11 17	56	11 56	48
10.2	Milepost 161¼		13 35	48	13 51	52	14 21	46	13 58	40	13 15	49	14 07	44
12.2	SIDMOUTH JUNC	17	16 02		16 23		17 12		16 52		15 49		16 55	
1.3	Milepost 158		2 55	46	3 06	45	3 05	45	3 02	48	2 46	48	3 07	45
4.6	Honiton		7 29	42	7 22	44	7 39	42	7 36	40	6 55	44	7 40	41
5.8	Milepost 153½		9 12	41	9 01	44	9 22	42	9 23	40	8 33	42	9 27	39
6.8	Milepost 152½		10 27	52/82	10 17	-/79	10 40	51/80	10 47	50/82	9 48	52/80	10 49	50/77
11.5	Seaton Junc		14 23	72	14 30	66	14 49	72	14 50	72	13 53	67	14 51	76
13.0	Milepost 146¼		15 40	78	15 56	73	16 06	78	16 07	80	15 13	80	16 08	90
14.8	Axminster		17 02	70	17 24	67	17 28	73	17 26	76	16 28	78	17 16	80
—					sigs									
19.9	Chard Junc		21 47	64	23 00	59	22 05	66	21 37	74	20 43	70	21 22	74
26.0	Milepost 133¼		27 47	57	29 12	64	27 55	60	27 06	64	26 32	62	26 51	68
27.9	Crewkerne		29 22	80	30 52	76	29 34	78	28 47	73	28 09	80	28 25	76
29.1	Milepost 130¼		30 12	90	31 47	83	30 25	86	29 41	80	29 01	86	29 15	91
33.1	Milepost 126¼		33 06	72	35 08	66	33 25	72	33 02	60	32 02	66	32 10	76
34.5	Sutton Bingham		34 12	82	36 21	72	34 33	80	34 20	70	33 11	75	33 15	80
36.7	YEOVIL JUNC	37	35 47	84	38 12	72	36 11	85	36 10	78	34 48	85	34 51	82
41.3	Sherborne		39 18	79	42 07	74	39 50	71/48	40 18	68/46	38 22	77/58	38 25	78
44.9	Milborne Port		42 50	55	45 27	62	43 40	52	44 22	51	41 53	60	41 40	62
45.9	Milepost 113½		43 46	59	46 18	62	44 39	55	45 22	40	42 49	58	42 29	64
47.4	TEMPLE-COMBE		45 10	75	47 36	73	46 03	70	46 47	68	44 10	75	43 44	78
49.7	Milepost 109¾		46 45	83	49 23	80	47 40	86	48 32	85	45 48	84	45 19	87
51.9	Milepost 107½		48 30	70	51 22	62	49 32	64	50 37	56	47 36	68	47 05	70
—			sigs	2										
54.2	Gillingham		53 00	39	53 20	76/62	51 28	78	52 45	70	49 25	80	48 51	83
—			sigs		sigs									
58.3	Semley ...		61 41	30	57 07	40	55 28	53	57 12	48	53 07	58	52 12	70
63.3	Tisbury ...		67 00	74/80	61 55	74	59 48	78	61 47	78/80	57 20	80	56 02	86
—			sigs											
67.6	Dinton ...		71 45	15	65 27	82	63 22	71	65 04	82/84	60 38	84	59 12	80/84 eased to 70½
73.3	Wilton	70	79 10		69 52		68 31		69 45		65 12		63 50	
—			sigs										sigs	
75.8	SALISBURY	74	84 20		74 18		73 04		74 13		69 35		68 18	
Net times (min)			70½		72		73		74¼		69½		68	

TABLE II
SOUTHERN REGION: SALISBURY–WATERLOO

Run No Engine No Load, tons (e/f)			1 35025 368/395		2 35025 368/390		3 35024 368/390		4 34002 368/395		5 35013 370/395		6 35025 368/395	
Dist		Sch	Actual	Speeds	Actual	Speeds	Actual	Speeds	Actual	Speeds	Actual	Speeds	Actual	Speeds
Miles		min	m s	mph	m s	mph	m s	mph	m s	mph	m s	mph	m s	mph
0.0	SALISBURY	0	0 00		0 00		0 00		0 00		0 00		0 00	
1.1	*Tunnel Junc*		3 35	33	3 27	37	3 26	38	3 41	33	3 40	33	3 28	33
5.5	Porton ...		9 21	47	9 05	49	9 06	46	9 43	42	9 28	45	8 57	50
8.1	*Allington*		12 40	48	12 12	54	12 14	54	12 56	52	12 43	54	12 06	52
11.1	Grateley		15 45	66	15 07	68	15 04	70	15 56	62	15 44	64/82	15 11	58
15.9	*Red Post Junc*		19 50	78	18 57	80	18 56	84	19 47	84	19 40	80	19 45	75
17.4	ANDOVER JUNC		20 55	80	20 02	78/86	19 59	78/83	20 49	81/86	20 45	76	20 49	80
21.2	*Milepost 62½*		23 52	70	23 00	70	22 58	73	23 42 pws	73	23 43 pws	73	23 52 pws	65
22.6	Hurstbourne		25 06	74	24 17	72	24 10	74	25 21	15	25 25	15	25 31	20
24.5	Whitchurch		26 40	72	25 57	70	25 44	72	29 02	45	28 58	45	28 46	48
28.1	Overton		29 43	72/70	29 11	68	28 40	76	33 04	62	32 46	65	32 23	66
31.3	Oakley ...		32 25	72	31 58	73	31 10	76	36 04	67	35 36	74	35 15	71
33.4	*Worting Junc*	34	34 08	74	33 43	74	32 48	78	37 50	74	37 21	74	37 00	72
35.9	BASING- STOKE		36 07	78/82	35 41	79/84	34 39	84/88	39 46	80/86	39 16	80/84	39 03	79/86
41.5	Hook		40 18	76	39 51	79	38 35	82	44 51	80	43 23	79	43 08	78/81
44.0	Winchfield		42 10	78	41 40	79	40 25	80	45 37	82	45 13	76	44 58	78
47.3	Fleet		44 41	78	44 03	80	42 53	80/78	48 00	82	47 44	80	47 29	80
50.5	Farnborough		47 13	78	46 33	82	45 22	80	50 26	80	50 15	78	50 01	79
52.7	*Milepost 31*		48 57	76	48 16	78	47 04	80	52 06 sig stop (2½ mins)	79	51 58	78	51 45	77
55.7	Brookwood		51 21	72	50 37	78/75	49 19	81/79	60 09		53 18 sigs	79	54 09	76/74
59.3	WOKING	54	54 21	78	53 34	78	52 09	82/84	63 32	78	58 26	40	57 05	78
62.0	West Byfleet		56 20	80	55 33	79	54 03 sigs	81	65 36	80	61 07	67	59 11	78
64.6	Weybridge		58 16	75	57 31	82	56 34	45	67 36	78	63 19	68	61 11	78
66.6	Walton		59 52	75	59 07	78	58 47	59	69 12	78	65 04	72	62 47	75/78
70.4	*Hampton Court Junc*		62 46	75	62 03	76	62 06	74	72 08	76	68 04	74	65 41	77
71.7	Surbiton		63 50	70	63 08	73	63 12	70	73 11	75	69 09	74	66 43	71
73.9	New Malden		65 41		64 59		65 01		75 02		71 03		68 32	
76.4	Wimbledon		67 51		67 11		67 09		77 12		73 18		70 41	
79.8	CLAPHAM JUNC	73	71 20		70 33		70 29		80 39		76 35		74 00	
83.7	WATERLOO	80	71 20 sigs 78 25		77 08		77 05		80 39 sigs 88 07		83 07		80 36	
Net times (min)			78		77¼		75½		76½		77½		77½	

and 64.9 mph from Salisbury to Waterloo. The running of Driver Hoare, of Salisbury shed, was thus very consistent throughout the week, irrespective of what engine he had, whereas on the Exeter-Salisbury section it is remarkable that the fastest run of all, No 6, was made by a run-down mileage engine, No 35025, most vigorously driven by Gidley of Exmouth Junction. Despite her condition, this engine produced the highest maximum speeds of any on the Exeter road, and apart from her ascent to Honiton she was the fastest uphill as well. The minimum speeds of 68 mph at Milepost 133¼, and 70 mph at Semley were brilliant, on any reckoning.

The unrebuilt 'West Country' class engine No 34002 did not appear to have much in hand on the Thursday, and lost fractionally on schedule from Sidmouth Junction to Salisbury. This looks like an example of driving technique or personality, however, because on the second stage of the journey, in the hands of Driver Hoare, the work of this engine was barely distinguishable from that of the 'Merchant Navy' 4-6-2s this same driver had on every other day of the week. The net time was the second fastest of the Salisbury-Waterloo series, and it was a great pity the stop at Pirbright Junction intervened to cause such a late arrival.

Hoare's finest run was made on the Wednesday, when he got a good road practically all the way, and was able to pull off an arrival a minute early. In the finer points of detail these runs will repay close study, as showing the work of one driver with four different engines, and the work of six individual crews between Exeter and Salisbury all in the same week, April 6 to 11, 1964.

On the Portsmouth line

There is next another interesting series of runs made over a route now very rarely worked by steam. In the autumn of 1962, because of heavy engineering work in progress at Swaythling, certain of the Sunday Bournemouth expresses were diverted to the Portsmouth Direct Line, and by

the courtesy of Mr Ian J. Turnbull I am able to publish details of the running made over the most interesting part of the line, between Havant and Guildford. This includes some heavy gradients. There is a continuous ascent from Havant to the summit just south of Buriton Tunnel. At first the inclinations vary with steep miles at 1 in 147, 1 in 120, to Rowlands Castle. But after Idsworth Crossing there is nearly a mile at 1 in 100 followed by 1¾ miles at 1 in 80. Then comes a fast descent through Petersfield, and a further steep fall to near Liss. This is followed by the climb to the flanks of the Hindhead ridge, near Haslemere, and includes two miles at 1 in 80 just after Liss; four miles of more gradual rise past Liphook; and a final two miles at 1 in 100 to the summit.

Table III gives details of three runs made on diverted Bournemouth expresses; and then, by way of comparison, a run with a 'Schools' class 4-4-0 that I made on the footplate when the Portsmouth expresses were still steam-hauled. The first run, with an unrebuilt 'West Country' 4-6-2, was from a standing start at Havant.

TABLE III
SOUTHERN REGION: HAVANT–GUILDFORD

Run No			1		2		3		4	
Engine No			34102		34021		73087		925	
Engine Name			Lapford		Dartmoor		Linette		Cheltenham	
Load, tons (e/f)			370/400		367/395		363/395		360/395	
Dist		Sch†	Actual	Speeds	Actual	Speeds	Actual	Speeds	Actual	Speeds
Miles		min	m s	mph	m s	mph	m s	mph	m s	mph
0.0	HAVANT ...	0	0 00		0 00		0 00*		0 00*	
3.1	Rowlands Castle		6 53	38½	7 08	38	4 50	45	5 20	41
5.2	Idsworth Crossing		9 41	47	10 12	44	7 48	47	8 10	45
8.1	Milepost 58¼		14 02	29	15 21	25	12 58	25	13 16	24½
—			sigs		—	65	—		—	
11.5	PETERSFIELD	20	18 44	52	19 19	61	16 59	64	17 13	75
14.9	Liss ...		22 10	66/57	22 44	61	20 21	58	19 51	83½/74
17.1	Milepost 49¼		24 51	40	25 19	41½	23 11	36	21 55	52½
19.5	Liphook ...		28 02	47	28 21	56	26 25	60	24 24	64½
23.6	HASLEMERE	35	33 08	40	32 59	35	30 52	39	28 25	48½
—			—	71 (max)		69 (max)	—	72	pws	74 (max)
27.9	Witley ...		38 10		38 13		35 36	69	32 48	30
—					sigs		—		—	65 (max)
31.9	Godalming ...		42 45		44 09		39 23	60	37 18	
—					sigs		—		pws	
36.1	GUILDFORD	52	49 07		53 04		44 57		43 02*	

* Passing Havant and Guildford. † Schedule of diverted Bournemouth trains.

Good work was done up to Buriton Tunnel with this load, but a slight signal check preceded the approach to Petersfield. After that no higher speed than 60 mph was attained on the racing descent to Stodham Crossing, and in consequence speed fell to a minimum of 40 mph on the sharp ascent at 1 in 80 after Liss.

The engine was not pressed at all on the easier pitch past Liphook, but it was good work to register no greater fall in speed than from 47 to 40 mph on the concluding pull up to Haslemere Summit. The descent to Guildford includes much curvature, and although in past days the more venturesome of the Fratton drivers have been known to take the 'Schools' up to nearly 90 mph here on occasions, generally one noted plentiful use of the brakes.

The second run, with a rebuilt 'West Country' Pacific, was not so good in its uphill work, and again there was some most restrained running between Buriton Tunnel and Liss. But both drivers were improving on the point-to-point times laid down for the diverted trains, and one could not really expect more in the circumstances.

The third run had the advantage of passing Havant without stopping, albeit at very slow speed. Because of this the 'BR5' 4-6-0, which now carries the name formerly on the 'Urie Arthur' 4-6-0 No 752, gained 2 min on the Pacifics to Rowlands Castle. She remained about this much ahead of *Dartmoor* throughout to Haslemere, and in consideration of the moderate speed run between Petersfield and Liss the final climb was quite good. This engine also got a clear run through to Guildford, and without exceeding 72 mph managed to gain 7 min on the special schedule over the 36.1 miles from Havant.

The fourth run somewhat naturally was in a different class altogether. It was made by a crack driver, working over his regular route, with an engine in first-class order; and this 4-4-0 was surpassed only by the unrebuilt 'West Country' on the ascent to Buriton. The point-to-point times of the 90-min Portsmouth non-stops were 18 min to Petersfield; 31½ min to Haslemere; and 45½ min to Guildford—which timing was kept by the 'BR5' 4-6-0 *Linette*. But my run on the 'Schools' class 4-4-0 was also made on a Sunday, and because of signal checks in the early stages we had passed Havant 4½ min late. With three permanent way checks to come the driver was going hard to make up some of the lost time; but one of the most extraordinary features of the run was his method of working

the engine. Throughout from Portsmouth to Waterloo the cut-off was unchanged, at 29 per cent; all variations in power output were made by adjusting the regulator. Yet again nothing more than the first valve was used.

This method of working seemed to suit the engine to perfection, and once through Buriton Tunnel some tremendous running began. Petersfield was passed at 75 mph, and a top speed of 83½ mph was reached at Stodham Crossing. Impetus from this took us up the sharp rise beyond Liss at a minimum of 52½ mph; there was a fine acceleration to 64½ mph beyond Liphook, and the final climb to Haslemere did not lower the speed below 48½ mph—still on 29 per cent cut-off and the first port of the regulator. By this time *Cheltenham* had gained 2½ min on *Linette*; but two of the expected permanent way checks came before Guildford, and this robbed us of something of our advantage. Reverting to the 'diversion' runs, although their running is not to be compared to what the 'Schools' used to do in their hey-day on the Portsmouth expresses, they can be considered as very satisfactory in the circumstances.

While in the neighbourhood of Havant, I must mention the Hayling Island branch, wor-ked so fascinatingly by the veteran Stroudley 'Terrier' 0-6-0 tank engines. While many enthusiasts have taken photographs of those delightful little engines, Mr D. W. Winkworth has also taken some logs of their running. The run of 4½ miles from Havant to Hayling Island includes the slow passage over Langston bridge. Once clear of that, however, the little engines used to go for it, good and hard.

The branch trains consisted of three modern coaches, weighing with passengers about 100 tons; but this was no mean tonnage for engines having cylinders 13 in x 20 in, 4 ft coupled wheels, and a total weight of about 25 tons. It was just about the same as they worked on the London suburban services of 80 years ago, when in their prime. No doubt there have been modifications to those original dimensions by now; the cylinder diameter is probably a little larger. But it is their extreme lightness that enabled them to be used over Langston bridge.

On August 6, 1960, when Mr Winkworth took his notes, three of these engines were at work, Nos 32640, 32650 and 32661. Schedule time for the non-stop run of 4.5 miles was 10 min, and in the down direction it was very closely observed on all three runs. Langston, 1.1 miles, was passed in times varying from

3 min 8 sec to 3 min 20 sec, after which each engine got away to attain maximum speeds of 44 to 45 mph near North Hayling. The passing times at the latter place, 2.4 miles from Havant, were 5 min 46 sec, 5 min 43 sec, and 5 min 46 sec by engines 32640, 32650, and 32661 respectively. All three engines clocked into Hayling Island terminus within a few seconds of the scheduled 10 min. In the reverse direction engines 32640 and 32650 both made smart runs, with top speeds of 48 and 46 mph; but No 32661 made an extraordinary start, passing North Hayling, 2.1 miles, in 4 min 32 sec, and attaining no less than 53 mph before slacking for Langston bridge. On this run Havant was reached in 9 min 17 sec.

Resuming my notes on main-line working, there are next two steam runs on the Brighton main line. The first, detailed in Table IV, is another fine trip on the 3.20 am newspaper train from London Bridge, clocked from Earlswood onwards by Mr M. W. G. Skinner. When I published a run on this train in my article for June, 1963, I commented on this gentleman's enthusiasm in rising so early in the morning, in order to log an interesting train. He wrote afterwards in a somewhat wistful vein, that it was not

TABLE IV
SOUTHERN REGION:
EARLSWOOD-BRIGHTON

Load: 1 coach, 10 vans; 220 tons tare, 275 tons full
Engine: Modified 'West Country' 4-6-2
No 34013, *Okehampton*

Dist		Sch	Actual	Speeds*
Miles		min	m s	mph
0.0	EARLSWOOD ...	0	0 00	
1.85	Salfords		2 59	
4.1	Horley		4 58	67.5
7.7	THREE BRIDGES...	10	7 49	75.7
10.0	Balcombe Tunnel ...		9 48	69.4
12.2	Balcombe		11 37	72.7
16.1	HAYWARDS HEATH		14 48	73.5
19.3	Keymer Junc	24	17 20	75.8
21.95	Hassocks		19 32	72.3
24.5	Clayton Box		21 49	55.1
27.7	Preston Park		24 37	68.5
29.0	BRIGHTON	37	27 04	

* Average speeds from point to point

enthusiasm, but necessity in order to take up his railway duties at Brighton at the appointed hour! Nevertheless, from the many pleasant letters I have received from him it is evident that he *is* an enthusiast of the first water.

In sending me his logs he raises the question of

The 'Devon Belle' passing Raynes Park, hauled by engine No 35016 Elders Fyffes. (Author's collection)

the mileages quoted in the engine performances published in these articles, where sometimes there is disagreement between the published figures and those quoted in the railway working timetables. There are times, of course, when the official chainage, converted to decimals, gives figures such as 15.86. Is one to quote to two places of decimals, or round it off to the nearest tenth? Rounding off would make the above mileage 15.9; but over short distances such rounding off can give misleading values of the average speed. If one had, for example, two timing points the mileage of which, from the chainage, worked out at 14.74 and 15.86, the rounded-off mileage between them would be 1.2, whereas more precisely it is 1.12. If the distance were covered in a level 60 sec the average speeds would work out at 67.2 and 72 mph!

Again, with exact chainages and two or three places of decimals the accuracy of the record can be completely lost if one does not time precisely to the point on the station at which the chainage is taken. An easy answer would be to say 'the middle'; but then how does one regard stations with staggered platforms like Hatfield, Northallerton, Dunball, or some of those on the South Eastern line east of Tonbridge? With closely-spaced timing points I do not think there is any answer save to clock points like signalboxes or mileposts that can be pin-pointed.

If station-to-station times are used they should, strictly speaking, be taken over a fairly long distance so that the variation in mileage taken, or actual timing points, becomes of less consequence. For example, if through rounding off of the second place of decimals a distance becomes 7.2 instead of 7.12, a recorded time of 6 min 0 sec between them gives 72 mph instead of 71¼ mph. The latter difference is practically down to the limits of accuracy to which the majority of recorders can get with an ordinary stop watch.

On the run detailed in Table IV the train was diverted to the Quarry line because of engineering work, and so called at Earlswood instead of Redhill. A very fast and undelayed run to Brighton followed, in which the driver recovered 10 min on schedule. In this log, it will be seen that I have quoted distances to two places of decimals at Salfords and Hassocks, both of which are places where Mr Skinner, from his long experience over this route, can pin-point his timings. In this relatively short run of 29 miles the train averaged 71.8 mph over the 25.85 miles from Salfords to Preston Park, and the average speed from start to stop was 64.5 mph—an excellent performance.

Mr Skinner has also sent me details of a good run in the reverse direction, on the 12.14 pm Saturdays only train from Hastings to Birmingham, as between Brighton and Redhill. On this run the driver was a Three Bridges man, Sayers by name, and he began normally up to Clayton Tunnel. Then there was some very slow running down to Keymer Junction, very likely because he was sighting adverse signals in the distance. With colour-light signalling this is often the case, and a driver can regulate his speed so as to avoid a pronounced slowing

TABLE V
SOUTHERN REGION: BRIGHTON–REDHILL
Load: 10 coaches, 350 tons gross
Engine: Unrebuilt 'Battle of Britain' 4–6–2
No 34057, *Biggin Hill*

Dist		Sch	Actual		Speeds*
Miles		min	m	s	mph
0.0	BRIGHTON	0	0	00	
1.3	Preston Park		4	02	
4.5	*Clayton Box*		8	42	41.2
7.05	Hassocks		11	48	49.4
9.7	*Keymer Junc*	14	15	03	48.9
12.9	HAYWARDS HEATH	17½	18	29	55.9
16.8	Balcombe		22	45	54.9
19.0	*Balcombe Tunnel*		25	06	56.2
21.3	THREE BRIDGES	27½	27	20	61.5
24.9	Horley		30	07	77.5
27.15	Salfords		31	54	75.6
—			sigs		
29.0	Earlswood		34	52	
29.9	REDHILL	39	37	11	

* Average speeds from point to point

TABLE VI
SOUTHERN REGION: REDHILL–HAYWARDS HEATH
Multiple-unit electric trains

Run No		1		2		3	
Dist		Actual	Av Speed	Actual	Av Speed	Actual	Av Speed
Miles		m s	mph	m s	mph	m s	mph
0.0	REDHILL	0 00		0 00		0 00	
0.9	Earlswood	2 12		1 59		2 07	
2.75	Salfords	4 14	55.1	3 54	57.8	4 01	58.4
5.0	Horley	6 04	73.6	5 47	71.3	5 49	75.0
8.6	THREE BRIDGES	8 59	74.0	8 49	71.8	8 37	77.2
10.9	*Balcombe Tunnel*	11 03	68.5	11 00	63.2	10 38	68.7
13.1	Balcombe	12 51	73.3	12 47	73.8	12 25	73.8
15.85	*Copyhold Junc*	15 03	74.9	14 58	75.3	14 43	71.8
17.0	HAYWARDS HEATH ...	16 35		16 31		16 13	

down. He ran harder up the 1 in 264 gradient to Balcombe Tunnel than he had done downhill from Clayton. But then, presumably by that time getting clear signals, he put on a tremendous sprint from Three Bridges down to Horley. With an average speed of 77½ mph between these two stations the maximum was 80 mph sustained for a full mile north of Horley. This of course was nothing unusual for a Bulleid Pacific, but as Mr Skinner remarks in his letter it was 'Not bad for a summer holiday extra'.

Lastly I come to the electrics, and again through the kindness of Mr Skinner I am able to give details of some fine running between Redhill and Haywards Heath on the 12.28 pm train from Victoria to Brighton. In sending these runs to me my friend refers briefly to some others on which the performance was 'spoiled', because the driver exceeded the speed limit of 75 mph laid down for multiple-unit stock over this line. On one journey, indeed, on an occasion which must remain unspecified, the 13.1 miles from Salfords to Copyhold Junction were covered in 10 min 16 sec—an average

speed of 76.7 mph. On the three runs tabulated, all with the '2HAP' stock, the averages over this same distance were 72.8, 71.2, and 73.5 mph. The last-mentioned had the making of a very fast run; but the driver eased off after Balcombe so as not to exceed the speed limit.

I am afraid I have reached almost the end of this article without giving the electrics very much space in the way of detailed running notes. I feel, however, that this is just how the Southern Region authorities would wish it to be. Day-to-day variations, and the problems of individual engines and runs, have contributed much of the perennial interest of steam locomotive practice and performance. It is this variation that has been virtually eliminated on the electrified system of the Southern Region, and one now finds men talking about runs being 'spoiled' if a driver goes faster than usual! This of course is an ideal state of affairs from the operating point of view, and it amply explains why the Southern, for all its sustained excellence and regularity, does not 'hit the headlines'.

100 mph and all that

In 1964, maximum speeds of 100 mph or more on British Railways had not been very frequent. I had been stop-watching myself then for 43 years, and until the days of the LMR electric service had recorded only four instances with steam traction, two with Gresley 'A4' Pacifics, one with a Great Western 'King' and the controversial 114 mph on the 'Invitation Run' of the 'Coronation Scot' in 1937. The present article, however, contains some of the first '100s' by the LMR electrics in ordinary service, and also the attempts, albeit unsuccessful, to reach the 'Ton' on two sections of the otherwise very successful 'Ian Allan Limited' from Paddington to Plymouth and back on the 60th anniversary of the 'Ocean Mail' record run of May 9 1904, when *City of Truro* actually did reach 100 mph, perhaps a shade over, down the Wellington bank.

A T the present time it is no more than natural that particularly close attention is being given to every step in the construction of the electrified main line from Liverpool and Manchester to Euston. The extension of regular electric running southwards to Nuneaton, the institution of very fast electrically hauled schedules, and the promise of a very enterprising timetable when the job is finished, all combine to produce excellent news. At the same time it is equally good to learn that the most careful attention is being given *now* to the quality of riding in the trains. I have emphasised the word 'now' to some purpose, because in certain phases of the British Railways Modernisation Plan, new services and new trains have been introduced, but attention to the riding qualities of the stock has become intensified only after much complaint from passengers.

The need to provide smooth riding cannot be over-stressed. Much of the high prestige value of the Blue Pullmans is lost through their bad riding, yet in talking to some railwaymen there can be detected a tendency to accept rough riding as an inevitable accompaniment of high speed. This of course is plain nonsense, and the beautifully smooth riding of some ordinary stock on the same routes traversed by the Pullmans also gives the lie to the suggestion sometimes made that the poor riding is because the track is not suitably fettled up for such high speeds.

I referred to the excellent riding of ordinary stock on the Midland line in my last article. Part of the present article has been written, most comfortably, in a Western Region express that in the course of a start-to-stop run from Swindon to Reading averaged 87 mph for 32¾ miles of the distance. This was by no means an isolated instance. A week earlier I had enjoyed an equally fast and comfortable journey on the same train, but in a different coach. To the defeatists one would feel like applying the Mikado's remedy making 'the punishment fit the crime'—and condemning them to ride ceaselessly in PLM expresses between Paris and Dijon till at length they admitted that perfectly smooth travel was not incompatible with continuous running at 85 to 90 mph!

In the sphere of passenger comfort the London Midland Region has a very high reputation to sustain. The LMSR, following the magnificent traditions of the London & North Western in this respect, was renowned for the good riding of its express trains, and to ensure the finest possible results from the new electric trains some high-speed tests have been carried out over the London–Liverpool route during the past summer. The object of the tests was to cover the entire route at speeds as nearly as possible equal to those that will apply to the express passenger trains when full electric working is introduced. It was felt necessary to get an impression of the effect on passengers of sustained high speed, and by measuring instruments to draw attention to any places on the track where work was necessary to bring it up to the required standards.

During the course of high-speed runs from London to Liverpool and back, at two places in each direction—namely, at Wolverton and Weedon—the curves were taken deliberately at higher speeds than normal to note the effect, so far as passenger comfort was concerned, of curves having an insufficient amount of super-elevation. A special seven-coach train was used, including a track recording coach, making up a

BR electric locomotive No E3164. (British Railways)

tare load of 230½ tons, and this was hauled by a BR/Sulzer type '4' diesel-electric locomotive No D2.

Hallade track recorders were included in two vehicles in the train, in addition to one in the track recording coach. Although these instruments have been in use on the railways of this country for some years it is perhaps not generally known what their precise function is, and how they work; so I may add that they consist of three pendulums, which respond to the various coach movements, and each records a trace on a roll of paper which passes through the machine at a constant speed. The lowest trace gives the vertical movements, excess of which indicates that the packing under the sleepers requires attention. The centre trace shows trans-verse movement and calls attention to places where lining up is desirable and where super-elevation needs adjustment. The top trace shows any rolling of the vehicle.

An observer, using a push-button and an electromagnetic device, records on the trace the passing of each quarter-mile post, and also stations, tunnels and water troughs. Checking each quarter-mile post is essential for the identification of places where faults occur, and also to keep a check on the speed of the train. A trail of blue-white marking fluid is automatically released on to any portion of the track which deviates from the high standard required for high-speed running. This enables the exact spot to be easily located and given further attention.

The outward journey from Euston to Liverpool was completed in 2 hr 54 min, an average of 66.5 mph. The test train was delayed on this trip by a mishap to a preceding train, but on the return journey it averaged 74.0 mph to cover the 193 miles from Liverpool Lime Street to

'Duchess' class 4-6-2 No 46254 City of Stoke-on-Trent *on a Birmingham–Glasgow express stopped at Tebay while a bank engine buffers up in rear.* (Derek Cross)

Euston in 2 hr 36½ min. On this latter journey the passing times and the corresponding point-to-point average speeds were as shown in Table I.

TABLE I
LMR TRACK TESTING SPECIAL
LIVERPOOL–EUSTON
Load: 7 coaches, 230½ tons tare
Engine: BR/Sulzer type '4' diesel-electric No D2

Dist		Actual	Av Speed
Miles		min	mph
0.0	LIME STREET ...	0	—
1.4	Edge Hill	5½	25.5
6.4	*Speke Junc* ...	10½	60.0
10.8	Ditton Junc ...	14	75.2
14.3	*Halton Junc* ...	17	70.0
19.3	Weaver Junc ...	21½	67.3
32.4	*Coppenhall Junc* ...	30	82.5
35.6	CREWE	34	48.0
24.5	STAFFORD ...	18½	79.5
41.7	Lichfield	33	71.2
60.9	NUNEATON ...	48	76.8
75.5	RUGBY	57½	91.4
98.1	Roade	75½	75.4
111.4	BLETCHLEY ...	84	95.0
116.4	Tring	97	69.4
140.6	Watford Junc ...	106½	88.5
158.0	EUSTON	117½	90.6

The above items are taken from the guard's journal and clearly include some inaccuracies on the section from Crewe to Euston. In passing, it is interesting to recall the times made by the Stanier Pacific engine No 6220, *Coronation*, on the Press run of the 'Coronation Scot', in 1937, when I personally clocked an overall time from Crewe to Euston, with a load of 270 tons, of 118 min 57 sec. The corresponding times to those quoted in Table I were:

				m	s
Stafford	..	..	..	21	05
Lichfield	..	..	..	34	35
Nuneaton	..	..	..	48	23
Rugby	..	..	..	59	20
Roade	..	..	..	76	13
Bletchley	..	..	..	85	00
Tring	..	..	..	95	12
Watford	..	..	..	104	39
Euston	..	..	..	118	57

On the face of it the finishing time of the track-testing special from Watford into Euston—11 min dead, against the 14 min 18 sec of the 'Coronation Scot'—seems most unlikely, seeing that on the latter train we passed Watford at 85 mph, touched a maximum of 96 mph at Wembley and were still doing 82 as near to the terminus as Queens Park. I may add that on the trip of the 'Coronation Scot' we reached a level 100 mph at Castlethorpe troughs, topped Tring summit at 87 mph, and ran at a sustained 99 mph near King's Langley.

But reverting to the present day, reference has been made in previous articles of this series to the improvements in track that are being made on many parts of British Railways, and particularly to the introduction of continuous-welded rail. At the time of these tests, 199 track miles of the London–Liverpool route had already been relaid with continuous-welded rail. It is the intention of the London Midland Region to extend the use of continuous-welded rail to the whole of the routes now being electrified. The programme provides for the completion of the work between Willesden and Crewe by the end of 1965, and the section between Rugby and Birmingham will have been completely renewed with continuous-welded rail by the end of 1966.

Two further examples of actual running with trains electrically hauled between Crewe and Nuneaton have been sent to me by different correspondents. The first of these, detailed in Table II, was made on the 10.30 am from Euston to Carlisle, which has some fairly sharp timings. Although the immediate start from Nuneaton was very fast, speed was not allowed to rise above 80 mph at first, in view of the restriction to 70 mph round the Atherstone curves. But some very fast running followed, with a full 100 mph between Polesworth and Tamworth, a sustained minimum of 90 mph on the 1 in 331 rise from Hademore troughs and through Lichfield, and a maximum of 98 mph before Rugeley. After that, with the train getting ahead of time, the engine was very markedly eased. Some further fast running took place between

TABLE II
LONDON MIDLAND REGION: NUNEATON–CREWE
Load: 12 coaches, 422 tons tare, 455 tons full
Engine: Bo + Bo electric No E3056

Dist		Sch	Actual		Speeds
Miles		min	m	s	mph
0.0	NUNEATON ...	0	0	00	—
2.9	*Milepost 100* ...		3	50	80
5.2	Atherstone ...		5	35	75
9.4	Polesworth ...		8	27	100
12.9	TAMWORTH	11½	10	36	92
19.2	Lichfield	16	14	45	90
—			—		98
27.2	Rugeley	22	19	58	—
30.05	Colwich	24	22	02	80
32.5	Milford ...		24	04	72
36.45	STAFFORD ...	32½	30	06	—
5.4	Norton Bridge ...	6½	6	08	86/90
—	*Whitmore Summit*		—		82
16.1	Madeley	15	13	40	92
18.45	*Milepost 151* ...		14	22	100
21.45	*Milepost 154* ...		16	10	100
24.45	CREWE	25	21	06	—

TABLE III
LONDON MIDLAND REGION: CREWE–NUNEATON
Load: 11 coaches, 394 tons tare, 415 tons full
Engine: Bo + Bo electric No E3061

Dist		Sch	Actual		Speeds
Miles		min	m	s	mph
0.0	CREWE	0	0	00	—
1.0	*Milepost 157* ...		2	32	46
2.0	*Milepost 156* ...		3	33	69
4.7	*Betley Road* ...		5	46	80
7.9	*Milepost 150* ...		8	03	86
14.6	*Standon Bridge* ...		12	28	100
19.05	Norton Bridge ...	17½	15	17	96
24.45	STAFFORD ...	21½	19	00	64*
28.4	*Milford*	25	22	28	—
30.85	*Colwich*	27	24	10	—
—			—		98
33.7	Rugeley	29	26	01	88
41.7	Lichfield	35	31	13	98
—			—		102
48.0	TAMWORTH ...	40	34	59	92/84
51.5	Polesworth ...		37	19	93
55.7	Atherstone ...		40	05	(slack)
—			—		92
60.9	NUNEATON ...	51	44	30	—

* Speed restriction

Stafford and Crewe. As far as Madeley the driver was running considerably below the maximum permitted on this part of the line, but there was a sustained maximum of 100 mph down the Madeley bank itself.

The second run, for which I am indebted to Mr W. Robertson, of Glasgow, was on the 8 am from Manchester to Euston. On the 1 in 177 gradient of Madeley bank speed rose to 86 mph and a maximum of exactly 100 mph was sustained for 1¼ miles approaching Norton Bridge. The details of the running on this occasion give a very good idea of the speeds likely to have been run on the track-testing train, when Stafford was passed in 18½ min against the 19 min on the electrically hauled trip. Over the Trent Valley line, however, the electric locomotive, hauling 415 tons, drew clean away from the diesel hauling 230, and very fast time was made throughout from Milford to Atherstone. The average speed between these two points was no less than 92.7 mph, and this included a maximum of 102 mph between Lichfield and Tamworth. Thus on a fairly sharp allowance of 51 min start to stop for the run of 60.9 miles there was a clear gain of 6½ min, showing an actual average speed of 82.2 mph. This was indeed a most impressive example of what the new electric locomotives can do.

The extension of the electrification from Weaver Junction northwards to Carlisle and Glasgow becomes a very attractive proposition in the light of such performances, and the prospect of what could be done with electric traction over Shap. The only sad reflection on this prospect, and it is a *very* sad one, is that the electrification of the West Coast Route would almost certainly sound the death-knell of the Settle & Carlisle line. And mention of both Shap and the latter magnificent route leads me on to a most fascinating piece of running over both these routes, recorded by Mr H. G. Ellison, on a special tour train organised by the West Riding Branch of the Railway Correspondence & Travel Society. Following the Three Summits Tour organised by the Society last year, a 'Merchant Navy' class Pacific was employed this

TABLE IV
LONDON MIDLAND REGION:
CARNFORTH–PENRITH
RCTS SPECIAL

Load: 9 coaches, 303 tons tare, 325 tons full
Engine: Rebuilt 'Merchant Navy' 4-6-2 No 35012,
United States Line

Dist		Actual	Speeds
Miles		m s	mph
0.0	CARNFORTH	0 00	—
—	Burton	—	54
7.3	Milnthorpe	10 15	63
9.2	*Hincaster Junc* ...	12 05	65
12.8	OXENHOLME ...	15 31	64
17.9	*Lambrigg Crossing* ...	20 55	60
19.9	*Grayrigg*	23 11	54½
25.9	TEBAY	28 00	82
28.9	*Scout Green Box* ...	30 33	59
	Shap Wells IBS*	32 36	sig stop
		35 50	
31.4	*Shap Summit*	41 49	—
—		—	75 (max)
44.9	PENRITH	60 05	—

*Intermediate block signal

Weymouth–London express near Brockenhurst hauled by rebuilt 'West Country' 4-6-2 No 34104 Bere Alston. (Derek Cross)

time, on a trip that included the mounting of both Shap and Aisgill summits. The load was no more than a moderate one for so large an engine, 303 tons tare: but there was extremely fine hill climbing on both the North Western and on the Midland route.

The log of the northbound run is detailed in Table IV, and begins from a dead start from Carnforth. The engine was not pressed at the start, and after climbing the 2½ miles at 1 in 134 out of Carnforth, speed did not rise above 63 mph on the 3½ miles descent and level to Milnthorpe. But here the engine was substantially opened out, and on the lower reaches of Grayrigg bank speed *increased* to a sustained 64–65 mph, held as far up as Oxenholme. On the long 1 in 124–131 to Lambrigg Crossing a sustained speed of 60 mph was recorded, and the final 2 miles at 1 in 106 to Grayrigg Summit brought speed down to 54½ mph. This would have involved an equivalent drawbar horsepower output of about 1,760.

It was evident that a terrific assault was to be made on Shap, for speed was worked rapidly up to 82 mph on the level at Tebay, and the special was past Scout Green box before the speed drop-

ped below 60 mph. Then, unfortunately, the train was stopped at the Shap Wells intermediate colour-light signal, and held there for 3¼ min. Had it not been for this the time from Oxenholme to Shap Summit could well have been something of a record.

The 'Merchant Navy' class engine took up the haulage of the special once more on the return journey from Carlisle, this time over the Midland route. Although the run once again suffered from signal checks, the Southern engine notched up yet another notable record in the very diverse saga of locomotive performance over this route. If indeed the day does eventually come when the Settle & Carlisle is closed it will be enthralling to recall again the great variety of locomotives that have worked over it, both in regular service, and on special and test occasions.

It has probably witnessed more full-dress test runs than any other line in the country, dating back to the extended indicator trials with the

pioneer Midland compound No 2631, in 1902, and finishing with the epic performance of the *Duchess of Gloucester*. Again, who could have foreseen, in the early 1900s, that in later years the top-line express passenger engines working over the route would at one time be of LNWR design, the 'Claughtons', and at another of Great Northern origin, the Gresley nonstreamlined Pacifics. Even the Caledonian had a go, in the early days of the LMSR.

The 'Merchant Navy' class 4–6–2, No 35012, *United States Line*, made a somewhat leisurely start out of Carlisle. But in the short break in the 1 in 132 ascent to Low House box she attained 50 mph at Cumwhinton, and once over the first summit she was soon galloping to pass Armathwaite at 71 mph. Nevertheless, it was clear the engine was not being in any way extended at this stage by the way speed fell off on the two-mile rise from Armathwaite, mostly at 1 in 220. Looking back at two 'Claughton' runs of my own clocked in 1931, with gross loads of 330 and

The down 'Golden Arrow' hauled by 'Merchant Navy' class No 35018 British India Line *near Knockholt passing a rebuilt 'West Country' class 4-6-2* Ilfracombe. (Derek Cross)

335 tons, although speeds were no more than 58–60 mph through Armathwaite the lowest speeds on the subsequent rise through Baron's Wood tunnels were 51 to 52 mph, whereas the 'Merchant Navy' 4-6-2 fell from 71 to a minimum of 51 mph.

The latter swept very quickly into high speed again in descending to river level beyond Lazonby, touching 75 mph, but after Culgaith a whole succession of signal checks was experienced, so that the 9.6 miles from Little Salkeld to Long Marton took as much as 14 min 50 sec. On the form shown by this engine on other parts of the line these checks cost fully 6 min between them.

TABLE V
LONDON MIDLAND REGION:
CARLISLE–HELLIFIELD RCTS SPECIAL
Load: 9 coaches, 303 tons tare, 325 tons full
Engine: Rebuilt 'Merchant Navy' 4-6-2 No 35012,
United States Line

Dist		Actual	Speeds
Miles		m s	mph
0.0	CARLISLE	0 00	—
0.9	*Petteril Bridge Junc*	3 20	—
3.9	Cumwhinton	9 07	50
10.0	Armathwaite	15 11	71
—	*Milepost 295*	—	51
15.2	Lazonby	21 02	73
18.3	Little Salkeld	23 33	75
—		sigs	20
23.4	Culgaith	30 00	—
—		sigs	—
27.9	Long Marton	38 23	—
30.8	APPLEBY	42 05	59
33.2	Ormside	44 25	73
36.1	*Griseburn Box*	47 10	56
38.3	Crosby Garrett	49 12	66
41.5	Kirkby Stephen	52 22	62
—	*Mallerstang*	—	54/56
48.3	Aisgill	59 49	51
51.4	Garsdale	62 42	64/60
54.6	Dent	65 20	70
59.5	*Blea Moor*...	70 44	50
			(min)
65.5	Horton	75 57	80
67.2	*Helwith Bridge*	77 15	84
71.6	Settle	81 05	eased
73.5	*Settle Junc*	83 40	sig stop
		84 57	—
76.8	HELLIFIELD	97 10	—

Even by comparison with the normal time-keeping speed of the 'Thames-Clyde Express' in 1931, the 'Merchant Navy' dropped 4¾ min on 'Claughton' standards between Little Salkeld and Appleby.

My friend does not state in his record the actual cause of this succession of delays, but from Appleby a clear road was obtained, and the driver then proceeded to cover the 17.5 miles up to Aisgill in 17 min 44 sec—a magnificent piece of running. Earlier in the day the engine, in climbing Grayrigg bank, had demonstrated her ability to climb a gradient of 1 in 131 at a sustained minimum speed of 60 mph, and now, on the gruelling climb to Aisgill, speed at no time fell below 50 mph. The ascent is 1 in 100 or slightly easier from Ormside viaduct to Griseburn Signalbox, and here speed fell from 73 to 56 mph. The next three miles witnesses a progressive easing of the gradient, first to 1 in 162, then to 1 in 215 to Crosby Garrett Station, and then to a short level over Smardale Viaduct. Here speed rose to 66 mph. The worst part of the ascent then follows: nine solid miles of it, all at 1 in 100, except for three-quarters of a mile at 1 in 302 past Mallerstang sidings.

In normal working one usually clocked the lowest speed of the ascent at the south end of Birkett Tunnel, topping the long 1 in 100 that extends almost unbrokenly from Smardale Viaduct. Here the 'Merchant Navy' class engine was making the fine speed of 54 mph; but she did not recover to more than 56 mph past Mallerstang, and fell away to 51 mph on the last three miles at 1 in 100 up to Aisgill summit. This was excellent work in itself, though in comparison with standard driving practice in Midland and early LMSR days one would normally expect a higher minimum speed at Aisgill summit than in leaving Birkett Tunnel. On the two 'Claughton' runs previously mentioned—the second in very bad winter weather—the speeds at Birkett Tunnel, Mallerstang and Aisgill were 31½, 39 and 34 mph on the first trip, and 28, 38½ and 29 mph on the second. Although there was obviously some considerable easing of No 35012 after Birkett Tunnel this

The celebrated and now preserved GWR 4-6-0 Pendennis Castle *as originally built.* (W.J. Reynolds)

engine made a very splendid climb. There was also a very pronounced easing after Dent, for speed fell so low as 50 mph in Blea Moor Tunnel. The trip ended with further delays—a signal stop at Settle Junction, and slow progress onwards to Hellifield with brakes leaking on.

Reference to trains organised for enthusiasts leads me on to some interesting correspondence I have had following the very successful Paddington–Plymouth round trip, the 'Great Western,' organised by Ian Allan Limited on the sixtieth anniversary of the Ocean Mail record run of May 9, 1904, and described in the July issue of *The Railway Magazine*. Mr J. H. Trounson, of Redruth, Vice-Chairman of the West of England Steam Engine Society, writes: 'After the heartbreaking mishap to poor old *Pendennis Castle*, the astounding performance of *Capel Dewi Hall* did much to put everybody in a good frame of mind again; tremendous credit is due to the bitterly disappointed crew for the work that they got out of that "Hall". Incidentally, one of the two firemen concerned, who was riding back as a passenger in the afternoon, told me that he and his mate were firing the "Hall"

as fast as they could handle the shovels and by the time they had reached Taunton the tender was empty and the fire only a foot thick!'

Then, referring to the very fine return trip from Plymouth to Bristol, he continues: 'I was in the second coach from the engine on the way up, and during the climb to Whiteball the roar from 7029's chimney became so colossal that even shouted conversation was all but impossible. The individual beats had merged into one continuous roar—I have never experienced such a thing before in my life. I ceased eating tea and sat back and tried to capture it all, realising that, as long as I lived, I should never know such a thing again. The scene with the coach crowded with fellow enthusiasts, the light becoming dim as the cutting deepened, the lineside objects flashing by, the pandemonium of sound, the dash through the tunnel with the exhaust note suddenly dying down as the cut-off shortened, and then the breathtaking rush down the other side—it was electrifying. As a distant relative of Richard Trevithick, I thought how proud the old man would have been to be on board that train that day!'

One of the firemen on *Clun Castle* wrote: 'I would not have missed the trip for anything, but as you know I am not Harry's regular mate and it was only that they insisted on two that I was on the job, but honestly speaking there was no need for two. The engine was very free and no effort was required to keep her steaming. The hardest job was holding her back. *Now you might think I am talking through my hat, but I am convinced that the engine was capable of going well over 100 mph on that day, in fact I will go as far as to say that she could have given* Mallard's *record a shake!*'

The question of the maximum speed individual engines could attain will be debated for many a year among locomotive enthusiasts, whether they be amateurs or men who have handled the shovel and the regulator. It is interesting to hear so tremendously enthusiastic a case being made for one of the double-chimneyed 'Castles'. In my own experience the 'Kings' were faster engines than the 'Castles' when it came to the attainment of really high maximum speeds; but whether a 'King' or a 'Castle' in the most favourable circumstances could equal the unique record of *Mallard* I am not prepared to say. Two other engine classes could seriously be considered as contestants for the honour of being the fastest British steam locomotive, namely the Stanier 'Duchesses' and the 'Merchant Navy' class. Both have topped the '100' in ordinary service, but neither on the London Midland, nor on the Southern, is there a stretch so favourable to the attainment of exceptional speed as that from Stoke Summit down towards Peterborough.

In 1937, on the Press run of the 'Coronation Scot', those on the footplate were definitely instructed to try for 120 mph down Madeley bank. But there was insufficient distance in which to attain such a speed and stop comfortably afterwards. From a maximum speed of 114 mph we certainly stopped precisely in the middle of Crewe Station, but the immediate approach through three successive crossover roads was hectic, to say the least of it! Now that the day of the express passenger steam locomotive is virtually over would it not be possible for an occa-

sion to be organised, on the one stretch where really high speed can be safely run, in which representatives of famous steam locomotives could be really extended, in competition with each other?

There are still 'Castles', 'Merchant Navy' 4–6–2s, and 'Duchesses' game for 100 mph or more, and just as Rainhill in 1829 signalised virtually the commencement of the steam era, could not its ending be appropriately rounded off by some fast running between Grantham and Peterborough? If well organised on a Sunday in the quiet season, it could create enormous interest: excursions from all parts of the country to witness such an event would be well patronised, and 'Essendine 1965' would become as much a mile-stone in railway history as 'Rainhill 1829'.

And what of the engine whose record in 1938 has ever since been the envy of men of the other railway groups? *Mallard's* epic flight was made down the bank from Stoke Summit towards Peterborough, but quite recently I have received from Mr M. N. Bland a log of a truly magnificent performance made in the reverse direction in the last years of *Mallard's* active service on the line. In Table VI herewith is detailed a log of the 2 pm Kings Cross-Newcastle express. This train then had the fairly sharp allowance of 111 min for the 105½ miles to Grantham; it included a total of 6 min recovery time, so that a driver woud be expected to make a net time of 105 min if lost time had to be regained. On this journey, however, there were two permanent-way checks to 20 mph in fast running locations, and worse than this a succession of signal checks culminating in a dead stand at Langley Junction. These checks between them caused a total loss of 13½ min in running; yet *Mallard* was in such good form, and so splendidly driven and fired, that they arrived in Grantham slightly before time.

Excellent work was done with this 415-ton train after a moderate start out of Kings Cross, with speed rising to 58 mph on the 1 in 200, and Hatfield was passed on time. Then came the succession of checks culminating in the stop at Langley Junction. Because of this, Hitchin was

TABLE VI
EASTERN REGION:
KINGS CROSS–GRANTHAM

Load: 11 coaches, 390 tons tare, 415 tons full
Engine: Class 'A4' 4-6-2 No 60022, *Mallard*
Driver: Coe (Kings Cross)

Dist		Sch	Actual		Speeds
Miles		min	m	s	mph
0.0	KINGS CROSS ...	0	0	00	—
2.6	Finsbury Park ...		7	19	—
5.0	Wood Green ...		10	24	55
12.7	Potters Bar ...	18	18	38	58
17.7	Hatfield	23	23	04	73
—			sigs		—
26.7	*Langley Junc* ...		32	20	sig
			34	45	stop
28.6	Stevenage ...		38	30	50
31.9	HITCHIN ...	37	41	34	75
37.1	*Arlesey*		45	19	86/83
41.1	Biggleswade ...		48	12	87
44.1	Sandy	46	50	18	84
47.5	*Tempsford* ...		52	39	87
51.7	St Neots ...		55	42	82
			pws		18
58.9	HUNTINGDON	60	66	29	59
62.0	*Milepost 62* ...		69	24	66
67.4	*Connington South*		73	34	84
69.4	*Holme*		75	16	62
			sigs		(slack)
76.4	PETERBOROUGH	80	83	00	20
					(slack)
79.5	*Werrington Junc*	85	87	22	62
—			pws		20
84.8	*Tallington* ...		94	11	69
88.6	*Essendine* ...	94	97	16	78
92.2	*Little Bytham* ...		99	58	82
96.0	*Milepost 96* ...		102	45	80
97.1	*Corby Glen* ...		103	34	82
100.1	*Stoke Box* ...	105	105	51	78
102.0	*Great Ponton* ...		107	18	83
					max
105.5	GRANTHAM ...	111	110	39	—

Net time 96½ min

celeration to 66 mph up the 1 in 200 bank to Milepost 62 a slight signal check approaching Peterborough prevented more than 3½ min being regained over the Huntingdon–Peterborough section, which had 4 min recovery time.

The checks had so far cost 11½ min between them, so that *Mallard* and her crew had to their credit an excellent net time of 71½ min for the 76.4 miles from Kings Cross to Peterborough. But with a booking of no more than 31 min for the 29.1 miles from Peterborough to Grantham stop, and an allowance of only 20 min for the 20.6 miles from Werrington Junction to Stoke Box, very hard work was going to be needed if the outstanding 3 min of arrears was to be made up, particularly as there was yet another permanent-way slack to be observed.

Fortunately the restriction near Helpston was not a long one, and after this had been duly observed *Mallard* was put to it in a style that was enough to make this climb of the Stoke bank almost as great a classic as her descent in 1938. Against the rising gradients speed was worked up to 78 mph at Essendine, and the slight descent afterwards raised the speed to 82 mph. Then, on the continuous 1 in 200 gradient to Milepost 96, speed settled to an absolutely sustained *eighty miles per hour*. Mr Bland clocked every milepost on this critical length and there is no doubt whatever about the accuracy of the speed claimed. This mighty effort gives an equivalent drawbar horsepower of 2,450.

There was a slight increase to 82 mph past Corby Glen, and on the last three miles up to Stoke Box where the gradient is 1 in 178 the minimum speed was 78 mph, indicating a continuation of the same standard of performance. This was no mere transitory burst of energy. It began from the moment they were clear of the Helpston check and continued for a full 15 min. With a smart run into Grantham the train arrived slightly ahead of time in a net time of 96½ min from Kings Cross. *Mallard* may indeed be remembered as well by this tremendous uphill effort as by her 126 mph down the bank.

passed 4½ min late, and the 2 min recovery time in the schedule between Sandy and Huntingdon was not nearly enough to cover the effects of the permanent-way slack near Offord. Huntingdon was passed 6½ min late, and although there was a most vigorous uphill ac-

What would Rous-Marten have said?

Even though he had died 56 years before I wrote this particular article, Rous-Marten was then still a legend in the world of train logging enthusiasts. The occasion that led me to use that sub-title was the ending of the historic name for the series of articles, which had hitherto always been 'British'. The increasing use of standard designs of locomotives, be they steam, diesel or electrics, was resulting in a diminution in the variety of subject matter for these articles, while at the same time evidence in the form of the correspondence reaching me showed greater awareness and interest in locomotive practice and performance overseas. The final purely British instalment contained a collection of fine runs, with all three types of traction, one indeed so spectacular by the standards hitherto prevailing that I commented, 'I wonder what Rous-Marten would have thought of that!'

IT is now more than 63 years since this series of articles was inaugurated in *The Railway Magazine* under the authorship of the ever-memorable Charles Rous-Marten. And of all the literary assignments that have come my way I have accepted none with a feeling of greater honour than this one, in which I am endeavouring to follow in the footsteps of that great pioneer, and no less in those of his successor of record longevity—Cecil J. Allen. But it would be a wanton waste of words to dwell on how circumstances have changed since the series was so inaugurated. What is important to appreciate is that the rate of change has been greater in the six years since I took over the authorship, in January, 1959, than at any time previously.

Then, the railways of Great Britain were operated almost entirely by steam locomotives; today, in express passenger service at any rate, a steam-hauled train takes some finding.

With this extraordinary metamorphosis there has come an equally marked shift of emphasis in the interests of those outside the railway service who study locomotive and train working with an enthusiasm that is in no way diminished with the passing of steam. There will, of course, always be a stubborn, indomitable rearguard action in progress from those who, Canute-wise, would try to stem the flowing tide; but on the other hand an interest and affection for relics and memories of the past is not in any way incompatible with enthusiasm for the latest developments of this present age. It is nevertheless becoming clear that subject matter for discussion in a serial article such as 'British Locomotive Practice and Performance' is becoming rapidly less. As experience with the various makes of diesel-electric locomotives has been gathered, certain designs have been chosen for standardisation, and in the future there will be less and less in the way of variety.

As with locomotives, so with the main lines themselves. Main-line electrification is an expensive business, and there is a natural desire to obtain the maximum utilisation from any route on which heavy capital investment has been made; and it is no secret that a number of studies is now being made towards the diversion of certain well-established services to the West Coast main line for at least some parts of their journeys. The lessening of traffic on other routes, not scheduled for electrification, will inevitably diminish their importance, to the point one imagines when closure, or demotion in other ways, may need to be considered. At the same time the example of certain overseas railways stand as a warning against undue precipitancy in the closing of 'parallel' routes.

All over the world there is a common experience that electrification brings more traffic. In France it was a matter of major policy to concentrate traffic for the south on to the former PLM main line, via Dijon, and to run down all parallel and subsidiary routes. But things have now reached almost to the point of saturation, and studies are being made towards the modernising of some routes that could provide relief. One can no longer afford to regard the railways of this country as a tight little entity, having their own problems, and solving them in their own way, and in their own time. Railway experience in many parts of the world is full of useful pointers, just as our own railways continue, as they have always been, to be a pattern for many.

'Jubilee' three-cylinder 4-6-0 No 45729 Furious *on the Settle and Carlisle line passing Stainforth with a Huddersfield–Helensburgh excursion.* (Derek Cross)

Glasgow–Liverpool and Manchester express diverted by Sunday working in March 1975 over the Settle and Carlisle line near Cotehill, hauled by Class 47/4 No 47454. (M. Bryce)

With all these factors in mind we have decided to make a small but significant change in the title of this serial article, and from January, 1965, the word 'British' will be omitted. As the series is foreseen, for the next few years at any rate, topics of British interest will predominate; but no hard and fast allocation of space, country by country, is contemplated. What Rous-Marten wrote in the first article of the series applies with equal cogency today:

'In the first place my purpose is, while giving such an account of locomotive practice in these islands as shall be interesting, and, I hope, "informing" to engineering readers and other scientific persons, also to non-engineering people connected or associated with railways, to present it, with authentic records of observed work, in such a shape as to be acceptable to readers who do not come under either of these categories. That is to say, I wish to make my notes readable by those who have no special personal interest in railways, either professionally or "hobbycally". In other words, I seek to please the railway enthusiast and the casual reader as well as the skilled specialist. This is, I am aware, a "large order". Still, I shall try to accomplish it.

'Secondly, I shall in the present instance depart from a rule which hitherto I have invariably followed when treating generally of the railways of any country—that is to say, the plan of taking them in the order in which they come in *Bradshaw's Guide*. I do so because, while I still deem that rule a good one as avoiding all suspicion of favouritism or undue preference, its limitations would be too stringent under my present plan, and would force upon me the adoption of too prim and didactic a method instead of the more free-and-easy mode which I prefer to pursue in recognition of the object to be kept in view, viz., readableness as well as instructiveness.

'Thus I do not pledge myself to confine my attention solely to the locomotive practice of any one engine or railway in any one article, or to limit my attention to either to a single article. In short, I approach my subject with an entirely free hand, and, as ever, wholly without prepossession, or prejudice, liking or disliking.

The prototype 'Deltic', en route *to its berth in the Science Museum.* (English Electric Co)

Everything will be treated on its merits, and on its merits alone, but necessarily on the merits revealed by my own personal study and observation.'

The study of historical aspects of locomotive development continues to provide interest and enjoyment for many enthusiasts in the comparisons it can provide with present-day practice; in this respect we are fortunate in that we shall be able to extend the scope of such comparisons in future years. The late Lord Monkswell, who was a most assiduous and enthusiastic recorder of locomotive performance, has made available to me, for use in *The Railway Magazine*, the majority of his old log books dating back to 1896, and these contain a wealth of information on contemporary British and French running, much of it recorded from the footplate. Furthermore, these notebooks contain certain intensely interesting items that obviously could not be published at the time they were recorded.

The privileged observer on the footplate is sometimes at a disadvantage. He is a guest of the administration concerned, and if he should witness some *contretemps*, or see a new engine failing to come up to the performance target of its designer, then courtesy to one's hosts precludes any literal reporting. In such cases it is sometimes better to write nothing at all, rather than give no more than half the story. Lord Monkswell's notebooks include one or two very interesting items of this kind, and now they can certainly be brought out into the light of day.

This month, so far as performance is concerned, there is first of all an interesting item reported to me by Mr Derek Cross, whose fine action photographs so often adorn the columns of *The Railway Magazine*. Cross was spending a week-end photographing at Shap, and each morning he was up bright and early to photograph the down 'Night Scot' ascending the bank. And he was pardonably astonished to find the train worked by steam on two successive mornings—not only so, but by the same engine! This was the Stanier Pacific No 46235, *City of Birmingham*. By a combination of circumstances—and his wife and son travelling from Ayr into Glasgow, and a friend travelling from Carlisle to the south—he was able to piece together a very strenuous week-end's work for the engine, thus:

Train	Section	Miles
11.40 pm Euston-St Enoch	Crewe-Glasgow	256¼ *
7.00 pm Glasgow-Euston	Glasgow-Crewe	243¼ †
11.35 pm Euston-St Enoch	Crewe-Glasgow	256¼ *

* Via Dumfries and G & SW line. † Via Beattock.

There was a comfortable turn-round time in Glasgow between the first and second trips; but between the second and third there would not be much more than 2½ hr. Mr Cross reports that on the second northbound run, when the load was about 540 tons tare, Shap was ascended at a very brisk and businesslike pace.

Next there are two more runs with Stanier 'Jubilee' class 4-6-0s, which had to be omitted from last month's article through lack of space. They are detailed in Tables I and II, and were with the same engine, No 45598, *Basutoland*; they date from the year 1957. The first was logged by Mr F. G. Cockman on the 12.36 pm from Leicester to St Pancras. There was a fine start on this trip, with speed rising to 57 mph on the rising gradient from Wigston, and being held at this figure over Kibworth summit. The maximum of 74 mph at East Langton was well sustained, right to the point of slowing for the Market Harborough curve, and it was then excellent work to fall no more than 3 mph—from 55 to 52 mph—in the 4½-mile ascent at 1 in 132 to Desborough North box. The checks were then most hampering, from 75 down to 30 mph for relaying south of Kettering; from 72 to 30 mph for adverse signals at Oakley; and finally a moderate check for permanent-way work just north of Ampthill Tunnel. In these circumstances it was fine work with a 375-ton train to be so near 'even time' at Cricklewood.

The second run was logged by Mr P. G. Barlow on the 10.30 am from Bradford to St Pancras, south of Nottingham. This train had some sharp timings, and with a bad permanent-way check at the start it was not possible to keep time to Kettering. Nevertheless some very hard running was made both uphill and down. The acceleration from the initial check to 51 mph at Widmerpool, and the continuous hard effort

TABLE I
LONDON MIDLAND REGION: 12.36 pm
LEICESTER–ST PANCRAS

Load: 10 coaches; 354 tons tare, 375 tons full
Engine: 3-cyl 'Jubilee' class 4-6-0 No 45598, *Basutoland*

Dist		Actual	Speeds
Miles		m s	mph
0.0	LEICESTER	0 00	—
3.7	Wigston	6 43	—
10.1	Kibworth	13 37	57
12.8	East Langton	15 46	74
16.2	MARKET HARBOROUGH	18 31	55*
21.0	Desborough	23 46	52 (min)
27.1	KETTERING	29 42	75
—		pws	30
—		—	74
34.0	WELLINGBOROUGH ...	36 47	60*
36.4	Irchester	38 54	65
39.4	*Milepost 59¾*	42 37	44
42.4	Sharnbrook	45 38	79
46.1	Oakley	48 47	72
—		sigs	37
49.3	BEDFORD	52 22	—
—		pws	45
57.3	Ampthill	61 53	51/56
61.8	Harlington	67 12	52 (min)
66.3	Leagrave	72 05	—
68.9	LUTON	74 22	71
74.5	Harpenden	79 05	74
79.2	ST ALBANS	82 53	75
83.9	Radlett	85 22	79
86.7	Elstree	88 37	67
92.2	Hendon	93 05	80 (max)
—		sigs	—
97.6	Kentish Town	102 04	—
—		sigs	—
99.1	ST PANCRAS	104 52	—

* Speed restriction

from Melton up the gradual rise to Ashwell; the dash downhill to Oakham; and the fine speed maintained on the climb out of the Welland valley from Harringworth Viaduct, all showed evidence of a keen and competent crew, and an excellent engine. But still finer work followed the restart at Kettering, and except for a slight check before Kentish Town the train was entirely undelayed. Outstanding points to note in the log, Table II, are the minimum of 55 mph at Milepost 59¾ summit, after three miles rising at 1 in 120; the minimum of 61 mph at Milepost

TABLE II
LONDON MIDLAND REGION:
NOTTINGHAM–ST PANCRAS

Load: 9 coaches; 312 tons tare, 340 tons full
Engine: 3-cyl 'Jubilee' class 4-6-0 No 45598, *Basutoland*

Dist		Sch	Actual		Speeds
Miles		min	m	s	mph
0.0	NOTTINGHAM ...	0	0	00	—
1.0	*Milepost 122½*		2	53	32
—			pws		22
2.8	Edwalton		6	55	27
8.2	Widmerpool		14	02	51
10.8	Upper Broughton ...		16	56	55/63
12.1	Old Dalby		18	07	61/59
14.3	Grimston		20	19	64/69
18.2	MELTON MOWBRAY ...	22	24	08	44*
22.0	Saxby		28	40	55
26.6	Ashwell		33	28	61
29.7	Oakham		36	21	71
33.4	MANTON ...	37	39	08	83/70*
38.6	Harringworth		43	25	74
44.0	Corby		48	31	61/59
46.4	Geddington		50	46	73/75
48.9	*Glendon South Junc* ...		52	49	66/68
—			sigs		—
51.5	KETTERING	55	56	27	—
3.8	Finedon		6	06	61
6.9	WELLINGBOROUGH ...	9	8	55	71/75
9.3	Irchester		10	53	71
12.2	*Milepost 59¾*	15	13	42	55
15.3	Sharnbrook		16	20	83
19.0	Oakley	20½	19	14	62
22.0	*BEDFORD NORTH JUNC*	23	21	51	76
30.2	Ampthill		28	50	62
31.8	Flitwick		30	19	68
34.7	Harlington		32	58	65
38.0	*Milepost 34*		36	06	61
41.8	LUTON	42	39	24	76
47.4	Harpenden		43	50	81 (max)
52.1	ST ALBANS	51	47	32	81
—			eased		—
56.8	Radlett		51	18	70
59.6	Elstree		53	54	62
65.1	HENDON	62	58	12	80 (max)
—			sigs		—
70.5	Kentish Town	68	64	12	—
72.0	ST PANCRAS	71	67	14	—

* Speed restriction

34, after many miles rising at 1 in 176; and the covering of 67 miles in the first hour from the dead start at Kettering.

In this last article under the old title I suppose it is natural to find oneself asking 'I wonder what Rous-Marten would have thought of this, or that, item of performance,' and on the very day of writing this part of the article I have clocked a run on the up Perth express due in Euston at 7.10 pm on which the electric section of 60.9 miles from Crewe to Nuneaton was covered in 49 min start to stop. There is nothing unusual in this nowadays, but what was unusual, I should imagine, was that the maximum speed on the journey occurred during the ascent of Madeley bank. That is, the highest speed was attained while we were climbing the steepest gradient on the line! With engine No E3004 and a load of 426 tons tare, 445 tons gross, we passed Betley Road, from the Crewe start, at 85 mph, and then continued to accelerate slightly on the 1 in 177 gradient to a maximum of 86½ mph. We were quite unchecked, and we did not need to exceed 85 mph anywhere else.

This journey was notable also in its overall results: exactly 165 min from Crewe to Euston, with the stop to change engines at Nuneaton, permanent-way checks between there and Rugby, and the Rugby passenger stop. At Nuneaton we had exchanged our electric locomotive for a type '4' English Electric diesel, No D214. Rugby was left a minute late, but the driver ran hard to keep the sharp sectional time of 48 min for the 50.9 miles to passing Tring. There were only a couple of trifling checks in the last 31.7 miles, and needing little or nothing of the 15 min recovery time provided we stopped in Euston precisely 15 min early by the public time. The question as to how recovery time is to be inserted into train schedules has been debated many times, and I have seen the London Midland Region criticised for the occasional very early arrival. But when a railway is being completely rebuilt, a certain degree of erratic time-keeping may amply be excused, and only a day earlier I had experienced a journey when things were very different.

I was travelling to Liverpool on the down 'Red Rose,' and for the first stage of the journey two type '4' diesels were provided for a train of 424 tons tare. This was a case of an unbalanced engine working; but on this occasion, even with two diesels, it was not possible to keep time to Nuneaton. This was one of the occasions when the train was re-routed via Northampton, so as to provide the electric traction constructional engineers with 'possessions' on the main line via Weedon. When this is done the 'Red Rose' is allowed an extra 13 min to Rugby, and all points north, though from my experience, and those of other recorders, the drivers seem to try and recover the extra time spent in running via Northampton and run in the normal schedule onwards. Altogether the present overall timing of 3 hr 36 min (working) from Euston to Lime Street includes a total of 22½ min recovery time, and an allowance of 8 min for changing engines at Nuneaton. So, if the checks experienced are not too bad, one ought to be able to regain the 13 min diversion time, and bring the train into Lime Street at any rate at the advertised time of 4.1 pm.

On this trip of mine we did not need the recovery allowances provided in the early stages, and without anything in the way of exceptional running we passed Roade 10 min early. The distance from Roade to Rugby via Northampton is only 2¼ miles farther than over the main line through Kilsby Tunnel, and the working time of 39 min for the 25 miles includes a generous amount of recovery margin. But we experienced a prolonged series of signal checks and eventually took no less than 42¾ min to cover the distance. So we passed Rugby 17¼ min late by the ordinary schedule, and 4¼ min late on the retiming. With one further check we reached Nuneaton at exactly 2.30 pm—18 and 5 min late respectively on the ordinary and retimed schedules. Smart engine changing saved 2¼ min, and I was then exceedingly interested to see what would happen subsequently.

The point-to-point times north of Nuneaton are the same for both schedules, and give a total of 96 min for the 96.7 miles to Lime Street. This

Western Region: 'The Inter-City' Birmingham to Paddington in 1953 hauled by engine No 6013 King Henry VIII. *(W. Blenkinsop)*

allowance includes 12½ min recovery time, so that if the driver really set about things there is a good chance of clocking into Liverpool certainly at the advertised time of 4.1 pm if not at the ordinary working time of 3.56 pm. Nevertheless, with the diversion via Northampton, the driver would still have been considered on time from the railway point of view if he had brought the train in at 4.9 pm. It was very soon evident that he was going for a *real* on time arrival, despite all the checks on the Northampton line. The very fast point-to-point times were observed with close precision, and taking advantage of the 5 min recovery time between Milford and Stafford we were ahead of the retimed schedule at the latter point. Here are our times, as far as Crewe:

					Sched min	Actual m	s
Nuneaton	...	...	...	...	0	0	00
Tamworth	...	...	...	...	11½	11	28
Lichfield	...	...	...	...	16	15	43
Rugeley	...	...	...	...	22	21	13
Milford	...	...	...	...	26	25	04
Stafford	...	...	...	...	34½	28	30
Norton Bridge	...	...	...	39	32	53
Madeley	...	...	...	...	47½	40	34
Crewe	...	...	...	...	54½	48	47

The maximum speed did not exceed 93 mph. At Winsford we were stopped by signal for 65 sec, and then had one of those exhibitions that would be phenomenal from anything except these blue electric locomotives. In three miles from our restart, with a trailing load of 450 tons, we were travelling at exactly 90 mph! After Weaver Junction it was a case of running to the limitations of speed permitted on the line; but the last 23.4 miles were covered nevertheless in exactly 20 min, without exceeding 75 mph at any point, and Lime Street was reached at 4.2½ pm—a trifling 1½ min late by the advertised time. I must not be tempted to go into the details of this fine run; so much has been published lately of the spectacular work of these locomotives. But taken overall it was an excellent example of present-day running on the Western Lines of the

London Midland Region.

Since then I have received details from a correspondent of a remarkable run on this same train when the 96.7 miles from Nuneaton to Lime Street were covered in 87 min exactly, inclusive of four signal checks and one dead stand. On this trip there were three independent maxima of 100 mph or more, and the net time was only 77 min—an average of 75½ mph. I wonder what Rous-Marten would have thought of that!

At the time Rous-Marten inaugurated this series of articles the idea of a 'standard' express passenger locomotive for service on all non-electrified main lines of this country—and moreover one that can tackle express freight trains with equal facility—would have been the remotest of pipe dreams. Engineers like F. W. Webb, S. W. Johnson, Dugald Drummond and Wilson Worsdell were still in the saddle, and coming up to succeed them, and others, were striking individualists like R. M. Deeley, Douglas Earle-Marsh, and G. J. Churchward, who in modern parlance could not have cared less what other railways were doing.

But today the 'standard' locomotive has arrived, in the form of the Hawker–Siddeley Brush 2,750 hp type '4' diesel-electric. It is a rather poignant commentary on the rate at which circumstances are changing that the new locomotives have virtually superseded the diesel-hydraulic locomotives on the Western Region. Against the 36-year innings of the 'Castles' on crack duties, the 'Warships' have nearly all gone after no more than five years. It will be interesting to see what sort of a show they make on the Southern, though the tasks they will have to perform can scarcely be compared on any basis with the duties undertaken by the Bulleid Pacifics, whether rebuilt or not.

On ordinary Western Region duties the sight of a Brush type '4' diesel-electric at the head of a train is usually a guarantee of a fast punctual run, and, sharp though the schedules are, the fact that these locomotives are permitted to run up to a maximum speed of 90 mph, against the 80 stipulated on all but a few of the 'Warships,' provides a margin for recovery from signal checks and relaying slacks. At the same time, good though these locomotives are, their maximum efforts cannot be compared with the 'Deltics'. I am indebted to Mr R. A. Gold for details of a number of runs on the East Coast main line between Kings Cross and Doncaster. With ten- and eleven-coach trains it is a commonplace nowadays to pass Hitchin inside 'even-time', and for this distance of 31.9 miles the time on three successive runs with Brush type '4s', and tare loads of 345, 385, and 390 tons, was 29 min 23 sec; 31 min 51 sec; and 31 min 51 sec again, the last-named after a signal check had caused the loss of about 1½ min in running.

It is nevertheless significant to compare the uphill speeds from Wood Green to Potters Bar with those of a similarly loaded 'Deltic'. The fastest of the 'Brush' runs, with the lightest load, included a fall in speed from 68 mph at New Southgate to a sustained 65 mph from New Barnet to the summit, and with the other engines speed was around 61 to 63 mph on the ascent. This of course was splendid work in itself; but then compare the 'Deltic', hauling 395 tons tare: from 63 mph at New Southgate this locomotive accelerated up the continuous 1 in 200 to Potters Bar to 73 mph over the summit. For a more detailed comparison between a 'Brush' and a 'Deltic', I have set out in Table III details of two runs with comparable loads from Grantham to Kings Cross. The first was on the up 'Yorkshire Pullman' from a flying start at Grantham, and the second was on a 'Deltic'-hauled train, working on a schedule of 101 min start-to-stop for the 105.5 miles up from Grantham.

The Brush locomotive, with a gross load of about 450 tons, passed Grantham at 75 mph, and then fell away gradually to a minimum of 66 mph at Stoke Summit. The 'Deltic', starting from rest at Grantham with a 480-ton train, accelerated to 64 at Stoke, and then put on a tremendous spurt to 100 mph before observing the relaying slack at Essendine. The 'Deltic' was indeed going in such style that by Werrington

TABLE III
EASTERN REGION: GRANTHAM–KINGS CROSS

Run No Engine No Engine Class Load, tons (e/f)		1 D1573 DE 4 430/445		2 D9015 DE 5 455/480	
Dist		Actual	Av Speed	Actual	Av Speed
Miles		m s	mph	m s	mph
0.0	GRANTHAM ...	0 00	*	0 00	†
3.5	Great Ponton ...	3 00	70.0	5 14	—
5.4	Stoke Box ...	4 42	77.1	7 03	62.8
8.4	Corby Glen ...	6 57	80.0	9 12	83.8
13.3	Little Bytham ...	10 27	84.0	12 10	99.1
—		pws	—	pws	—
16.9	Essendine	14 57	48.0	15 58	56.8
20.7	Tallington ...	19 40	48.4	20 39	48.6
23.6	Helpston	22 01	74.1	22 43	84.2
26.0	Werrington Junc	24 14	65.3	24 48	69.1
—		sigs	—	—	—
29.1	PETERBOROUGH	29 52	—	29 00	—
—		pws	—	pws	—
30.5	Fletton Junc ...	33 23	—	—	—
32.9	Yaxley	36 59	40.0	35 52	—
36.1	Holme	39 54	65.9	38 43	67.3
38.1	Connington South	41 33	72.7	40 17	76.8
42.0	Abbots Ripton ...	44 46	72.7	—	—
46.6	HUNTINGDON ...	48 20	77.3	46 30	82.2
49.6	Offord	50 41	76.6	48 47	78.8
53.8	St Neots ...	54 12	71.9	52 07	75.8
58.0	Tempsford ...	57 19	80.9	55 05	85.0
61.4	Sandy	59 41	86.3	57 21	90.2
64.4	Biggleswade	61 43	88.5	59 22	89.5
68.4	Arlesey	64 38	82.4	62 05	88.4
73.6	HITCHIN ...	68 21	84.0	65 32	90.5
76.9	Stevenage ...	70 59	75.3	67 51	85.6
80.5	Knebworth ...	73 42	79.6	70 20	86.7
—		sigs	—	—	—
87.8	HATFIELD ...	82 17	—	76 15	71.9
92.8	Potters Bar ...	86 19	74.5	80 15	75.0
96.3	New Barnet ...	89 09	74.2	82 56	78.1
99.0	New Southgate ...	91 26	70.9	85 00	78.3
100.5	Wood Green ...	92 44	69.3	86 13	74.0
102.9	Finsbury Park ...	95 02	62.6	88 48	55.7
105.5	KINGS CROSS ...	99 26	—	94 26	—

* Times from passing Grantham at 75 mph. † Times from dead start at Grantham.

Junction she was close on the heels of the 'Brush', despite the fact that the latter engine had the big advantage of a flying start through Grantham. In certain cases the speeds quoted by

A diesel test special climbing southbound to Shap hauled by Class 47 No D1815 in original painting style. (Derek Cross)

my correspondent seem to be somewhat on the low side; so I have quoted the point-to-point average speeds in the logs.

After climbing the Abbots Ripton bank, and checking the speed down to the 70 mph limit at Offord, both engines put on some very fine running to Knebworth. The average speeds over the 26.7 miles from St Neots to the former station were 82.2 and 88.8 mph respectively. There was, however, a most significant difference between the minimum speeds at Stevenage, namely 73 mph by the 'Brush' locomotive and 83 mph by the 'Deltic'. The uphill averages over the 12.5 miles from Biggleswade to Stevenage were 81 and 88.2 mph. The latter figure is indeed a remarkable tribute to the capacity of the 'Deltics' with so heavy a load as 480 tons. After Knebworth the prowess of both locomotives was restricted by the limitations of the road, but both continued to run smartly. The 'Brush' locomotive was working closely to the schedule of the 'Pullman', and completed the 156 miles from

Doncaster to Kings Cross in 150 min 49 sec against the 152 min scheduled. The allowance from Grantham to Kings Cross of the 'Deltic'-hauled train was 101 min.

My correspondent has also sent me details of three other 'Brush'-hauled runs from Peterborough to Kings Cross made in June of this year and all with eleven-coach trains of about 410 tons gross trailing load. The three runs gave overall times of 74 min 30 sec, 73 min 27 sec and 67 min 3 sec from Peterborough to Kings Cross, 76.4 miles. The first of the three, with engine No D1572, had the easiest schedule, of 82 min; and after a fast and undelayed start the driver was able to take things relatively easily. Nevertheless he passed Wood Green, 71.4 miles, in 65 min 33 sec. The other two runs were delayed by the same permanent-way check that affected the two runs detailed in Table III. On the second of the three runs engine No D1518 did some very good work between St Neots and Knebworth, averaging 84.3 mph,

TABLE IV
WESTERN REGION:
HIGH WYCOMBE–BANBURY
Load: 10 coaches; 351 tons tare, 370 tons full
Engine: Brush type '4' diesel-electric No D1717

Dist		Sch	Actual	Speeds
Miles		min	m s	mph
0.0	HIGH WYCOMBE ...	0	0 00	—
2.3	West Wycombe		4 44	44½
—			pws	10
5.0	Saunderton		10 48	—
8.2	PRINCES RISBOROUGH	12½	16 18	66
10.8	Ilmer Halt		18 33	87
13.6	Haddenham		20 18	98
17.5	*Ashendon Junc*	19½	22 51	96
20.9	Brill		25 00	98½
23.9	Blackthorn		26 49	102
26.9	BICESTER NORTH ...		28 41	93
30.7	Ardley	30	31 22	81
—			pws	20
35.9	*Aynho Junc*	34½	37 08	52
37.4	Kings Sutton		38 39	74
—			—	84
40.9	BANBURY	40	42 24	—

while No D1501 was no more than fractionally slower, at 83.8 mph. The respective minimum speeds at Stevenage were 77 and 75 mph.

Lastly I am indebted to another correspondent for details of a most exciting run with one of these locomotives on the Birmingham route of the Western Region. The time allowance from High Wycombe to Banbury—40 min for the 40.9 miles—is not unduly sharp, but it was another matter when two permanent-way checks of some severity were in operation. The first one, over Saunderton summit, was so slow and so long that the train took no less than 16¼ min to clear Princes Risborough, 8.2 miles. After that the driver put on a terrific spurt, aided by the fact that the old slack of Great Western days at Ashendon Junction is no longer called for. My correspondent clocked a maximum of 102 mph at Blackthorn, which is well supported by an average speed of 97.8 mph from Brill to Bicester. Yet despite this, time could not be kept. The net time was 36¼ min—perhaps even a little less—showing a start-to-stop average speed of 67.8 mph.

By way of contrast I turned up a couple of runs on a Great Western equivalent of this train of 36 to 37 years ago. On the first of these, engine No 4016, *Knight of the Golden Fleece*, had a load of 250 tons. That engine had then recently been rebuilt as a 'Castle', and she passed Ardley in 31 min 10 sec, after having slackened from 77 to 60 mph at Ashendon. She was running very easily after Aynho, and passed Banbury in 41 min 50 sec at no more than 56 mph. The 60.8 miles from High Wycombe to Leamington were completed in 60¾ min after a maximum of 82 mph down Fosse Road bank. At that time a coach was slipped at Banbury, leaving a load of only 220 tons to go forward.

On the second of the two runs we were hauled by a 'Star', and the running was interesting enough to be tabulated here. The engine was originally named *King Richard*, but this run was made in 1928 after the introduction of the 'King' class, and the 'Stars' of the 4021–4030 series had been renamed as monarchs. On this occasion

TABLE V
GWR: HIGH WYCOMBE–LEAMINGTON
Load: 7 coaches; 236 tons tare, 255 tons full*
Engine: 'Star' class 4-6-0 No 4026, *Japanese Monarch*

Dist		Actual	Speeds
Miles		m s	mph
0.0	HIGH WYCOMBE ...	0 00	—
2.3	West Wycombe	4 45	—
—		sigs	—
5.0	Saunderton	9 00	41
—		sigs	—
8.2	PRINCES RISBOROUGH	13 10	50
13.6	Haddenham	18 30	72½
17.7	*Ashendon Junc*	22 10	60†
20.9	Brill	25 20	71½
23.9	Blackthorn	27 50	76½
26.9	BICESTER	30 20	68
30.7	Ardley	34 05	58½
35.9	*Aynho Junc*	38 40	79
40.9	BANBURY	42 55	70½
44.6	Cropredy	46 15	61 (min)
49.7	Fenny Compton	50 50	83½ (max)
54.7	Southam Road	54 35	79
59.9	*Milepost 105*	58 20	85
60.8	LEAMINGTON	60 15	—

* One coach slipped at Banbury. † Speed restriction

the train was checked by signal between West Wycombe and Princes Risborough; but after that we went like the wind. Because of the slow speed at Princes Risborough we did not reach a very high speed on what used to be the fastest stretch of all, and the slack at Ashendon Junction was carefully observed. Then came some grand speeding, with Banbury passed in 42 min 55 sec and Leamington reached in 60¼ min from High Wycombe. Our driver certainly turned the blind eye to the speed restriction at Aynho, and it was a thrilling experience to sweep across the 'flyover' at nearly 80 mph and take the junction with no more notice than a momentary shutting off steam! But so far as I can remember the riding was not unduly rough. There is nothing in my old notebook by way of comment at this point.

I am afraid that in those days we took smooth and immaculate riding for granted, and I remember very well my consternation when I made my first trip on the Great Central main line by the fast 2.15 pm from Manchester to Marylebone. It was then allowed 110 min from Leicester, via Aylesbury. We had a load of six heavy Robinson corridors, with the anti-telescoping jaws, and when the 'Director' class 4-4-0 No 434, *Earl of Kerry*, really got going on the downhill stretches the coach in which I was travelling developed an occasional bout of hunting, with much jangling noise from the bogies. As one whose travelling experience at that time was mainly confined to the London & North Western and to the Midland, I was shocked —not to say alarmed! I wonder what we should have thought of the Blue Pullmans in those days!

But I must not end the long run of 'British Locomotive Practice and Performance' on a sarcastic or derogatory note. During this long run the railways of this country and their engineering has been the admiration of the world, and the pattern for very many other administrations. I believe—not from any pious hope or facile optimism, but from a knowledge of what is going on today—that British railways will in their new form be an example and an inspiration, and I look forward with keen anticipation to recording in these columns the results of the great electrification project on the London Midland Region, and of the newly authorised electrification project on the Bournemouth route of the Southern.

With these 'home' activities are many interesting developments abroad. Before we have progressed very far into these new fields it will be appreciated, among other things, that some railways overseas are not *quite* so free from troubles as occasionally visitors might imagine them to be. I am sure that one outcome of this change will be to show British Railways in a broader perspective than has been possible up to now, and the result will be, I hope, a better appreciation of all that has been done here in the last six or seven years.

The remarkable Bulleid Pacifics

At that time, to the dismay of Southern enthusiasts, the old London & South Western main line from Salisbury to Exeter, which had seen so many stirring feats of express locomotive performance, was in progress of relegation to secondary status. It was clearly a time for a further appraisal of the work of the Bulleid Pacifics, and as I wrote in the article that eventuated, 'In recent years I have received from correspondents more logs of runs with the Bulleid Pacifics than with any other type of locomotive—steam, diesel or electric'. This itself was astonishing, not only because of the relatively small stud in relation to the British Railways 'fleet' *in toto*, but also because the Bulleid Pacifics generally were not among the most popular of locomotives, either with the enthusiasts or the members of the motive power department of the railway themselves.

WITH the relegation of the West of England main line of the Southern Region to secondary status, and the approaching electrification of the Bournemouth lines, the last duties of the Bulleid Pacifics will soon come to an end, and thus also will end one of the most remarkable episodes in the history of the British steam railway locomotive. In years before the war, when it was clear that Maunsell's time as Chief Mechanical Engineer was drawing to a close, it might have seemed also that the sun was setting on steam locomotive operating all over the Southern Railway. Its sphere of activity was rapidly contracting as more and more lines were electrified, and the role of mechanical engineers on the Southern looked like becoming nothing more exciting than maintaining the existing stock in reasonably good order until successive lines were electrified, and still fewer steam locomotives were required.

Individually the 'King Arthur' and the 'Schools' class engines were doing magnificent work. Unfortunately, however, the same could not be said for the 'Lord Nelsons', although from the viewpoint of maintenance costs and freedom from troubles on the road these locomotives also had an excellent reputation. With the 'King Arthurs' able to work the heaviest trains the traffic department desired to run on the West of England service, and the 'Schools' performing prodigies of weight haulage on the Bournemouth line, there seemed, down to the year 1937, no reason why these two types should not carry on until they were displaced by electrification.

Then ill health compelled the resignation of Mr Maunsell and, by one of those coincidences of railway history, his retirement came to coincide with that of Sir Herbert Walker as General Manager. In the meantime, however, the management of the Southern Railway had been seeking a successor, and to the surprise of quite a number of onlookers the choice fell on O. V. S. Bulleid, who, since 1923, had been assistant to Sir Nigel Gresley on the LNER. The choice was surprising because Bulleid seemed to be about the last man to fit in with the passive, defensive role to which the Chief Mechanical Engineer's Department of the Southern Railway had gradually been committed. Although Bulleid's 'light' had, outwardly at any rate, been very much hidden under the 'bushel' of Sir Nigel Gresley, it was well known that he was an ex-

ceedingly dynamic character and a prolific inventor.

It is no exaggeration to say that, through his personal influence, drive, and enthusiasm, he completely transformed the position of his department within a very few months of taking office at Waterloo. His extensive rebuilding of the 'Lord Nelson' class was extraordinarily successful; he immediately drew attention to the locomotives and carriages under his supervision by painting them in a new, gay, and even startling colour; but his most epoch-marking achievement was reserved for the war years.

One would have thought that with all the difficulties and hindrances of a great national emergency, and the responsibilities he had to shoulder in connection with the ordinary day-to-day work of his department, that there would be little time for the development of an entirely new

The Interchange Trials of 1948: 'Merchant Navy' class No 35017 Belgian Marine *fitted with an LMS-type tender for water pick-up on an Eastern Region King's Cross–Leeds express near Potters Bar.* (M.W. Earley)

Inward-bound Continental boat train in the Folkestone Warren, hauled by 'Battle of Britain' class 4-6-2 No 21C157 Biggin Hill. (Rev A.C. Cawston)

locomotive design. But Bulleid not only did this, but packed into that design an extraordinary number of novel features, all calculated to react towards the utilisation of those locomotives in conditions that were only just developing on British railways in 1941, but which were to hit the railway network from end to end of the country with almost overwhelming effect several years later.

In its broad conception, the 'Merchant Navy' class locomotive, the first of which appeared in 1941, represented a most imaginative excursion into future requirements; and although its ultimate use was to be wholly in express passenger service, the prototypes were definitely designated as 'mixed traffic', with the twofold object of getting them fully tried out in both passenger and freight service during the war years, and of obtaining authority for them to be built at all, during a period of great national stringency in railway expenditure.

Bulleid envisaged in the immediate post-war

years a prolonged use of inferior fuel, coupled with a shortage of labour, a shortage of the choicest engineering materials, and yet a demand for a quick return to pre-war standards of service on the British railways. His first concern was to have the largest possible boiler that could be accommodated within the limitations of length and weight imposed by civil engineering restrictions on the Southern. Whereas at the formation of the railway itself, after grouping, in 1923, the traffic department had desired a locomotive that would haul train loads of 500 tons at start-to-stop average speeds of 55 mph, Bulleid designed the 'Merchant Navy' class with the object of hauling train loads of 550 to 600 tons at average speeds of 60 mph between London and Dover, and at start-to-stop average speeds of 70 mph between Waterloo and the West of England.

The very large boiler and all-welded steel firebox fitted with two Nicholson thermic syphons proved the most prolific steam raiser; in fact, when one of the 'Merchant Navy' class engines was subsequently tested on the stationary plant at Rugby the ultimate limit of evaporation was never finally established.

Plymouth–Brighton express at Seaton Junction hauled by 'West Country' class 4-6-2 No 34106, then not named. (Derek Cross)

Mechanical conditions both on the test plant and on the Settle & Carlisle line made it unwise to attempt to press the locomotive to its limit of steaming. Taken by and large, Bulleid succeeded, in the most striking manner, in producing a locomotive that would steam freely under the most adverse conditions, and by use of the five-nozzle multiple-jet blastpipe would steam while causing very little back pressure from the exhaust.

Having designed this very large boiler and firebox he had to get the weight down in other respects, and one method was to support the outer casing for the boiler lagging on the frames rather than on the boiler itself. This gave rise, coupled with Mr Bulleid's natural flair for publicity, to the outer 'air smoothing' which bestowed on the engines so unusual and distinctive an appearance—and led to their being nick-named 'Spam-cans'. When the smaller 'West Country' class engines were introduced in 1945 and were specially designated 'lightweight', there were some who criticised the use of the so-

called air-smoothing as being a contradiction in principles. It had been noted in the case of the 'Duchess' class Pacifics on the LMSR that streamlining added several tons to the overall weight of the locomotive, and it was assumed that the 'air-smoothing' on the Bulleid Pacifics did the same. On the contrary, the form of construction used actually resulted in a *reduction* of weight, as compared with conventional boiler-lagging practice.

Further advanced ideas

If Bulleid had been content with this magnificent boiler, and had proceeded rather more cautiously towards his further advanced ideas, one feels that the 'Merchant Navy' class engines would have been a far greater success than they actually were. But with a view to reducing maintenance and the attention needed at running sheds in the course of ordinary day-to-day performance, he introduced the completely-enclosed valve motion, and he enclosed also the piston rod and connecting rod of the inside cylinder. It was a difficult task to design an oil bath which would be adequate for running conditions in ordinary locomotive practice; but this was achieved, though because of the confined space available an entirely novel arrangement of the valve gear had also to be designed, which was chain driven. Another novel feature was the driving of the piston valves themselves from a point midway along the valve rather than by a valve spindle in the conventional manner. It was this ingenious—almost daring—conception that led to a lot of trouble in service, and eventually led the nationalised British Railways to the drastic step of rebuilding the engines entirely with a conventional front end and three sets of ordinary Walschaerts valve gear.

When the original Bulleid Pacifics were newly shopped and everything at the front end was tuned up to concert pitch, they could do remarkable work. The front end provided for a very free flow of steam into and out of the cylinders, and they were not only very fast, but very powerful engines. But deterioration with increasing mileage proved to be much more rapid than on normal types of locomotives, and not only did the coal consumption become heavy, but very considerable trouble used to develop because of leakage of oil. This made the engines particularly prone to slipping, and was the source of great anxiety to the test engineers at Rugby when one of these engines was being put through full-dress trials on the stationary plant. It was the inherent characteristics of the front end that prevented the enormous steam raising capacity of the boiler from being used to its full effect, and in consequence the locomotives were never able to attain in service a haulage capacity anything approaching that for which they were originally designed. Their rebuilding with conventional valve gear turned them into good reliable machines, but lacking that little 'extra' which they possessed in their earlier days. Certain engines that were very well looked after could produce reasonably high outputs of power, even after running long mileages; an example of this is given later in this article. But many of the engines on which I rode, particular-

Rebuilt 'West Country' 4-6-2 No 34028 Eddystone *at Bath.* (Ivo Peters)

ly the 'West Country' class, appeared to be well off their beat at the front end and very heavy coal burners in relation to the actual work they were doing. At the same time of their rebuilding the boiler pressure was reduced to 250 lb per sq in to lessen the maintenance costs of the boiler.

In recent years I have received from correspondents more logs of runs with the Bulleid Pacifics than with any other type of locomotive—steam, diesel, or electric. The great majority of these include examples of smart and sometimes very fast running; but the loads are relatively light—very light indeed in comparison with the specific performance standards laid down by Mr Bulleid when the locomotives were being designed. With the reduction in boiler pressure that accompanied their rebuilding, it is obvious that one could not expect the maximum efforts of the rebuilt engines to equal the best put up by the originals, and when the rebuilt engine no 35020, *Bibby Line*, was put through a series of dynamometer car tests between Waterloo and Exeter, as I described in *The Railway Magazine* for February, 1960, the traffic authorities would

not permit any excess over the regular loads of the trains concerned; to compensate for the inclusion of the dynamometer car there was one coach less in the ordinary passenger part of the train. Thus there was no opportunity to observe what the engine could have done if really opened out.

The most interesting trip I ever had with one of the original 'Merchant Navy' class engines was with No 35028, *Clan Line*, out and home on the 'Golden Arrow' in the spring of 1954. The engine had then covered 100,000 miles since last general overhaul, and 35,000 miles since last intermediate. She was in reasonably good nick at the front end, but more important than that was we had a pair of thorough-going enthusiasts in charge, Driver J. Brewer and Fireman D. Ward of Stewarts Lane shed. It was a tonic to ride with them. The logs of these two journeys are set out in Tables I and II herewith. On the down journey I was interested to see the driver using wide openings of the regulator and relatively short cut-offs, and when linked up to 15 per cent the action of the engine was quite smooth at the

The preserved rebuilt 'Merchant Navy' class 4-6-2 No 35028 Clan Line. (British Railways)

front end. At the same time one cannot accept the readings of cut-off read from the reverser

TABLE I
SR: VICTORIA–FOLKESTONE JUNCTION
'The Golden Arrow'

Load: 9 Pullmans, 3 other vehicles; 406 tons tare, 420 tons full

Engine: 'Merchant Navy' Class 4-6-2 No 35028, *Clan Line*

Driver J. Brewer, Fireman D. Ward (Stewarts Lane)

Dist		Sch	Actual		Speeds
Miles		min	m	s	mph
0.0	VICTORIA	0	0	00	—
0.7	*Grosvenor Road 'D' Site* ...		1	56	—
2.3	Clapham		5	50	—
4.0	Herne Hill	8½	8	57	—
5.7	Sydenham Hill		12	15	30½
8.7	Beckenham Junc	16	16	06	62/50
10.9	BROMLEY SOUTH ...		18	35	56
12.6	*Bickley Junc*	22	20	58	30
14.9	Orpington	27	24	45	41
16.4	Chelsfield		26	54	43
17.7	Knockholt		28	40	41
21.7	Dunton Green		32	52	67½
			sigs		15
23.2	SEVENOAKS	37	35	28	
28.1	Hildenborough		41	33	72
30.6	TONBRIDGE	44½	44	15	—
32.1	*Milepost 31*		46	10	49½
35.9	Paddock Wood	50	49	42	75
40.5	Marden		53	22	77/75
43.0	Staplehurst		55	22	78
			sigs		81
					(max)
46.3	Headcorn		58	35	35
51.5	Pluckley		64	40	54½
					66½
55.0	*Chart Siding*		67	58	64½
57.2	ASHFORD	69½	69	57	72
			—		75
61.5	Smeeth		73	16	75
			—		77½
65.3	Westenhanger		76	20	72
66.5	*Sandling Junc*		77	24	69
69.2	*Cheriton Junc*		79	42	72
71.0	FOLKESTONE CENTRAL		81	13	—
			sigs		
72.0	Folkestone Junc Sta ...		82	18 ⎫	sig
			83	02 ⎭	stop
72.4	FOLKESTONE JUNC SIDINGS	86	85	35	—

Net time: 78 min

scale as precise, because the Bulleid Pacifics, above all engines, were subject to considerable variations in the actual cut-offs obtaining in their cylinders.

There was nothing special about the outward journey until we were heavily checked by adverse signals at Headcorn. With the rails wet, and the engine slipping repeatedly, we took some time to get into speed again. The reverser indicated 20 per cent cut-off; but on the rising gradients from Pluckley a steam-chest pressure of 160 lb per sq in was the maximum the engine would take without slipping, and we passed Ashford slightly behind time. The speed was then 72 mph and with all going well the driver then opened the regulator much wider to give 230 lb per sq in in the steam chest. The response was terrific. Up the rise to Smeeth, averaging 1 in 300, we accelerated to and *sustained* 75 mph; the brief easing of the grade past Smeeth Station raised the speed to 77½ mph, and even though cut-off had to be reduced to 15 per cent we cleared the four miles at 1 in 266-286 to Westenhanger without falling below 72 mph— this with a load of 425 tons behind the tender. This very big effort would have brought us into Folkestone Junction Sidings well ahead of time; but the road was not clear, and we were stopped for 3/4 min waiting to cross over from the main line.

The return trip was from Dover, and involved some magnificent running, with the same load. Cut-off was fixed at 20 per cent from the western end of Shakespeare's Cliff Tunnel, and with wide openings of the regulator we steadily accelerated up the long 1 in 266 gradient to 62½ mph at Westenhanger summit. Some fast work followed to Tonbridge, intercepted by a bad signal check at Pluckley; but it was after Tonbridge that the most extraordinary feat took place. With cut-off at 25 per cent and the regulator absolutely full open, we sustained 53 mph on the 1 in 122 gradient up to Sevenoaks Tunnel. This performance, involving an equivalent drawbar horsepower of between 1900 and 2000 was, of course, not up to the level of the maximum feats of the Stanier 'Duchess' class

TABLE II
SR: DOVER MARINE–VICTORIA
'The Golden Arrow'

Load: 406 tons tare, 425 tons full
Engine: 'Merchant Navy' 4-6-2 No 35028 *Clan Line* (unrebuilt)

Dist		Sch	Actual		Speeds
Miles		min	m	s	mph
0.0	DOVER MARINE ...	0	0	00	—
7.0	FOLKESTONE CENT		12	44	55½
11.5	Sandling Junc ...		17	18	61
12.7	Westenhanger ...		18	29	62½
16.5	Smeeth		21	35	80
20.8	ASHFORD	26½	24	47	84
			sigs		15
26.5	Pluckley		30	10	—
31.7	Headcorn		37	35	68
35.0	Staplehurst ...		40	20	75
37.5	Marden		42	23	74
42.1	Paddock Wood ...	44½	45	54	82
45.9	*Milepost 31* ...		48	49	75
47.4	TONBRIDGE ...	49½	50	08	47*
			—		53
49.9	Hildenborough ...		53	13	57½/53
			sigs		10
51.8	*Weald Box* ...		56	35	—
54.8	SEVENOAKS ...	60½	62	51	—
56.3	Dunton Green ...		64	30	64½
60.3	Knockholt ...		68	40	51
63.1	Orpington ...	69	71	07	75
65.4	*Bickley Junc* ...		73	43	30*
69.3	Beckenham Junc ...	78	79	55	—
72.3	Sydenham Hill ...		83	47	—
			sigs		—
74.0	HERNE HILL ...	85	85	57	—
			sigs		—
78.0	VICTORIA ...	92	92	07	—

Net time 83 min
* Speed restrictions

TABLE III
SR: 8.40 BOURNEMOUTH
CENTRAL–WATERLOO

Load: 13 coaches; 450 tons tare, 485 tons gross
Engine: Rebuilt 'West Country' 4-6-2 No 34004, *Yeovil*

Dist		Sch	Actual		Speeds
Miles		min	m	s	mph
0.0	BOURNEMOUTH CENT	0	0	00	—
1.2	Boscombe		3	47	40
3.7	Christchurch ...		6	37	62*
7.0	Hinton Admiral ...		10	05	56½/51
9.5	New Milton ...		12	55	56½/68
12.5	Sway		15	47	67½
15.2	BROCKENHURST		18	24	62/77
20.0	Beaulieu Road ...		22	31	74
22.6	Lyndhurst Road ...		24	43	62*/73½
26.2	Redbridge... ...	28	28	12	47/56
28.8	SOUTHAMPTON CENT	33	32	18	—
1.0	*Northam Junc* ...	3½	3	22	16*
1.9	St Denys		5	24	39½
3.4	Swaythling ...		7	25	47½
5.6	EASTLEIGH ...	10	9	59	60
10.2	*Shawford Junc* ...		14	31	63
12.6	WINCHESTER CITY ...	20	17	12	—
2.1	*Winchester Junc* ...	5½	5	03	43
8.5	Micheldever ...		12	21	58½
10.4	*Roundwood* ...		14	16	60
14.0	*Wootton*		17	43	68/70
16.3	*Worting Junction* ...	23	19	47	61*
18.8	BASINGSTOKE ...		22	05	70/75
24.4	Hook		26	48	72½
26.6	Winchfield ...		28	45	76½
30.1	Fleet		31	31	71½
33.4	Farnborough ...		34	13	76
35.6	*Milepost 31* ...		36	00	74/82½
38.6	Brookwood ...		38	20	80½
42.3	WOKING		41	17	71½/66
46.2	Byfleet		44	43	77½
47.5	Weybridge		45	43	76½/74
49.5	Walton-on-Thames ...		47	18	81½
52.2	Esher		49	19	83
53.3	*Hampton Court Junc* ...	55½	50	05	82
			sigs		50
54.6	SURBITON		51	30	53½
56.8	New Malden ...		53	55	60½
			sigs		5
59.4	Wimbledon		58	33	22
61.0	Earlsfield		61	21	50
62.7	CLAPHAM JUNC ...	65	63	38	39*
66.6	WATERLOO	72	70	25	—

Net time from Winchester: 65¾ min
* Speed restrictions

Pacifics in climbing the Grayrigg and Shap inclines; but it was nevertheless a very thrilling affair to experience on the footplate.

Red-hot arrival at Victoria

Unfortunately we were badly checked by signal at Weald intermediate box, and our chances of making quite a record time from Tonbridge up to Knockholt spoiled. But despite further checks, and cautious running in the London suburban area, we reached Victoria on time. I said in my first reference to this day's running that the engine was not in her first bloom of youth. I can now tell also that we arrived in Victoria with all the metal out of one of the side-rod bushes, and a red-hot smokebox door! But No 35028 had a strenuous programme to fulfil. The shed staff at Stewarts Lane rendered effective 'first-aid' on the following day, and she was turned out, as immaculate as ever, for a VIP Special the day after!

I have not left myself much space for the tabulation of recent runs, and must conclude with reference to a very fine performance with one of the rebuilt 'West Country' class on the up 'Royal Wessex', for details of which I am indebted to Mr B. C. Smith. The log is set out in Table III. The load was a heavy one of 485 tons gross behind the tender, and the departure from Bournemouth 2¾ min late. The initial booking of 33 min start to stop for the run to Southampton is tight, in view of the four intermediate speed restrictions, at Christchurch, Lymington Junction, Lyndhurst Road and over Redbridge Viaduct and curve. But by dint of an excellent climb of Hinton Admiral bank, with a minimum speed of 51 mph on the 1 in 111 gradient, and some fine bursts of speed on the section through the New Forest, nearly ¾ min was gained, and the train left Southampton a shade under 2 min late. Splendid work followed with an acceleration to 60 mph at Eastleigh and a further increase to 63 mph on the 1 in 250 that begins shortly after that station. Thus Winchester was left on time.

On the continuous 1 in 250 gradient that extends from the start to Roundwood Box speed was gradually worked up to 60 mph and, with a brief maximum of 70 mph beyond, Worting Junction was passed more than 3 min early, at a reduced speed of 61 mph. Then, on the generally favourable gradients that extend to the outskirts of London, some fast running was made with an average speed of 73 mph between Worting Junction and Hampton Court Junction. At the latter point the train was 5½ min early, and paid the penalty by getting involved in signal checks. But although some 4½ min were lost in running there was sufficient time in hand to offset the effects of this delay, and Waterloo was reached 1½ min early. This was a really splendid example of the work of the rebuilt 'West Country' Pacifics, and the net time of 65¾ min from Winchester showed an average speed of 60.8 mph with this heavy train of 485 tons.

Euston–Crewe : dawn of a new age?

The inauguration of the full electric service between Euston, Liverpool and Manchester was greeted in the higher railway circles with misgivings as much as enthusiasm. The Government of the day was not by any means convinced of the merits of main-line electrification, or the cost of it, and there was then a very real risk that the planned extension from Weaver Junction to Carlisle and Glasgow would be abandoned. In the article in question I detailed some fine examples of LMR electric locomotive performance; but where high speed on this route is concerned, one's thoughts inevitably go back to the days of the old 6.12 pm from Crewe to Willesden Junction, booked at a start-to-stop average of 64 mph, and I concluded this article with details of two thrilling runs in which the regular engines were not available and the substitutes put in some heartwarming performances.

BY the middle of this month the end-product of the long years of planning, hard work, and rising hopes and disappointments will at last materialise on the Euston electrified route, with the introduction of the long-promised high-speed services between Euston, Liverpool and Manchester. It needs some courage and faith to say that this is not the culminating point of the enterprise—or even the penultimate step, having regard to the work still in progress in the Black Country and on the North Staffordshire line. Once the momentum of electrification was well under way, and its benefits could already be seen, there were high hopes that finance would be forthcoming for the logical extensions to Carlisle, to Glasgow, and over feeder routes for freight traffic into the Eastern Midlands. But unfortunately these hopes are felt to be waning, and there is more than a risk that the Euston-Liverpool-Manchester scheme may also be the end, as well as the beginning, of long-distance main-line electrification in this country.

Diesels are surely not the ultimate answer to main-line motive power in this country. Even if their present shortcomings can be finally overcome—and the whole fleet tuned-up and maintained to yield monthly mileages and mileages between failure approaching those which we were promised when the urge to dispense with steam was at its height—there is still the risk, for inland transport, of depending in such wholesale manner on imported fuel, especially in a coal-producing country. Furthermore, good though the best of the diesels are on their day, their maximum performance cannot hold a candle to the London Midland 'AL5' and 'AL6' electrics. Imagine, for example, how the development of uniformly high-speed services in France would have been stillborn, if the electrified area had been terminated at Dijon! If no further work is undertaken our boundary point, so far as Anglo-Scottish traffic is concerned, will remain at Crewe.

I am quite aware that the London Midland electrification has cost a great deal more than the original estimates; but that is in some measure due to the 'stop-go' policy of Government authority. Furthermore, if future extensions are decided on in the future, they will cost vastly

more still if the organisation already existing is allowed to run down and be dispersed, and the plant made idle. However, this is perhaps a rather dismal and dispiriting note on which to open comment on the inauguration of the fine new services; and one must pause to congratulate the engineers in many diverse branches of the profession, who have worked so long, and sometimes in such frustrating and difficult circumstances, to carry the job through to its conclusion.

In recent months I have received many logs of the running of electrically-hauled trains, which, with one exception, show clearly that the new schedules should include a comfortable margin in reserve to the fine 'AL5' and 'AL6' locomotives. The exception was a curiosity. It took place when a new 'AL6' replaced an English Electric type '4' diesel on the up 'Royal Scot', at Crewe, on a 420-ton train. With some

Electric No 86006 at Manchester Piccadilly on arrival with the 06.55 ex-Euston. (Brian Morrison)

TABLE I
LMR ELECTRIC LOCOMOTIVE PERFORMANCE

Section				Loco	Load full	Dist	Sch	Actual	Net time
				No	tons	miles	min	min	min
Euston–Rugby	...	...	...	E3090	505	82.5	110	66¼	61¾
Rugby–Crewe	...	...	...	E3075	445	75.5	60½	59½	56½
Rugby–Crewe	...	...	...	E3039	415	75.5	60½	60½	56½
Stafford–Rugby	...	...	...	E3078	365	51.0	—	43	37
Crewe–Bletchley	...	...	...	E3035	515	111.3	106	105¾	92
Crewe–Rugby	...	...	...	E3197	485	75.5	65	67¾	61
Bletchley–Liverpool	...	...	...	E3187	505	147.1	150	151½	117½
Nuneaton–Crewe	...	...	...	E3072	450	60.9	54	45½	45½
Crewe–Euston	...	...	...	E3187	375	158.0	151	132¼	118

strangely unenterprising running, and no speed above 77 mph at any point, there eventuated a loss of 4 min on the present schedule. There was no doubt good reason for this peculiar performance—so totally unlike the usual order of things with the electric locomotives.

Rather than anticipate the accelerations that are to come with detailed accounts of further runs in the transition period, I am tabulating herewith summary particulars of a number of

Down West Coast express passing Tebay hauled by Class 86 electric loco No 86036. (Brian Morrison)

typical runs, received from correspondents. One of these, from a friend whose accuracy of recording is beyond any question, did however include one unintentionally comic item. By a slip of the typewriter, no doubt, his log reads as though the speed on a down journey rose from 92 mph at Lichfield to no less than 1,000 mph at Armitage!

The faster of these runs all show net average speeds of between 80 and 82½ mph, start to stop, even with loads exceeding 500 tons, and they are a clear indication of what we can expect later this month. The fastest run that I have experienced personally since electrification was made about a year ago when, by the kindness of Mr W. F. Beatty, Chief Civil Engineer, LMR, I was invited to travel on a track-testing special. At that time there was no regular electric running south of Rugby, and to enable the high speed required for test purposes to be obtained with diesel traction the load had to be kept down to six coaches, only 213 tons all told. The 'Peak' class engine, No D2, *Helvellyn*, did well, sustaining speeds of 90 to 92 mph on the 1 in 335 gradients to Tring, in both directions on the round trip from Euston to Liverpool and back, and her time of 37 min from passing Bletchley to arrival in Euston, with a 20 mph permanent-way check at Bushey, included two maximum speeds of 102 mph.

But it was the down electric run from Hillmorton to Liverpool that provided the greatest thrills, and details of it are set out in Table II. As will be seen from the log there was some very fast running over the Trent Valley section, deliberately in excess of some of the present speed restrictions so as to examine the effect of the riding in the coaches and in the 'whitewash car' at the rear of the train. From Brinklow to Milford we averaged 97 mph and there were maximum speeds of 108 mph near Tamworth, and 105 at Hademore Crossing; but even on this special occasion we did not quite reach 1,000 mph at Armitage—the best we could do was 107! Ultimately we arrived in Lime Street Station in 84½ min from Hillmorton Sidings, where we had changed locomotives

TABLE II
LMR TRACK-TESTING SPECIAL: RUGBY–LIVERPOOL
Load: 6 coaches; 211 tons tare, 213 tons full
Engine: 25 kV Bo-Bo electric No E3087

Dist			Sch	Actual		Speeds
Miles			min	m	s	mph
0.0	Hilmorton Sdgs	...	0	0	00	—
2.3	RUGBY	...	2½	3	43	60
11.0	Shilton	...		9	49	103
16.9	NUNEATON	...	13½	13	20	90
				—		97
22.1	Atherstone	...		—		70*
26.3	Polesworth	...		19	37	108
29.8	TAMWORTH	...	22¼	21	35	95
				—		105½
36.1	Lichfield	...	26¼	25	17	95
40.8	Armitage	...		28	04	107
44.1	Rugeley	...	32	30	00	89
47.0	Colwich	...	34	31	52	98
49.4	Milford	...		33	32	81
53.4	STAFFORD	...	39	36	50	60*
58.7	Norton Bridge	...	43	40	10	98/101
69.8	Madeley	...	50½	47	07	—
77.8	CREWE	...	58½	53	45	20*
82.8	Milepost 163	...		58	05	97
86.7	Winsford Junc	...		60	28	104½
89.7	Hartford	...		62	11	100
92.3	Acton Bridge	...		63	44	105
94.1	Weaver Junc	...	71	64	57	71*
				—		65
97.2	Sutton Weaver	...		67	27	84
100.3	RUNCORN	...		69	46	67
102.6	Ditton Junc	...	77½	71	53	—
107.0	Speke Junc	...	81	75	10	85†
109.4	Mossley Hill	...		76	59	78
112.0	EDGE HILL	...	86¼	80	55	—
113.4	LIVERPOOL LIME ST		90	84	35	—

* Slack. † Maximum.

from diesel to electric haulage. Our start to stop average speed was 80½ mph.

Before the final curtain falls on the old days between Euston and Crewe it is appropriate that we should remind ourselves of what was once done with steam, not so much in the now-legendary era of the LNWR but in the period just before dieselisation commenced, and by way of a comparison to the summary of electric runs set out in Table I. I have collected details of some steam runs of fine quality all made with engines of LMSR design. The first in Table III,

TABLE III
LMR STEAM LOCOMOTIVE PERFORMANCE

Section	Loco No	Type	Load (full) tons	Dist miles	Actual min	Net min	Net Av mph
Rugby–Watford	46221	4–6–2	500	65.0	53¼	53¼	73.3
Crewe–Euston	46239	4–6–2	490	158.0	152¼	147	64.7
Crewe–Euston	46208	4–6–2	490	158.0	145½	139	68.2
Crewe–Euston	46209	4–6–2	490	158.0	153	140½	67.7
Nuneaton–Crewe ...	46164	4–6–0	540	60.9	66¼	63	58.0
Nuneaton–Crewe ...	46241	4–6–2	590	60.9	70¾	61¾	59.2
Nuneaton–Crewe ...	46132	4–6–0	545	60.9	60	60	60.9
Nuneaton–Crewe ...	45534	4–6–0	530	60.9	63½	61½	59.5

with engine No 46221, *Queen Elizabeth*, was a truly magnificent performance, from a dead-slow passage through Rugby on the up 'Red Rose', after which the average speed over the 54.3 miles from Welton to Kings Langley was 78.6 mph. The maximum was 95 mph near Hemel Hempstead, though this maximum was notably exceeded on the run with the 'Princess Royal' class engine No 46209 on the fourth run, when the speed was 98 mph near Kings Langley. The four runs from Nuneaton to Crewe were made on the 7.30 pm 'Royal Highlander' from Euston, and all showed splendid work in view of the heavy loads conveyed. Particularly good was the work of the 'Royal Scots'.

Dover–Stirling motorail express passing Crawford hauled by Class 86 electric No 86018. (Derek Cross)

Manchester–Glasgow express climbing Shap behind 'Patriot' class No 45515 Caernarvon *banked in rear.* (Derek Cross)

But where high speed on the Euston-Crewe route is concerned, one's thoughts always go back to the running of the old 6.12 pm from Crewe to Willesden, booked to cover the 152.7 miles in 142 min. On this service the loading regulations were naturally strict, and the 'Royal Scots' were originally limited to 380 tons when the train was first put on to the accelerated schedule in the summer of 1932. When the Pacifics were available gross loads up to 500 tons were taken unassisted, but in their early days the big engines were not always available, and with the train loading heavily at weekends there was a certain amount of double-heading. At first, with that promiscuity in locomotive allocation that had always existed on the West Coast Route, even in the most elegant of LNWR days, all kinds of passenger engines were put on as pilots; but one night, so the story goes, a 'George the Fifth' was in such a run-down condition as to be in danger of shedding its cab *en route*! And from that time the edict went forth that *ex*-LNWR engines were not to be used as pilots on the 6.12 pm—apart, of course, from 'Claughtons'

which, as will be shown later, were sometimes used as train engines.

I tried the 'flyer' personally on a number of occasions; but as my travelling was confined to weekends I had many disappointments, in the shape of double-headed runs, division of the train, and of delayed running. On one journey the pioneer 'Royal Scot', No 6100, ran short of steam with a minimum load train; on another, No 6101, *Royal Scots Grey*, had to contend with dense fog and lost time. On a Saturday journey with a Pacific we did reasonably well to Rugby, but then ran into a shocking succession of checks. My log records that we took 159¼ min to pass Watford, and that I then gave up timing, with the comment 'prolonged delays after'. Then after an Easter in Scotland I made my way south from Edinburgh in order to make yet another attempt on the 'flyer', hoping that on Easter Tuesday I might catch a maximum load with a Pacific. Once again, however, I thought my luck was out, for the train was divided, and the first part, Pacific-hauled, ran through Crewe, non-stop from Lime Street to Euston.

One of the original 'Claughton' class 4–6–0s, built in October 1920 and named after the designer, C. J. Bowen Cooke, *who died in that same autumn.* (British Railways)

The second part was also loaded to 12 coaches, and came into Crewe double-headed with a 'George the Fifth' and a brand-new Stanier 'Jubilee', No 5673, at that time unnamed. The second part was also running to the 142-min schedule. We duly changed pilot engines, and got a 'Baby Scot', No 5524, *Sir Frederick Harrison*, in exchange for the 'George'. Two class '5X' 4-6-0s for a load of 415 tons did not seem to promise anything very exciting, but to summarise what happened we made the astonishing net time of 126½ min to Willesden—a net gain of 15½ min on this very fast schedule, and an average speed of 72½ mph.

The division of the load into 208 tons apiece to the two 4-6-0s made comparison with the high-speed 'Silver Jubilee' of the LNER, which was then conveying a load of 230 tons, and scheduled at an average speed of 70 mph, or slightly over, between Kings Cross and York. I remember discussing the details with W. A. Willox, who was then Editor of *The Railway Magazine*, and I recall clearly his comment: 'This is "Silver Jubilee" standards of running with "5X" 4-6-0 engines'. Certainly it was. Brief details of the run were published in a note in *The Railway Gazette*, and from a friend who was then at Euston House I learned that the details caused no end of a 'flap' in high LMSR circles. The Chief Civil Engineer was already poised to come down like a ton of bricks on the Operating Manager, for he was convinced that such an overall net time could not possibly have been made without grossly exceeding the speed limits at Stafford and Rugby. Fortunately the Operating Department had ready access to a copy of my detailed log, which showed that far from exceeding the speed limit at Stafford and Rugby the train had been stopped dead at both places!

I have been a long time coming to the log itself, which is detailed in Table IV, and which shows some pretty startling performance, even for two engines. The start was several minutes behind time, and although vigorous the two

TABLE IV
LMSR: 6.12 PM CREWE–WILLESDEN JUNC
(Second Portion)
Load: 12 coaches; 391 tons tare, 415 tons full
Engines: 4–6–0s Nos 5524, *Sir Frederick Harrison*,
and 5673 (unnamed)

Dist		Sch	Actual	Av Speed
Miles		min.	m s	mph
0.0	CREWE	0	0 00	—
4.7	Betley Road ...		7 07	56½
7.9	Madeley		10 28	58
10.5	Whitmore... ...		12 55	65
14.6	Standon Bridge ...		16 12	80½
19.2	Norton Bridge ...		19 31	85
21.2	Gt Bridgeford ...		20 58	83½
24.1	*Milepost 134* ...	sig	23 28	—
		stop	23 45	—
24.5	STAFFORD ...	26	25 42	—
28.6	Milford		31 01	68
31.0	Colwich		33 04	72½
33.8	Rugeley	36	35 19	82
37.1	Armitage		37 44	84/81
41.8	Lichfield	42	41 11	84
44.7	*Hademore*		43 13	86½
48.1	TAMWORTH ...	47	45 42	80½
			Pitfall	
			severe	30
51.6	Polesworth ...		49 55	45
55.9	Atherstone ...		54 25	64½
61.0	NUNEATON ...	60	58 38	79
64.6	Bulkington ...		61 25	76½
66.8	Shilton		63 08	83½
70.0	Brinklow		65 27	85
73.1	*Newbold*		67 38	88
74.8	*Rugby No 7* ...	sig	—	—
		stop	69 10	—
			70 22	—
75.5	RUGBY	73	72 37	—
79.3	*Kilsby North* ...		77 17	58
82.8	Welton		80 35	71½
88.4	Weedon		84 45	88
95.3	Blisworth	91	89 36	85
98.2	Roade	94	91 45	79
100.6	*Hanslope*		93 32	90
			sigs slight	53
103.3	Castlethorpe ...		95 55	64½
105.7	Wolverton ...		98 04	72½
111.4	BLETCHLEY ...	105	102 39	83½
115.9	*Chelmscote Bridge*		105 59	79
117.9	Leighton Buzzard ...		107 31	81
120.0	*Sears Crossing* ...		109 04	82½
122.0	Cheddington ...		110 34	79½
126.4	Tring	119	114 00	75

Dist		Sch	Actual	Av Speed
Miles		min.	m s	mph
130.1	Berkhamsted ...		116 49	83½
			—	85
131.9	*Bourne End* ...	sig	118 20	—
		stop	118 55	—
133.6	Boxmoor		123 59	56
137.1	Kings Langley ...		127 19	72½
140.6	WATFORD ...	131	130 10	77½
142.1	Bushey		131 18	82
143.3	Carpenders Park ...		132 12	79½
144.8	Hatch End... ...		133 19	85
146.7	Harrow		134 38	87
148.1	*Milepost 10* ...		135 35	90
150.0	Wembley		136 57	80½
152.7	WILLESDEN JUNC	142	140 33	—

crews did not really get going until after the first signal stop, outside Stafford. Then we averaged 67 mph to the next stop, at Rugby No 7 box, despite a pitfall check to 30 mph at Polesworth which cost us at least 2 min. This is not allowed for in the net time for it was more or less permanent then, and provision was understood to be made for it in the schedule.

From Rugby the going was, if anything, harder than ever, with speeds of 88 mph at Weedon, 90 before Castlethorpe, a minimum of 75 mph over Tring Summit, and 85 mph before the train was stopped a *third time*—at Bourne End. The enginemen were obviously beyond anything in the way of discouragement, and when the signals cleared they tore into it for the fourth time to average 82.7 mph from Watford to Brent Junction. On this most thrilling journey 99 miles in the aggregate were covered at an average of 80 mph.

For a final memory of the 'Liverpool Flyer' we must go back three years earlier, to an occasion of which I received complete details only a short time ago. My home was at Bushey at the time and one evening in June, 1933, I was within sight of the line and waited to see the 'flyer' pass. When it did come, a few minutes behind time, I was surprised to see an unrebuilt 'Claughton' on the job, with an eleven-coach train. She seemed to be travelling fast, but I was more than half a mile away and could not judge things properly. The slight lateness I put down to an overloaded engine, not quite up to the job. It was only recently, through the kindness of Mr E. L. Bell, that I learned what had actually happened, and through the hunting-up of old diaries was able to connect the log he sent with the occasion I had witnessed myself, now nearly 33 years ago.

This was a mid-week occasion, and the train was loaded to 351 tons tare. Neither a 'Royal Scot' nor a 'Baby Scot' was apparently available, and with an ordinary 'Claughton' a pilot was naturally considered essential. A class '2P' standard 4-4-0 was therefore put on, and the two engines made no more than a modest run as far as Tamworth. Although Rugeley had been passed slightly ahead of time, despite a permanent-way check near Stafford, a minute was dropped on to Tamworth, apparently without cause, and the usual pitfall slack at Polesworth put them further behind at Nuneaton. But there was a good recovery after this, and Rugby was passed less than a minute late despite the two checks. Then, 3½ min later, the train stopped at Hillmorton box, under clear signals. Something had gone amiss with the pilot engine, and it was quickly detached.

The 'Claughton' was 51 tons overloaded on this booking, and being so near to Rugby one could have imagined the driver sending out an SOS for help and waiting till it arrived. But the spirit of the old LNWR was evidently abroad that night, and after a stop of only 3 min 24 sec engine No 5967 was away again, unassisted, and soon going in terrific style. The subsequent performance is detailed in Table V. No maximum and minimum speeds are quoted in the details supplied to me; but I have worked out the average speeds, and it is evident that the maximum must have been close on 80 mph at Weedon and Castlethorpe, while the minimum at Tring cannot have been less than 60. No wonder I thought the train was travelling fast when I saw it between Watford and Bushey, for

TABLE V
LMSR: 6.12 PM CREWE–WILLESDEN JUNC
Load: 351 tons tare, 370 tons full
Engine: 'Claughton' class 4–6–0 No 5967, *L/Corpl J. A. Christie, VC*
Run from Hillmorton Box, from emergency stop to put off class '2' 4–4–0 pilot which had failed.

Dist			Sch*	Actual		Av Speed
Miles			min.	m	s	mph
0.0	Hillmorton ...	...		0	00	—
5.1	Welton	...		7	35	—
10.5	Weedon	...		12	15	69.3
17.4	Blisworth	...		17	45	75.2
20.3	Roade	...	21	20	10	72.1
25.4	Castlethorpe	...		24	10	76.5
27.7	Wolverton ...	...		26	13	67.4
33.5	Bletchley	...	32	31	11	71.2
40.1	Leighton Buzzard	...		36	35	73.3
44.2	Cheddington	...		39	57	73.1
48.5	Tring	...	46	44	00	63.7
55.7	Hemel Hempstead			49	53	73.3
62.7	Watford Junc	...		55	00	82.0
66.9	Hatch End			58	15	77.4
68.8	Harrow	...		59	45	76.0
74.8	Willesden Junc	...	69	65	48	60.0

* From passing Rugby, 2.1 miles north of Hillmorton (usual passing time from Rugby to Welton was 7¾ to 8 min)

the speed must have been very near 85 mph!

The outcome of this tremendously sporting effort on the part of the crew of No 5967 was that the train was only 4½ min late in arriving at Willesden, and the total running time from Crewe was 143 min 14 sec. The run of No 5967 from Hillmorton to Willesden showed a start-to-stop average speed of 68.2 mph—one of the finest pieces of LNWR locomotive performance I have ever known. The engine was named after one of the three company's men who won the Victoria Cross in the first world war. The driver and fireman on this 1933 occasion certainly deserve a 'mention in dispatches', but at this distance in time it is not possible to trace their names. With this run I ring down the curtain on steam over the Euston-Crewe route. It is now up to the electrics.

The London–Edinburgh non-stops

The 40th anniversary of the inauguration of the celebrated non-stop run of the morning Anglo-Scottish express between King's Cross and Edinburgh Waverley always puts one in mind of the amusing prelude by which the LMS broke the long-distance record before the LNER had made theirs, and with a Midland compound hauling a six-coach second portion of the 'Royal Scot' non-stop from Euston to Edinburgh Princes Street. Between the two World Wars, the East Coast non-stop was always the 'Flying Scotsman', and so it continued afterward until the summer season of 1951, when the 'Capitals Limited' was introduced, leaving King's Cross at 9.30 am instead of the historic 10 am. In Coronation year, 1953, the name was changed to the 'Elizabethan', and thus it remained to the end of steam traction.

O N May 1 falls the fortieth anniversary of the inauguration of the most notable steam locomotive working ever operated in this country, or anywhere else. Looking at a railway map of the world, and noting the size of the British Isles in comparison with the many great countries having large and important railway systems, it is remarkable that the longest non-stop run ever regularly scheduled with steam should have been made here. The inauguration of the London-Edinburgh non-stops, on May 1, 1928, was the culmination of the 'longest non-stop' competition between the LMSR and the LNER after these two companies had wrested the honour from the Great Western, in the summer of 1927.

The LNER made the first move, with the London-Newcastle run of the relief 'Flying Scotsman' in 1927. The LMSR then surpassed this with the London-Carlisle run of the 'Royal Scot' in the autumn of the same year; but the London-Edinburgh record run programmed for May 1, 1928, had—if I may commit an Irishism—its record broken before it was made, by an amusing, if isolated, counter-stroke of the LMSR. The outstanding nature of the forthcoming LNER schedule was widely publicised, with a fully justified fanfare of trumpets, when suddenly the news 'broke' that the LMSR had already eclipsed the new record-to-be.

On Friday, April 27, the 'Royal Scot', which was usually a 15-coach train, was divided, and the Glasgow and Edinburgh sections run separately throughout. Both portions were run non-stop. The first, a nine-coach train hauled by the 'Royal Scot' class 4-6-0 No 6113, *Cameronian*, ran non-stop from Euston to Glasgow Central, 401.4 miles, while the second, of six coaches, and hauled by Midland Compound No 1054, ran non-stop from Euston to Edinburgh Princes Street, 399.7 miles. The schedules, like those of the forthcoming non-stop 'Flying Scotsman', were very easy, allowing 8¼ hours in each direction between London and the Scottish cities.

In this article I am concerned with the LNER, and I well remember travelling south by the 5.30 pm from Leeds Central to Kings Cross on Tuesday, April 10, 1928, Easter Tuesday that year, and seeing the newly-equipped 'A1' Pacifics Nos 4472, *Flying Scotsman*, and 4476, *Royal Lancer*, standing resplendent outside Doncaster Works, and attached to them were two of the first corridor tenders. On May 1, No 4472 worked the inaugural train from London, while the corresponding up train was hauled by one of the earliest Pacifics to be rebuilt with a 220-lb boiler, No 2580, *Shotover*.

The crews are worth recalling, for three out of four drivers were famous men. Albert Pibworth, of Kings Cross, took No 4472 on the first half—he who had taken No 4474 to Plymouth in the 1925 exchange with the Great Western —and at Tollerton, the changeover point, he was relieved by the great Tom Blades of Gateshead, who fired to Bob Nicholson on the 'M' class 4-4-0 No 1620 in the 1895 Race to the North, and who shared in the making of the great record run from Newcastle to Edinburgh in the early hours of August 22, 1895. Coming South, *Shotover* was worked from Edinburgh to Tollerton by Tom Henderson, of Haymarket, who in former years drove the North British Atlantic No 878, *Hazeldean*, and who put up some very fine performances in the Atlantic trials of 1923, against North Eastern and Great

The 'Non-stop' in the 1930s, near Barkston on the up journey, hauled by a celebrated Haymarket 'A3' of that period, No 2795 Call Boy. *(M.W. Earley)*

Northern rivals. The London driver who completed the first up non-stop run was J. Day.

In 1928, contemporary observers seemed rather to discount the merit of the London-Edinburgh non-stop, because the overall speed of 47.7 mph was slow. It was contrasted with the 54½ mph of the 'Cornish Riviera Express' between Paddington and Plymouth. Nevertheless, a great amount of experience had to be gained in the making of so long a run. The coal consumption was generally no worry. Not all the Gresley Pacifics had then been rebuilt with the long-lap long-travel valves, but enough were available to provide stand-by engines to the crack units specially reserved for the job, and with the demands for steam fairly light, and the use of a thin fire, things could usually be kept comfortably clean in the firebox with a minimum of formation of clinker. Lubrication was one of the main worries. Machinery in constant motion for 8¼ hours could easily develop a tendency to run hot, and the quantity of oil available on the 'non-stop' engines, and its quality, were given the closest attention.

Although I was travelling frequently on the East Coast Route at the time, I did not have occasion to make a through journey from Kings

'A4s' on the pre-war 'Flying Scotsman': No 4901 Capercaillie *southbound near Low Fell on a sunny December day in 1938.* (W.B. Greenfield)

Cross to Edinburgh until the late summer of 1935, and by that time three-quarters of an hour had been cut from the original non-stop schedule. One Saturday in the height of the tourist season I had a splendid trip on the down train with the 'A3' engine No 2795, *Call Boy*. The drivers were George Haygreen, of Kings Cross, and J. Scott of Haymarket. The schedule, to fit in with other trains, was then somewhat uneven, with a fast initial allowance of 114 min passing Grantham to keep ahead of the 10.5 am 'Junior Scotsman', and then an easy 95 min for the 82.7 miles on to York. The margins ahead were very tight on this stage, and any attempt to get time in hand would have involved checks, and possibly a dead stand for signals. This was the last thing anyone wanted, because a signal stop would have destroyed all the publicity value of the non-stop run.

On my run, with a load of 14 coaches, 449 tons tare and 480 tons full, Driver Haygreen ran very closely to the scheduled point-to-point times, doing fast and excellent

TABLE I
LNER: THE NON-STOP 'FLYING SCOTSMAN' AUGUST 1935

Load: 14 coaches, 449 tons tare, 480 tons full
Engine: Class 'A3' 4–6–2 No 2795, *Call Boy*
Drivers: Haygreen (Kings Cross)
Scott (Haymarket)

Dist		Sch	Actual		Speeds
Miles		min.	m	s	mph
0.0	KINGS CROSS ...	0	0	00	—
2.6	Finsbury Park ...		7	27	—
5.0	Wood Green ...		10	52	53
12.7	Potters Bar ...		21	08	43/46
17.7	Hatfield ...	25	26	02	75
23.5	*Woolmer Green* ...		31	13	59
31.9	HITCHIN ...	39	38	49	76
41.1	Biggleswade ...		45	54	82
51.7	St Neots ...		54	22	66
56.0	Offord ...		57	59	74½
58.9	HUNTINGDON ...	61	60	23	71
62.0	*Milepost 62*		63	23	55
69.4	Holme ...		70	07	72½
76.4	PETERBOROUGH	79	78	15	10*
84.8	Tallington ...		90	05	58
92.2	Little Bytham ...		98	06	53
97.1	Corby Glen ...		104	02	48/52
100.1	*Stoke Box* ...		107	43	46
105.5	GRANTHAM ...	114	113	22	60
120.1	NEWARK ...	130	129	03	easy
133.7	*Markham Box* ...		144	19	46
138.6	RETFORD ...	151	149	27	—
156.0	DONCASTER ...	170	168	48	—
174.4	SELBY ...	191	190	30	—
186.2	*Chaloners Whin Junc*		205	27	—
—			sigs		—
188.2	YORK ...	209	209	20	—
197.9	Tollerton ...		221	17	60
210.4	Thirsk ...	234	233	33	66
218.2	NORTHALLERTON	242	240	27	61/68
232.3	DARLINGTON ...	256	254	01	70
254.3	DURHAM ...	282	277	40	—
268.3	NEWCASTLE ...	300	298	25	—
284.9	Morpeth ...	325	322	53	—
293.9	Chevington ...		332	40	69 (max)
303.1	Alnmouth ...	345	341	03	65
307.7	Little Mill ...		346	22	42½
314.3	Chathill ...		353	12	69
319.9	Belford ...	363	358	53	55
326.9	Beal ...		365	14	75
335.2	BERWICK-UPON-TWEED	380	374	13	—
351.5	Grantshouse ...		401	51	39
358.9	Innerwick ...		409	25	82½
363.6	DUNBAR ...		413	20	eased
374.9	DREM		421	13	64½
389.7	Portobello ...		441	30	—
392.7	EDINBURGH WAVERLEY	450	447	23	—

* Speed restriction

work to Peterborough, and filling out his easy schedule onwards to York. Even so there was a signal check in the approach to York, though the road was kept wonderfully clear for a summer Saturday. Haygreen afterwards said to me that if he had been half a minute earlier he would have been stopped. The continuation involved steady but unspectacular going, with 91 min allowed for the 80.1 miles from York to Newcastle, and 150 min for the final 124.4 miles from Newcastle to Edinburgh. I was able to spend some time on the footplate north of Alnmouth, and *Call Boy* was sailing along in the most effortless manner, working in 15 per cent cut-off steaming very freely, and the cab as fresh and clean as if the engine had come on at Newcastle, instead of having already run over 300 miles non-stop. A skeleton log is given of this journey, including a little more detail of the more strenuous working in the early stages.

In the last seasons before the second world war when 'A4' Pacifics were available for the job, the schedule was cut to seven hours, but I was not able to make a trip at this period. Non-stop running was restored in the summer of 1948, with the train then running through three Regions of the nationalised British Railways—the Eastern, the North Eastern and the Scottish. During that first post-war season of non-stop running the allowance was 7 hr 50 min, but that summer was marked by the terrific storms that swept over south-eastern Scotland on the afternoon of August 12, and left the East Coast main line between Berwick and Dunbar completely breached in *ten* places: seven bridges swept away, and three major landslips. The 'Flying Scotsman', and all other East Coast services, had to be diverted via Kelso and Galashiels, and for a short time all thoughts of non-stop running bet-

Above *'The Elizabethan' northbound near Monktonhall Junction in 1954, hauled by engine No 60009* Union of South Africa *(now preserved).* (E.D. Bruton)

Below *'The Elizabethan' southbound, passing the old excursion platform south of York, hauled by engine No 60017* Silver Fox. (Real Photos)

'The Elizabethan' southbound, leaving Peascliffe Tunnel hauled by engine No 60011 Empire of India. (M.W. Earley)

ween Kings Cross and Edinburgh vanished. The distance between Waverley and Lucker water troughs by this route was 90 miles, and it was generally considered desirable in the up direction to provide rear-end banking assistance from Hardengreen Junction up the long 1 in 70 ascent to Falahill summit. A stop was usually made for water at Galashiels.

Then, the drivers, with supreme confidence in their 'A4' engines, began to take things into their own hands, and on August 24, Driver Stevenson of Haymarket shed, with engine No 60029, *Woodcock*, and the standard load of 13 coaches, 435 tons tare and 460 tons full, decided to try a non-stop run. He succeeded, and duly participated in making the longest non-stop run ever achieved, 408.6 miles. Following this it was made eight times in the down direction, and nine times in the up. Of these 17 runs Driver Stevenson was responsible for six, Driver Swan for seven, and Driver McLeod for four. Having regard to the heavy grading of the Waverley route these were remarkable feats of enginemanship.

Unfortunately none of these runs was logged

in detail, but I have the journal times of the up journey on September 7, with engine No 60029, *Woodcock*, and Driver Swan. With the usual load of 460 tons the initial 9.5 miles from Waverley to Hardengreen Junction took 17 min and the very severe 8.4 miles up to Falahill 31 min. A total of 6 min on the emergency schedule had been lost to that point, but by omitting the 5 min water stop at Galashiels the train was on time at Kelso. Despite some incidental checks the emergency schedule was thereafter kept and Kings Cross reached on time.

It is of interest to set down here the engines that were concerned in these splendid pieces of train working, on the 17 occasions:

60029	*Woodcock*	…	…	…	9 runs
60012	*Commonwealth of Australia*	…			3 runs
60028	*Walter K. Whigham*	…		…	2 runs
60027	*Merlin*	…	…	…	1 run
60031	*Golden Plover*	…	…	…	1 run
22	*Mallard*	…	…	…	1 run

The load in every case was one of 13 coaches, 435 tons tare, 460 tons full.

In the summer of 1951, the working was altered. The 'Flying Scotsman' continued to run to its normal timing, and intermediate stops, and the non-stop run was made by a new train called the 'Capitals Limited', leaving Kings Cross at 9.30 am, and allowed 7 hr 20 min to Edinburgh. I had a most interesting footplate run during the 1951 summer season, with engine No 60029, *Woodcock*, and struck a day when a succession of unusual circumstances led to some late running. First of all, because of some contretemps at the now-demolished Kings Cross 'top-shed' the engines for both the 'White Rose' and the 'Capitals Limited' were late in arriving in the station, and we got away 13 min late. The engine of the 'White Rose' was not doing well, and we were several times checked by her signals. Then, for once, an 'A4'—and a crack engine selected for the non-stop—was not steaming well, and the gauge needle was drooping even before we passed Potters Bar. Then finally we were pulled up dead, at Corby Glen, where a 'stop and examine' signal had been received for a southbound train.

In addition to our 13 min late start a further 16 min had been lost by the time we passed Grantham. How that somewhat ailing engine was coaxed through to cover the 287.2 miles from Grantham to Edinburgh in 299 min 48 sec,

and bring us in only 4¼ min late, was an epic of locomotive enginemanship. There was nothing spectacular about the running—indeed there could not be with an engine constantly shy for steam—but the skill and team work of the drivers and firemen was beyond praise. They were Driver Simmons and Fireman Hemmings of Kings Cross, and Driver Anderson and Fireman Inglis of Haymarket. The overall time was 7 hr 11½ min but this included 5¼ min standing at Corby, the many checks experienced from the 'White Rose', and a 10 mph permanent-way check near Acklington. The net time was about 402 min, a net gain of no less than 38 min on schedule—all with a poor steaming engine. I should add, however, that mechanically *Woodcock* was in superb condition.

In Coronation year, 1953, the name of the non-stop was changed to the 'Elizabethan', and in the following summer the time was cut to 6½ hours. The load was limited to one of 11 coaches, having a tare weight of 403 tons, and with this substantial train an average speed of 60 mph had to be maintained throughout. This was the culmination of all the experience gained in running the 'non-stop' since its inauguration in 1928. The 'A4s' never did a finer job than in working the 'Elizabethan' and I was fortunate in logging a splendid run on the south-bound ser-

TABLE II
EAST COAST ROUTE: THE 'ELIZABETHAN'
Load: 11 coaches, 403 tons tare, 425 tons full
Engine: Class 'A4' 4-6-2 No 60030, *Golden Fleece*
Drivers: Paterson (Haymarket)
Tappin (Kings Cross)

Dist		Sch	Actual		Speeds	Dist		Sch	Actual		Speeds
Miles		min	m	s	mph	Miles		min	m	s	mph
0.0	EDINBURGH WAVERLEY	0	0	00	—	41.2	Grantshouse	44	45	46	38½
3.0	Portobello...	5	4	39	—	46.2	Reston Junc	49	50	30	76½
—			pitfall		—	51.9	Burnmouth		55	07	66/81
6.1	*Monktonhall Junc* ...	10	8	46	—	56.4	*Marshall Meadows* ...	58	58	58	—
13.2	Longniddry		16	46	62	57.5	BERWICK-UPON-TWEED	60	60	10	15*
17.8	DREM	19	21	00	70/77	60.9	Scremerston		64	31	61½
23.5	East Linton		25	35	69	65.8	Beal		68	23	82½
—			pws		15	72.8	Belford	74½	73	57	66
29.2	DUNBAR	29	32	22	61½	78.4	Chathill		78	53	72½
31.3	*Oxwellmains*		34	25	56	81.4	Christon Bank		81	22	71½/61
33.8	Innerwick		37	04	67	85.0	Little Mill		84	41	66/75

Dist		Sch	Actual		Speeds	Dist		Sch	Actual		Speeds
Miles		min	m	s	mph	Miles		min	m	s	mph
89.6	ALNMOUTH	90	88	32	(slack)	243.2	Milepost 149½ ...		238	00	58½
92.5	Warkworth		91	24	64	245.0	Bawtry		239	40	74
95.9	Acklington...		94	24	70½	254.1	RETFORD	254	248	51	—*
104.2	Longhirst		101	27	75	258.7	Milepost 134 ...		253	03	51½
107.8	MORPETH	107	104	46	30*	265.3	Crow Park		258	50	82
110.5	Stannington		108	34	60	—			pws		40
114.5	Cramlington		112	47	54½	272.6	NEWARK	270½	265	36	55
119.4	Forest Hall... ...		117	17	69	277.3	Claypole		270	18	64½
123.8	Manors		122	28	—	283.0	Barkston	279½	275	48	56
124.4	NEWCASTLE	125	124	08	—*	287.2	GRANTHAM	283½	280	10	62½
125.0	King Edward Bridge Junc	127	125	56	—	292.6	Stoke Box		285	44	53
128.2	Lamesley		129	54	61	295.6	Corby Glen		288	30	76
—			sigs		—	300.5	Little Bytham		292	02	92/96
132.6	Chester-le-Street ...		135	52	—	304.1	Essendine		294	20	93/95
—			pws		—	307.9	Tallington		296	46	90
138.4	DURHAM...	141	144	40	—	—			pws		40
142.6	Croxdale		150	17	68/62	316.3	PETERBOROUGH ...	308½	305	28	20*
147.5	Ferryhill	151½	155	01	64	323.3	Holme...		313	13	75
150.2	Bradbury		157	28	78	—			pws		40
155.0	Aycliffe		161	15	63*	329.2	Abbots Ripton ...		319	22	50
160.4	DARLINGTON	163½	165	44	82	333.8	HUNTINGDON ...	325½	323	58	79
163.0	Croft Spa		167	38	84	336.7	Offord		326	14	70*
165.6	Eryholme	168	169	33	77½	341.0	St Neots		329	52	68
170.8	Danby Wiske		173	27	82	345.2	Tempsford		332	21	79
174.5	NORTHALLERTON ...	175½	176	21	75	348.6	Sandy		335	56	75
182.3	Thirsk	182	182	16	82	351.6	Biggleswade		338	17	76½
188.4	Pilmoor		187	00	77	354.1	Langford Bridge ...		340	20	70
193.3	Alne	191	190	47	80/79	357.0	Three Counties ...		342	46	75
199.0	Beningbrough ...		195	04	82	360.8	HITCHIN	348½	346	01	63
202.9	Skelton Box	198½	198	18	—	364.1	Stevenage		349	33	52½
204.5	YORK	201½	200	03	—*	367.7	Knebworth	355	353	29	—
206.5	Chaloners Whin Junc		202	53	—	370.7	Welwyn North ...		356	09	72 (max)
214.2	Riccall		210	17	73½	375.0	HATFIELD	362	359	46	—
218.3	SELBY	216½	214	15	—*	—			pws		—
222.9	Templehirst		219	21	64	380.0	Potters Bar	370	366	23	—
229.7	Moss		225	37	73½	—			sigs		—
232.5	Shaftholme Junc ...	232½	227	56	69	387.7	Wood Green... ...		377	01	—
236.7	DONCASTER ...	237	231	48	60	390.1	Finsbury Park		380	24	—
239.5	Black Carr Junc ...		234	30	64½	392.7	KINGS CROSS ...	390	385	10	

Net time: 369 min
* Speed restrictions

vice when we finished with a net gain of 21 min, even on this fast service. The log of this journey is tabulated herewith. It is worth close study, because although it includes some spells of very fast running the engine developed the effort in her normal stride at every point.

Chief Inspector Jenkins of the Eastern Region was travelling on the train and at his invitation I went through to the footplate after Newark. I then saw how easily the engine developed the high speed between Stoke and Peterborough, working in 15 per cent with regulator eased back after passing Stoke summit. The analysis of the high-speed sections is also interesting, as showing that an aggregate of 308.3 miles was covered at an average speed of 66.8 mph.

ANALYSIS OF HIGH-SPEED RUNNING

Dist	Stretch	Actual		Av speed
Miles		m	s	mph
17.4	Monktonhall–East Linton	16	49	62.3
27.2	Dunbar–Marshall Meadows	26	36	61.3
47.2	Tweedmouth–Pegswood	40	45	69.5
12.2	Stannington–Heaton	11	56	61.4
64.5	Relly Mill Junction–Skelton	51	38	73.8
9.7	York–Riccall	10	14	56.6
42.4	Templehirst–Crow Park	39	29	64.4
35.3	Newark–Tallington	31	10	68.0
7.6	Fletton Junction–Connington Sth	7	11	63.5
45.8	Abbots Ripton–Hatfield	40	24	68.3
308.3		276	12	66.8

Net actual average from start to stop = 63.9 mph

Intermediate stretches	Dist	Actual		Net	Net av speed
	miles	m	s	min	mph
Edinburgh–Newcastle	124.4	124	08	121½	61.6
Newcastle–Darlington	36.0	41	36	38	56.8
Darlington–York	44.1	34	19	34½	77.3
York–Grantham	82.7	80	07	78½	63.2
Grantham–Hatfield	87.8	79	36	76½	68.8

The running of the 'non-stop' was the last remnant of the heroic age of British steam railways: a memorial for all time to the foresight and enterprise of Sir Nigel Gresley. The writing of this article has brought many personal memories, quite apart from the actual journeys, and that first sight of the two engines 4472 and 4476, newly equipped with their corridor tenders outside Doncaster works. Until then 4472 had been a Doncaster engine, but it was natural that she should have been specially selected for the inauguration of the 'non-stop'.

I have seen the train at many parts of the line: at Berwick and Alnmouth; weaving its way through the purlieus of Newcastle; and coming into Kings Cross many times, invariably a few minutes ahead of time. But perhaps the most vivid memories are of the control room at York, seeing how much care was taken to give her a clear road, and there to see her route set in a chain of white lights from end to end of that immense panel. Professionally one watched her approach on the diagram, seeing the route lights change from white to red as successive track circuits were entered; but I could never resist the temptation of the enthusiast to go to the door of the cabin, and actually see her pass below. The 'non-stop' is now no more, but her memory will always remain among East Coast railwaymen and enthusiasts alike.

NOVEMBER 1968

Steam finale : some reflections

Writing in the year of grace 1988, it seems indeed strange that as long ago as November 1968 I should have used the phrase 'Steam finale'. When this article was first published in *The Railway Magazine* there were many who really believed that the farewell trips on 11 August 1968 were the last. Many of the boffins at British Railways headquarters fervently hoped that they would be! Far from it. Quite apart from the magnificent recent restoration of *Mallard*, my current issue of *The Railway Magazine* shows three preserved locomotives 'going great guns' on BR tracks. Long may it continue.

WITH some extensive overseas travelling on my immediate agenda, which will involve my absence from this country for the best part of five weeks, this particular article had to be written earlier than usual. Drafting it at the end of August it is the stupendous event that took place in the middle of that month that transcends everything else in the minds of those who have railways at heart. I refer of course to the end of steam traction on British Railways. It was signalised by some remarkable scenes during the running of the farewell train-tour on Sunday August 11, scenes that demonstrated once again the extraordinary emotional appeal that the steam locomotive has for so many people.

We are nevertheless a little too near to events to appreciate to the full the profound significance of the epoch that has now ended. Many scribes have written nostalgically about the days of steam; albums of superb photographs have been published; and historians of all kinds—your humble servant among them—have been busy chronicling many diverse aspects of locomotive history. There is no doubt that the fascination of locomotive history will increase, as the steam era recedes further into history. Hardly a month passes without some diligent researcher turning up some 'find' in the way of a hitherto unknown document, and I have remarked before now on the frequency with which steam is still likely to form the centrepiece of discussion in these articles.

However, it is not detail, either in historical data or in actual running, that is uppermost in my own thoughts just at the moment. It is the immensity of the pageant that is now closed, and its world-wide implications. The steam locomotive, invented and developed in Great Britain, made world history on a colossal scale, not so much in speed records, power output and all the minutiae of detailed engineering, as in the advancement of civilisation in almost every continent the world over. In Africa, Australia, the Far East; in India, and South America, British engineers built railways for operation by steam locomotives, and it was the *British* steam locomotive, and its reliability in the superb quality of its workmanship and in its longevity that enabled pioneer railways in developing countries to be successfully operated.

In every country of the world the steam locomotive was the very cornerstone of the great sociological developments of the nineteenth century. A vast project like the Canadian Pacific Railway would never have been enterprised had there not been the certainty that once built there would be reliable power to work it. It was the same certainty of eventual sound operation when railroads were pushed westwards from Chicago, in the teeth of violent native opposition, or when the first railways were built in tropical Africa, and in the swamps and dense forests of countries like Burma. It is of course the British steam locomotive, above all others, that is foremost in our thoughts at the present time;

and by British I mean not merely those that have worked on the home railways, but the products of the locomotive building industry. It is as well to ponder for a while on the extraordinarily wide ramifications of the great export trade in locomotives that was built up during the nineteenth century, and which reached its zenith in the years before the first world war.

At home, those who study railway history are familiar with the lines that were built with the specific purpose of opening up tracts of country that from one reason or another were lying derelict, or depopulated. The northern extensions of the Highland Railway and the West Highland line and its extension to Mallaig are very familiar examples. Abroad, the steam-operated railway was the basis of the strategic growth of modern India. In South America the establishment of steam-worked railways changed the Argentine from a remote, sparsely populated virgin land into a thriving economic community: indeed, so far as railways themselves were concerned the Buenos Aires Great Southern grew to be the largest British-owned joint stock corporation outside the Commonwealth.

The 'Golden Arrow' arriving at Dover Marine hauled by 'West Country' class 4-6-2 No 34039 before the engine was named Boscastle. (Rev A.C. Cawston)

Again, so far as Great Britain was concerned, the steam railways of the world not only provided an immense market for export trade in locomotives, but the ancillary needs of steam railways led to other large exports. Welsh coal was the finest locomotive fuel to be found anywhere in the world, and huge tonnages were exported to South America for the British-built locomotives operating there. The equipment of the South Wales ports for mass-handling of export coal facilitated its despatch to many other countries, and its qualities were so well appreciated by the Paris, Lyons & Mediterranean Railway, for example, that colliers of its own used to ply between Marseilles and Cardiff conveying the choicest locomotive fuels. To descend to the colloquial, it was a case of: 'Big fleas have little fleas...'

One day, I hope, the full history of steam railways may be written: not a catalogue of locomotives built, a recital of leading dimensions, nor of record runs, but the story of what steam railways have done towards the development of civilisation. I shall always remember the Presidential Address of W. S. Graff-Baker to the Institution of Locomotive Engineers on October 26, 1944. He was then Chief Mechanical Engineer of London Transport, and far more concerned with electric trains than with steam haulage, and while he rather horrified some members of his audience by the forward-looking nature of his views, one passage in the opening stages of his address can always send a glow of pride through the hearts of those who have never lost their affection for steam.

He said: 'It appears now to have become unsafe to say that the steam locomotive will necessarily continue to have the monopoly of hauling long distance passenger and goods trains—it has already lost the monopoly it once held of handling the suburban traffic.

'The steam locomotive as we know it is a machine with certain physical limitations and certain detrimental features. It is limited in power by the loading gauge and in efficiency by a relatively limited temperature range. It has detrimental effects on track and structures due to the extreme difficulty—or even impossibility—of obtaining a mechanical balance at varying speeds, and in this connection it is only proper to observe that the track and structures are as essential parts of a railway as the locomotive.

Flashback to Aspinall days on the LYR: one of the celebrated Atlantics as originally built and lettered on the tender, No 708. (W.J. Reynolds)

Sir Nigel Gresley *in its last months at Grantham, after having worked 'The Northumbrian' down from King's Cross.* (K.H. Leech)

With these difficulties the fact remains that the steam locomotive is a magnificent machine and has done more for the cause of civilisation than any other effort of the mechanical engineer—far more than the internal combustion engine which seems now to have a heavy debit as well as a credit entry in its balance sheet.'

I need hardly remind older readers, yet must necessarily explain to my younger friends, that Graff-Baker's Presidential Address was delivered at a stage in the second world war when, having survived the night 'blitz' and seen the Allied armies successfully launched on the liberation of Western Europe, London was enduring the ordeal of the flying bomb, and rocket attacks.

Graff-Baker succeeded Bulleid as President of the Institution, and at the conclusion of the meeting a vote of thanks was passed thanking him for his services. Bulleid replied in characteristic and mildly provocative style, and is thus reported:

'Personally, he was a quite unrepentant steam engineer. He had listened to rosy views of the marvels of other modes of traction, so rosy that they ignored the thorns which were always there, and, though he knew that a Presidential Address must not be discussed, he would like to say that five years' experience of the Presidency, during which he avoided delivering a Presidential Address, tempted him to remind the present President that he had no business to introduce into his address anything which could be considered controversial; and especially in the Hall of the Institution of Mechanical Engineers, where the Stephenson tradition was so strong and so carefully preserved.'

Behind the badinage, which was typical of that impish sense of humour with which Bulleid used occasionally to delight his audience, lay of course his implacable opposition to the diesels, and indeed to anything except steam. But as one turns back the pages of railway history one finds that some of the greatest steam locomotive engineers had a completely open mind towards other forms of traction.

This amusing manifestation of Bulleid's attitude was borne out more and more in the years following nationalisation, when he was seen fighting an ever more desperate rearguard action against the advancing forces of newer forms of motive power. Then he was virtually standing alone. In looking back over the past 60 or 70 years, however, it is interesting to see how quite a number of famous steam locomotive designers were far-seeing enough to give the most serious consideration to newer forms of power. While one could hardly include Brunel in the ranks of engine designers, the daring and disastrous experiment with the atmospheric system certainly merits a mention; but the first British locomotive designer of any standing who began seriously to turn away from steam was Sir John

Aspinall—one of the greatest railwaymen of all time. He had that rare quality of broad managerial outlook combined with his outstanding qualities as an engineer, and this priceless blend of talents carried the Lancashire & Yorkshire Railway along the crest of the wave for many years. At a time when many alternative forms of transport in teeming urban areas were being introduced he sponsored the electrification of two of the busiest of commuter lines, Liverpool-Southport and Manchester-Bury. As a designer of good, dividend earning steam locomotives like the 2–4–2 tanks, the 7 ft 3 in 4–4–0s, and the historic inside-cylindered Atlantics, he might have given thought to a 'Lanky' version of the Decapod, to keep electrification at bay; but under his direction the LYR went in exactly the opposite direction.

As General Manager, Aspinall had an

Another flashback: an LNWR 'Experiment' class 4-6-0 No 1413 Henry Cort *on an up West Coast express south of Preston.* (Real Photos)

overall, rather than a detailed responsibility for both forms of traction, but on the North Eastern Sir Vincent Raven took direct responsibility for both. From the time when he was Locomotive Running Superintendent, under Wilson Worsdell, he showed himself to be very electrically minded, and the ingenious arrangements of cab signalling were due to him. Electrically-operated semaphore indicators in the cab not only showed the positions of signals ahead, but also indicated the routes to be taken at a diversion. It was on his recommendation and to his designs that the intensely used Shildon-Newport freight line was electrified, in 1915; this was of inestimable value during the war years in liberating many steam locomotives for other duties, and permitting the North Eastern to lend the entire stud of class 'T1' 0-8-0s for service with the Railway Operating Division, in France—50 invaluable heavy freight engines.

Raven, who so superbly continued the old North Eastern tradition of handsome steam locomotives, invariably kept in spotless condition, was nevertheless a very strong advocate of electric traction, and to the Tyneside suburban and the Shildon-Newport freight schemes he advocated, and eventually obtained Board sanction, for the electrification of the main line between York and Newcastle. Unfortunately this great project, which the wealthy and profitable North Eastern Railway could comfortably have financed on its own, lapsed after grouping when the inclusion of certain impecunious concerns within the LNER group put a very different complexion on the overall finances. Before grouping took place, however, Sir Vincent Raven had designed a prototype express passenger electric locomotive which is as much a monument to his life's work as the army of three-cylinder steam locomotives of the 4-4-2,

A 'Precedent' class 2-4-0 No 477 Caractacus *on an up Central Wales express near Kenton – the third and fourth vehicles are Cambrian Railways stock running through to Euston.* (C. Laundy)

4-6-0, 0-8-0, 4-4-4 T and 4-6-2 T types by which he is perhaps better remembered.

Sir Nigel Gresley will always be regarded as one of the greatest exponents of steam traction; but he was above all a *railwayman*, and forever sought to give good service to the public. To Gresley service meant speed, and with his breadth of outlook he was immediately attracted by the performance of the high-speed diesel multiple-unit trains put into service on the German State Railways in 1933. He went to Germany and travelled on 'The Flying Hamburger', which maintained a start-to-stop average speed of 77.4 mph between Berlin and Hamburg. Just as Churchward 30 years earlier had recommended the purchase of a de Glehn compound Atlantic from France for trials on the Great Western, so Gresley seriously considered purchasing a train similar to the 'Flying Hamburger' for trials on the LNER. The outcome is well known. The magnificent performances of the 'A3' Pacific engine *Papyrus* in March 1935 so surpassed anything that the manufacturers of the 'Flying Hamburger' could promise that steam haulage of the proposed 'Silver Jubilee' express was assured. But the point for emphasis is that as early as 1935 Gresley was prepared to consider diesel traction.

On the Great Western, Hawksworth introduced the gas-turbine-electric locomotive, while H. G. Ivatt, with the ready assistance of the English Electric Company, pioneered the first British diesel-electric main-line locomotives on the LMSR. All these projects, like Hawksworth's introduction of oil firing on the Great Western, had limited objectives. They were conceived as rational experiments, designed to provide comparative data on a like-for-like basis, on which wider decisions on policy could be made when the relevant information had been gathered. The oil-firing episode should have been a lesson. The Great Western's 'limited objective' programme looked like being very successful when the government of the day—or rather one ministry—stepped in, and without consulting anyone else authorised a large-scale adoption of the Great Western pro-

posals. Only when a vast amount of public money had been spent, or rather utterly wasted, was the scheme brought to a grinding halt, because another ministry of the same government had not enough foreign exchange to buy the necessary oil!

It has been much the same, in a different way, with the wholesale scrapping of steam, and its replacement with expensive diesels which were introduced on a large scale before maintenance facilities were properly developed. There was a definite case for the gradual change in motive power; but with the proven longevity of steam, and the high cost of the diesel replacements, one must be pardoned for doubting if there was sound actuarial justification for such summary slaughter of engines like the BR standard types after little more than ten years of service. However, once any organisation comes under national ownership, propaganda becomes of greater importance than sound economics, and propaganda decreed that steam must go. And that was that!

I have left myself very little room for performance this month, but there is an item of great historical interest that I have had by me for some time, none other than a full dynamometer-car record of two of the runs made in the 1909 interchange trials on the LNWR between the 'Experiment' class 4-6-0 No 2630, *Buffalo*, and the Caledonian 4-6-0, *Cardean*, working the 9.15 am express from Crewe to Carlisle. The record is contained on a drawing made at St Rollox and signed by J. F. McIntosh himself. Unfortunately, it relates only to the down journey. When this drawing came to light, in response to my urgent enquiries the Scottish Region authorities very kindly made a thorough search to try and find a companion drawing giving details of the much-harder southbound runs on the 12.58 pm up express from Carlisle. Unfortunately no such drawing could be traced.

I must admit that I have always had some doubt whether the competing engines really *did* work the 12.58 pm up *on the same day* as their corresponding down journeys. The first details of these tests ever to see the light of day, outside official circles, were published in *The Railway Magazine* in November, 1936, in a serial article of mine. The details were given to me by the late Sir William Stanier, and the dates of the comparison runs appear to admit of no doubt, except to leave one furiously wondering how on earth the competing engines *and* the dynamometer car were turned in the time. *Buffalo*, for example, did not arrive from the south till 12.43 pm and yet is reported as leaving on time with the 12.58 pm up! *Cardean* had 3 min more in which to turn. The quickest way would probably have been to set back through the Citadel station and round the Maryport line to Currock Junction; then to go forward on the goods connection to M & C & NE Junction, thence going eastwards till reaching the North Eastern passenger line from the Citadel station. Then the engine and car could back up into the station. From the centre of the station the distances involved in this manoeuvre would have been 78 chains backing to Currock Junction; 69 chains forward to North Eastern Junction, and then 36 chains backing up to the station. It *could* have been done, but it would have needed some good organisation to keep the various lines clear.

The 9.15 am from Crewe was a fairly light train as far as Preston and really formed no passenger connection with the forward working, which was the 10.51 am Liverpool and Manchester 'Scotsman'. The only vehicles which went through from Crewe to Carlisle were two WCJS brake vans, one marshalled at the front and one at the rear of the train. The 10.51 am *ex*-Preston had a sharp timing, for those days, of 102 min for the 90 miles from Preston to Carlisle. The accompanying logs have been prepared from the St Rollox drawing. Having regard to the difference in loads there was not a great deal to choose between the times of the two engines as far as Grayrigg summit was concerned; but *Cardean* was giving a distinctly better performance in the dynamometer car. On the faintly rising length from Garstang to Galgate she was sustaining a steady drawbar pull of 2 tons at 64 mph, against *Buffalo's* 1¾ tons. Climbing Grayrigg both engines gradually increased their

LNWR: 10.51 am PRESTON–CARLISLE

Dist			Sch	6-7-09 903 *Cardean* 301		9-7-09 2630 *Buffalo* 321	
Date Engine No Engine Name Load, tons tare				Actual	Speeds	Actual	Speeds
Miles			min	min	mph	min	mph
0.0	PRESTON ...	...	0	0	—	0	
4.7	Barton	...		7¾	55	8	54
7.4	Brock	...		10½	64	11	62½
9.5	Garstang	...		12¼	63	13	62
12.7	Scorton	...		15¼	63	16	60
15.3	Bay Horse ...			17¾	64	18½	61
16.6	Galgate	...		19	63½	20	62
21.0	LANCASTER	...	23	23¼	64	24	65
24.1	Hest Bank ...			26¼	63	27	66
25.5	Bolton-le-Sands	...		27½	63	28	65
27.3	CARNFORTH	...	30	29¼	63	30	63
31.8	Burton	...		34	60	34¾	58½
34.6	Milnthorpe ...			36¾	59	37¼	58
40.1	OXENHOLME	...	44	43¾	37	44½	40
47.2	Grayrigg	...		56	33	57	29½
48.9	Lowgill	...		58	52	59½	50½
53.2	TEBAY	...	...	61	62½	63	64	—
				—		Stop BE	—
58.7	*Summit*	...	70	72	31	76	33
60.7	Shap	...		74½	60	78¾	56½
68.0	Clifton	...		81½	65	85½	66½
72.3	PENRITH ...		84	85½	56½	89½	54
77.0	Plumpton ...			90	65½	94½	62
79.3	Calthwaite ...			92	71	96½	65
82.7	Southwaite ...			95	73	99½	73
85.2	Wreay	...		97	67½	102	56
90.1	CARLISLE ...		102	104	—	108	—

efforts to a drawbar pull of 3⅜ and 3¾ tons, approaching the summit. The actual drawbar horsepowers were 720 by *Cardean* and 650 by *Buffalo*. Correcting these figures for gradient the equivalent drawbar horsepowers were 970 for *Cardean* and 820 for *Buffalo*.

The Caledonian engine scored a big point over her rival by taking Shap without assistance, and her drawbar pull approaching the summit was 5⅜ tons. This gave the high actual drawbar horsepower of 1,000, while the equivalent figure, after making the correction for gradient, was 1,320—a really splendid effort. *Buffalo* showed a drawbar pull of 11 tons when starting from Tebay, but the effort gradually tailed off to 3¼ tons at Shap Summit. As the train was travelling at 33 mph at the summit the banker must have been putting forth a mighty effort, yet the St Rollox drawing shows this assistant engine to have been a 2–4–0 'Jumbo'! What fascinating records there still are to be unearthed relating to the great age of steam!

——————————— · · · ———————————

Index

No 35016 Elders Fyffes *on the 'Devon Belle' at Raynes Park* (Author's collection)